Leadership in Psychiatry

Leadership in Psychiatry

Edited by

Dinesh Bhugra

Professor of Mental Health & Cultural Diversity
Institute of Psychiatry
King's College London
London, UK

Pedro Ruiz

Professor and Executive Vice Chair
Director of Clinical Programs
Department of Psychiatry & Behavioral Sciences
Miller School of Medicine
University of Miami
Miami, Florida, USA

Susham Gupta

Consultant Psychiatrist
East London NHS Foundation Trust
London, UK

WILEY Blackwell

Library of Congress Cataloging-in-Publication Data

Leadership in psychiatry / edited by Dinesh Bhugra, Pedro Ruiz, Susham Gupta.
    p. ; cm.
  Includes bibliographical references and index.
  ISBN 978-1-119-95291-6 (cloth)
  I. Bhugra, Dinesh.   II. Ruiz, Pedro.   III. Gupta, Susham.
  [DNLM: 1. Leadership.   2. Mental Health Services–organization & administration.   3. Communication.
4. Medical Staff–organization & administration.   5. Professional Competence.   WA 495]
  RC467.95
  616.890068–dc23

                                                                                    2013015838

A catalogue record for this book is available from the British Library.

Wiley also publishes its books in a variety of electronic formats. Some content that appears in print may not be available in electronic books.

Cover image: iStockphoto.com/Dmitry Merkushin
Cover design by Sarah Dickinson

Set in 10/12.5pt Times by Aptara® Inc., New Delhi, India
Printed and bound in Malaysia by Vivar Printing Sdn Bhd

1   2013

Contents

List of Contributors

John P. Baker
Assistant Professor
Center for Leadership Excellence
Western Kentucky University
Bowling Green, Kentucky, USA

Dinesh Bhugra
Professor of Mental Health and Cultural
Diversity
Institute of Psychiatry, King's College
London
London, UK

Kenneth G. Busch
Psychiatrist
Chicago, Illinois, USA

Nicholas Deakin
Academic Foundation Year
Barts Health NHS Foundation Trust
London, UK

Klement Dymi
Research Assistant
Psychiatric Centre Ballerup
Hellerup, Denmark

Cindy L. Ehresman
Program Manager
School of Leadership Studies
Western Kentucky University
Bowling Green, Kentucky, USA

Wolfgang Gaebel
Professor, Department of Psychiatry and
Psychotherapy
LVR-Klinikum Düsseldorf
Medical Faculty
Heinrich Heine University
Düsseldorf, Germany

Patrick Gatonga
University of Nairobi
Nairobi, Kenya

Maja Gawronska
Stein Institute for Research on Aging
University of California, San Diego
(UCSD)
Department of Psychiatry
San Diego, California, USA

Susham Gupta
Consultant Psychiatrist
East London NHS Foundation Trust
Assertive Outreach Team – City &
Hackney
London, UK

Denise Harris
Clinical Facilitator
Professional and Practice Development
Team
Sussex Community NHS Trust
Zachary Merton Hospital
Rustington, West Sussex, UK

Dilip V. Jeste
Estelle and Edgar Levi Chair in Aging
Director, Sam and Rose Stein Institute for
Research on Aging
Distinguished Professor of Psychiatry and
Neurosciences
Director of Education, Clinical and
Translational Research Institute
University of California, San Diego
San Diego, California, USA

Marianne Kastrup
Competence Center for Transcultural
Psychiatry
Psychiatric Centre Ballerup
Hellerup, Denmark

Andreas Kuchenbecker
LVR-Academy for Mental Health
Solingen, Germany

Levent Küey
Associate Professor of Psychiatry
Istanbul Bilgi University
Istanbul, Turkey

Juan José López-Ibor
Departamento de Psiquiatría, Facultad de
Medicina
Universidad Complutense, Instituto de
Investigación Sanitaria del Hospital
Clínico San Carlos (IdISSC)
Fundación Juan José López-Ibor
Madrid, Spain

María Inés López-Ibor
Director, Departamento de Psiquiatría,
Facultad de Medicina
Universidad Complutense, CIBERSAM
(Centro de Investigación Biomédica en
Red de Salud Mental)
Fundación Juan José López-Ibor
Madrid, Spain

David M. Ndetei
Professor of Psychiatry
University of Nairobi
Director, Africa Mental Health
Foundation
Nairobi, Kenya

Ahmed Okasha
Director of WHO Collaborating Center
for Research and Training in Mental
Health
Okasha Institute of Psychiatry, Ain
Shams University
Cairo, Egypt

Zoë Reed
Director of Strategy and Business
Development
South London and Maudsley NHS
Foundation Trust
London, UK

Blanca Reneses
Deputy Director
Instituto de Psiquiatría y Salud Mental
Instituto de Investigacion Sanitaria
(IdISSC)
Hospital Clínico San Carlos
Departamento de Psiquiatría, Facultad de
Medicina Universidad Complutense
Madrid, Spain

Robert Roca
Vice President and Medical Director
Sheppard Pratt Health System
Baltimore, Maryland, USA

Hugo Rodriguez
Head of Inpatient Unit
Institute of Psychiatry
National University of Asunción
Asunción, Paraguay

Wulf Rössler
Professor Emeritus, University of Zurich,
Switzerland
Senior Professor, Leuphana University,
Lüneberg, Germany
Professor of Post-Graduation, University
of Sao Paulo, Brazil

Pedro Ruiz
Professor and Executive Vice Chair
Director of Clinical Programs
Department of Psychiatry and Behavioral
Sciences
Miller School of Medicine – University of
Miami
Miami, Florida, USA

Norman Sartorius
President, Association for the
Improvement of Mental Health
Programmes
Geneva, Switzerland

Steven S. Sharfstein
President and Chief Executive Officer
Sheppard Pratt Health System
Baltimore, Maryland, USA

Alex Till
Foundation Year 1
Leicestershire, Northampton & Rutland
Foundation School
East Midlands Workforce Deanery
Northampton, UK

Julio Torales
Professor of Psychiatry
Professor of Medical Psychology
School of Medical Sciences

National University of Asunción
Asunción, Paraguay

Rebecca Viney
Coaching and Mentoring Lead
Associate Dean
Professional Development Department
London Deanery
Stewart House
London, UK

Hugo de Waal
Consultant Old Age Psychiatrist
Norfolk & Suffolk NHS Foundation Trust
South London & Maudsley NHS
Foundation Trust
Associate Postgraduate Dean, East of
England Deanery
The Julian Hospital
Norwich, UK

Sidney Weissman
Professor of Clinical Psychiatry
Feinberg School of Medicine
Northwestern University
Chicago, Illinois, USA

Noemi Wulff
LVR-Academy for Mental Health
Solingen, Germany

Jürgen Zielasek
Department of Psychiatry and
Psychotherapy
LVR-Klinikum Düsseldorf
Medical Faculty
Heinrich Heine University
Düsseldorf, Germany

Preface

Clinical leadership is vital in looking after patients, managing resources and responding to the needs of families and carers of patients. However, only in the last few years has attention increasingly been paid to aspects of leadership and training. In medical schools, as well as other training environments, very limited exposure to leadership situations is made available. Hence, often those in clinical leadership situations learn on the job.

There is always a tension regarding whether leaders are born or made. The truth is somewhere in the middle. Certain leadership skills can be learnt, such as managing teams, managing resources and communication skills. On the other hand, certain personality skills are present from birth. This combination of nature and nurture can make a good leader who is capable of doing the best for their patients and making the most of the available resources. Leadership does not occur in a vacuum and leaders need followers. Why followers choose one leader rather than another depends upon a number of factors. Charisma, passion, courage and communication, along with technical competence, are some of the qualities possessed by successful leaders.

At the core of clinical leadership is the patient, whose clinical needs must be paramount. Services need to revolve around the patient, and the clinical leader has to take these into account in acquiring and managing resources. Clinical leaders must remain focused on clinical matters, but also on the social, political and economic context within which they may provide services.

Clinical leadership in mental health services carries with it certain responsibilities, and specific competencies and skills are required. Planning and delivering services, whether these are in the public sector or the private sector, is a critical aspect of the role the clinical leader plays. In addition, the task for the leader is to set the direction for the planning and delivery of services. This focus requires personal qualities such as self-awareness, self-management and self-development. Part of the continuing professional development must focus on these skills. Keeping up to date and being technically competent is vital for any clinical leader so that they can convey professional values and views with confidence. Any worker in a clinical setting must work with integrity and honesty.

Clinical leaders also need to have vision about the healthcare delivery, along with the passion to communicate their vision to the key stakeholders. Leaders also need the skills to mentor team members and support them when needed. Managing teams and resources is an important function of the leader's role. The leader must maintain professional standards and understand decision-making processes as well as theories of leadership.

It is part of the profession's responsibility to ensure that the next generation of leaders have the appropriate skills mix and are fully aware both of theoretical and practical aspects of leadership. Humility with wisdom must be the hallmark of a good leader, and we hope that this volume will contribute to obtaining these skills.

This volume brings together a team of international experts with clinical and non-clinical backgrounds to pull together the theories and practical skills required to be a successful leader. Inevitably, there is some overlap between chapters, but we have deliberately left this so that chapters can be read independently of each other. We are grateful to our contributors, who in spite of their busy schedules managed to deliver their chapters and have been a source of inspiration as well as support. Our thanks also go to Joan Marsh and her team at Wiley-Blackwell.

Andrea Livingstone brought sterling support and energy to the project. Without her steer and hard work, this volume would not be in the wonderful shape it is in now. We are grateful to her.

Dinesh Bhugra, Pedro Ruiz and Susham Gupta

Part A
The Role of the Leader

Chapter 1

What is Leadership?

Dinesh Bhugra, Susham Gupta and Pedro Ruiz

Introduction

Leadership is crucial in any sphere of life. The meaning and functions of leadership are influenced by a number of factors, including culture and the role of leadership. Leaders lead because their role is to act with vision related to an organization or an institution. The task of the leader is to provide a blueprint for members or people to follow. This may include political parties, business organizations, membership organizations and social organizations. Leaders exist because there are followers. Often individuals put themselves up for such roles, or are thrust into leadership positions.

There has to be some degree of self-awareness in the first instance, whereas in the second instance it is the status of the individual or the family/kinship or organization they come from which pushes them into leadership roles. The latter has been repeatedly shown in politics, for example, in the Indian subcontinent, where children, spouses or siblings of leaders who die in harness are encouraged to take on their leading responsibilities, or in the United States, where the family names can provide a platform for entry into local or national level politics. Furthermore, leaders may take on the task for a single specific objective, whatever it is, for practical ends, or to deliver a specific result. The leadership styles will differ in a number of ways and may be influenced by the specific purpose for which leadership is sought or offered.

In this chapter, we propose to set out some broad principles for the readers of this book. The focus of the book remains on leadership in the mental health profession.

What is leadership?

Leadership can be conceptualized in a large number of ways.[1] Leadership is the focus of the group processes as described by Bass.[2] But it is more than that. It is a concept and a process, both of which are embedded in a single person, but rarely in a body of individuals. Northouse[3] illustrates leadership by the power relationship that exists between leaders and their followers. Leadership can be transformational, involving management of change, and carries with it a skills set to influence individuals, events and processes. The specific

Leadership in Psychiatry, First Edition. Edited by Dinesh Bhugra, Pedro Ruiz and Susham Gupta.

task(s) related to leadership roles can be carried out only with the implicit or explicit consent of followers.

Northouse[3] asserts that while some are leaders, those towards whom the leadership is directed can be seen as followers. Both are needed in our understanding of the process of leadership. Neither the leader nor the followers can exist in a vacuum. However, who initiates this relationship is an interesting question. Embedded within the question is the purpose, function or goal of leadership. Leaders are not above their followers, but often, in politics especially, the power differential is so great that there may be a chasm between the leader and the followers.

Leadership is both a trait and a process. Development of leader and leadership skills and traits can be attributed to the family and early life.[4] According to Zaleznik,[4] provision of adequate gratification in childhood can lead to a harmony between what individuals expect from life and what they achieve. On the other hand leadership skills can be developed within organizations due to the need for changes, or be honed through mentorship.

Skills needed in and for leadership roles

Leadership requires a certain set of skills. In an impressive explanation of skills approach, Northouse[3] points out that the skills needed are technical, human and conceptual, although levels required in different roles will vary. In some settings and at some levels the skills mix will be different. A crucial element is the role of technical competence. Technical skills are about proficiency in a particular specialized area with analytical ability in that field and to use appropriate tools and techniques.[5] Technical competence becomes incredibly significant in the field of mental health, where the leader has to be able not only to understand technical aspects but also be able to communicate these to the key stakeholders. Technical competence is critical in convincing the funders if services are to be developed in a certain framework. In the Northouse modified model of Katz,[5] it is argued that at higher levels (e.g. top management), technical aspects are not as critical; but in the field of clinical sciences as well as mental health, technical knowledge is helpful. In their model, technical skills are concerned with working with things. In clinical matters, it is useful to know about conditions and potential treatments, which also gives the leader a degree of credibility. Understanding of the complexities and nuances of mental health is crucial in understanding, advocating and garnering of accurate resource allocation. Interestingly, along with technical competence, clinicians also have to possess human and communication skills, which are concerned with dealing, negotiating and working with people. These skills enable the leader to work with followers, delegate tasks appropriately and mentor followers. With these skills, it is possible for the leader to trust others and create an environment of trust, where followers can express their views and feel listened to. A good leader is sensitive to the needs of others and will take them into account. These skills become increasingly relevant higher up the leadership ladder.

The third set of skills are conceptual and deal with the ability to work with ideas and concepts.[3] It can be argued that in some ways these are the most significant skills. These are at the core of strategic thinking and are central to creating a vision and plan for an organization or functionality of the organization. These are the central essential skills that allow a leader to express their vision and bring about changes.

Individual style and competencies in problem-solving, effective communication, passion and courage are important attributes of leadership. Clinicians are aware of and trained in developing hypotheses and then testing these to devise diagnostic and management strategies. Therefore, they are better placed at problem-solving and looking at problems 'outside the box'. Creative abilities for solving complex management problems in the organization include good judgement in defining problems and formulating solutions, which is essential in the armoury of leadership skills.[6] Identifying problems and solutions is one aspect, but communicating these effectively and gaining the support of others are equally important in achieving change. Along with problem-solving and social judgement skills, the capacity to understand people and social systems is helpful. Mental health professionals, by virtue of their training, must be able to utilize these skills in working with others, enthusing, supporting and mentoring them. Part of the conceptual ability is to take a perspective that is equivalent to social intelligence[7] or emotional intelligence.

Northouse[3] points out that, at an individual level, general cognitive ability, crystallized cognitive ability, motivation and personality all will play a role in leadership skills. Career experiences and environmental influences will also play a role in decision-making and leadership abilities.

A major challenge to this model is its breadth, which not every leader may be able to match. Although Northouse[3] indicates that its predictive value is weak, it is not entirely clear whether this poor predictive value also applies to clinical settings. Furthermore, an added problem with any competencies model is the actual level of competencies obtained. The behaviour of the leader may not be related to skills. The style approach of leadership focuses both on tasks and relationships. Both the task and the relationship will also depend upon the context within which leadership works – and this is where the situational approach to leadership may work. The situational approach sees the leader as having directive and supportive dimensions. Northouse[3] classifies leadership styles into:

- high directive–low supportive;
- high directive–high supportive;
- high supportive–low directive;
- low supportive–low directive.

These are self-explanatory.

Leaders: born or made?

As noted earlier, organizations help to identify and develop leaders. Peer review and training can be both productive and destructive, depending upon how it is carried out. Zaleznik[4] notes that peer reviews may influence managerial skills more than leadership skills. There is no doubt that our individual personality traits allow us to develop certain skills. For example, extrovert individuals may find it easier to communicate than introverts. In addition, other personality traits, such as aggression, may be more inherent. This means that some skills needed for leadership are innate, whereas others can be learned.

The abilities to manage conflict, to negotiate and to manage resources can be acquired through direct observation, training and mentoring. Learning to develop strategy and develop expertise in a field is possible through training. Leaders have to learn how to manage change and how to make the most of opportunities that can emerge from such change. Strategic direction for an organization can develop from extensive analysis of the functions of the organization and testing strategic scenarios in the context of complexity, technological advances, geographical factors and organizational structures.[8]

Some leaders, by virtue of their own personality traits, can manage change effectively, whereas others feel the need to maintain the status quo irrespective of what might be the needs of the organization at that particular time. Challenges related to change are strategic, technical, adaptive or rejecting. Individual personality traits will influence the type of approach used. Managing distress related to change and inherent ambiguity in change is important for any leader. Psychiatrists, by virtue of their training, should be more capable at sensitively dealing with ambiguity and uncertainty. It is also helpful that psychiatric training teaches individuals to deal with group dynamics and to explore not only what is being conveyed openly, but also what is not. These can help individuals and the organizations adapt to change. Heifetz and Laurie[9] observe that, at first, a leader must be able to create a holding environment which is a temporary 'place' or an ongoing safe space where ideas can germinate and grow. These skills are both inherent and acquired.

Heifetz and Laurie[9] propose that in adaptive work leaders have to take on the responsibilities for direction, protection, orientation, managing conflict and shaping norms requiring technical and adaptive skills. These authors suggest that good leaders encourage those below them to speak up, participate actively and contribute their skills. In addition, good leaders must also maintain disciplined attention to their views, and be able to give constructive feedback and justify their decision-making. Pilot training and working on a flight crew provide an excellent example of where any member of the team can point out problems without fear or ridicule, the primary aim of which is to reduce overall risk. In the healthcare services, certainly in the United Kingdom, whistle-blowing is still not widely encouraged. Technical orientations of the leadership role can be learned and this competence stands the leader in good stead.

Team leadership and managing teams

Different styles and competencies are needed work in teams. The structure and function of the team and the personalities of team members will play key roles in determining how the leader is allowed to lead. In this context, we identify a single leader for the team rather than the (entire) team in a leadership role. The latter model may work in some executive committees but a leader is still required to play a central role in allowing decision-making by the group and to liaise and negotiate with outside agencies and stakeholders, and to communicate outcomes back to the group. In mental healthcare delivery teams the leader is the driver in ensuring that the team is effective. Hill[10] points out that leaders must have a 'model' of a situation wherein the model reflects not only the components of the problems faced by the team but also the environmental and organizational contingencies affecting the smooth functioning of the team. Flexibility, vision and a broad range of skills are required for this. As mentioned earlier, mental health professionals are trained to understand group dynamics; so, theoretically, they should be able to run teams effectively by managing them. However, this observation does not take into account individual personalities as well as their roles and functions within the team. A range of options is available to leaders. They will have to assess internal and external factors and monitor the situation and reach decisions. Mentoring team members and enabling them is part of the responsibility of the leader to ensure that the team works as an effective functional unit.

Manager or leader?

Mintzberg[11] notes that if managers are asked what they do, they are most likely to say that they plan, organize, coordinate and control; but when observed in their role, what they actually do often does not correspond to what they say they do. Managerial activities are said to be characterized by brevity, variety and discontinuity. Mintzberg[11] goes on to highlight that managers have formal authority and status and their interpersonal role as figurehead has associated informational roles as monitor and decisional roles as negotiator, allocator of resources and entrepreneur.

Leadership complements management and does not replace it

Kotter[12] argues that management is about coping with complexity, and its practices and procedures are in general a response to the development of large and complex organizations, whereas leadership is about coping with change. Both leadership and management require decisions, especially as to what needs to be done, thus creating networks of people and relationships that can accomplish an agenda and ensure that these tasks are carried out effectively. However, the manager and the leader do these differently: a manager will identify resources, whereas a leader will set the direction. Zaleznik[4] observes that the managerial culture emphasizes nationality and control and may adapt passive attitudes towards goals. The role of the manager and the leader may be entirely separate, embedded in each other, or may have slight overlap.

Psychodynamic understanding of leadership

Leadership as a process itself can be understood by looking at psychodynamic aspects. Similarly, the dynamic aspects of the personality of the leader are also of interest in explaining decision-making and leading. There have been various studies of leaders using psychoanalysis as a process by which the leader's actions can be understood.[4, 13, 14] There have also been studies of illnesses (physical and psychiatric) that various leaders have suffered and how these may have influenced their decisions in leadership roles.[15, 16]

There is no doubt that childhood experiences and child rearing patterns will influence how an individual develops. In early life children start by idolizing their parents and older siblings and then, as they grow older and attempt to find an individual identity, they tend to identify external figures as role models, for example pop stars, teachers, leaders, film stars or other celebrities. Hero worshipping can influence their subsequent behaviour, thinking, values and development. There is always a risk of attributing leadership roles to these role models, even if they are not true leaders. Stech[17] points out that the psychodynamic approach starts with the analyses of human personality, and these are then related to leadership levels and types. These personality traits are deeply ingrained. The psychodynamic approach also explores unconscious motives both of leaders and their followers. Stech[17] provides further details of transactional analysis and Freudian theories, which readers will find extremely helpful. Jungian personality types also provide an insight into the way a leader behaves.

Krueger and Theusen[18] remark that leadership involves the use of power, comprising both the personal and organizational. This is especially relevant when looking at the leadership roles of clinicians, particularly psychiatrists, as the latter have the legal power to deprive patients of their liberty and have the organizational power to medicate them against their will. The personality traits of the leader – whether they are an extrovert, introvert, thinker, intuitor, etc. – dictate the way they may respond to crises and how they reach decisions.

Leaders also have different ways of dealing with followers. In some cases, especially with extreme right-wing political ideology, the use of uniforms may be used to give a definite message,[19] as will wearing a white coat. The primary aim of the psychodynamic approach is to make both the leader and the follower aware of personality types and of underlying motives. In working with others, there may be unconscious motives that need to be identified, understood and explained if pragmatic decisions are to be reached. Stech[17] highlights the strength of the psychodynamic approach in analysing the relationship between the leader and the follower. Stech also recognizes weakness of the psychoanalytic approach due to its focus on personality traits. The approach remains attractive as it explores both the personality and the unconscious motives.

Key qualities of successful leaders

Communication

Even if the leader has an excellent vision of the development and direction of the organization, they may not be able to communicate their decisions effectively for the followers to realize and accomplish the vision. Charismatic leaders are good at listening and communicating with others. Effective and successful leaders convey their message in a straightforward way that allows followers to understand their roles and tasks clearly. Communication style may be intuitive but can also be learned. The basic communication model as described by Weightman[20] is about encoding the message, transmitting it in the context of the environment on the one hand, and decoding information and providing feedback on the other. The communication feedback loop is helpful in conveying even the most complex messages.[21] Communication networks can be of different varieties, such as chain, circle, wheel, all-channel, Y or inverted Y.[22] In order to succeed, good leaders follow both upward and downward methods of communicating with their followers. Effective communication within an organization means giving the same clear message to everyone, changing behaviour, improving motivation or sharing information.[23] Active listening and paraphrasing are important aspects in the stages of learning.[24] Leadership carries with it ethical and confidential responsibilities. Informed decision-making is discussed in Chapter 8.

Managing conflict

In professional settings in clinical practice, it is inevitable that conflicts may arise within teams. Clinical leaders need to be aware of potential areas that may lead to conflict and have strategies in mind to deal with these situations.

Barr and Dowding[24] point out that conflict may be seen as negative and confrontational, but also can be a positive way of bringing growth to the team. Obviously it depends on the type of conflict, the reasons for it, and how the conflict is managed and resolved. These authors go on to describe various levels of conflict, which are: intrapersonal (i.e. within the individual); interpersonal (between two or more people perhaps related to their beliefs, values, roles and rules); and intergroup conflict, which may be across professional groups or organizations. The responses as a result of conflict also vary both at individual and group levels. Conflict can result from overt and covert objectives and motives, differences in perceptions at various levels of organizations, resource management, and poor clarity of roles and responsibilities. The 'symptoms' as a result of conflict can be poor communication, frustration, rivalry, jealousy, friction at individual and professional levels, and loss of control or increased control as a response to conflict. If not tackled appropriately, the conflict can adversely affect the organization as well as the individual.

A leader can manage conflict using a number of strategies. These include: creating a friendly atmosphere; helping everyone to feel valued and part of the team; supporting and looking after colleagues; showing public acknowledgement and appreciation; and demonstrating respect and consideration towards others.[24]

Conflict can be avoided but in some settings it may be worthwhile building this up constructively to reach a satisfactory conclusion. Various options available to the leader include avoidance, accommodation, compromise, creative management and collaboration. Conflict management style may be active or passive. Thus leaders have to choose a way of dealing with the conflict according to their personality style.

Clinical leaders may need to use both personal and organizational strategies to manage conflict. Within such management, skills related to negotiation, ethics, confidentiality and objectivity are critical. Furthermore, cultural conflicts may become more relevant if team members are not aware of cultural nuances and differences. Hofstede[25] described cultural context in five dimensions while studying culture within IBM. These five dimensions are: distance from the centre of power, uncertainty avoidance, individualism-collectivism, femininity-masculinity and long-term orientation. They are vital in the understanding of cultural values and managing conflict that may be related to cultural variations.

Most professional organizations and regulatory bodies have policies on working in teams and collaborating. A competent clinical leader will thus be fully aware of potentials for tensions and negative conflicts, how these can be avoided, and if they happen how best these can be managed. Teams will have their own stages, whether they are new or old, mature and experienced. The type and degree of conflict therefore may be related to this setting as well, and the clinical leader may have to take this into account in managing conflict.

Gender and leadership

It is well known that gender plays a key role in leadership styles (also see Chapter 17). Rosener[26] argued that men were more transactional leaders and women had transformational styles. However, as Barr and Dowding[24] point out, in the last two decades this approach may well have become less evident. Certainly gender plays a key role in communication, collaboration and conflict management styles. Men and women socialize differently,[27] and their roles, how they relate to colleagues, and their perceived and real power in teams will also vary. These differences are important in our understanding of leadership styles.

Solving problems as leader

Problem-solving is part of the clinical role of the clinical leader. This allows a degree of conflation between decision-making and problem-solving, which is not entirely accurate. As problem-solving focuses on the root cause of the problem so that it can be understood and dealt with, this process is different from decision-making, which itself may be a part of the problem-solving activity. However, the organizational approaches of problem management are four-fold.[24] These include classical management, human relations, systems and contingency. Recognition of the nature of the problem is the first step, followed by assessment of the impact and the implication of the problem with an understanding of identifying outcome success criteria, actual decision-making and communicating solutions. The type of problem will obviously dictate how it is identified and solved. Problems have been described as simple (also called difficulties) or hard (complex) problems.[28] Complex problems may have more than one component and may be interrelated or even interdependent.

The steps in problem-solving are related to correct identification of the problem and gathering the right information and data, which will lead to the exploration of a range of alternative solutions, selecting the right option, implementing it, evaluating the success and communicating it effectively. Some of the solutions may have to be found by delegating matters to other members of the team.

Delegation of responsibilities

No leader can manage all the activities expected of them. It is inevitable that some matters will have to be delegated. This process is key in managing time as well as in managing teams, where the ultimate responsibility continues to rest with the leader but the person to whom the task has been delegated becomes responsible to the superior for carrying this out. Leaders may retain authority and responsibility as well as a degree of accountability. Accountability within the healthcare delivery system is within the regulatory structures of the individual's profession as well as civil, employment and criminal law. The culture of any organization and type of leadership will determine what type of delegation is allowed to occur. The act of delegation is also part of the process by which individuals within the team are supported and, indeed, encouraged to develop skills to take on additional responsibilities. Leaders influence the culture of the organization and the organization itself will allow the development of leadership skills and strategies.

Conclusions

Leadership means different things to different individuals in different settings. The art of leadership can be both acquired and influenced by a number of factors. Theories of leadership provide an overview of tasks that a leader may face. The culture of the organization on the one hand, and gender, personality traits, education and experience of the leader on the other, will produce an interaction that will affect the growth and the strategy of the organization. Leaders need followers, and leadership styles will be determined by the type of task that needs to be completed. Skills related to problem-solving and conceptual and strategic skills are all key in any leadership role. Clinical leadership can mean both leadership by clinicians as well as by those leading on clinical matters in clinical settings and healthcare structures. Clinicians are generally aware of decision-making and problem-solving, which makes it relatively easier for them to take on leadership roles. Various models of leadership provide an insight into our understanding of clinical leadership.

References

1   Fleischman E, Mumford M, Zaccaro S, Levin K, Korothis A, Heim M. Taxonomic efforts in the description of leader behaviour: a synthesis and functional interpretation. *Leadership Quart* 1991; **2**:245–87.
2   Bass BM. *Bass and Stogdill's Handbook of Leadership*. New York: Free Press, 1990.
3   Northouse P. *Leadership: Theory and Practice*. Thousand Oaks, CA: Sage, 2007.
4   Zaleznik A. Managers and leaders: are they different? In: *Harvard Business Review on Leadership*. Boston, MA: HSB Press, 1977; reprinted 1998; pp. 61–88.
5   Katz RL. Skills of an effective administrator. *Harvard Bus Rev* 1955: **33**:33–42.
6   Mumford MD, Zaccaro S, Harding F, Jacobs T, Fleischman EA. Leadership skills for a changing world: solving complex social problems. *Leadership Quart* 2000; **11**:11035.
7   Zaccaro S, Gilbert J, Thor K, Mumford M. Leadership and social intelligence: linking social perspectiveness and behavioural flexibility to leader effectiveness. *Leadership Quart* 1991; **2**:317–31.
8   Farkas CM, Wetlaufer S. The way chief executive officers lead. In: *Harvard Business Review on Leadership*. Boston, MA: HBS Press, 1998; pp. 115–46.
9   Heifetz RA, Laurie DL. The work of leadership. In: *Harvard Business Review on Leadership*. Boston, MA: HBS Press, 1998; pp. 171–98.
10 Hill SEK. Team leadership. In Northouse P (ed.), *Leadership: Theory and Practice*. Thousand Oaks, CA: Sage, 2007; pp. 207–36.

11   Mintzberg H. The manager's job: folklore and fact. In: *Harvard Business Review on Leadership*. Boston, MA: HBS Press, 1998; pp. 1–36.

12   Kotter JP. What leaders really do. In: *Harvard Business Review on Leadership*. Boston, MA: HBS Press, 1998; pp. 37–60.

13   Berens L, Cooper S, Ernst L *et al. Quick Guide to the 16 Personality Types in Organisations*. Huntingdon Beach, CA: Telos, 2001.

14   Maccoby M. *The Leader: A New Face for American Management*. New York: Ballantine, 1981.

15   L'Etang H. *Fit to Lead*. London: William Heinemann Medical Books, 1980.

16   L'Etang H. *The Pathology of Leadership*. London: William Heinemann Medical Books, 1969.

17   Stech EL. Psychodynamic approach. In: Northouse P (ed.), *Leadership: Theory and Practice*. Thousand Oaks, CA: Sage, 2007; pp. 237–64.

18   Kreuger O, Theusen JW. *Type Talk at Work*. New York: Dell, 2002.

19   Bhugra D, de Silva P. Uniforms: fact, fashion, fantasy or fetish. *Sexual and Marital Therapy* 1996; **11**: 393–406.

20   Weightman J. *Introducing Organisational Behaviour*. Harlow: Addison Wesley Longman, 1999.

21   Shannon C, Weaver W. *The Mathematical Theory of Communication*. University of Illinois Press, 1954.

22   Leavitt HJ. Some effects of certain communication patterns on group performance. *J Abnorm Soc Psychol* 1951; **46**:38–41.

23   Greenbaum HW. The audit of organisational communication. In: Weightman J (ed.), *Introducing Organisational Behaviour*. Harlow: Addison Wesley Longman, 1999; p. 70.

24   Barr J, Dowding L. *Leadership in Health Care*. London: Sage, 2008.

25   Hofstede G. *Culture's Consequences*. Thousand Oaks, CA: Sage, 2001.

26   Rosener J. (1990) Ways women lead *Harvard Business Review*. In Markham G. Gender in leadership. *Nursing Management* 1996; **3**:18–19.

27   Grohar-Murray ME, Di Croce H. *Leadership and Management in Nursing*. London: Prentice-Hall, 2002.

28   Ackoff A. The art and science of mass management. In: Mabey C, Mayon-White B (eds), *Managing Change*. London: Paul Chapman, 1981; pp. 47–54.

Chapter 2

What Makes a Leader? Skills and Competencies

Juan J. López-Ibor, Blanca Reneses and María-Inés López-Ibor

None of the different ways to approach the study of leadership cover all the diverse characteristics of a subject that is key in management. The traditional perspective emphasizes the personal characteristics of the leader, that is, the personality traits that facilitate or hinder his or her function. A second approach focuses on the behaviour that 'makes' the leader effective. The third perspective considers the situation in which the leadership process takes place, and therefore the group the leader runs and the context in which the process happens.

In this chapter we will consider the more personal aspects of leadership in its broadest sense, and how to put them into practice, while considering the crucial role of the context in which leader and workforce function. Of course we will highlight the specific requirements for leadership in the field of psychiatry and mental health.

Leader and leadership

The English words *leader* and *leadership* have been incorporated exactly so in most of the languages of the world. The reason is that putative translations may convey a very negative meaning. *Caudillo* in Spanish, *führer* in German or *duce* in Italian are good examples. Etymologically *caudillo* comes from the Latin *caput* 'head', from where also derives captain. The German *führer*, derived from *fahren* 'to drive', and the Italian *duce* from *ducere*, also 'to drive', denote persons who guide unchallenged. Instead, in the managerial jargon, leader and leadership have a positive meaning as they are fundamental elements of good quality management. Leadership is put into practice taking into account the best interests of the organization, basically because the organization's roles serve the best interests of the individuals in the organization, the clients and society at large. Therefore we have to keep in mind this distinction between a 'leader' and a *caudillo*, to say the least.

Leadership in Psychiatry, First Edition. Edited by Dinesh Bhugra, Pedro Ruiz and Susham Gupta.
© 2013 John Wiley & Sons, Ltd. Published 2013 by John Wiley & Sons, Ltd.

Leader

In its purest sense a leader is somebody whom people follow, someone who drives or directs other people. However, the term 'leader' is used in many different senses and has been abused to include anyone having any responsibility involving people in an organization. Yet there is far more involved in the fact of being a leader than simply holding a role.

A leader[1] is a person who holds a dominant or superior position within their field, and is able to exercise a high degree of control or influence over others. The leader may or may not have any formal authority, and more often than not they surpass the institutional role that they hold.

A pragmatic point of view considers an effective leader 'as an individual with the capacity to consistently succeed in a given condition and be viewed as meeting the expectations of an organization or society'.[2] A leader comes to the forefront in case of crisis, and is able to think and act in creative ways in difficult situations. Unlike management, leadership flows from the core of a personality and cannot be taught, although it may be developed and enhanced through coaching or mentoring.

Some organizations follow a traditional model of profitability, based on figures (i.e. the bottom line, number of visits, length of stay) while others adopt a more innovative approach, with leaders that strive to bring out the best in their teams, in order to enable people to contribute to the goals of the organization more creatively. This approach is essential in the healthcare sectors, where one of the functions of (clinical) leaders is to confront the economic demands of their superiors, namely the administrators of a Managed Care Organization or of a National Health Care System approach.

Leadership

Leadership is the ability to organize a group of people to achieve a common goal. Leadership is also the process of social influence whereby one person can enlist the collaboration and support of others in the achievement of a common task.[3]

Leadership has also been defined as:[1]

1   The activity of leading a group of people or an organization, or the ability to do this. In its essence, leadership in an organizational role involves: (i) establishing a clear vision, (ii) sharing that vision with others so that they will follow willingly, (iii) providing the information, knowledge, and methods to realize that vision, and (iv) coordinating and balancing the conflicting interests of all members or stakeholders.
2   The individuals who are the leaders in an organization, regarded collectively.

The so-called ontological–phenomenological model for leadership[4] (see below) considers leadership as 'an exercise in language that results in the realization of a future that wasn't going to happen anyway, which future fulfils (or contributes to fulfilling) the concerns of the relevant parties'. Therefore, leadership is about the future and includes the fundamental concerns of all the relevant parties instead of considering the dualism of a leader and their followers.

Every organization needs leaders at every level. The corroboration of leadership is in the following of the followers. Leadership is all about the influence to change wills, not just about dominance.[5] Leadership is a service, not a right nor a position in a hierarchy. A leader should never forget President Kennedy's chiasmus: 'Ask not what your country can do for you, ask what you can do for your country'. A leader should also convey this attitude to their team.

Management versus leadership[6]

A manager and a leader function in very different ways,[7,8] although they may share common responsibilities. The fact is that not all managers are leaders, but all leaders are, or should be, managers.

To manage is a designated and structural competence, which must comply with rules and regulations, is hierarchical and tries to control and influence people. In management as such, decisions are routines and are taken within the framework of a strategy already established, based on retrospective analysis, aiming to solve problems and to reduce uncertainty.[9,10]

To lead, on the other hand, is to manage wills, to provide the framework, values, resources and motivation to members of an organization to enable them to achieve previously agreed goals. Decisions are made from a strategic perspective with a prospective analysis method and tuning the culture of the organization.

Very often a manager is considered a replica of the leader, responsible for communicating the rules and philosophies of the organization to individual employees, and ensuring that they abide by them. A manager is a component in a hierarchical decision-making system. Managers are responsible for maintaining the day-to-day operations of the organization. The functions of a manager are to plan, organize and coordinate. A manager asks 'how' and 'when' in a passive way and expects to get answers about 'what' and 'why'.

In contrast, the main objective of leadership is to generate changes.[11] Leadership is emergent and personal, and has a modus operandi that has moral and ethical components.[9,10] A leader has to inspire and motivate and their agenda concerns interpersonal relationships. As implied above, a genuine leader should also be willing to surpass or confront hierarchies and 'bottom-line' short-range demands, keeping in mind and encouraging a long-range perspective. Leaders are considered 'fearless innovators' in that they challenge the status quo and are unafraid to take big risks in search of excellence.

In other words, management is a kind of a 'transactional' leadership (characterized by emphasis on procedures, contingent reward, management by exception) while true leadership is 'transformational' leadership (characterized by, e.g., charisma, personal relationships, creativity).[12] Table 2.1 summarizes the differences between management and leadership, although we have to insist that a leader is also a manager, whereas the opposite should not be sustained.

The Managerial Grid,[13,14] which we would prefer to call a 'Leadership Grid', is a graphical tool for evaluating leader behaviour along two basic attributes: concern for

Table 2.1 Management versus leadership. Modified from Lease[77]

	View of manager	View of leader
Goals	• To maintain and exploit business advantages[78] • To plan and budget • To organize and staff[79] • To keep the current system functioning[80] • Goals arise out of necessity[8]	• To successfully achieve organizational transformation[78] • To manage wills, to provide the framework, values, resources and motivation • To generate useful changes[11] • Goals arise out of vision[8]
Kind of competence	• A designated, hierarchical and structural competence, which must comply with rules and regulations[10, 11] • To solve problems[81]	• Decisions are made from a strategic perspective • To manage dilemmas[81]
Methods of work	• To control and influence people • To create stability[82] • Surrenders to the context, focus on the bottom line, on systems and structure, on tactics, accepting the status quo[83] • Controlling and problem-solving[79]	• Prospective analysis method, tuning the culture of the organization[9, 10] • Masters the context, focus on the horizon, on people. Challenging the status quo[83] • Motivating and inspiring people • To explore opportunities[84]
Attributes of work	• Facilitator[84] • Emphasis on rationality and control[82]	• Innovator, risk-taking, flexible, active[83] • Emphasis on inspiration
Required personal characteristics	• Intelligence, analytical ability, persistence, tolerance, goodwill[8]	• Tolerance of chaos, passion, intensity, empathetic[8]
Expected outcomes	• Predictability, order, consistent production of key results[85]	• Dramatic and useful changes (new products, new approaches, new processes)[85]

production (straightforward management) and concern for people (authentic leadership). The managerial grid model[13] distinguishes five leadership styles with varying concerns for people and production (Figure 2.1):

• The *impoverished style* (point 1,1), is characterized by low concern for both people and production; its primary objective is for managers to stay out of trouble.
• The *country club style* (point 1,9), is distinguished by high concern for people and low concern for production; its primary objective is to create a secure and comfortable atmosphere where managers trust that subordinates will respond positively.

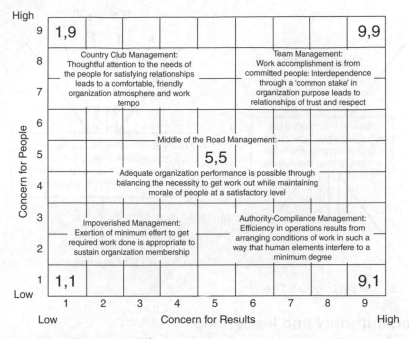

Figure 2.1   The managerial grid[1, 13]

- The *authoritarian style* (point 9,1), is identified by high concern for production and low concern for people; its primary objective is to achieve the organization's goals, and employee needs are not relevant in this process.
- The *middle-of-the-road style* (point 5,5) maintains a balance between workers' needs and the organization's productivity goals; its primary objective is to maintain employee morale at a level sufficient to get the organization's work done.
- The *team style* (point 9,9), is characterized by high concern for people and production; its primary objective is to establish cohesion and foster a feeling of commitment among workers.

The grid is a chiasmus (again) of theory X (management assumes employees are inherently lazy and will avoid work if they can and that they inherently dislike work. As a result, workers need to be closely supervised, and systems of controls implemented, and managers should rely heavily on threat and coercion to gain their employees' compliance)[15] and theory Y (management assumes that employees are ambitious, *self-motivated*, able to exercise *self-control*, and that they possess the ability for creative problem-solving, but their talents are underused in most organizations). Managers believe that the satisfaction of doing a good job is a strong motivation. Many people interpret theory Y as a positive set of beliefs about workers.[16]

Effective leadership styles exhibit high levels of both attributes (Figure 2.2).

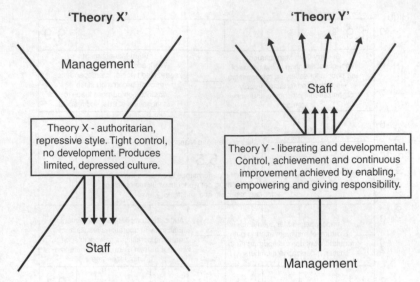

Figure 2.2   The McGregor XY theory[86]

Power, authority and leadership

Power is the ability to influence others in their behaviours, attitudes or beliefs. Effective leaders develop and use power. The traditional manager's power comes from their position within the organization. There are various forms of power used by managers to change employee behaviour.[17,18]

1   *Legitimate power* stems from a formal management position in an organization and the authority granted to it. Subordinates accept this as a legitimate source of power and comply with it.
2   *Reward power* stems from the authority to reward others. Managers can give formal rewards, such as pay increases or promotions, and may also use praise, give attention, and recognition to influence behaviour.
3   *Coercive power* is the opposite of reward power and stems from the authority to punish or to recommend punishment. Managers and leaders have coercive power when they have the right to fire or demote employees, criticize them, withhold pay increases, give reprimands, make negative entries in employee files, and so on.

Legitimate power and reward power are most likely to generate compliance, where workers obey orders even though they may personally disagree with them. Coercive power most often generates resistance, which may lead workers to deliberately avoid carrying out instructions or to disobey orders.

Leaders also possess other kinds of power.[19] *Personal power* is the tool of a leader who is followed because of the respect, admiration or care that workers feel for this individual and his or her ideas. The following two types of personal power exist:

• *Expert power* results from a leader's special knowledge or skills regarding the tasks performed by followers.

- *Referent power* results from leadership characteristics that command identification, respect and admiration from followers who then desire to emulate the leader. When workers admire a supervisor because of the way he or she deals with them, the influence is based on referent power. Referent power depends on a leader's personal characteristics rather than on his or her formal title or position, and is most visible in the area of charismatic leadership.

The most common response to expert power and referent power is commitment. Commitment helps team members to overcome fear of change, and it is especially important in those instances.

Another way to describe power is making the distinction between formal and informal power. This dichotomy is closely linked to the concept of formal and informal leadership. Formal power is legitimate power conferred by the hierarchical position in the organization.[18] Informal power is instead the result of personal characteristics and integrates 'referential power'.[20] Authentic leadership is associated with personal characteristics and therefore with informal leadership.[21]

In the healthcare world, and specifically in psychiatric services, the informal power and the expert power lie sometimes with physicians who are not at the highest hierarchical level; conversely, it is not always the professional with the 'legitimate power' who has the greatest expert power or referent power. The balanced combination of different types of power is important in a leadership position. Therefore, it is necessary that the leaders of the medical services in general, and psychiatric and mental health in particular, cultivate not only the expert power, but also the power of reference.[22, 23] The skills specific to reference power can be learned. Leaders with significant medical expert power can develop skills that increase their power of reference such as communication skills, to negotiate differences or for conflict management.

Leadership and charisma

Charisma is a leadership feature that is difficult to define. Charisma is all about personal traits and skills that are hard to acquire because they cannot be easily learned; rather, charisma is regarded as a personal gift that seduces or attracts others. The charismatic leader is able to influence how individuals or the group identify with the goals.[21]

Charisma can be defined by taking into account the personality of the leader or those powers conferred by the group. Charisma is an attribute that followers confer on the leader as a result of certain behaviours of the leader, such as the formulation of how a project differs from the status quo of the organization, the ability to take risks to achieve that vision, and the skill to articulate and convey the vision through good communication skills.[24–26] Charisma would then depend on the leader's talent to get his or her 'vision' shared by the followers.

Nowadays it is generally accepted that what attracts followers is the project (vision) of the leader and not his or her personal characteristics, in contrast to the traditional concept of charisma.[12] From charismatic leadership, transformational leadership theory evolved,[13] which has become the basis for a far-reaching research roadway.

The ability of charismatic leaders is based on creating an emotional bond with a critical mass of the group. From a psychoanalytic perspective, identification is the core feature in the relationship between the leader and the group.[14] Therefore, a key factor in charisma is the possibility that the origin of the ability to inspire arises from the evocation of features reminiscent of a significant figure from the past.[5]

Aberbach, based on attachment theory, describes how the charismatic ability of some great leaders during crises may be a creative exit to early emotional loss.[27,28].

Personal skills in leadership: traits of a leader

The study of leadership contains a lot about the traits of leaders[29] – situational interaction, function, behaviour, power, vision and values,[30] charisma, and intelligence, among many others. Because workplace situations vary, leadership requirements vary too

Critics of the trait theory of leadership point to the fact that recent research concentrates on a limited number of traits – i.e. the 'Big Five Factors'[31] – while it ignores other characteristics such as cognitive abilities, motives, values, social skills, expertise and problem-solving skills; fails to consider patterns or integrations of multiple attributes; does not distinguish between those leadership attributes that are generally not malleable over time and those that are shaped by, and bound to, situational influences; and does not consider how stable leadership attributes account for the behavioural diversity necessary for effective leadership.[32] As a result, it seems more appropriate to consider what effective leaders do rather than what effective leaders are, that is, merely distinguishing between effective and ineffective leaders.

The personality traits that characterize a leader encompass the following.[19,33]

Openness to the unvarnished truth[34]

This trait includes the following:

- *Credibility* – this is the foundation of leadership.[19] Leaders do what they say they will do. When a leader is believable, people are more likely to be committed and to provide their time, energy, intelligence and support.
- *Honesty* – leaders are truthful.
- *Integrity* – authentic leaders not only tell the truth, they also live using a set of ethical principles and clear standards.
- *Discretion* – leaders must always adopt a discreet position. They usually move alone as they cannot involve the organization in their concerns and weaknesses. They must inhibit their need to share and communicate emotions or risk losing authority with their peers.[26]
- *Self-mastery* – the key to growing one's leadership presence, building trusting relationships with followers and overcoming one's limiting beliefs and habits, thereby enabling behavioural flexibility as circumstances change, while staying connected to one's core values (i.e. while remaining authentic).[35] Self-mastery reflects a well-adjusted personality.[36] About 10% of office workers are relentlessly problematic,[37] and anyone can learn how to cope with these troublesome individuals. Although troublemakers cause problems, they often see themselves as the solution to problems or tensions, with

consequent disruption of the team's dynamic. Several types have been described (the plotter, the tease, the gossip, the escape artist, the know-it-all, etc.) and several coping mechanisms to confront them have been described, all of which necessitate a well-adjusted personality.

Implicit in the concepts of integrity and personal honesty is a consistency between words and deeds. A leader's behaviour cannot distance itself too much from his or her theoretical standpoint. Altruism and tolerance are further attributes described in the literature.[32]

Commitment

This trait includes:

- *Drive* – leaders are ambitious and take initiatives.
- *Motivation* – leaders want to lead and are willing to take charge.
- *Self-confidence* – leaders are assertive and decisive and enjoy taking risks. They admit mistakes and foster trust and commitment to a vision. Leaders are emotionally stable rather than recklessly adventurous.
- *Forward-looking* – good leaders have a vision for the future that is the basis for a strategic vision, for the ability to imagine a better future, clearly articulate it and involve others to attain goals.[31,32]
- *Openness to experience*[38] – one of the domains used to describe human personality in the '(Big) Five Factor Model'.[31] Openness involves active imagination, aesthetic sensitivity, attentiveness to inner feelings, preference for variety, and intellectual curiosity.
- *Conscientiousness*[38–40] – has been defined as extending from the virtual world into the real world. Conscientious people have strong moral principles and absolute certainty. They are concerned primarily with getting jobs done and getting them done right. They are loyal, hardworking, achievement oriented; they love to work, thrive on challenge, and are bound for success.[41] Highly valued characteristics of this type include attention to detail, self-discipline, emotional control, perseverance, reliability and politeness.[42]

Inspiring skills

Skills that inspire others include the following:

- *Motivating* – good leaders not only have a vision for the organization, but also connect that vision to others' hopes and aspirations. When people share in a future vision, they are more likely to willingly follow a leader. Inspiring leaders share their excitement about future possibilities. This excitement is accompanied by a positive attitude.
- *Ability to provide safety* – knowing how to create a safety culture to encourage the personal growth of the members of the organization.[33]
- *Determination and ability to delegate tasks* are personal characteristics required to be a good leader.[28–30]
- *Extraversion*[32,36] – organizations tend to celebrate and promote extroverted personalities, as opposed to introverts, who draw energy from ideas or one-on-one interactions. Such quiet types are often not as visible within companies, but by some calculations, introverts make up half of the population.

Competency

Competent individuals have a proven track record for getting things done. This generates confidence in a leader. Competency is based on:

- *Cognitive ability* – leaders are intelligent, perceptive and conceptually skilled, but are not necessarily geniuses. They show analytical ability, good judgement, and the capacity to think strategically.
- *Business knowledge* – leaders tend to have technical expertise in their field of business.
- *General self-efficacy*[43, 44] – this refers to one's confidence in executing courses of action in managing a wide array of situations. Individuals with higher work self-efficacy are more likely to look forward to, and to be successful in, workplace performance.

A combination of curiosity, creativity, perseverance and intelligence leads to competency. These traits are present in a set of behaviours that have often been described to provide expertise in training seminars and courses. For instance, leaders are:[32]

1 Readily willing to listen and make decisions based on a diverse range of views.
2 Acting as a guide or a coach, as opposed to those who dictate.
3 Providing credit for success to subordinates (rather than accepting it for themselves).
4 Enabling and empowering by providing free rein on business functions.
5 Enlightening people through development and education, whether based on the leader's personal experience or outside resources.
6 Inspiring others through a level of personal belief in the business venture.
7 Motivating people through positive reinforcement and rewards.
8 Leading by example.
9 Serving people, looking out for their best interests.

Leaders who make use of 'The Five Practices of Exemplary Leadership'[19] are perceived to be better leaders. These practices are:

1 Model the way
2 Inspire a shared vision
3 Challenge the process
4 Enable others to act
5 Encourage the heart

According to the functional leadership theory[19,45–47] the leader's main job is to see that whatever is necessary for the group's needs is taken care of; thus, a leader can be said to have done their job well when they have contributed to group effectiveness and cohesion. There are five functions a leader performs when promoting an organization's effectiveness: environmental monitoring, organizing subordinate activities, teaching and coaching subordinates, motivating others, and intervening actively in the group's work.[48]

In the specific field of psychiatry, both in academia and in healthcare settings, one might think that psychiatrists have advantages for the leadership role based on their understanding of group phenomena and experience in relational behaviour.

What sets up a leader?

The traditional approach to the research of leadership focuses on the leader's personality traits, idiosyncrasies and *Weltanschauung* ('worldview') – that which led him or her to become what they are – considering that leaders have some innate qualities, traits, talents, skills and physical characteristics that raise them to power.[49] For instance, Galton[50] was able to show in families of powerful men that the number of prominent relatives declined when moving from first-degree to second-degree relatives and that therefore leadership was inherited.

Although there have been plentiful retrospective studies on the great leaders of history (see Box 2.1 as an example), the ingredients of personality that predict success as leaders have not been clearly identified. Those studies reveal great variability, and although the need to take into account certain individual characteristics for a good leader is an issue that offers little controversy, leadership depends to a significant extent on the context in which it occurs – the nature of the organization and the people involved. As a result, nowadays it is generally accepted that there are certain conditions that facilitate a personal leadership role but, by themselves, these are not sufficient for success and that leadership effectiveness does not depend exclusively or predominantly on the personality of the leader. Personal attributes must be interwoven with knowledge and skills learned.[26]

Box 2.1 Sun Tzu's and Niccolo Machiavelli's lessons in leadership[6]

Sun Tzu and Machiavelli were the masters of leadership, and their philosophies, through their respective masterworks, *The Art of War* and *The Prince*, have taught generations of leaders the basics of being effective in their roles; their philosophies still hold true today. Here are a few key points:

- Consistency is the key to all leadership decisions. Setting the rules and abiding by them to the letter is the primary foundation for establishing an effective, time-tested leadership. Once the rules are set, they must be enforced unflinchingly and with an iron fist. When team members realize that even the leader is subject to the rules, then they will fall in line.
- Mixing personal relationships with leadership roles should be avoided: 'It is better to be feared than loved' (Machiavelli).
- Effective leaders do not waste their resources on unattainable goals: 'If troops lay siege to a walled city, their strength will be exhausted' (Sun Tzu). Leaders set realistic goals and centralize priorities for employees in order to prevent morale from falling.
- In order to maintain morale the leader should convey the message that he or she knows the plan, even when he or she hasn't the faintest idea.
- A leader has to be ready to make difficult decisions and sacrifices when necessary in order to attain the set goal. This is often a lonely path, but the path of a true leader is rarely one filled with friends, not forgetting Machiavelli's motto, 'The end justifies the means'.

Recent studies have revealed that individuals can and do emerge as leaders across a variety of situations and tasks,[43] and that this process is fostered by the presence of specific traits such as described above.

Great leaders are rarely born; rather they are created through rigorous trial and error. Great leaders grow into their roles and remain dedicated to their mission, regardless of the personal costs. In other words, times produce the person and not the other way around;[51]

different situations call for different characteristics and no single optimal psychographic profile of a leader exists. 'What an individual actually does when acting as a leader is in large part dependent upon characteristics of the situation in which he (or she) functions'.[52]

Any theory of leadership should include four key elements:[5]

- To explain why different contexts require different forms of leadership.
- To analyse the leadership as an interaction between leaders and followers.
- To address the role of power in the leadership process, not only as input but also as a result.
- To explain the transformational component that succeeds in bringing changes in both the followers and the leaders.

Leadership styles

An important consequence of the discussion above is that although some common traits are present in leaders, leaders in one situation may not necessarily be leaders in other situations.[53,54] In other words, the influence of individual characteristics on outcomes is best understood by considering the person as an integrated totality rather than a summation of individual variables.[32,43,53–56]

Early theories about leadership and organizations[57] were task oriented. The aim was to improve efficiency and production regardless of the human factor in the organization. In contrast to this approach, in the 1960s, Douglas McGregor,[16] among others, introduced a humanistic model of leadership in which human relationships and motivation of workers had a starring role.

The recent focus on situational leadership is the result of the combination of different styles of leadership, which integrates scientific and human relations dimensions and argues that it is necessary to adopt different leadership styles, taking into account the degree of maturity of the organization and the nature of the work environment.[58]

The effort to combine the trait and situational approaches led to the definition initially of three leadership styles (items 1–3 below), each being more effective in some situations and less effective in others. The number of styles has been constantly growing, often attached to specific models or theories about leadership. As a consequence they may overlap partially. Those more relevant in the healthcare sector are:

1 The *autocratic* or *authoritarian* style is highly efficient in periods of crisis but fails to empower teams in creative day-to-day management. It can also be called the *commanding* style because it is the classic model of traditional military-style leadership. Although it is probably the most often used it is often the least effective. Because it rarely involves praise and frequently employs criticism, it undercuts morale and job satisfaction.

2 The *participative* or *democratic* style is more suited to situations that require consensus building. This style draws on people's knowledge and skills, and creates a group commitment to the resulting goals. Engagement is the key to participative leadership.[59] It works best when the direction the organization should take is unclear, and the leader needs to tap the collective wisdom of the group. Nevertheless this

consensus-building approach can be disastrous in times of crisis, when urgent events demand quick decisions.

3   The *free-rein*, or *laissez-faire*, style is welcomed by teams due to the degree of freedom it provides, but often it fails to steer the organization to efficiently achieve its goals.

4   The *visionary* style is most appropriate when an organization needs a new direction. Its goal is to move people towards a new set of shared dreams. 'Visionary leaders articulate where a group is going, but not how it will get there – setting people free to innovate, experiment, take calculated risks.'[60]

5   The *coaching* style focuses on personal development, showing people how to improve their performance, and helping to connect their goals to the goals of the organization. Coaching works best with people who show initiative and want more professional development, but it can backfire if it's perceived as 'micromanaging' an employee, and undermines his or her self-confidence.

6   The *affiliative* style emphasizes the importance of teamwork, and creates harmony in a group by connecting people to each other. This approach is particularly valuable when trying to heighten team harmony, increase morale, improve communication or repair broken trust in an organization, but it may backfire if it becomes an opportunity to increase tolerance to mediocrity.

7   The *pace-setting* style is based on demanding high standards of performance for the leader as well as the followers. This style should be used sparingly, because it can undercut morale and make people feel as if they are failing.

8   The *engaging* style is where the aim is to engage both leaders and employees in understanding the existing conditions and how they can collectively assist in addressing them. This can be attained by reaching out to employees during difficult times to better understand their concerns and interests.[61] The engaging style is a variant of the participative style.

9   The *narcissistic* style is a common leadership style among academics and clinicians. It is accomplished when the leader is only interested in him/herself, at the expense of their people/group members.The narcissism may range anywhere between healthy and destructive.

10   The *toxic* style is present when the leader is someone who has responsibility over a group of people or an organization, and abuses the leader-follower relationship by leaving the group or organization in a worse condition than when he/she joined it.

11   The *ontological-phenomenological* style focuses on the future and on the fundamental concerns of the relevant parties, avoiding the dualism of leader and followers. A future that addresses the concerns of the relevant parties is no longer a vision of the leader, but rather is the outcome of putting upfront the concerns of those who are headed by the leadership.[4]

Informal leaders

An informal leader[1] is an individual within an organization who is viewed as someone worth listening to due to their perceived experience and reputation among peers. The informal leader does not hold any position of formal authority or power over the peers choosing to follow his or her lead but can influence the decisions of others. Informal leaders emerge in disaster situations, but sometimes they can interfere with rescue activities and interventions.

Some authors argue that leaders in the field of psychiatry tend to adopt interpersonal (democratic) leadership-based styles rather than power relations.[62, 63]

Relationship-oriented versus task-oriented leaders

These two types of leadership are based on the situational contingency theory. Relationship-oriented leaders tend to accomplish the task by developing good relationships with the group, while task-oriented leaders have as their prime concern the performance of the task itself considering that there is no ideal leader for all situations. Both task-oriented and relationship-oriented leaders can be effective if their leadership orientation fits the situation. Task-oriented leaders are more effective in extremely favourable or extremely unfavourable situations, whereas relationship-oriented leaders perform best in situations with intermediate favourability.[64]

Public, private and personal leadership

The Integrated Psychological theory of leadership is an attempt to integrate the strengths of other theories by introducing a new element – the need for leaders to develop their leadership presence, attitude toward others and behavioural flexibility by practising psychological mastery.[35] In order to do so the theory has defined three levels of leadership:[35, 65] public, private and personal leadership. The first two, public and private leadership, are 'outer', or behavioural, levels that address the four dimensions of leadership: (i) a shared, motivating group purpose; (ii) action, progress and results; (iii) collective unity or team spirit; and (iv) individual selection and motivation.

Personal leadership is an 'inner' level and concerns a person's growth towards greater leadership presence, know-how and skill. Personal leadership has three facets: (i) technical know-how and skill; (ii) developing the right attitude towards other people (servant- or service-oriented leadership); and (iii) psychological self-mastery (authentic leadership).

Transactional and transformational leadership

Eric Berne first analysed the relations between a group and its leadership in terms of transactional analysis.[66] Transactional leadership includes the following core elements:

- contingent reward;
- management-by-exception active;
- management-by-exception passive.

The transactional leader influences the motivation of his or her followers by exchanging rewards. He or she tries to determine the followers' needs and expectations and respond to them accordingly. Curiously enough, transactional leadership is nothing but *laissez faire*, which characterizes leaders not actually engaged in a leadership role.

Transformational leadership has five core elements:[67,68]

- Idealized influence (attribution) – a form of charismatic leadership based on admiration, respect and appreciation of subordinates for the leader.
- Idealized influence (behaviour).
- Inspirational motivation – motivation to promote a common vision and to stimulate members of the organization to have a commitment that goes beyond performing the regular tasks and duties. At the same time this kind of leadership provides staff with the resources to behave so.
- Individualized consideration.
- Intellectual stimulation promotes new ways of working supported by innovation and creativity.

Transformational leadership shares some elements with charismatic leadership: the importance of identification with the leader and the dissemination of the leader's vision to all members of the organization. Besides, transformational leadership incorporates new elements that contribute to the intellectual and personal development of the members of the organization, namely intellectual stimulation and individualized consideration. Intellectual stimulation promotes new ways of working based on innovation and creativity.

Transactional and transformational leadership are not mutually incompatible; on the contrary, a combination of both strategies is ideal. Transformational leadership includes an ethical dimension, consisting of the leader's commitment to strive for the benefit of the group and society while transcending any personal interest dimension; this aspect is not so significant under charismatic leadership.

The Multifactor Leadership Questionnaire (MLQ),[68] which quantifies the essential factors of transactional and transformational leadership styles, has been validated.

Transactional and transformational leadership styles have proved their effectiveness in the health sector in order to achieve the implementation of evidence-based medicine.[69,70] Besides, transformational leadership has proved to be a protective factor against burnout in healthcare organizations,[71,72] and is positively associated with different processes and outcomes such as job satisfaction and responsibility towards the organization.[73,74]

An account of contrasting leadership styles is given in Box 2.2.

Box 2.2 Contrasting leadership styles drawn from real life

During the process of planning the ICD-10 Primary Health Care Version Field Studies in Spain one of us, the Director of the WHO Training and Education Centre in Madrid, organized a meeting with Norman Sartorius, the person responsible for the development and implementation of chapter F (V) on Mental and Behavioural Disorders, and the presidents of the three societies in the field from Spain. They had never met together before and they were strongly competing among themselves in the profession, in society and in their aspirations to gain influence on the Health Care Administration reorganized after the establishment of democracy in Spain.

The three were top leaders, but their style was manifestly different. One was president of an old-established society mainly consisting of rural doctors working in a traditional way and identified with conservative political positions. The President spoke elegantly, was dressed in formal attire, wore a tie and no beard, and had no problem in taking all the decisions about the research study as, so he said, he had the full trust of the members of his society.

The second belonged to a recently created society that had a strong socio-democratic approach to healthcare and maybe other problems of society. The President spoke in a barely noticeably pedantic way, was dressed more informally, but in clothes that were elegant and casual, and of course no tie. He wore a short and carefully trimmed beard. He stated that although he was in favour of participating in the study with the two other societies, he had to go his Executive Committee for a collegial decision.

The third belonged to a left-wing society that was trying to reorganize itself. The President spoke with clear determination, was dressed informally, wore a beard (of course), this time in old Dutch style, but not so long as to obscure the chest hair revealed by his open-neck shirt. In his case the important decisions had to be taken at a General Assembly of his comrades.

In the end the three societies participated enthusiastically. Each of them designated a member for a steering committee of the research project. The resulting Spanish language study had by far the greatest number of participants of any similar study conducted throughout the world.

The impact of leadership on the organization

The leadership style largely determines the behaviour of the group and the results of the task its members are responsible for. But, as mentioned above, the personal characteristics of the leader and his or her leadership style are only one ingredient influencing the final result. To achieve effective leadership, the characteristics of the group, its internal organization, a clear definition of the task of the organization, and its organizational and administrative structure must also be taken into account. Given these elements, it is known that effective leadership can have a moderate positive influence. But the consequences of bad leadership are more extreme.[75]

The motivation of professionals is another element when considering the impact of leadership style. The motivational framework for health professionals, in particular physicians, has distinctive characteristics when compared to other professions. The most relevant is the importance of intrinsic and transcendental motivation, that is, the desire for a job well done and the satisfaction of its positive impact on others.[58] This means that the leader should give significant value to knowledge, to openness to innovation and to human factors that lead to greater commitment.

Demoralization and demotivation in clinical staff occur especially when individual and professional goals are thwarted for various reasons. One such reason may be an authoritarian, hierarchical and bureaucratic management style that is the opposite of participatory leadership. The demotivation and burnout may lead to worse patient care and greater staff turnover. The leader of a healthcare organization must know that one of the main challenges is to promote the motivation of his or her team members, and healthcare services need a leadership style that includes the value orientation and the commitment of professionals.[6, 33]

The positive effect of leadership seen in the climate of the organization

In the specific field of psychiatry and mental health the analysis of empirical data has shown that the organizational climate is closely related to the successful implementation of evidence-based practice[38, 39] and of positive clinical outcomes in general.[31] Healthcare organizations with a more competent culture, and that are more committed and have a less stressful work environment, are associated with more positive attitudes from the clinicians. Specifically, transformational leadership has been directly associated with an improved attitude towards innovation.[39]

Another indirect measure of the effect of leadership on the work climate in healthcare organizations is the degree of professional burnout. In the specific field of psychiatric services, transformational leadership has been associated with lower burnout rates and greater cohesion of professional teams, whereas an opposite association was observed with a leadership style based on laissez faire, with a higher levels of burnout and deleterious effects on the organizational culture.[76]

Personal traits that hinder leadership

In essence the personal characteristics that are described as obstacles to effective leadership are the mirror image of the positive attributes. An extensive survey of academic leaders of psychiatry in the United States[58] identified the following risk factors for a lack of leadership:

- Lack of vision.
- Indecision.
- Excessive narcissism that prevents enough attention being paid to other people.
- Lack of sufficient maturity to perform as a professional mentor.
- Giving precedence to personal needs over those of the organization.

Certain abnormal personalities and particular pathologies can interfere significantly in leadership effectiveness. This is especially so in the case of paranoid and narcissistic personalities, having the highest difficulty handling tensions and aggressivity.[26] Excessive impulsivity has also been described as a numbing feature.[28]

The leadership role entails the risk of burnout due to several reasons, including excessive commitment to work, lack of personal space and the need to be constantly solving problems.[35, 36]

References

1   BusinessDictionary.com. Available at: http://www.businessdictionary.com [accessed 27 March 2013].
2   Ogbonnia S. The political party system and effective leadership in Nigeria: a contingency approach. Dissertation, Walden University, 2007.
3   Chemers MM. *An Integrative Theory of Leadership*. Mahwah: Lawrence Erlbaum Associates, 1997.
4   Erhard W, Jensen MC, Granger KL. Creating Leaders: An Ontological Model. Harvard Business School: Working Knowledge (on-line newsletter), 2010. Available at: http://hbswk. hbs.edu/item/6570.html [accessed 27 March 2013].
5   Haslam S, Reicher S, Platow MJ. El liderazgo como gestión de la identidad social. In: Molero F, Morales J (eds), *Liderazgo: hecho y ficción*. Madrid: Alianza, 2012; pp. 77–116.

6   Leo Sun. Management vs. Leadership. BusinessDictionary.com. Available at: http://www. businessdictionary.com [accessed 27 March 2013].

7   Kotte JP. *A Force for Change: How Leadership Differs from Management.* New York: Free Press, 1990.

8   Zaleznik A. Managers and leaders: are they different? *Harvard Bus Rev* 1977; **55**:67–78.

9   Shortell SM. The evolution of hospital systems: unfulfilled promises and self-fulfilling prophesies. *Med Care Rev* 1988; **45**:177–214.

10 Shortell SM, Kaluzny A. *Essentials of Health Care Management.* Albany: Thomsom Learning, 1997.

11 Kellerman B. Thinking about...leadership. Warts and all. *Harvard Bus Rev* 2004; **82**:40–5, 112.

12 Burns JM. *Leadership.* New York: Harper & Row, 1978.

13 Blake R, Mouton J. The Managerial Grid: The Key to Leadership Excellence. Houston: Gulf Publishing Co, 1964.

14 BusinessDictionary.com. Available at: http://www.businessdictionary.com [accessed 27 March 2013].

15 Papa MJ. *Organizational Communication. Perspectives and Trends.* London: SAGE Publications, Inc., 2008.

16 McGregor D. *The Human Side of Enterprise.* New York: McGraw Hill, 1960.

17 French JRP Jr, Raven B. The bases of social power. In: Cartwright D (ed.), *Studies in Social Power.* Ann Harbor, MI: Institute for Social Research, 1959.

18 Raven BH. The bases of power and the power/interaction model of interpersonal influence. *Analyses of Social Issues and Public Policy* 2008; **8**:1–22.

19 Kouzes JM, Posner BZ. *The Leadership Challenge.* San Francisco: Jossey-Bass, 2002.

20 Gabel S. Addressing demoralization in clinical staff: a true test of leadership. *J Nerv Ment Dis* 2011; **199**:892–5.

21 Pielstick CD. Formal vs informal leading: A comparative analysis. *J Leadership Stud* 2000; **7**:99–114.

22 McKenna MK, Gartland MP, Pugno PA. Development of physician leadership competencies: perceptions of physician leaders, physician educators and medical students. *J Health Adm Educ* 2004; **21**:343–54.

23 Williams SJ. What skills do physician leaders need now and in the future? *Physician Exec* 2001; **27**:46–8.

24 Conger JA, Kanugo RM. Toward a behavioral theory of charismatic leadership in organizational settings. *Acad Manage Rev* 1987; **12**:647.

25 Conger JA, Kanugo RM. Behavioral dimensions of charismatic leadership. In: Conger JA, Kanugo RM (eds), *Charismatic Leadership.* San Francisco: Jossey Bass, Inc., 1988; pp. 78–97.

26 Pearce CI, Conger JA. *Shared Leadership: Reframing the Hows and Whys of Leadership.* Thousand Oaks: Sage, 2003.

27 Bowlby J. *Attachment and Loss.* New York: Basic Books, 1982.

28 Aberbach D. Charisma and attachment theory: a cross-disciplinary interpretation. *Int J Psychoanal* 1995; **76**:845–55.

29 Locke EA, Kirkpatrick S, Heeler JK, *et al. The Essence of Leadership.* New York: Lexington Books, 1991.

30 Richards D, Engle S. After the vision: Suggestions to corporate visionaries and vision champions. In: Adams JD (ed.), *Transforming Leadership.* Alexandria, VA: Miles and River Press, 1986; pp. 199–215.

31 McCrae RR, John OP. An introduction to the Five-Factor Model and its applications. *J Pers* 1992; **60**:175–215.

32   Zaccaro SJ. Trait-based perspectives of leadership. *Am Psychol* 2008; **62**:6–16.

33   Kirkpatrick SA, Locke EA. Do traits really matter? *Acad Manage Perspect* 1991; **5**:48–60.

34   Eisenstat RA, Beer M, Foote N, Fredberg T, Norrgren F. The uncompromising leader. *Harvard Bus Rev* 2012; **86**:50–7.

35   Scouller J. *The Three Levels of Leadership: How to Develop Your Leadership Presence, Knowhow and Skill*. Cirencester: Management Books, 2000, 2011.

36   Zaccaro SJ. Trait-based perspectives of leadership. *Am Psychol* 2012; **62**:6–16.

37   Bramson RM. *Coping with Difficult People: The Proven-Effective Battle Plan That Has Helped Millions Deal with the Troublemakers in Their Lives at Home and at Work*. New York: Dell Publishing, 1981.

38   Judge TA, Bono JE, Ilies R, Gerhardt MW. Personality and leadership: A qualitative and quantitative review. *J Appl Psychol* 2002; **87**:765–80.

39   Arvey RD, Rotundo M, Johnson W, Zhang Z, McGue M. The determinants of leadership role occupancy: Genetic and personality factors. *Leadership Quart* 2006; **17**:1–20.

40   Tagger S, Hackett R, Saha S. Leadership emergence in autonomous work teams: Antecedents and outcomes. *Pers Psychol* 1999; **52**:899–926.

41   Torgersen S. Epidemiology. In: Oldham JM, Skodol AE *et al.* (eds), *Textbook of Personality Disorders*. Washington, DC: American Psychiatric Publishing, 2005; pp. 129–41.

42   Beck AT, Freeman A, Davis DD. *Cognitive Therapy of Personality Disorders*, 2nd edn. New York: Guilford, 2004.

43   Foti RJ, Hauenstein NMA. Pattern and variable approaches in leadership emergence and effectiveness. *J Appl Psychol* 2007; **92**:347–55.

44   Smith JA, Foti RJ. A pattern approach to the study of leader emergence. *Leadership Quart* 1998; **9**:147–60.

45   Hackman JR, Walton RE. Leading groups in organizations. In: Goodman PS (ed.), *Designing Effective Work Groups*. San Francisco: Jossey-Bass, 1986; pp. 72–119.

46   McGrath JE. *Leadership Behaviour: Some Requirements for Leadership Training*. Washington, DC: US Civil Service Commission, 1962.

47   Adair J. *Effective Leadership*. London: Pan Books, 1988.

48   Klein KJ, Ziegert JC, Knight AP, Xiao Y. Dynamic delegation: Shared, hierarchical, and deindividualized leadership in extreme action teams. *Admin Sci Quart* 2006; **51**:590–621.

49   Carlyle T. *On Heroes, Hero-Worship, and the Heroic in History*. Boston: Houghton-Mifflin, 1849.

50   Galton F. *Hereditary Genius*. New York: Appleton, 1869.

51   Heifetz R. *Leadership Without Easy Answers*. Cambridge, MA: Harvard University Press, 1994.

52   Hemphill JK. *Situational Factors in Leadership*. Columbus: Ohio State University Bureau of Educational Research, 1949.

53   Stogdill RM. Personal factors associated with leadership: A survey of the literature. *J Psychol* 1948; **25**:35–71.

54   Mann RD. A review of the relationship between personality and performance in small groups. *Psychol Bull* 1959; **56**:241–70.

55   Gershenoff AG, Foti RJ. Leader emergence and gender roles in all-female groups: A contextual examination. *Small Group Res* 2003; **34**:170–96.

56   Magnusson D. Holistic interactionism: A perspective for research on personality development. In: Pervin LA, John OP (eds), *Handbook of Personality: Theory and Research*. New York: Guilford Press, 1995; pp. 219–47.

57   Taylor F. *The Principles of Scientific Management*. New York: Harper & Row, 1911.

58   Marcos LR, Silver MA. Psychiatrist-executive management styles: nature or nurture? *Am J Psychiatry* 1988; **145**:103–6.

59   Collaborative Leadership (website). Leadership Development National Excellence Collaborative. URL: http://www.collaborativeleadership.org/pages/modules_description.html [accessed 27 March 2013].

60   Goleman D. Leadership that gets results. *Harvard Bus Rev* 2000 March-April: 82–3.

61   Alimo-Metcalfe B, Alban-Metcalfe J, Bradley M, Mariathasan, J, Samele, C. The impact of engaging leadership on performance, attitudes to work and wellbeing at work: A longitudinal study. *J Health Organ Manag* 2008; **22**:586–98.

62   Lipton A, Loutsch E. A reconsideration of power in psychiatric administration. *Hosp Community Psychiatry* 1985; **36**:497–503.

63   Racy J. Psychiatrist and administrators: problems on leadership and the exercise of power. *Hosp Community Psychiatry* 1975; **26**:528–9.

64   Fiedler FE. *A Theory of Leadership Effectiveness*. New York: McGraw Hill-Harper and Row Publishers, Inc., 1967.

65   Businessballs.com. Integrated psychological approach. Available at: http://www.businessballs.com/leadership-theories.htm#integrated-psychological-leadership[accessed 27 March 2013].

66   Berne E. *The Structure and Dynamics of Organizations and Groups*. Philadelphia: Lippincott, 1963.

67   Bass B. From transactional to transformational leadership: Learning to share the vision. *Organ Dyn* 1990; **18**:19–30.

68   Avolio BJ, Bass B. *Multifactor Leadership Questionnaire*, 3rd edn. Palo Alto: Mind Garden, 2004.

69   Aarons GA. Transformational and transactional leadership: association with attitudes toward evidence-based practice. *Psychiatr Serv* 2006; **57**:1162–9.

70   Aarons GA, Sommerfeld DH. Leadership, innovation climate, and attitudes toward evidence-based practice during a statewide implementation. *J Am Acad Child Adolesc Psychiatry* 2012; **51**:423–31.

71   Green AE, Miller EA, Aarons GA. Transformational leadership moderates the relationship between emotional exhaustion and turnover intention among community mental health providers. *Community Ment Health J* 2011 [epub ahead of print].

72   Stordeur S, D'hoore W, Vandenberghe C. Leadership, organizational stress, and emotional exhaustion among hospital nursing staff. *J Adv Nurs* 2001; **35**:533–42.

73   MacKenzie SB, Podsakoff PM, Rich GA. Transformational and transactional leadership and salesperson performance. *J Acad Market Sci* 2001; **29**:115–34.

74   Walumbwa FO, Orwa B, Wang P, Lawler JJ. Human Resource Development *Quarterly* 2005; **16**:235–256.

75   Molero F. La investigación del liderazgo en psicología. In: Molero F, Morales J (eds), *Liderazgo: hecho y ficción*. Madrid: Alianza, 2011; pp. 21–45.

76   Corrigan PW, Diwan S, Campion J, Rashid F. Transformational leadership and the mental health team. *Adm Policy Ment Health* 2002; **30**:97–108.

77   Lease DR. Management reviled: is leadership just good management repackaged? Academy of Business Education Conference, 6–7 April 2006. Available at: http://drdavidlease.com/uploads/MANAGEME.PDF [accessed 28 March 2013].

78   Ackoff RL. The opportunity quest separates real leaders from managers. *Strategy & Leadership* 2003; **31**:39–40.

79   Kotter JP. What leaders really do. *Harvard Bus Rev* 2001; **79**:85–97.

80   Kotter JP. *John P. Kotter on What Leaders Really Do*. Boston: Harvard Business School Press, 1999.

81   Nicolaou-Smokoviti L. Business leaders' work environment and leadership styles. *Curr Sociol* 2004; **52**:407–27.

82 Alvesson M, Sveningsson S. Managers doing leadership: The extra-ordinarization of the mundane. *Human Relations* 2003; **56**:1435–59.

83 Bennis W. *On Becoming a Leader*. Reading, MA: Addison-Wesley Publishing Co., Inc., 1989.

84 Caldwell R. Change leaders and change managers: Different or complementary? *Leadership Organiz Dev J* 2003; **24**:285–93.

85 Kotter JP. *A Force for Change: How Leadership Differs from Management*. New York: Free Press, 1990.

86 Businessballs.com. Douglas McGregor's XY theory. Available at: http://www.businessballs.com/mcgregor.htm [accessed 28 March 2013].

Chapter 3

Medical Professionalism, Leadership and Professional Judgement

Dinesh Bhugra, Alex Till, Nicholas Deakin and Pedro Ruiz

Introduction

Professionalism is the hallmark of professionals. How a profession defines its standards, skills and knowledge base is critical in the development of professionalism in its members. Professionalism in medicine has a long history and, in spite of attacks on it, has managed to survive relatively intact. Built within the concept of professionalism is the expertise and judgement on professional matters. The relationship between clinical leadership and clinical or medical professionalism is an intricate one.

Professionalism has certain core components, including self-regulation, team working, good communication skills, and managing time and resources. However, different professions may place different emphases on different components. Part of the responsibility of the professional (as well as leaders) is social contact. This concept deals with the contract between the society at large and the professional group or body. Society defines deviance and normality and allocates resources accordingly for dealing with individuals who need help of one kind or another. Mental health professionals have a specific responsibility dealing with risk assessment and risk management. In some ways the level of risk changes according to society's concerns. It is helpful to ascertain what society expects of psychiatrists and what the profession expects in return. Professionalism thus defined has key concepts of the role of the leader and critical timing. In this chapter we propose to explore the links between professionalism, critical timing and styles of leadership.

Historical account

Gough[1] provides an interesting overview of the concepts of the social contract. He points out that although the contract started in ancient Greece in Aristotelian times, its heyday was in the seventeenth and eighteenth centuries. In an age of monarchy rooted in the divine right of kings (monarchs), 'social contract' covered two different kinds of contract – the

Leadership in Psychiatry, First Edition. Edited by Dinesh Bhugra, Pedro Ruiz and Susham Gupta.

social contract proper (a group of individuals living together agreed to form a society) and the contract of government or submission (contract between the King and the people). The latter contract, Gough[1] argued, was to do with specifying views that determine the people's relations with the King. They promise him obedience and in return he promises them protection and good government. The contract therefore determined what was needed and what was required from both sides. Although it can be argued that 'contract' is a legal term and legally binding, medicine's contract with society is not explicit but implicit. The contract has to be differentiated from obligation. Interestingly, Gough[1] also argues that the contract theory was the expression of an exaggerated individualism that recognized no ultimate reality but force. Cruess and Cruess[2] describe medicine's contract with society, which, with a few amendments, can be applied to psychiatry.

Professionalism

Medical professionalism – defined as an occupation governed by ethics with its members working on the basis of their mastery of a complex body of knowledge and skills – dates back to Hippocrates in the late fifth century BC. Since then, our commitments as medical professionals have been at the very heart of being a good doctor and have formed the basis for a moral contract between the profession and society, whereby we belong to 'a moral community whose defining purpose is to respond to and advance the welfare of those who are ill, in need of help, healing, or relief of suffering, pain or disability' with a doctor's knowledge, clinical skills and judgement utilized to protect and restore human well-being.[3–5] This moral community was formalized by the evolution of medieval guilds bringing a covenant between society and the medical profession.[6] They provided a specialized service for society and self-regulated their membership in exchange for autonomy, respect and a fair livelihood as long as society's needs were met.[7] Our current medical professional bodies, for example the Royal College of Physicians in the UK, are a derivation of the guilds, established in 1518 as the Company of Physicians. With extraordinary stringency they regulated and licensed doctors in the practice of medicine and were responsible for setting and maintaining professional standards.[5] Through this formalization it was clear that professionalism lay at the heart of being a good doctor and became 'an ideal to be sustained'.[8] Going back to Hellenic Greece and Hippocrates, we see the origins of the Declaration of Geneva, which in response to changes in society's expectations, replaced the better-known Hippocratic Oath in 1948.[9] This oath, taken by graduands throughout the world, presents the unique demands and expectations that are placed on the doctor as a leader; the graduands, on its proclamation, are said to have attained their professional status. As a result of this, one has a 'binding commitment to place one's specialist knowledge and skills at the service of their patients' and adhere to the General Medical Council's (GMC's) duties of a doctor as set out in 'Good Medical Practice', the formal expression of this professionalism in the United Kingdom.[3, 10] Weissman and Busch in this volume (see Chapter 18) emphasize the cardinal relationship between the clinical leader and the patient, outlining clear responsibilities for a doctor to uphold this relationship.[11] As Richard Horton, prime author of 'Doctors in Society', states:

'professionalism is medicine's most precious commodity' and it is this that separates the physician as a medical professional from a skilled medical worker.[12, 13]

The Royal College of Physicians has recently redefined medical professionalism as 'a set of values, behaviours, and relationships that underpins the trust the public has in doctors.' It involves multiple commitments – to the patient, fellow professional and the institution or system within which healthcare is provided to collectively support the patient.[5] Inculcated into us through a 'process of professionalization and teaching of professional behaviour'[3] by our medical school and postgraduate training, we begin to encompass these values and define our relationship with our patients and society as a medical professional.[6]

Published simultaneously in the United Kingdom and United States of America was the Charter on Medical Professionalism.[14] Here, the values, behaviours and relationships were described further as a set of fundamental principles and a set of 10 professional responsibilities or 'commitments' that a doctor should uphold. The fundamentals refer to:

- 'primacy of patient welfare', whereby the dedication to altruism is outlined and how as doctors we must not let external factors compromise this;
- 'patient autonomy', whereby the importance of being honest and respecting our patients' decisions must be upheld; and
- 'social justice', whereby we have a duty to fairly distribute resources and eliminate discrimination.

The 10 commitments required by the charter in order to achieve the basic components integral to a good medical professional are summarized as follows:

1 *Professional competence* – ensuring all members of the profession can achieve and maintain competence with a commitment to lifelong learning in order to sustain the knowledge and skills necessary for quality care.
2 *Honesty with patients* – ensuring honesty with patients allowing informed consent and decisions on care to be made whilst additionally taking responsibility, informing them of adverse events of medical care and implementing measures to prevent recurrence.
3 *Patient confidentiality* – ensuring the strictest of confidence is upheld regarding patient information, particularly with increasing use of computer-based systems.
4 *Maintaining appropriate relations with patients* – ensuring the vulnerability of patients is not exploited for personal gain, particularly sexually or financially.
5 *Improving quality of care* – ensuring continuous active involvement in quality improvement for systems, individuals and institutions within healthcare.
6 *Improving access to care* – ensuring throughout society there is an equitable access to an adequate standard of healthcare including the promotion of public health and preventative medicine.
7 *Just distribution of finite resources* – ensuring cost-effective allocation of resources and avoidance of superfluous services.
8 *Scientific knowledge* – ensuring scientific evidence and technology is appropriately used clinically whilst promoting an active involvement in research.

9   *Maintaining trust by managing conflicts of interest* – ensuring professional responsibilities are not compromised by personal gains.

10   *Professional responsibilities* – ensuring self-regulation and collaboration to maximize patient care.[14]

These recommendations, combined with guidance from the Royal College of Physicians and General Medical Council in the United Kingdom, provide doctors with the responsibility and framework to assess their own personal values, behaviours and relationships against its description, now considered the 'gold standard', to ensure they meet the standard of modern professionalism expected in daily clinical practice.[5]

Motivation in professionalism

Professionalism has both individual and collective aspects to it. Collective aspects come from regulatory bodies, professional associates and an ethical framework. The components of professionalism can be and should be included in the curriculum at an early stage. These components include not only technical knowledge but also expertise, with a clear commitment to the values of the profession. These competencies must keep patient welfare at the core of professionalism and include clinicians acting honestly on a par with the patients. Maintaining appropriate relations and confidentiality with patients, their carers and families is critical. Focus on improving quality of care with just distribution of finite resources while managing conflicts of interest and professional responsibilities are skills that can be learnt.

In virtually all cultures and societies, a gulf has developed between the medical profession and the public's expectations of their doctors.[8] We now have 'a better informed community asking for accountability, transparency and sound professional standards'.[15] This turbulence has presented unprecedented challenges to the medical profession as patients are becoming increasingly aware of the meaning of poor professionalism and associating it with poor medical care.[5] With this in mind, what is key is the need to maintain one's practice and reaffirm one's professional values and commitments to professionalism in order to meet the prevailing expectations of society and sustain the fidelity of medicine's contract with society.[14, 16]

The deprofessionalization of medicine in general and psychiatry in particular throughout Western countries during the last decade or so can be related to a number of social and economic factors. Holsinger and Beaton[17] identify loss of autonomy, emergence and growth of managed care models, increasing specialization within each medical specialty, variance in expectations by society and increasing litigations (over trivial matters at times), as some of the factors contributing to a sense of deprofessionalization. Often the profession's response has been to become defensive or aggressive rather than engage in a dialogue.

The accumulation of threats and perceived loss of autonomy to the medical profession have led to dissatisfaction and disillusionment among clinicians and ultimately their demoralization. This presents a serious risk to the relationship between patients and professionals as well as being incompatible with an effective healthcare system.[18, 19] Bhugra and Gupta list some of the external factors influencing this.[18] Worthy of note are the lapses in professional standards and the erosion of public trust in the profession through highly publicized medical scandals in the United Kingdom, leading to inquiries such as The Shipman Inquiry,[20] The Bristol Inquiry[21] and The Royal Liverpool Children's Hospital Inquiry,[22] where the public perception is one of the medical profession failing to self-regulate and guarantee the competency individuals deservedly expect.[23] There is a feeling among some doctors that the criticisms and increased scrutiny of the profession as a result of these have led to the profession being unfairly treated, to the point where they see themselves as victims.[24]

The recent intrusion of the state and corporate sector into healthcare in the United Kingdom has further compromised medicine's autonomy and, when combined with ever-expanding political imperatives, prescriptive centralized policies and managerial pressures, has caused many clinicians to feel frustrated at their attempts to deliver ideal care against what are primarily financially based outcome measures with monetary restraints and incentives, so-called 'accounting logic', that strain and increasingly compromise their personal principles.[25,26] These appear to be undermining and progressively threatening the traditional image and values a doctor holds as a medical professional, and perhaps causing clinicians to feel they are being forced into being 'technicians rather than healers' due to a loss of control over their clinical decision-making and the increasing emphasis on tasks unrelated to the practice of medicine.[18]

Inextricably linked to this is the implementation of formal medical revalidation in the United Kingdom by the General Medical Council. Its introduction seeks to demonstrate that each doctor is practising in a way that merits relicensure and specialist recertification, and acts as a process through which doctors can demonstrate their fitness to practise on a regular basis.[27] The overwhelming advantage of this is not only to secure the basic guarantees that modern society demands of the profession, but also to provide doctors as individuals with the self-confidence and self-respect to boost morale by proving to colleagues that they are up to date, fit to practise, and meet the principles and values set out in 'Good Medical Practice'.[28,29]

The challenge the medical profession now faces is how to counter further disillusionment, combat demoralization and foster the vision of a new modern professionalism. Swick *et al.*[30] suggest that the increasing interest in professionalism is related to external factors (such as the government and insurance companies) and internal factors (such as alienation and frustrations). In order to prevent medicine becoming a commodity in a market-orientated world, physicians must participate in shaping the profession's future and understand the principles and obligations associated with being a member of a profession.[8] We must put in place measures that support a genuinely positive, patient-centred and life-enhancing professional culture.[31] We must return to a state where professionalism connotes everything that we admire in our colleagues and that we strive for in ourselves. We must deem it 'an ideal to be constantly pursued', with individuals motivated by conscience to achieve this.[7,23,32,33] It is vital that all doctors recognize the importance of mutual respect, individual responsibility and appropriate accountability in creating a partnership with their patients. Through a commitment to integrity, altruism, continuous improvement and a partnership with the wider healthcare team, we can achieve excellence and Sir Donald Irvine's ideal, whereby we 'encourage and celebrate good practice to protect patients and the public from suboptimal practice'.[4,5]

Inspiration

Irvine points out that patients want doctors they can trust, and see the covenant of trust as lying at the core of our profession and being a central component of professionalism, which is at the heart of our healing relationship with patients.[34] With the integrity of the medical profession as a whole being both predicated and reflected upon by the professional behaviour of the individual physician, it is vital that we nurture a clear sense of identity, pride and higher self-esteem in belonging to a group where there is a shared acknowledged aim and desire to always put the patient first ahead of other interests.[6, 18]

Professionalism is a powerful and valuable concept with a strong value-based framework.[35] Provided doctors commit to this and work in the best interests of the public and their patients, it can be a powerful mechanism for shaping health policy, healthcare improvement, and ensuring safety in the millions of daily individual interactions between doctors and patients. We must share responsibility for maintaining and protecting the quality of our healthcare system as a whole and help shape improvements wherever possible by exercising a constructive influence on health policy in the public interest.[36]

To achieve this successfully and become more responsive to our patients needs, we must ensure this is given through both the individual doctor providing care and the institutional system in which that care is given.[5] Formalizing this to ensure active participation by clinicians, the government introduced the programme of clinical governance to all National Health Service (NHS) organizations in 1999. However, despite this, there is still reluctance by clinicians to take up this 'corporate responsibility' and it is still frequently a neglected aspect of modern medical practice.[5, 37] One of the potential reasons for this was highlighted in the inquiries into recent scandals mentioned earlier. These inquiries identified that current undergraduate teaching was not producing fully 'fit for purpose' doctors and that education and training have critical but neglected roles in strengthening the ethos of professionalism.[31]

Real cultural change is largely achieved through medical education, and despite Stephenson *et al.*[38] emphasizing the importance of a commitment to the teaching of professionalism, many of its defining qualities are not taught or reflected on systematically in the undergraduate medical curriculum or in postgraduate training.[31, 38, 39] In order to overcome this, it became clear that professionalism needed a well-articulated and clearly expressed definition, being explicitly incorporated and promoted as a critical and integral part of medical education, training and the teaching of young doctors to prepare individual doctors to manage professionally.[23, 35, 36] Committed to meeting this need, the Modernising Medical Careers team and Postgraduate Medical Education and Training Board (PMETB) – both of which no longer exist – were established in the United Kingdom, thereby creating further layers of control and bureaucracy.[40] However, further measures may still be necessary to establish an enabling environment where the Physicians' Charter can flourish and we can secure the future of medical professionalism.[5]

Source credibility, that is, establishing role models, is an important principle of adult learning. The recognition of positive role models by medical students, the custodians of medical professionalism, is widely accepted as one of the most powerful ways of inculcating professional values, demonstrating excellence in medical professionalism and ensuring the next generation of doctors are inspired to provide high professional standards of care to patients.[35,36,41] In medical schools in the United Kingdom, NHS trusts and postgraduate deaneries should utilize the power of role modelling and take the lead in nurturing and delivering strong professionalism;[23] the same principles can be applied in healthcare and training systems elsewhere. With clinical teachers consciously or unconsciously acting as role models for students, they require detailed knowledge of professionalism in order to promote the values and beliefs integral to it. Heightened attention to the professionalism of medical students through GMC guidance, such as 'Medical Students: Professional Behaviour and Fitness to Practice', has led to increased awareness of the need for teaching and the modelling of professionalism amongst faculty, residents and staff;[35,42] again, similar principles can be applied across other countries and healthcare systems. Alongside a shared responsibility by the profession for promoting professionalism, it is vital that medical institutions create a framework and supportive learning environment in which the personal and professional development of their staff is more likely to occur and is conducive for clinicians to be truly professional.[13,32,43–46]

Clinicians recognized as excellent role models are those who not only provide excellent clinical care but who also are active participants in shaping the future landscape of healthcare and, importantly, make time to facilitate feedback and reflection, and make a conscious effort to articulate what they are modelling to their students, including professionalism, which is best learnt through experiencing and discussing exemplary professional behaviour.[31,35,47]

In addition, wherever possible, a relevant framework for professionalism must also include a governing council framework, and values.[48] These values include essential values of fair access, quality, efficiency, patient advocacy, and provision of autonomy and consumer sovereignty and personal security of care.[49]

Professional judgement

Professional judgement plays a critical role in making decisions as a leader. Two main approaches have been identified by Elstein and Bordage.[50] These are the problem-solving approach (where information processing aims to characterize the process by which steps are analysed to understand the psychological elements) and the judgement approach (which investigates the possibility of representing judgemental policy using correlational statistical methods).

Information processing includes both technical knowledge and expertise, and involves making sense of information given and asking the right questions to gather further information. Elstein and Bordage[50] point out that the psychological principle basic to the understanding of clinical reasoning is the concept of bounded or limited rationality, as suggested by Newell and Simon.[51] The principle emphasizes that limits exist to the human capacity for rational thought that are *not* results of unconscious motives or psychodynamic capabilities. However, intuition or gut instinct plays an important role in the process but is often ignored. Obviously, small capacity of working memory plays a key role in this process. Direct observation of behaviour and technical knowledge or competence will influence the thought process and the information processing. At the heart of information processing is the clinician's ability to generate multiple hypotheses and accept or reject these according to the available information.[52]

Leadership and professional judgement go hand in hand. In the role of leader, an individual has multiple sources of information and a major task is to prioritize these and utilize them in making appropriate decisions. Steps in reaching decisions are related to cue acquisition (from history, investigation and tests); generating hypotheses (retrieved from memory so that alternative options can be set up); interpreting cues (checking alternative hypotheses under consideration); and, lastly, evaluating each hypothesis and accepting or rejecting them accordingly.[50,52] Hypothesis generation is a key aspect in decision-making and may be related to expertise, technical competence and long-term memory. An ideal number of hypotheses is four or five; common diagnoses and situations may be higher up in the list of hypotheses. The most salient hypotheses are the most provable ones and much harder to repudiate or reject. Clearly, generation of hypotheses can, especially if done at an early stage, lead to narrowing of the repertoire, and formation of opinions sooner rather than later.

Professional judgement depends upon how the information is collected and analysed and what weight is given to each bit of information. Clinical problem analysis depends upon a number of factors. As Kassirer *et al.*[53] point out, clinical problem-solving requires a store of medical knowledge and reasoning processes with which knowledge can be applied to a specific clinical situation.

Decision analysis is most applicable to clinical questions that cannot be answered by appealing directly to the results of a clinical trial or to a large database.[54] This approach applies especially to decision-making in leadership roles where trials or databases may not be easily available or applicable. Furthermore, hindsight (or experience) may further influence decision-making. Arkes *et al.*[55] point out that clinicians do carry a hindsight bias but this bias is variable and not applicable equally to every situation. Emotions, cognitions and mood all play a role in influencing how decisions are made. Arkes *et al.*[55] also suggest that knowledge of hindsight is important for medical education.

As in clinical decision-making, where the patient may play a key role in influencing decisions, followers of the leader may play a similar role. As patients may misunderstand questions, withhold information or give wrong information, it becomes necessary to understand the role of the followers in decision-making by the leader. Clinical leaders often have to take into account other factors while making decisions. Critical thinking and evaluating the evidence available will also impact upon decision-making. However, there remain personal and socio-cultural biases in decision-making.

The ethics of decision-making cannot be separated from the professional values and regulatory factors. Bhugra and Deakin[56] suggest that with the practice of medicine becoming increasingly complex (as has the process of decision-making) new ethical issues have emerged. Beauchamp and Childress[57] propose *four key principles of ethics*:

- respect for autonomy
- non-maleficence
- beneficence
- justice.

Autonomy is seen as the individual (patient) being an independent moral agent as is the clinician. Cultural values will influence autonomy of the individual, which is often embedded in the concept of the self. In egocentric societies and with egocentric individuals, notions of autonomy are likely to be very different than those of sociocentric individuals in sociocentric societies. The other three principles are clearly beyond dispute. Non-maleficence (not causing harm); beneficence (benefiting others) and justice (treating everyone in a fair and equal manner) are clearly at the core of clinical practice but can also be applied to any leader as well. These four principles should guide and justify all matters of decisions and carry equal weight.

The application of these four principles in a coherent and cohesive manner is possible in individual and organizational settings. The four principles are at the heart of any clinical decision-making. These have been described as the moral DNA[58] and can be applied at both individual and institutional levels.

Shweder *et al.*[59] argue that cultures and societies rely on the three principles of autonomy (incorporating harm and justice), community (incorporating duty, respect and interdependence) and divinity (incorporating traditions and purity). Thus additional dimensions have to be borne in mind. This has been challenged by Walker,[60] who points out that the four principles are easily applicable in healthcare but not necessarily in other settings. These ethical principles also need to be applied in the context of decision-making in leadership roles. There is a potential for conflict between the four principles, and managing this conflict may add further complications to the leader's roles.

Bhugra and Deakin[56] take the role of 'speciation' further. Speciation is defined as further enhancement of the utility while analysing specific cases. Were this to be successful, it could mediate the weakness that may occur as a result of internal conflict.[61] Speciation may allow an amalgamation of the four principles. For example, maximizing benefits to the patient and minimizing harm by using interventions that may help may supersede the principle of autonomy. Therefore, a danger lurks in the decision-making process of the leader that autonomy may make way for other principles thereby changing the speciation. Obligations to the patients or the followers may bring with them certain moral values and perspectives.

With the economic downturn and other social and cultural factors, autonomy and personal choice may take on a different role, especially across different healthcare systems. The tension between individual autonomy and the policies – especially the notions of greater good – will determine how health professionals behave in the face of patient demands and needs. These principles raise further dilemmas in the field of public mental health. Although the idea of public mental health dates back over a century, it is only recently that prevention strategies are being developed and used actively in a variety of settings. This approach looks at the broader population base as well as those at risk but also at the individual level. The potential for conflict across all these levels can add to pressures on leaders who may be trying to deliver public mental health. Another potential conflict is whether society prefers prevention or treatment. Special ethical considerations may well be dictated by local social and cultural mores and expectations. Childress *et al.*[62] have suggested that there are general moral considerations required for public health-related decision-making (by the leader) that may well go beyond the four principles outlined above. They propose that these additional factors include protecting privacy and confidentiality (but again definitions of privacy may well differ across the profession). Bhugra and Deakin[56] also caution that the four principle theory is seriously undermined by the inner conflict that can occur between the four principles.

Professionalization has been criticized as the profession fighting back and taking back control. Larson[63] argued that the successful professional project was a 'monopoly of competence, legitimized by officially sanctioned expertise' and a 'monopoly of credibility with the public'. There is obviously a debate to be had regarding the monopolistic nature of healthcare delivery. Evetts *et al.*[64] point out that in the previous two decades more extreme versions of the 'professional project' had become apparent. They highlight that even though professions may initiate projects and influence governments, just as often professions are responding to external demands for change and these demands can be political, economic, cultural and social. Thus it is inevitable that stakeholders will influence the professions, but the leadership must use a formal ethical structure to negotiate and deliver expertise.

Evetts *et al.*[64] indicate that an appraisal of professionalism has to be normative and functional, but with new directions, including creating a commercialization dictated by governments.[65] The state may have a variable role, depending upon the type of profession. Professionalism in some branches within the healthcare system may be related to bringing about social change. Under these circumstances, the key components of the four principles may not be seen as sacrosanct. The argument that professionalism includes exclusive ownership of an area of expertise and knowledge and the control of access to potential solutions needs to be revisited. Evetts *et al.*[64] suggest that additional aspects of collegiality, autonomy in decision-making, discretion in work practices and self-regulation are essential to professionalism.[19] Accountability, audits, targets and performance indicators appear to have become a part of the new professionalism.[66] As more and more professionals are becoming pushed into meeting targets, especially as a result of the economic downturn, it is inevitable that groups of different professionals will be responding to these demands in different ways. Individuals may deal with the targets either by embracing them and modifying professionalism within an ethical framework; or by rejecting them outright as a challenge to their professional skills, turning them into pen-pushers, an action that may be seen as a rejection of professional values. It is inevitable that under pressure and stress the professionals may respond by turning inwards. Professions may hold heterogeneous and divergent views, which may make it extremely difficult to deal with them. Furthermore, the ethical framework may be seen as flexible in dealing with external pressures. The accountability of the leader is an important aspect of the role, where the leader may well have to explain the likely deviations from the ethical framework to other stakeholders. Evetts *et al.*[64] also suggest that the appeal of professionalism as a discourse of disciplinary control at the micro level must be considered. Using strategies to delineate alternative approaches may help the leader to consolidate any gains. Interestingly, McClelland[67] classifies professionalization as from within or from above. Medical professionalism used to be from within, but is gradually giving way to from above, where external factors dominate the group. From within, the group can achieve substantial gains in position and achievement.

The onus on the leader can thus be multi-faceted. Some of the pressure on the leader may relate to their role as the leader and the other pressures may result from the demands made of them by the profession. The changes in regulatory processes across different professions add a further complex dimension to the ethical framework, whether these ethics come from within or are imposed from above. Evetts *et al.*[64] make a cogent point that the discourse of professionalism is being used to convince, cajole and persuade key stakeholders about the role of the organizations and institutions and, in turn, the latter are imposing strictures, targets and control. The changes in professionalism therefore have a major impact on individuals and organizations and the ethical framework within which leaders work.

Leadership and professionalism: vision, strategy, values, empowerment in teams, influence, team working

'Regulating doctors, ensuring good medical practice' – the strapline for the UK's regulatory body, the General Medical Council – emphasizes the urgency of the medical profession to reaffirm and redefine precisely what medical professionalism means in modern society. Augmented by the Royal Colleges, specialist societies and medical schools, this clear leadership by the GMC can help to facilitate the implementation and dissemination of the new definition and description of medical professionalism of the Royal College of Physicians (RCP).[28] The clear, modern and measurable definition of professionalism, published by the RCP, when combined with revalidation and the revised publication of the hugely influential *Good Medical Practice* (which sets out the principles and values describing 'medical professionalism in action'), will help doctors articulate a clearer and renewed vision of exactly what it means to be a modern medical professional.[36] However, alongside this institutional leadership, in order to achieve the cultural transition necessary to meet societal expectations, we require stronger individual medical leaders to act as the vehicle to strengthen professionalism.[35] They must act with the courage and determination to take the agenda forward, without sacrificing the best interests of patients or the longer-term interests of the medical profession on the altar of short-term political expediency, whilst actively promoting engagement between doctors, patients and a variety of other stakeholders to produce a shared vision of how to improve healthcare.[18,28,68]

Integral to promoting modern professionalism, the working party on 'Doctors in Society' identified six major themes: leadership, teams, education, appraisal, careers and research.[5] It identified the need for individual as well as collective leadership and 'followership' to create a cohesive vision for the NHS across the front-line clinical team, local service entity and the national policy stage.

An integral composite to good leadership is forming an interprofessional partnership between the key stakeholders to produce a strong, effective clinical team, operating in patients' best interests to provide excellence of care despite the inherent fluidity involved in working within the NHS. The GMC and medical schools must therefore strengthen interprofessional education and training to develop a cadre of clinical leaders where professionalism is seen not as a perk or a luxury but a central component to the covenant of trust between patient and doctor. There must be caution, however, to avoid elitism, as within any group this may lead to the exclusion of individuals who may be experts in their own right but who through their status or position are not allowed to become part of the said elite. A leader, by definition, once in the position of power, may become part of the elite or establishment, which may lead to alienation of the people the leader may be purporting to represent. Embedded within both the profession and the leader are what Weber[69] describes as charisma, heredity and merit. The role of the ethical framework and thinking will influence the merit of the argument, and the leaders can therefore encourage, entice or enthuse their followers and consequently deliver what is needed.

In order to provide a richer atmosphere for professional development and produce a sustainable, positive, patient-centred and life-enhancing professional culture, one's professional values must be assessed, reflected upon and developed throughout training and clinical practice to ensure fitness to practice. We are seeing these increasingly through systems of appraisal and revalidation, where one's professional and personal development needs are agreed alongside assessment of one's contribution to the quality improvement of services to achieve delivery of high-quality care. Without protected time for this intervention, we are likely to experience, as Hilton and Slotnick discuss, an inevitable degree of natural decay in professional values.[70] With these professional values constituting the social capital of medicine, we must ensure its long-term viability by establishing a forum for research into how it can best be used to improve health outcomes and create an enabling environment where professional values can flourish.

Conclusions

The tension between the professional group and the role of the leader must not be underestimated. This tension can lead to creative thinking within the ethical framework. Both followers and leaders are bound by an ethical framework within their professional values and expectations. Irrespective of the pressures on the professions from above, it is important that the profession also carries with it values from within. The three fundamental principles outlined earlier form the core of good clinical practice. For mental health professionals, it is essential to determine how these principles can be applied across different cultures and socio-economic settings. Human rights and values must be universal, but there needs to be a culturally relative application. Mental health professionals and leaders must establish a framework of ethical clinical practice and ethical leadership. These values must be embedded in training at an early stage.

References

1 Gough JW. *The Social Contract: A Critical Study of its Development*, 2nd edn. Oxford: Clarendon Press, Oxford University Press, 1963.
2 Cruess SR, Cruess RL. Medicine's social contract with society: its nature, evolution and present state. In: Bhugra D, Malik A, Ikkos G (eds), *Psychiatry's Contract with Society: Concepts, Controversies and Consequences*. Oxford: Oxford University Press, 2010; pp. 123–46.
3 Pellegrino ED. Professionalism, profession and the virtues of the good physician. *Mt Sinai J Med* 2002; **69**:378–84.
4 Irvine DH. New ideas about medical professionalism. *Med J Australia* 2006; **184**:204–5.

5   Royal College of Physicians. *Doctors in Society: Medical Professionalism in a Changing World*. London: Royal College of Physicians, 2005.
6   McDonagh D. Medical professionalism. *Northeast Florida Medicine Supplement*, 2008; January; pp. 6–7.
7   Sox HC. The ethical foundations of professionalism: a sociologic history. *Chest* 2007; **131**:1532–40.
8   Cruess RL, Cruess SR, Johnston SE. Professionalism: an ideal to be sustained. *Lancet* 2000; **356**:156–69.
9   Lasagna L. (1964): A modern version of the Hippocratic Oath. Available at: http://www.pbs.org/wgbh/nova/body/hippocratic-oath-today.html [accessed 19 April 2013].
10 General Medical Council. *Good Medical Practice*, 5th edn. London: GMC, 2013.
11 Weissman S, Busch K. (2013): Leadership for good versus good leadership in mental health. In: Bhugra D, Gupta S, Ruiz P (eds), *Leadership in Psychiatry*. Oxford: John Wiley & Sons, Ltd, pp. 217–225.
12 Horton R. Medicine: the prosperity of virtue. *Lancet* 2005; **366**:1985–7.
13 Sethuraman KR. Professionalism in medicine: Human resources for health. *Regional Health Forum* 2006; **10**:1–9.
14 Medical Professionalism Project. Medical professionalism in the new millennium: A physicians' charter. *Lancet* 2002; **359**:520–1.
15 Dunning AJ. Status of the doctor – present and future. *Lancet* 1999; **354**(suppl. IV): SIV18.
16 Rosen R, Dewar S. *On Being a Doctor: Redefining Medical Professionalism for Better Patient Care*. London: King's Fund, 2004.
17 Holsinger JW, Beaton B. Physician professionalism for a new century. *Clin Anat* 2006; **19**: 473–9.
18 Bhugra D, Gupta S. Medical professionalism in psychiatry. *Adv Psychiatr Treat* 2010; **16**:10–13.
19 Freidson E. *Professionalism Reborn: Theory, Prophecy and Policy*. Chicago: University of Chicago Press, 1994.
20 Shipman Inquiry. *Safeguarding Patients: Lessons from the Past, Proposals for the Future*. Dame Janet Smith (chairman). London: Stationery Office, 2004.
21 Bristol Royal Infirmary Inquiry. *Learning from Bristol: the Report of the Public Inquiry into Children's Heart Surgery at the Bristol Royal Infirmary 1984–1995*. London: Stationery Office, 2002.
22 *The Royal Liverpool Children's Inquiry Report*. London: Stationery Office, 2001.
23 Cruess S, Johnston S, Cruess R. Professionalism for medicine: opportunities and obligations. *Med J Australia* 2002; **177**:208–11.
24 Edwards E, Kornachi MJ, Silversin J. Unhappy doctors: what are the causes and what can be done? *Brit Med J* 2002; **324**:835–8.
25 Kassirer J. Doctor discontent. *N Engl J Med* 1998; **339**:1543–4.
26 Broadbent J, Laughlin R. "Accounting logic" and controlling professionals. In: Broadbent J, Dietrich M, Roberts J (eds), *The End of Professions? The Reconstructing of Professional Work*. London: Routledge, 1997; pp. 34–49.
27 Department of Health. Trust, assurance and safety – the regulation of health professionals in the 21st century; Health & Social Care Bill. London: Department of Health, 2007.
28 Irvine D. Success relies on winning hearts and minds. *Brit Med J* 2006; **333**:965–6.
29 General Medical Council. *The Good Medical Practice Framework for Appraisal and Revalidation*. London: GMC, 2011.
30 Swick HM, Bryan CS, Longo LD. Beyond the physician charter: reflections on medical professionalism. *Perspectives in Biology and Medicine* 2006; **49**:263–75.
31 Royal College of Physicians. *Leading for Quality: The Foundation for Healthcare over the Next Decade*. London: Royal College of Physicians, 2010.

32   Irvine DH. Patients, professionalism, and revalidation. *Brit Med J* 2005; **330**:1265–8.

33   Kultgen J. *Ethics and Professionalism*. Philadelphia: University of Pennsylvania Press, 1988.

34   Irvine D. Doctors in the UK: their new professionalism and its regulatory framework. *Lancet* 2001; **358**:1807–10.

35   Levenson R, Atkinson S, Shepherd S. *The 21ˢᵗ Century Doctor: Understanding the Doctors of Tomorrow*. London: King's Fund, 2010.

36   Levenson R, Dewar S, Shepherd S. *Understanding Doctors: Harnessing Professionalism*. London: King's Fund, 2008.

37   Department of Health. *Supporting Doctors, Protecting Patients*. London: Department of Health, 1999.

38   Stephenson A, Higgs R, Sugarman J. Teaching professional development in medical schools. *Lancet* 2001; **35**:867–70.

39   Irvine DH. Time for hard deisions on patient-centred professionalism. *Med J Australia* 2004; **181**:271–4.

40   Brown N, Bhugra D. 'New' professionalism or professionalism derailed? *Psychiatr Bull* 2007; **31**:281–3.

41   Passi V, Doug M, Peile E, Thistlethwaite J, Johnson N. Developing medical professionalism in future doctors: a systematic review. *Int J Med Educ* 2010; **1**:19–29.

42   General Medical Council and Medical Schools Council. *Medical Students: Professional Behaviour and Fitness to Practise*. London: GMC and MS, 2009.

43   Paice E, Heard S, Moss F. How imortant are role models in making good doctors? *Brit Med J* 2002; **325**:707–10.

44   Weissmann PF, Branch WT, Gracey CF, Haidet P, Frankel RM. Role modeling humanistic behavior: learning bedside manner from the experts. *Acad Med* 2006; **81**:661 7.

45   Kahn MW. Etiquette-based medicine. *N Engl J Med* 2008; **358**:1988–9.

46   Jones WS, Hanson JL, Longacre JL. An intentional modeling process to teach professional behavior: students' clinical observations of preceptors. *Teach Learn Med* 2004; **16**:264–9.

47   Wright SM, Kern DE, Kolodner K, Howard DM, Brancati FL. Attributes of excellent attending-physician role models. *N Engl J Med* 1998; **339**:1986–93.

48   Schmutzler DJ, Holsinger JW. New professionalism. In: Bhugra D, Malik A (eds), *Professionalism*. Cambridge: Cambridge University Press, 2011; pp. 127–39.

49   Preister R. A values framework for health system reform. *Health Affairs* 1992; **11**:84–107.

50   Elstein AS, Bordage G. Psychology of clinical reasoning. In: Dowie J, Elstein A (eds), *Professional Judgement: A Reader in Clinical Decision Making*. Cambridge: Cambridge University Press, 1988; pp. 109–29.

51   Newell A, Simon HA. *Human Problem Solving*. Englewood Cliffs, NJ: Prentice-Hall, 1972.

52   Elstein AS, Shulman LS, Sprafka SA. *Medical Problem Solving: An Analysis of Clinical Reasoning*. Cambridge, MA: Harvard University Press, 1978.

53   Kassirer JP, Kuipers BJ, Gorny GA. Toward a theory of clinical expertise. In: Dowie J, Elstein A (eds), *Professional Judgment: A Reader in Clinical Decision Making*. Cambridge: Cambridge University Press, 1988; pp. 212–25.

54   Doubilet P, McNeil B. Clinical decision making. In: Dowie J, Elstein A (eds), *Professional Judgment: A Reader in Clinical Decision Making*. Cambridge: Cambridge University Press, 1988; pp. 255–76.

55   Arkes HR, Saville PD, Wortmann RL, Harkness AR. Hindsight bias among physicians weighing the likelihood of diagnoses. In: Dowie J, Elstein A (eds), *Professional Judgment: A Reader in Clinical Decision Making*. Cambridge: Cambridge University Press, 1988; pp. 374–8.

56   Deakin N, Bhugra D. Four principles approach to medical ethics. *Indian J Psychiatr* (in press).

57   Beauchamp T, Childress J. *Principles of Biomedical Ethics*, 6th edn. New York: Oxford University Press, 2009.

58   Gillon R. Medical ethics: four principles plus attention to scope. *Brit Med J* 1994; **309**:184.

59   Shweder N, Much N, Mahapatra M. The 'big three' of morality (autonomy, community, divinity) and the 'big three' explanations of suffering. In: Brand A, Rozin E (eds), *Morality and Health*. New York: Routledge, 1997; pp. 119–72.

60   Walker T. What principlism misses. *J Med Ethics* 2009; **35**:229–31.

61   Beauchamp T. Methods and principles in biomedical ethics. *J Med Ethics* 2003; **29**:269–74.

62   Childress J, Faden R, Gaare R, *et al*. Public health ethics: mapping the terrain. *J Law Med Ethics* 2002; **30**:170–8.

63   Larson M. *The Rise of Professionalism: A Sociological Analysis*. Berkeley, CA: University of California Press, 1997.

64   Evetts J, Mieg HA, Felt U. Professionalization, scientific expertise and elitism: a sociological perspective. In: Ericsson KA, Charness N, Feltovich PJ, Hoffman RR (eds), *The Cambridge Handbook of Expertise and Expert Performance*. Cambridge: Cambridge University Press, 2006; pp. 105–23.

65   Hanlon G. *Lawyers, the State and the Market: Professionalism Revisited*. Basingtoke: Macmillan, 1999.

66   Evetts J. Professionalization and professionalism: explaining professional initiatives. In: Mieg HA, Pfaedenhauer M (eds), *Professionelle Leistung (Professional Performance)*. Konstanz: UVK, 2003; pp. 49–69.

67   McClelland CE. Escape from freedom? Reflections on German professionalism 1870–1933. In: Torstendahl R, Burrage M (eds), *The Formation of Professions: Knowledge, State and Strategy*. London: Sage, 1990; pp. 97–113.

68   Salvage J. *Rethinking Professionalism: The First Step for Patient Focused Care*. London: IPPR, 2002.

69   Weber M. *Economy and Society* (trans. G Roth & C Wittich). Berkeley, CA: University of California Press, 1979.

70   Hilton S, Slotnick H. Proto-professionalism: how professionalization occurs across the continuum of medical education. *Med Educ* 2007; **39**:58–65.

Chapter 4

Leadership Theories and Approaches

John P. Baker

Introduction

The ancient Chinese philosopher Lao-tzu stated, 'When the best leader's work is done the people say: we did it ourselves.' Leadership appears very simple on the surface until one delves into the complexities of influencing others to do what needs to be done. There exists a plethora of guidance originating with Sun-tzu (400–320 BC), who wrote *The Art of War* prescribing to us the best leadership path for a given context.[1] A simple Google Scholar search produces over 2.3 million books and publications on the topic of leadership. Often, when faced with overwhelming guidance on how to proceed with a given challenge, the best place to begin is by exploring the basic theories, approaches and constructs of the task. Understanding the theoretical basis for leadership provides insights that, when coupled with leadership self-awareness, allow one to determine the best leadership path to follow.

The intent of this chapter is not to describe the best way to lead, but to provide readers with an overview of leadership theories and approaches that can help leaders better understand the best approach to use given their strengths or weaknesses and the given situation. This chapter divides theories and approaches into two categories: The first, entitled *classical,* includes those theories and approaches prevalent through the mid-1970s, and the second, entitled *modern,* includes those emerging since the mid-1970s. A logical point to begin a discussion of leadership theories and approaches is to define leadership.

Definition of leadership

Many scholars and leadership practitioners have defined leadership. Northouse[2] defines leadership as 'a process whereby an individual influences a group of individuals to achieve a common goal'. In *Leadership for the 21st Century,* a book devoted to conceptualizing leadership, Rost[3] defines leadership as 'an influence relationship among leaders and followers who intend real change that reflects their mutual purposes'. Dwight Eisenhower,[4] one of the foremost practitioners of leadership, stated that leadership is 'the art of getting someone else to do something you want done because he wants to do it.'

Leadership in Psychiatry, First Edition. Edited by Dinesh Bhugra, Pedro Ruiz and Susham Gupta.
© 2013 John Wiley & Sons, Ltd. Published 2013 by John Wiley & Sons, Ltd.

The common theme in all definitions of leadership is influence. Regardless of the leader, follower or context, the ability of one person (a leader) to create influence with another person (a follower) is leadership. Leadership is both an art and a science based on an influence relationship. Leaders' ability to create and maintain effective relationships with those they intend to influence is the basis of any effective leadership process. With an emphasis on influence relationships, are leaders managers, or are managers leaders? A review of the differences and similarities between leadership and management sets the stage for a review of leadership theories, approaches and aspects that impact the ability of one to influence another.

Leadership versus management

Leadership is similar to but also much different from management. Peter Drucker[5] stated, 'Management is about doing things right, leadership is about doing the right things.' Through the end of the 1980s, many leadership scholars and authors blended the concepts of leadership and management, viewing leadership as good management.[3] Both management and leadership involve influence, achieving goals, creating a sense of responsibility and accountability, and bringing about change. However, leadership does differ from management. Table 4.1 provides a summary of the differences between management and leadership.

Table 4.1   Management versus leadership

Management	Leadership
Process and procedures focused on efficiencies to meet requirements	**Inspirational motivation** based on leaders influencing others to achieve more than they think possible
Human resource functions providing for the needs and rights of employees	**Establishing effective relationships** building trust and commitment to the leader and organization
Routines focused on maintaining the status quo and meeting expectations	**Taking risks,** creating opportunities, and exceeding expectations
Systemic approach toward the future based on a strategic plan	**Providing a way ahead** by creating and communicating a vision for the future

The two disciplines are closely related, yet vastly different as leadership focuses on the intangible aspects of influencing others while management focuses on controlling and directing others. Good leaders use management techniques, and good managers exhibit leadership behaviours. Together, good management and good leadership provide a foundation for effective organizations to develop followers and achieve goals.

Classical leadership theories and approaches

Early leadership theories focused primarily on the leader and did not consider the context or those whom the leader wanted to lead. Most equated leadership to the leader, not realizing the complexity and number of variables that impact the leadership process. Over time, leadership studies progressed as a discipline, and scholars realized that the follower and situation greatly impacted the leadership process. A review of leadership theories and approaches provides a historic timeline and evolution of leadership thought to the present day.

Great Man and trait approach

One of the earliest Western leadership theories to emerge was the Great Man approach where the 'Great Men' of history were studied and exemplified. The Great Man approach framed the argument that leaders were born, not made. The traits and characteristics of great leaders such as Alexander the Great, Napoleon Bonaparte and Winston Churchill were studied and believed to define effective leadership. The Great Man approach was the prevalent thought through the latter part of the nineteenth century, but came into question as industrialization and professional managerial groups emerged in the early twentieth century.[1] From the Great Man approach evolved the trait approach.

The trait approach emphasizes that there are certain qualities or characteristics of a person that explain why certain individuals are effective leaders. Early researchers identified a multitude of traits, some redundant and some contradictory. A review of the traits listed indicates that certain traits, such as intelligence, self-confidence, determination, integrity and sociability, were included in most lists of traits determined as needed for effective leadership. Although the trait approach focuses only on the leader and does not consider the follower or situation, the trait approach is still valid and provides insight to effective leadership.

Style approach

A set of classical theories emerged during the 1940s and 1950s that focused on a leader's behaviour. Research conducted at Ohio State University and the University of Michigan analysed the two broad leadership constructs of a leader's task behaviours and relationship behaviours. Relationship behaviours were the actions leaders took to comfort followers as they interacted with other followers and the context. Task behaviours focused on the actions of a leader to accomplish the assigned requirements. Both of these lines of research further defined the leadership process but did not fully embrace the importance of the situation and context. Also, although well researched, it is difficult to link the specific leader behaviours to desired outcomes as both approaches are broad and cannot account for other variables that may influence results.

One of the best known uses of the style approach is captured in the Managerial Grid®, which first appeared in the early 1960s and was later renamed the Leadership Grid®. The Leadership Grid® graphically illustrates the extent of a leader's concern for people (relational) and results (task). Various self-reflection surveys allow leaders to plot their leadership style on the Leadership Grid®. The extremities for the Leadership Grid® include Impoverished Management (low concern for people and task), Team (high concern for people and task), Country Club (high concern for people, low concern for task) and

Authority-Compliance (low concern for people, high concern for task). In reality, good leaders will adapt their style depending on the situation and usually lead with a more balanced concern for both people and tasks, called Middle-of-the-Road style.

Skills approach

While the trait approach focused on innate characteristics of the leader, the skills approach emphasized leadership performance. The skills approach suggests that effective leadership requires leaders to utilize knowledge and abilities.[2] Katz[6] suggested that leaders need three basic types of skills: (i) technical, (ii) human and (iii) conceptual. Leaders at different levels use varying amounts of the three skills, with lower-level leaders using more technical than conceptual skills while higher-level leaders need more conceptual than technical skills. A constant need at all levels is human skills.

Empirical research by Mumford *et al.*[7] described a capabilities model that examined the relationship between a leader's knowledge, abilities and performance. Both the Katz[6] and Mumford *et al.*[7] skills approaches further advanced leadership studies thought and began a movement to diverge from the prevalent thought at this time that leadership was reserved for those who were born leaders. The skills approach also illustrated that a leader's behaviour was important and spurred research that examined the task and relational nature of leaders.

Contingency theory

Contingency theory is a neoclassical approach developed in the late 1950s and 1960s that advanced our understanding of leadership by incorporating certain aspects of a situation into the leadership process. Fiedler's[8] research incorporated the relationship between the leader and followers, the complexity of the task, and the positional power the leader had for a given situation. Based on the leader's style, determined by a self-assessment, and the three aspects of the situation, the leader is either a good or a poor match to lead in that situation. Although proven valid, contingency theory does not explain why leaders are effective in a given situation and does not consider other situational variables including the characteristics of the follower.

Situational approach

The situational approach, as the name suggests, focuses on the situation facing the leader with an emphasis on the follower. Researchers[9, 10] determined that effective leaders must understand their followers and apply the correct balance between direction and support that followers require for a given situation. The situational approach defined four leader styles: (i) directing (high direction, low support); (ii) coaching (high direction, high support); (iii) supporting (low direction, high support); and (iv) delegating (low direction, low support).

The key to the situational approach lies in the relationship between the leader and the follower. The leader must assess the follower's needs based on an effective relationship and then provide the needed direction and/or support. The situational approach is dynamic as a follower's need for direction and support fluctuates. In a normal situation, a person new to an organization initially requires high direction and low support as the leader must direct the follower. After gaining experience, the follower understands his or her responsibilities, and the leader can engage the follower with more two-way conversations and provides more support to build commitment to the organization and loyalty to the leader. Over time, the follower becomes comfortable with the requirements, and the leader provides more support while increasing the focus on building commitment and loyalty. As the follower increases his or her commitment to the organization and loyalty to the leader, the leader can delegate tasks and responsibility. This process regresses or can even begin over if the situation changes and the follower encounters obstacles or new requirements. While research findings have not fully supported all the dimensions of situational leadership, the situational approach is practical and pragmatic and has enjoyed popularity in many organizational leadership development programmes.

Research through the mid-twentieth century on leadership progressed scholarly thought regarding the leadership process. However, researchers failed to account for critical aspects impacting effective leaders and leadership. A review of more current thought on leadership can provide more practical and effective approaches to leadership for today's leaders.

Modern leadership theories and approaches

Leadership research and thought have progressed rapidly since the mid-1970s as leadership scholars focused attention on a more encompassing leadership process. Classical leadership theories and approaches were developed in a society influenced by hierarchical organizations such as organized religion and the US military. Modern leadership theories and approaches tend towards a more shared leadership process that emphasizes values and relationships.[11] The following provides an overview of the modern leadership theories and approaches.

Path-goal theory

Path-goal theory focuses on how leaders create conditions for followers to self-motivate and achieve their goals. Based on their style and the task, leaders apply the correct motivation that results in follower performance and accomplishing the goal. Effective leader-follower relationships are essential in path-goal theory. Leaders base their actions on how well they know the follower and correctly apply the right form of motivation. Path-goal theory emphasizes expectancy theory, which suggests that people want to accomplish tasks if they feel they are capable of successfully completing the task, believe their efforts will result in achieving a certain outcome, and value the task, believing it is a worthwhile accomplishment. The success of path-goal theory lies in the leader's ability to provide what is missing in a situation to bridge the gap between the follower's abilities and the goal.

Path-goal leadership starts with the leader and follower defining the goal and determining the path to accomplish the goal. The leader monitors the follower and either clears or assists in clearing obstacles that may occur as the follower pursues the path toward the goal.[2] As the follower pursues the goal, the leader applies the appropriate leader behaviour to motivate the follower. The appropriate leader behaviour depends on the follower and what that follower needs according to the expectancy theory. Four general leader behaviours include directive, supportive, participative and achievement-oriented; however, others may exist.[12] Path-goal leadership is one of the first prescriptive leadership theories by suggesting ways to lead.

Path-goal leadership is simple to understand and practical, but does present several challenges. While path-goal defines four leader behaviours, the leader is left to judge which behaviour to apply and when, based on the relationship between leader and follower. Path-goal does not define the requirements or prerequisites to apply to any leader behaviour, and leaders must rely on their knowledge of what followers need to accomplish their goal. Although conceptually straightforward, path-goal is complex in reality as the leader must understand expectancy theory, have a good relationship with the follower, and adjust for any variables that may occur during the path-goal process. While path-goal theory illustrates the importance of both the leader and the follower, the leader-member exchange theory provides insight to the interactions created by leaders and followers.

Leader-member exchange theory

Leader-member exchange (LMX) theory focuses on the relationship between the leader and the follower and how leaders create and utilize relationships to advance both personal and organizational leadership effectiveness. The leader-follower relationship becomes the focal point for LMX. Leaders develop a relationship with followers and, in the process, determine how each follower can best assist the leader and organization to accomplish tasks and organizational goals.

Based on the nature of the leader-follower relationship, it is not uncommon for *in-groups* and *out-groups* to develop. The leader usually demands more from in-group members than from those in the out-group, and in return, the leader provides more rewards to the in-group than to out-group members. Leaders constantly assess their relationships with followers through time and make adjustments to the membership of both in- and out-groups to ensure both the leader and the organization are using the strengths of each member. Likewise, members in both the in- and the out-group may desire membership in the other group, requiring the leader to adjust group membership.

Ideally, it is valuable for leaders to engage in leadership making, which is a process of developing high-quality relationships with each follower.[2] Leadership making consists of three phases: (i) the stranger phase, (ii) the acquaintance phase and (iii) the partner phase.[13] In the stranger phase, interactions between leader and follower are scripted, directive in nature (from leader to follower) and low quality. As leaders and followers develop their relationship, interactions become less formal and more participative. In the partner phase, leaders and followers have high-quality interactions as both become comfortable with the relationship and better understand each other's strengths.

LMX on the surface appears unfair.[2] Leaders must guard against personal bias in using in-groups and out-groups to accomplish tasks. Regardless of the context of the organization and its leaders and followers, LMX will occur. The leadership challenge within an organization is for leaders and managers to acknowledge, understand and take advantage of the LMX process.

Transformational and charismatic leadership

Leadership can be thought of as existing along a continuum from an absence of leadership (laissez-faire) to what many consider its ultimate form – transformational leadership. Transactional leadership links laissez-faire to transformational leadership by providing a means for leaders to accomplish routine tasks. The continuum of leadership provides a frame of reference for leaders by defining the type of leadership needed for a given situation.

Laissez-faire leadership is an absence or lack of leadership and defines one extreme of the options available to leaders – do nothing. Transactional leadership is simply what the description implies: a transaction. Leaders are transactional when they provide followers with rewards for good performance and punish them for failing to meet standards.[14] A transactional process can assist in developing relationships that can evolve into transformational leadership, but to a limited degree as the process does not involve personal or organizational values.

Transformational leadership is a process that raises a follower's level of maturity, commitment and sense of well-being toward others, the organizations to which he or she belongs, and to society.[14] The term *transformational leadership* was originally proposed by James Downton in 1973 but brought to prominence in 1978 by James MacGregor Burns[15] in his Pulitzer Prize-winning book *Leadership*.[16] Leaders establish strong emotional relationships with followers and use these relationships to inspire followers to go beyond what they believe they can accomplish. The transformation process has at its centre the ability of the leader to communicate a mutually desirable vision of the future and a way to achieve that future. Transformational leaders, through an inspirational leadership process, create a greater sense of commitment and loyalty within the follower toward the organization as the leader and follower pursue the future vision.

Four aspects leaders can use to bring about transformational leadership include inspirational motivation, intellectual stimulation, idealized influence and individualized consideration.[14] All four aspects of transformational leadership require a tremendous commitment and involvement by leaders to ensure followers correctly understand the vision that provides the connection between the four aspects. The method of communicating the vision and creating a sense of commitment from the four aspects requires leaders to know their followers and passionately believe in the mutually desirable vision for the organization.

Charismatic leadership is closely related to transformational leadership and the essence of the 'inspirational motivation' factor in transformational leadership.[2] Conger and Kanungo[17] provide a three-stage model of charismatic leadership. In the first stage, the leader assesses the environment for deficiencies in the status quo or poorly exploited opportunities. During the second stage, the leader defines goals based on perceived opportunities and conveys the goals using unique and inspirational methods. The leader demonstrates how the organization can achieve the goals during the third stage. Although the three stages may appear linear, a charismatic leader can deviate and accomplish the defined goals utilizing the charismatic skills he or she possesses.

Charismatic leaders have unique skills that fall within three general competencies. First, charismatic leaders are keenly sensitive to environmental constraints and opportunities. Second, charismatic leaders have great self-awareness of their strengths and weaknesses that allows them to craft compelling goals that incites commitment and loyalty by followers to both the goals and the leader. Finally, charismatic leaders have the ability to convey defined goals to followers in a way that is unique, compelling and inspirational. The charismatic leader understands the situation and utilizes his or her unique skills to create the commitment needed to accomplish the defined goals to optimize the desired leader outcome.[17]

Servant leadership

Greenleaf[18] stated:

> The servant-leader *is* servant first . . . It begins with the natural feeling that one wants to serve, to serve *first*. Then conscious choice brings one to aspire to lead. That person is sharply different from one who is *leader* first, perhaps because of the need to assuage an unusual power drive or to acquire material possessions . . . The difference manifests itself in the care taken by the servant – first to make sure that other people's highest priority needs are being served. The best test . . . is: do those served grow as persons? Do they, *while being served,* become healthier, wiser, freer, more autonomous, more likely themselves to become servants? *And*, what is the effect on the least privileged in society: will they benefit, or, at least, not be further deprived?

Servant leadership has enjoyed increased popularity recently, even during these times of leadership failures by corporate leaders who have portrayed an elitist attitude with little regard for others. Greenleaf,[18] credited with beginning the discussions regarding servant leadership, developed the concept of servant leadership and formalized his thoughts on this leadership approach in his book titled *Servant Leadership* (1970). Spears[19] further developed the concept of servant leadership by defining 10 practical servant leadership constructs:

1   Listening – developing the discipline of communicating by listening first.
2   Empathy – leaders place themselves in another's situation to best understand that person.
3   Healing – caring about others and assisting them with personal and professional problems.
4   Awareness – understanding the situation and its impact on others.
5   Persuasion – convincing others without forcing them to adopt a certain view.
6   Conceptualization – creating a vision that defines goals and provides direction.
7   Foresight – the ethical responsibility to know the future and act appropriately.

8 Stewardship – effectively manage organizations for the good of society.

9 Commitment to the growth of people – assisting others to advance themselves.

10 Building community – creating a safe and comfortable place to connect with others.

Servant leadership focuses on putting others first, for the leader to serve others and, in this leadership process, accomplish tasks and achieve goals. The key to servant leadership resides with the leader and his or her ability to authentically convey to others the intent to serve them. Building trust and credibility allows the leader to influence others. Servant leaders share power and encourage a participative style of leadership that is inclusive and altruistic.

Although this approach is appealing for many contexts, leaders should fully understand the situation and context before deciding to employ a servant leadership approach. Many contexts and organizations would not respond favourably to a servant leadership approach. Organizations with a rigid hierarchical structure usually do not lend towards effective use of servant leadership. Leaders must understand both the organization and their own leadership style, ensuring a good *match* before attempting to employ a servant leadership approach.

Authentic leadership

Authentic leadership stresses the moral component of leadership and is a relatively new topic for leadership research, having emerged in the early twenty-first century.[20] However, since the beginning of mankind, leaders have provided countless examples of ineffective or bad leadership resulting from a lack of morality or a self-centred morality. As our world becomes more connected and information is disseminated at mind-boggling speed, the need for authentic leaders becomes more apparent.

Authentic leadership has its roots in psychological research and ancient Greek philosophy that focused on knowing oneself and acting in accord with that true self. Authentic leadership exists in three forms that are inclusive: (i) personal, (ii) as a leader and (iii) as an encompassing phenomenon. Many[21, 22] argue the three forms of authentic leadership are hierarchical as one cannot embrace authentic leadership and lead authentically if one is not personally authentic. Authentic leaders lead from a utilitarian ethical perspective trying to do what is good for the greatest number in a given situation. In summary, authentic leadership requires self-awareness, having an internal moral perspective, and leading transparently while balancing competing demands.[2]

Complexity leadership

Just as concepts from complexity theory have changed thought regarding the physical sciences, leadership studies appear as another realm expanding its boundaries to critically examine the possibilities of leveraging new views to improve human social performance.[23] Complexity in regard to leadership focuses on re-examining concepts of informal organization and leadership emergence. The importance of complexity leadership provides another perspective as present leadership thought struggles to adapt to the dynamics evolving in our rapidly changing world.

Complexity leadership comes from the study of complexity science and not complex or mismanaged bureaucratic processes. It assumes that the leadership foundation results from interconnections between individuals and is not based on authority and control. The interconnections occur from shared values and visions and common purposes that create a natural attraction facilitating productive relationships. Complexity leadership occurs with the leader existing as part of the organizational system, not external to the dynamic processes bringing about change. Leaders do not design formal organizational structures specifically to facilitate complexity leadership, but are aware of and encourage the natural associations that occur, allowing solutions to problems and productive ideas to evolve from interconnected relationships. This new emphasis on complex relationships 'takes leadership out of the Industrial Age and places it into the modern, connectionist Knowledge Era' with Knowledge Era organizations posed at the fringe of chaos.[24]

Leadership thought can focus on controlling conflict, maintaining order and achieving goals while inspiring others to commit to a vision that will bring about increased organizational performance. Complexity leadership focuses on a divergence from systematic processes and organization and allows a more free-flowing exchange of ideas and interconnectedness that creates more adaptive systems and organizations. Within the context of larger organizations, complexity leadership allows smaller, complex, dynamic processes to emerge and provide solutions. In summary, studying complexity leadership provides leaders with another way to better understand possible solutions to help organizations operate more like adaptive systems.[24] Much work remains on developing complexity leadership as research must better define the role of leaders, how others interact with leaders to produce desirable outcomes in complex environments, how organizations engage in complexity leadership, and other aspects not yet discussed.

Adaptive leadership

Adaptive leadership focuses on people and organizations adjusting to survive and thrive. Leadership scholars since the mid-1990s have observed and conducted research on evolutionary processes and systems that adjust to their changing environment and context, and then explored ways for leaders to adopt an adaptive mindset to facilitate change. Central to bringing about the ability to adapt and thrive is to change the priorities, thoughts, patterns and commitment of those involved in the change process. Adaptive leadership mobilizes leaders and followers to develop unique solutions to tackle tough challenges and thrive.[25]

The important constructs of adaptive leadership include building on rather than expunging the past, experimenting to bring about organizational refitting, embracing and leveraging diversity, rearranging and displacing old habits and ways, and developing patience as adaptation requires time. One of the greatest challenges for leaders employing adaptive leadership is to shift their perspective and realize that often change represents a sense of loss to those involved in the change process. A simple shift in perspective regarding change as loss can allow those leading adaptive change to accommodate others through behaviour modification that adapts to the fear and ambiguity associated with a sense of loss. Adaptive leadership also embraces conservation as leaders must preserve those critical elements from the present needed for future adaptation and growth.

Adaptive leaders observe, interpret observations, and develop interventions based on the observations.[25] Leaders must also manage themselves in their environments while minimizing the anxiety and ambiguity others experience from the synergies caused by the change process. An important leader function is to ensure enough stress occurs to bring about the desired adaptation while guarding against the threat of chaos for those involved in the evolution occurring within the context or situation. The art of balancing the boundaries of adaptive leadership challenges leaders and provides a growth opportunity for everyone. The balancing act necessitates leaders who are not afraid to take risks and experiment, follow a designed course of action, and yet not become fixed on the course of action allowing threats to emerge and opportunities to expire.

Summary

Leadership is a relatively new academic discipline, but the act of leading has existed for centuries. Since Sun-tzu, many have examined and explored various ways to influence others and lead them. Leadership and leader development success occurs through observation and understanding common principles that lend toward effective influence. Awareness at both the personal and organizational levels must occur before leadership advances. Good leadership occurs through accurate and honest assessments, knowledge of the various ways to lead, and an understanding of the environment and context. Leadership can act as a powerful force multiplier or be the cause of utter failure.

Case Study 4.1 Marine Sergeant Dakota Meyer

Just before dawn on September 8, 2009, while on a patrol with Afghan forces, Corporal Dakota Meyer and Staff Sergeant Juan Rodriguez-Chavez heard over their radio of an ambush involving their squad. Taliban fighters unleashed a firestorm from the hills, from the stone houses, even from the local school. The squad was quickly pinned down, taking ferocious fire from three sides. Men were being wounded and killed, and four Americans, Dakota's friends, were surrounded. Four times, Dakota and Juan asked permission to go into the ambush to help; four times they were denied. It was, they were told, too dangerous. Dakota and Juan defied orders; Juan jumped into a Humvee and took the wheel as Dakota climbed into the turret and manned the gun. They drove straight into a killing zone, Dakota's upper body and head exposed to a blizzard of fire from AK-47s and machine guns, from mortars and rocket-propelled grenades.

Coming upon wounded Afghan soldiers, Dakota jumped out and loaded each of the wounded into the Humvee, each time exposing himself to enemy fire. They turned around and drove those wounded back to safety. Those who were there called it the most intense combat they'd ever seen. Dakota and Juan would have been forgiven for not going back in. But as Dakota says, you don't leave anyone behind. Juan and Dakota returned to the firefight *five* more times, retrieving wounded and killed Afghan soldiers. On the fifth trip, they finally got to the trapped Americans, and Dakota jumped out and ran toward them. Drawing enemy guns on himself, bullets kicking up the dirt all around him, he kept going until he came upon those four Americans, lying where they fell, together as one team. Dakota and the others, who had joined him at this point, knelt down, picked up their comrades, and – through all those bullets, all the smoke, all the chaos – carried them out, one by one, because, as Dakota says, 'That's what you do for a brother.'

Discussion questions

1 Were the actions of Dakota and Juan transactional or transformational? Why?
2 Explain Dakota and Juan's actions in terms of path-goal leadership.
3 Explain how Dakota and Juan illustrated LMX leadership.
4 Did Dakota and Juan illustrate servant leadership? Please explain in terms of the 10 servant leader constructs.

Case discussion: Marine Sergeant Dakota Meyer

1 Were the actions of Dakota and Juan transactional or transformational? Why?

   Most actions by Dakota and Juan were transformational. The values instilled into them by the Marine Corps created a sense of commitment and loyalty to their comrades in danger greater than their value of personal safety. Transformational leadership focused on developing an internal desire to achieve organizational goals more than personal goals. In this case, both Dakota and Juan placed the Marine Corps values before personal values, prompting their actions to disobey orders. The two Marines' actions also illustrate the difference between management and leadership as both Dakota and Juan did what was right, not the right thing.

2 Explain Dakota and Juan's actions in terms of path-goal leadership.

   The goal for both Dakota and Juan was to retrieve the soldiers and Marines in harm's way. The path included making multiple trips into enemy fire to retrieve wounded and dead soldiers and Marines. There were many obstacles along the path that both Dakota and Juan had to overcome to achieve their goal. The leader behaviours used were mainly participative as both Dakota and Juan worked together to accomplish the goal. Both Dakota and Juan also used directive behaviour in defying orders and commandeering equipment to accomplish the goal.

3 Explain how Dakota and Juan illustrated LMX leadership.

   The in-group for both Dakota and Juan consisted of the other Marines in harm's way. The out-group included the Taliban fighters and those ordering them not to go into the firefight. The leadership making had already occurred as both Dakota and Juan were at the partner phase before the firefight started.

4 Did Dakota and Juan illustrate servant leadership? Please explain in terms of the 10 servant leader constructs.

   Both Dakota and Juan illustrated servant leadership. Instructors should review the 10 servant leadership constructs and discuss how both Marines either illustrated or could not illustrate each construct during the battle. The constructs illustrated by both Marines included:

1 Listening – they heard the firefight and quickly understood what they had to do.
2 Empathy – both Dakota and Juan could feel what the others were experiencing.
3 Healing – both cared about the other Marines and chose to assist them;
4 Awareness – both understood the situation and their impact on others;
5 Persuasion – Dakota convinced Juan to take action.
6 Conceptualization – both quickly developed a plan to save the others.
7 Foresight – both understood the ethical responsibilities and acted appropriately.
8 Stewardship – both knew the impact their actions would have on the Marine Corps values if they did nothing.
9 Commitment to the growth of people – both were willing to sacrifice themselves to assist others and allow them to advance in the future.
10 Building community – in a way, both were continuing the Marine community through their actions.

References

1 Grint K. *Leadership: A Very Short Introduction*. New York: Oxford University Press, 2010.

2 Northouse PG. *Leadership Theory and Practice*, 6th edn. Thousand Oaks, CA: Sage, 2013, p. 5.

3 Rost JC. *Leadership for the Twenty-First Century*. London: Praeger, 1991; p. 102.

4 Eisenhower DD. Cited on Thinkexist.com. Available at: http://thinkexist.com/quotation/leadership-the_art_of_getting_someone_else_to_do/147507.html[accessed 29 March 2013].

5 Cohen WA. *Drucker on Leadership: New Lessons From the Father of Modern Management*. San Francisco: Jossey-Bass, 2010, p. 10.

6 Katz RL. Skills of an effective administrator. *Harvard Bus Rev* 1955; **33**:33–42.

7 Mumford MD, Zaccaro SJ, Harding FD, Jacobs TO, Fleishman EA. Leadership skills for a changing world: Solving complex social problems. *Leadership Quart* 2000; **11**:11–35.

8 Fiedler FE. A contingency model of leadership effectiveness. In: Berkowitz L (ed.), *Advances in Experimental Social Psychology*, Vol. **1**. New York: Academic Press, 1964; pp. 149–90.

9 Hersey P, Blanchard KH. Life-cycle theory of leadership. *Train Dev J* 1969; **23**:26–34.

10 Reddin WJ. The 3-D management style theory. *Train Dev J* 1967; April: 8–17.

11 Pearce CL, Conger JA. *Shared Leadership*. Thousand Oaks, CA: Sage, 2001.

12 House RJ, Mitchell RR. Path-goal theory of leadership. *J Contemp Bus* 1974; **3**:81–97.

13 Graen GB, Uhl-Bien M. The transformation of professionals into self-managing and partially self-designing contributions: Toward a theory of leadership making. *J Manage Syst* 1991; **3**:33–48.

14 Bass BM. *The Bass Handbook of Leadership Theory, Research and Managerial Applications*, 4th edn. New York: Free Press, 2008.

15 Burns JM. *Leadership*. New York: Harper & Row, 1978.

16 Diaz-Saenz H. Transformational leadership. In: Bryman A, Collinson D, Grint K, Jackson B, Uhl-BienM (eds), *The Sage Handbook of Leadership*. Thousand Oaks, CA: Sage, 2011; pp. 299–310.

17 Conger JA, Kanungo RN. *Charismatic Leadership in Organizations*. Thousand Oaks, CA: Sage, 1999.

18 Greenleaf RK. *Servant Leadership: A Journey Into the Nature of Legitimate Power and Greatness*. Mahwah, NJ: Paulist Press, 1977; pp. 13–14.

19 Spears LC. Tracing the past, present, and future of servant-leadership. In: Spears LC, Lawrence M (eds), *Focus on Leadership: Servant-Leadership for the 21st Century*. New York: John Wiley & Sons, Inc., 2002; pp. 1–16.

20 Caza A, Jackson B. Authentic leadership. In: Bryman A, Collinson D, Grint K, Jackson B, Uhl-Bien M (eds), *The Sage Handbook of Leadership*. Thousand Oaks, CA: Sage, 2011; pp. 352–64.

21 Shamir B, Eilam G. "What's your story?" A life-stories approach to authentic leadership development. *Leadership Quart* 2005; **16**:395–417.

22 Yammarino FJ, Dionne SD, Schriescheim CA, Dansereau F. Authentic leadership and positive organizational behavior: A meso, multi-level perspective. *Leadership Quart* 2008; **19**: 693–707.

23 Uhl-Bien M, Marion R. Complexity leadership theory. In: Bryman A, Collinson D, Grint K, Jackson B, Uhl-Bien M (eds), *The Sage Handbook of Leadership*. Thousand Oaks, CA: Sage, 2011; pp. 352–64.

24 Uhl-Bien M, Marion R. Complexity leadership theory. In: Bryman A, Collinson D, Grint K, Jackson B, Uhl-BienM (eds), *The Sage Handbook of Leadership*. Thousand Oaks, CA: Sage, 2011; p. 473.

25   Heifetz R, Grashow A, Linsky M. *The Practice of Adaptive Leadership: Tools and Tactics for Changing Your Organization and the World.* Cambridge, MA: Harvard Business Press, 2009.

Further reading

26   Kouzes J, Posner B. *The Leadership Challenge*, 4th edn. San Francisco: Jossey-Bass, 2007.
27   Northouse PG. *Leadership Theory and Practice*, 6th edn. Thousand Oaks, CA: Sage, 2013.

Chapter 5

Clinical Leadership

Ahmed Okasha

The UK General Medical Council (2012), on the duties of a doctor registered with the GMC, states that patients must be able to trust doctors with their lives and health and to justify that trust the doctor must show respect for human life.[1]

Excellent leadership creates a vision that engages all staff, works across professional boundaries and ensures that patients and the public are truly involved in creating health. Whilst many good clinical leaders do exist within our clinics, hospitals and communities, these individuals are at a premium, and will become increasingly so with the rising public expectations, a global economic downturn, an ageing population and rapidly advancing technologies that will result in the pace of change within the health service increasing. If organizations are going to survive in this rapidly changing future environment, they will have to be able to adapt quickly whilst remaining focused on the health service key aim, which is to improve the quality of care we deliver to our patients and public.

This will require exceptional clinical leaders, able to take a macroscopic view (helicopter effects, bird's eye view) on health systems and resource allocation, and with an understanding of the political, economic, social and technological drivers for change that are going to influence healthcare provision throughout their careers.

Aspiring clinical leaders, many of whom have been taught little of the organizational structure of healthcare, will need to learn about the funding, governance and management that are integral to the system; but simply having knowledge and information will not be enough. Future clinical leaders will require, and will need to utilize, a range of non-technical skills to allow them to manage and lead others, not just within their specialty but also across all professional boundaries. These include creating vision and setting clear direction, together with skills in service redesign and quality improvement, adaptability, self-awareness and awareness of others, working collaboratively and networking.[2] The complementary skills of leadership and 'followership' need to be incorporated into doctors' training to support professionalism.[3] Leadership by clinicians is set to become an increasingly respected and sought-after quality.[4]

Definitions of leadership

There is no universally accepted single definition of 'leadership'. It often means different things to different people in different contexts. Common themes include exerting influence

Leadership in Psychiatry, First Edition. Edited by Dinesh Bhugra, Pedro Ruiz and Susham Gupta.
© 2013 John Wiley & Sons, Ltd. Published 2013 by John Wiley & Sons, Ltd.

over the thoughts, attitudes and behaviors of others; setting a direction; motivating and inspiring; helping others realize their potential; leading by example; selflessness and making a difference. Peter Drucker,[5] in the Foreword to the Drucker Foundation, tells us: 'The only definition of a leader is someone who has followers'.[5] John Maxwell sums up his definition of leadership as: 'Leadership is influence – nothing more, nothing less'.[6] By contrast, Warren Bennis defines it thus: 'Leadership is a function of knowing yourself, having a vision that is well communicated, building trust among colleagues, and taking effective action to realize your own leadership potential'.[7] Former US President Dwight Eisenhower defines leadership as 'the art of getting someone else to do something you want done because he wants to do it'. Definitions of leadership are heavily influenced by the context in which leadership is taking place. Thus it is likely that clinicians would look at Eisenhower's definition and identify strongly with it, yet many would, in the same breath, denounce their own leadership skills.

We have to differentiate between leadership and management. Warren Bennis summarizes the differences with 12 distinctions between managers and leaders:[7]

- The manager administers; the leader innovates.
- The manager is a copy; the leader is an original.
- The manager maintains; the leader develops.
- The manager focuses on systems and structure; the leader focuses on people.
- The manager relies on control; the leader inspires trust.
- The manager has a short-range view; the leader has a long-range perspective.
- The manager asks how and when; the leader asks what and why.
- Managers have their eyes on the bottom line; leaders have their eyes on the horizon.
- The manager imitates; the leader originates.
- The manager accepts the status quo; the leader challenges it.
- The manager is the classic good soldier; the leader is his own person.
- The manager does things right; the leader does the right thing.[7]

What is clinical leadership?

The United Kingdom's Department of Health, in the publication *Our Future*, describes the essence of clinical leadership in the UK National Health Service (NHS) as being to motivate, to inspire, to promote the values of the NHS, to empower and to create a consistent focus on the needs of the patients being served.[8]

Leadership is necessary not just to maintain high standards of care, but to transform services to achieve even higher levels of excellence. The working definition of clinical leadership is empowering clinicians to have the confidence and capability to continually improve healthcare on both the small and the large scale.[9] There is a feeling amongst some clinicians that they should be advocates for their patients and should make treatment decisions on clinical grounds, remaining independent of financial and political concerns; and thus involvement in management or leadership is seen to stand in direct opposition to this. Similarly, there may be conflicting interests between clinicians, their own departments and practices, and their umbrella organizations. All practising doctors are responsible for the use of resources, many will also lead teams or be involved with the supervision of colleagues, and most will work in managed systems. Doctors have responsibilities to their patients, employers and those who contract their services. This means that doctors are managers and are managed.[10]

Clinical leadership and group dynamics

The psychologist Kurt Lewin introduced the term 'group dynamics' in 1939, following classic studies on different styles of leadership. Schoolchildren were assigned to one of three groups, with an authoritarian, a democratic or a laissez-faire leader.[11] Democratic leadership was shown to be the most effective leadership style, but this conclusion is too simplistic, and warrants further consideration. There is agreement from different industries about the 'organizational context' in which quality improvement techniques are most likely to be effective. In healthcare, this requires the involvement of health professionals, especially doctors.[12] Clinical leaders in healthcare organizations, through bridging the divide between 'them' and 'us', are able to more effectively align improvements in the quality of care with wider organizational strategy. Teamwork in healthcare can be defined as: a dynamic process involving two or more health professionals with complementary backgrounds and skills, sharing common health goals and exercising concerted physical and mental effort in assessing, planning or evaluating patient care. This is accomplished through interdependent collaboration, open communication and shared decision-making.[13] This in turn generates value-added patient, organizational and staff outcomes. There is growing evidence from health services research that there is more to improving quality than the technical aspects of care. For a team to be effective, it requires the right mix of people performing the task in a coordinated manner, with regular effective communication, in the context of clearly understood shared objectives, known as goal orientation.[14]

Clinical leadership and decision-making

It is important for teams to have an agreed process for making decisions. For example, in psychiatry, responsibility for the care of referrals to a multidisciplinary team is distributed among the clinical members of the team. Contrary to the notion that doctors always dominate group discussions, Gair and Hartley[15] found that doctors were more likely than other healthcare professionals to have their proposals questioned and were more likely to accept decisions contrary to their initial suggestions. The value of teams truly making decisions together is that it creates collective ownership, which enhances commitment to implementing the outcome.[15]

Leaders should encourage their team members to develop psychological safety, which is a 'shared belief that the team is safe for interpersonal risk taking'.[16] In order for this to happen, individuals need to feel confident that they will not suffer for speaking up. Mutual trust and respect amongst team members takes time to develop – a particular challenge for clinical leaders, where team membership changes frequently

Although a degree of inter-team conflict can be beneficial, such as through competition between wards to achieve the lowest infection rates or confusion, this can be detrimental if it leads to a 'winners and losers' situation. Negative inter-group conflict can be reduced by rewarding teams, rotating membership of teams and ensuring high levels of communication between teams. Intra-team conflict commonly transitions through the stages of disagreement, confrontation, escalation, de-escalation and then resolution through negotiation and compromise.[17]

'Tribalism' of health and social care professions leads to some professional groups trying to gain dominance over others in multidisciplinary settings. One of the suggestions for producing more effective teams is to encourage different professions to learn together at different stages of their careers. Different professions, such as doctors and managers, general practitioners (GPs) and specialists, have their own languages, and have been socialized into specific ways of seeing and accepting the world.[18]

Personality and leadership

Personality provides us with an approach to understanding why some people are driven to attain leadership status, and why their ascent is supported by others. Personality is an important consideration since it tends to be relatively stable over adulthood, and is, therefore, a robust driver of characteristics relevant to leadership. Personality shapes individual work interests, preferences for dominance (and thus motivation for leadership positions), and leadership style.

The most commonly used model of personality is the Five Factor Model of Cloninger.[19] This is not meant to define personality but rather to aid understanding of personality and its effect on behaviour. The factors are as follows:

- emotional stability
- extroversion
- openness
- agreeableness
- conscientiousness.[20]

It is clear that personality is relevant to leadership (see also Chapter 2). However, personality alone is not enough to explain how some people become leaders. People might have the drive to be a leader and set ambitions from their early career; both their personality and drive shape their motivation to become a leader. Nicholson[21] summarizes the three main processes through which people attain leadership positions:

- *Emergence* – people emerge through the organization ranks. These people are characterized by their motivation and skills.

- *Selection* – elections or selection by others using a range of criteria can be used to select leaders. Managers from across an organization and human resource (HR) specialists could contribute to this process.
- *Designation* – leadership roles may be designated. The advantage of this approach is that leadership can be allocated fairly and sequentially to people of equal talent and expertise. An example is a university department where the head of department position is rotated among professors. A disadvantage is that leaders may not necessarily be driven to excel at their given role.[21]

Transformational leaders have to provide inspirational motivation, should have an idealized influence, should create intellectual stimulation, and show individualized consideration.[20]

There are two ethical challenges for the aspiring clinical leader: self-interest and self-sacrifice. It is also the job of a leader to bring about change where change is needed, to identify inadequacies and to put the delivery of high-quality patient care above the interests of themselves or their colleagues. The very notion of becoming a clinical leader can generate conflict between the needs of the individual to conform (in order to progress) and the interests of the patients they aspire to serve, the patient in front of you and the population. The tension between the needs of any individual patient and the limited resources of any individual healthcare organization is not unfamiliar to any practising doctor. Leading change for fairer allocation of resources within an organization could result in the patient in front of you losing out. To meet that challenge, the ability to articulate the overt and hidden values at work and to use your experience and knowledge to resolve them – to 'do ethics' –is essential.[22]

The primary responsibility of leaders is to provide for the safety and quality of care, treatment and services. The purpose of the hospital's mission, vision and goals is to define how the hospital will achieve safety and quality. The leaders are more likely to be aligned with the mission, vision and goals when they create them together. The common purpose of the hospital is most likely achieved when it is understood by all who work in or are served by the hospital.[23]

Leaders as change agents

Leaders have a key role as 'change agents' and role models. Change agents can be described as requiring several skills to manage change effectively.[24] These are:

- the ability to work independently, without the power, sanction and support of the management hierarchy;
- the skills of an effective collaborator, able to compete in ways that enhance rather than destroy cooperation;
- the ability to develop high-trust relationships, based on high ethical standards;
- self-confidence, tempered with humility;
- respect for the process of change, as well as the content;

- the ability to work across business functions and units, to be 'multi-faceted and ambidextrous'.[24, 25]

The most effective leader is the one who can accomplish the group purpose while carrying out the main tasks of leadership critical for success. In order to attain such a level of leadership and success, several important issues come into play. The most essential and commonly known are: motivation, shared vision, good communication, good time management, and a situational approach to leadership. Appreciating these points and knowing how to enforce them within the relevant context of healthcare management makes all the difference in the success of a leader.[26]

To motivate people, a leader needs to understand their needs.[27] People expend effort on behalf of their physiological needs, family, group loyalty, money, security and deeply held beliefs like religion. Though the tasks of a leader with respect to motivation are many, he/she should recognize the needs of followers and help them see how those needs could be achieved. The leader must be an effective communicator to achieve a high-level of motivation and visionary success. Good communication skills are a must in building confidence and loyalty among the group. It should be the goal of the organization to create a two-way communication system that allows information to flow from leader to follower and vice versa, including dissent, should it occur. This provides the opportunity for followers to attain a degree of empowerment and authority in their own right. Achieving such communication requires a leader to have emotional intelligence in order to work with the basics of needs-based motivation, and to encourage a cooperative teamwork. Managing relationships and communication delivery with people is an unquestionable facet of leadership.[26]

The umbrella that holds the previous conditions of leadership together is effective time management. 'Time is life. It is irreversible and irreplaceable. To waste time is to waste life, but to master time is to master life and make the most of it.' Time management is essential for achieving desired results. Therefore, leaders should emphasize upon themselves and their followers the importance of deadlines in order to effectively accomplish organizational activities.[28]

Leadership is best characterized by vision and mission, and the courage, character and ability to put the precepts of this vision and mission into sustainable action. Leaders combine their ideas and values with the necessary energy and effectiveness to implement them. As noted by Drs Meyer[29] and Greiner,[30] most leaders at any level also function as middle managers. Being able to maintain quality and effect growth is a challenge.[29, 30] Good leadership allows institutions and organizations to grow, plan for, and keep pace with environmental changes. No growth means stagnation. The best leadership proactively addresses and implements change, and sustains success for the future. Such success also involves developing (producing and nurturing) the next generation of leaders. As Greiner states, 'leadership is a moral enterprise'.[30] Though the effectiveness of good leadership is not always immediately apparent, its absence is felt at many levels and has long-lasting effects.[31]

Developing a team is one of the first tasks, especially for the leader joining a department or institution with deeply entrenched views, beliefs, values and loyalties. A team broadens perspective, helps movement in the direction of change, provides moral and concrete support, and also can give feedback (positive and negative) and help in planning and anticipating consequences.

Maintaining a focus on priorities, learning to delegate and teaching others to perform these tasks well while protecting time for personal growth and for emergencies, all support good time management.

Can we measure success?

Typically, popularity (love/respect) is one measure; it is better for a leader to be respected and loved than respected and feared, but this is insufficient. Meeting goals and fulfilling the mission is the best measure. Is there a modification of the prevailing culture that will ensure that these outcomes can be sustained? The leader's success reflects the success of the team, and consequently the team's success will support the success of the leader. Thus, generosity with praise is not simply window dressing, but an acknowledgement of contributions and fact.

In any measure of success, especially of leadership, it is important to know when to say goodbye. Clearly, very important irresolvable conflicts, such as ethical issues, can prompt departure, as can a change in mission. Recognizing limits to personal competence (which can be determined through introspection as well as feedback from colleagues) may prompt a change. For some leaders, the need for change, creativity and growth occurs regularly, no matter how well a current experience is progressing, leading to exploration of new and challenging (sometimes better) opportunities. Change can foster fresh ideas, energy and resources; new leaders can redress mistakes, adapt, clean house and restructure. Finally, no matter how elevated or important leaders are, they need to remember that life exists outside of work and find fulfillment in family and friends.[32]

We need to focus on clinical leadership, on responsibility and accountability, and on the ability to manage complexity – within ourselves, within the team and for the most severely challenged patients. We need to help psychiatrists demonstrate resilience in the most difficult of circumstances, and to maintain a constant drive for quality in mental health services for the benefit of patients.[33] We need to ensure excellence across the domains that matter most to the well-being of our patients, and demonstrate to fellow healthcare professionals, commissioners and policy-makers the unique role and added value of the consultant psychiatrist. There are many frameworks that can be used to make this case.[34]

Psychiatrists are best placed to use integrated biopsychosocial models in understanding the aetiology of mental illness and managing mental illness, emotional disturbance and abnormal behaviour. This is what makes them different from other disciplines, even in clinical leadership.[35] Clinical leadership is:

- vision;
- self-sacrifice;
- role modelling;
- acting as spokesperson;
- expectations of high performance;

- recognizing the contribution of others;
- clinical expertise;
- accountability;
- rational argument.[36]

Education and training for clinical leadership

> Contrary to the opinion of many people, leaders are not born. Leaders are made, and they are made by effort and hard work
>
> Vince Lombardi, 1913–70, professional football coach

There are many and varied opportunities for postgraduate trainees to develop their leadership capacity in the context of their clinical training (see Chapter 19). It is vital that developing as a clinical leader and being a clinical leader become core elements in the day jobs of some doctors. However, there are also paths to becoming a clinical leader that involve stepping outside standard clinical training, often temporarily.[37] While the experience of shadowing, of leadership development programmes and of short courses are undoubtedly of value, there are a growing number of clinicians who have decided to pursue more formal training in management or business. The core curriculum for master of business administration generally includes the following areas:

- Accountancy – involves an understanding of how to record, verify and report on financial statements about a business.
- Economics – the study of the production, distribution and consumption of goods and services.
- Finance – the study of managing money and risk.
- Strategic management – the study of drafting, implementing and evaluating decisions about how an organization can achieve its aims.

Clinicians often attend management training courses prior to consultant interviews. This is because management is a common area of question for interviews. Clinicians are now expected to have an understanding of the structure of healthcare organizations, and an overview of what is involved in running them. There is a wide array of choices regarding whether to study an MBA or a Masters, or to gain practical hands-on management experience through local projects or a placement in industry. The decision depends on both personal circumstances and individual preferences.[38]

Compassion and personality attributes

Compassion, the essence of caring for others, is a fundamental and sometimes neglected interaction in developing clinical leadership. Here, patients describe what it feels like to be treated as a collection of symptoms rather than an individual, to have their need for privacy ignored or to be spoken to without respect or kindness. This section also examines the powerlessness of being a patient, and how practitioners who are successful in demonstrating compassion are able to empower and build confidence in those they care for.[39]

Goleman identifies five elements of emotional intelligence that are crucial to leaders: self-awareness, self-regulation, motivation, empathy and social skills.[40]

The individual attributes that have an impact on leadership skills and knowledge include: general cognitive ability, which is an individual's intelligence; crystallized cognitive ability, a form of intellectual ability that is learned or acquired over time; and motivation, which indicates a leader's need to be proactive, seeking to influence a situation and then show willingness to tackle complex organizational problems. Personality traits undoubtedly play a role in leadership development; for example, charisma is a common trait of many successful leaders.[41]

Clinical leadership, in this sense, is about adding continuous service improvement to the day-to-day job of being a patient-facing clinician.[42] Beyond this, a small number of clinicians will make leadership a major part of their professional identity, and take on formal positions, such as clinical director and medical director. It is important that some of the brightest and most respected clinicians assume these roles. But since the heart of medicine will always be in the doctor–patient interaction, it is even more important that clinical leadership, in the form of understanding and systematically improving your own practice, becomes a natural part of what it means to be a good clinician.

Conclusion

Clinical leadership requires some traits of personality including persistence, dedication, emotional intelligence, empathy and the power to influence people not through fear but through respect and love. Emotional stability, resilience, innovation and the capacity to perceive future perspectives and devise new strategies are necessary requirements. Although some of these traits are possibly genetic, many can be acquired through training. Medicine is considered to be both an art and a science, but no medical specialty fulfils those two aspects more than psychiatry. It was stated by Sir Martin Roth that psychiatry is the most humanistic branch of medicine and the most scientific of human sciences. Leadership in psychiatry requires a wide horizon of cultural, spiritual and scientific knowledge. This does not mean psychiatric leaders should be angelically perfect, but at least should aspire to the above traits.

Leadership in psychiatry requires dedication, and clinical affluence which cannot be afforded in many parts of the world, where the clinical leader cannot allocate most of his or her time to clinical work. In emerging countries, the clinical leader has to do research, teaching and clinical work apart from supervising psychiatric theses for early career psychiatrists. Such leaders are not devoted solely to clinical leadership. In some developing countries, private practice is an addition to the tasks previously described, which means that clinical leaders in psychiatry can face burn out. However, they have a key role in promoting psychiatry, whether academic, research or teaching. In some countries, clinical psychiatric leaders can influence policy-making, promote psychiatric services, and assign budgets for mental patients and research through their connections with policy-makers, media professionals and celebrities. Remember that when the film director Alfred Hitchcock released his film *Psycho* in the 1960s, the budget for psychiatric services increased by 500% in the United States![29]

References

1 General Medical Council. Good medical practice (2013). Available at: www.gmc-uk .org/guidance [accessed 29 March 2013].
2 Lord Darzi. Foreword. In: Stanton E, Lemer C, Mountford J (eds), *Clinical Leadership: Bridging the Divide*. Quay Books, 2010; pp. xi–xiii.
3 Working Party of the Royal College of Physicians. Doctors in society: medical professionalism in a changing world. *Clin Med* 2005; **5**(6 Suppl. 1): S5–40.
4 Cave J, Cooke M, Chantler C *et al. High Quality Care for All: NHS next stage review final report.* London: Department of Health, 2008.
5 Drucker PF. Foreword. In: Hesselbein F, Goldsmith M, Beckhard R (eds), *The Leader of the Future: New Visions, Strategies and Practices for the Next Era.* New York: John Wiley & Sons, Inc., 1996.
6 Maxwell J. *The 21 Irrefutable Laws of Leadership Workbook.* Nashville: Thomas Nelson Publishers, 2002.
7 Bennis W. *On Becoming a Leader.* Perseus Books, 1989.
8 NHS Institute for Innovation and Improvement. Enhancing Engagement in Medical Leadership 2007. Available at: http://www.institute.nhs.uk/building_capacity/enhancing_engagement/ enhancing_engagement_in_medical_leadership.html[accessed 15 April 2013].
9 Stanton E, Lemer C, Mountford J. *Clinical Leadership.* Quay Books, 2010.
10 General Medical Council. Leadership and management for all doctors (2013). Available at: http://www.gmc-uk.org/guidance/current/library/management_for_doctors.asp[accessed 29 March 2013].
11 Lewin K, Llippit R, White RK. Patterns of aggressive behavior in experimentally created social climates. *J Soc Psychol* 1939; **10**:271–301.
12 Marshall M. Applying quality improvement approaches to health care. *Brit Med J* 2009; **339**:b3411.
13 Jelphs H, Dickinson H (2008) *Working in Teams (Better Partnership Working).* Policy Press.
14 Dawson J, West M, Yan X. Positive and negative effects of team working in healthcare: real and pseudo teams and their impact on healthcare safety. Aston University, 2009.
15 Gair G, Hartley T. Medical dominance in multidisciplinary teamwork: a case study of discharge decision making in a geriatric assessment unit. *J Nurs Manage* 2001; **9**:3–11.
16 Edmonson A. Psychological safety and learning behavior in work teams. *Admin Sci Quart* 1999; **44**:350–83.
17 Stanton E, Chapman C. Teamworking and clinical leadership. In: Stanton E, Lemer C, Mountford J (eds), *Clinical Leadership: Bridging the Divide.* Quay Books, 2010; chapter 4.
18 West MA, Borrill CS, Dawson JF. Leadership clarity and team innovation in health care. Leadership Quart 2003; **14**:393–410.
19 Cloninger CR, Svrakic DM, Przybeck TR. A psychobiological model of temperament and character. *Arch Gen Psychiatry* 1993; **50**:975–90.
20 Bicknell C, Soane E. Personality and leadership. In: Stanton E, Lemer C, Mountford J (eds), *Clinical Leadership: Bridging the Divide.* Quay Books, 2010; chapter 5.
21 Nicholson N. *Managing the Human Animal.* London: Random House, 2001.
22 Elias R. Ethics and clinical leadership. In: Stanton E, Lemer C, Mountford J (eds), *Clinical Leadership: Bridging the Divide.* Quay Books, 2010; chapter 6.

23 Schyve PM. *Leadership in Healthcare Organizations: A Guide to Joint Commission Leadership Standards*. The Governance Institute, 2009.

24 Dale C, Gardner J, Philogene S. Overcoming barriers to change: case of Ashworth Hospital. In: Howkins E, Thornton C (eds), *Six Steps to Effective Management; Managing and Leading Innovation in Health Care*. London: Baillière Tindall, 2002; pp. 220–46.

25 Kanter RM. *When Giants Learn to Dance*. London: Unwin, 1989.

26 Al Haddad MK. Leadership in healthcare management. *Bahrain Med Bull* 2003; **25**:1–3.

27 Bass BM. *Leadership and Performance Beyond Expectation*. New York: The Free Press, 1985.

28 Lakein A. *How To Get Control of Your Time and Your Life*. New York: New American Library, 1973.

29 Meyer R. The tripartite mission of an academic psychiatry department and the roles of the chair. *Acad Psychiatry* 2006; **30**:292–7.

30 Greiner C. Leadership for psychiatrists. *Acad Psychiatry* 2006; **30**:283–8.

31 Buckley P. Reflections on leadership as chair of a department of psychiatry. *Acad Psychiatry* 2006; **30**:309–14.

32 Robinowitz CB. Psychiatrists as leaders in academic medicine. *Acad Psychiatry* 2006; **30**: 273–8.

33 General Medical Council. Good medical practice: good doctors. Available at: http://www.gmc-uk.org/guidance/good_medical_practice/good_doctors.asp[accessed 29 March 2013].

34 Academy of Medical Royal Colleges & NHS Institute for Innovation and Improvement. *Medical Leadership Competency Framework. Enhancing Engagement in Medical Leadership*, 2nd edn. NHS Institute for Innovation and Improvement, 2009.

35 Bhugra D. *Role of the Consultant Psychiatrist: Leadership and Excellence in Mental Health Services*. London: Royal College of Psychiatrists, 2010.

36 Fisher N. Psychiatrists As Leaders (Powerpoint presentation), 2008. Available at www.rcpsych.ac.uk/docs/3-Spk2-NFisher.ppt[accessed 15 April 2013].

37 Klaber B, Bridle D. Education and clinical leadership. In: Stanton E, Lemer C, Mountford J (eds), *Clinical Leadership: Bridging the Divide*. Quay Books, 2010; chapter 7.

38 Woolcock C. MBA or not? In: Stanton E, Lemer C, Mountford J (eds), *Clinical Leadership: Bridging the Divide*. Quay Books, 2010; chapter 9.

39 e-Learning for Healthcare. Leadership for clinicians. Available at: http://www.elfh.org.uk/docs/projects/lead/wip_compassion.pdf[accessed 29 March 2013].

40 Goleman D. *Emotional Intelligence: Why it Can Matter More than IQ*. London: Bloomsbury, 1996.

41 Leff DR, Humphris P. Survival skills for leadership. In: Stanton E, Lemer C, Mountford J (eds), *Clinical Leadership: Bridging the Divide*. Quay Books, 2010; chapter 10.

42 Berwick D. A primer on leading the improvement of systems. *Brit Med J* 1996; **312**:619–22.

Chapter 6

Leadership and Clinician Engagement in Service Development

Hugo de Waal

The medical model and psychiatric services

The term 'medical model' can still be regularly heard, but mostly in a derogatory fashion. Although its pedigree in psychiatry goes back to Ronald D. Laing's critical analysis of psychiatric practice, which he published in 1960,[1] one rarely detects it being used by psychiatrists: it seems not to have survived into modern medical psychiatric discourse, although it is alive and well in the non-medical variant: I have heard non-medical colleagues refer to it regularly, although often it was not quite clear what precisely they meant by it (at least to me).

It was of course not the only critical analysis of a medical discourse: the sixties were a fertile era for these shifts in paradigms. Foucault published his *Naissance de la clinique: une archéologie du regard médical* in 1963.[2] His term *le regard médical* (the medical gaze) denoted the dehumanizing medical separation of the patient's body from the patient's person or identity, and Laing in many ways presented a similar critique about psychiatric medical practice: the psychiatric diagnostic action becomes in his view emblematic of dehumanization and represents a particularly malicious version of stigmatization. He questioned the nosological status of schizophrenia, alleging that it was unethical and irrational to treat psychiatric symptoms using biological interventions: his reasoning was based on the fact that psychiatric diagnoses were mainly based on behaviours and narratives, rather than on objectively established biological abnormalities, as is assumed to be the case in most other medical disciplines.

Laing's description of psychiatric practice is now of course markedly out of date: on the one hand he has been proven wrong in many of his arguments (the biological basis of much of psychiatric symptomatology is now not in question, although much remains to be clarified), whereas on the other hand psychiatric practice is today noticeably broad-based, having absorbed elements from many other disciplines and non-medical theories. Curiously then, whilst psychiatry is now more scientifically underpinned than ever before, psychiatrists are far less restricted to any particular model (biological or otherwise) than ever before. Yet, regularly non-medical (and sometimes even medical) colleagues express

Leadership in Psychiatry, First Edition. Edited by Dinesh Bhugra, Pedro Ruiz and Susham Gupta.

views as if Laing's caricature is still as valid as it was in the sixties (even if those colleagues may not know of his work directly).

Nowadays specialist psychiatric trainees in the United Kingdom (and not just in the United Kingdom) are constantly reminded of the value and necessity of multidisciplinary and 'holistic' approaches to patient care: one would be forgiven therefore for assuming that as a result of these emphases in medical training Laing's critical terminology had become obsolete, simply as a 'symptom' of its own success. Why then are some non-medical practitioners and others still using it?

To understand this phenomenon better, it is first necessary to understand the caricatured nature of the term and the settings in which it appears still to have some function: I take as an example the multidisciplinary team in psychiatric secondary care, but the term is heard in non-health services dealing with people with psychiatric problems (e.g. social services) as well. In those settings practitioners are regularly dealing with complex problems, which are likely – at least in part – to have arisen as a result of someone's mental illness. Whilst then the starting point of the contact between patient and service is likely to be articulated through a psychiatric diagnosis, that particular diagnosis does not fully predict the nature of someone's problems or the solution to them: instead, someone's social background and circumstances, past and current experiences, hopes and expectations, personality and views about him or herself and the world in general, are likely to be at least as relevant and probably more so. This appears to be reflected in the configuration of the majority of modern psychiatric services in the United Kingdom in the form of 'functional teams': nowadays teams usually do not provide a service targeting a particular diagnosis (with the possible exception of certain specialist services, such as dementia, anorexia or learning disability), even if that diagnosis is the first criterion to access any services. Instead they are configured along the lines of the particular clinical effort it aims to provide: brief intervention teams, assertive outreach teams, early intervention teams, reablement teams, recovery and rehabilitation teams, well-being services and so on.

In short, the practitioner is dealing with high levels of subjectivity, ambiguity, risk, unpredictability and idiosyncrasy and services are configured in an attempt (however unsuccessful at times) to reflect the predominance of those aspects, rather than psychiatric diagnostic categories. If then the term 'medical model' is understood in the narrow fashion Laing criticized, then it is clear that such a model is not going to be of much use.

This is precisely the reason why in modern undergraduate and postgraduate medical training much attention is given to 'holistic' approaches. This receives further articulation through other medical educational approaches, such as problem-based learning.[3] Furthermore, complexity is not exclusively the realm of psychiatric practice and therefore of psychiatric training: the literature on complexity in medicine is large and medical training pays particular attention to it: see, for example, Cook *et al.*[4] Historically therefore, one can discern in medical education and practice a reaction to the previously held belief that medical practice was predominantly reductionist.

In that original 'medical model' the doctor was thought to function in a specifically choreographed, linear practice: with each successive patient he or she was to establish the complaint, take a history, carry out investigations, establish a diagnosis and finally treat the patient. That therefore seems to depict a clinical world in which the doctor has contact with a succession of individual patients (as still is the case in quite a few areas around the world, where little or no systematization of healthcare services may have taken place), and his or her clinical engagement focuses on one person at a time. Decisions are then largely made with respect to 'this particular patient', taking into account the possibility that any idiosyncrasies may dictate deviating to some degree from usual practice. In and of itself that clinical encounter may therefore well be perfectly 'holistic' (in that sense defying the restraints of the caricatured depiction of the medical model), but the clinician nevertheless operates as a one-man retail outlet, dispensing his or her advice to a linear succession of customers, with a high level of clinical autonomy: the clinician is in charge of what gets done and how it is done.

That does not mean that complexity cannot play an important role in a singular patient-doctor relationship, as becomes clear once we realize how simple actions can convey powerful symbolic meanings, particularly when there are any number of hidden assumptions at work. The example of the singer Michael Jackson and his doctor is not 'normal' by any means in any culture, although the case appears medically quite simple: one patient (in this case a rich one) who hires one doctor to provide generic medical services. Apart from the monetary side there is philosophically not much difference with a more usual patient-doctor contact in primary care. However, it didn't take a medical philosopher to analyse powerful symbolic mechanisms: after the death of the client/patient, a non-medical journalist was able to detect all manner of complications in the quite straightforward prescribing actions (even if these were medically questionable) of Jackson's personal physician.[5]

In dealing with ambiguity, unpredictability and idiosyncrasy the medical model of problem-solving (delineate problem, establish diagnosis, identify cause, treat accordingly), whilst on the one hand running the danger of being over focused and blinkered, may on the other appear to convey a sense of security and safety. After all, it does provide a firm and seemingly secure framework and focus for one's clinical thinking. With this in mind, let us explore how a typical psychiatric clinical setting makes use of this caricature of medical practice (for perfectly understandable reasons) and how this contrasts with the classical 'medical model'.

Ambiguity, uncertainty, insecurity and multidisciplinary team-working

A well-functioning multidisciplinary team shares a particular feature with a modern cabinet-based government: there is the assumption that decisions are made with a degree of 'collective responsibility' (I desist here from being seduced in a political analysis of the truth of this concept in reality). Obviously individual practitioners are responsible for their own actions and decisions, but this responsibility is at least partially shared with the team. One can discern at least three assumptions, underlying this style of practice:

1 A range of views 'around the table' can only be helpful, enriching the discussions and maximizing on the available expertise and clinical experience.
2 Decisions reached through debate are more likely to have covered all angles, anticipated all pitfalls and identified the main risks.

3   Responsibility is shared, particularly when things go wrong (this is often a hidden assumption, but it may be deployed overtly, such as when a colleague states: 'I only need this done, because I need to cover my back').

When one takes the time to scrutinize these components more closely, it can be seen that – although these assumptions are perfectly reasonable in themselves – they serve a particular purpose: team-working creates a sense of completeness, professional security and clinical safety. The issue of clinical safety cannot be overemphasized and it is note-worthy how the possibility of adverse events at times seems to occupy with obsessional intensity even the most senior of clinical minds in psychiatry. This is likely to result more or less directly from the essential ambiguity and unpredictability innate to medical practice in general and psychiatric practice in particular. It is perhaps for this reason that some colleagues in various psychiatric disciplines find it difficult to make the move from, for example, an inpatient ward to a community team, given that in the latter situation prac-titioners often work alone when meeting patients: it takes time to learn how to transfer clinical insecurity as felt by a 'lone worker' to the presumed safety of the team meeting.

Psychiatric teams are markedly democratic: hierarchical structures are flat and one rarely, if ever, encounters teams that have a leader who in matters of doubt is the designated person formally tasked with taking a 'final' decision. That characteristic adds to the sense of ambiguity and uncertainty. Consider a situation in which a team engages in lengthy discussions, apparently 'going around the houses': it is likely that the relevant clinical case is too complex for normal decision-making procedures to provide the clarity and clinical safety needed to arrive at a shared decision. At that point the flat construction and 'democratic' lack of hierarchy in a team becomes problematic: there is – at least ideologically – no one person ultimately tasked with taking full responsibility for the more difficult and potentially contentious decisions and actions. Thus we see a merging of complex clinical ambiguity with 'democratic' (and therefore uncertain) decision-making processes, and this may lead to high levels of clinical insecurity.

At this point a curious phenomenon may occur: in such situations it often falls to the psychiatrist to guide the team through these hazardous waters. Despite our culture's tendency to deprofessionalize the expert,[6] doctors are still assumed to be the most senior practitioner in teams, in the sense of advising on what to do or not to do when matters are not clear. Why should this be so? Part of the answer lies in the sort of training med-ical students and postgraduate medical trainees are subjected to: they undergo extensive training in a large number of topics and discourses, gaining exposure and experience in a wide variety of clinical settings. Indeed, an often heard concern from medical students and trainees is how to integrate all they learn from completely different sources into one cohesive corpus of knowledge.

In short, from the very first day in medical school an important task lies in integrating disparate fields of knowledge, skills and competencies and developing the ability to deploy all or some of that in situations that may vary from one moment to the next. That implies that a doctor first and foremost is trained to analyse a clinical situation, not just to be able to arrive at a diagnosis and ensuing management plan, but also to be able to select which bits of her or his 'corpus of expertise' are relevant and should be used. One could therefore conclude that doctors are particularly trained in 'situational analysis' and are able to see the wood despite the trees (although obviously many senior non-medical practitioners may well be equally proficient).

It could be argued then that doctors are (ideally) able to anchor their thinking in this wide discourse, enabling them to navigate through complexity and ambiguity, sail between the cliffs of uncertainty and unpredictability, focus on creating clarity in misty surroundings and moor the boat safely. Their extensive background of knowledge and wide range of skills and competencies serve to provide a sense of safety and clarity, which may be far more difficult to achieve for someone who has been largely trained 'on the job' or has completed a three-year university degree course, no matter how worthy such education in itself may be. It is therefore natural that at such times as described above multidisciplinary teams expect to be able to rely on this source of safety, and it is an essential part of the doctor's role. This is a particular example of Erhard's terminology (see below): 'those who granted leadership'. Let us therefore examine the nature of leadership more closely.

The nature of clinical leadership

For the purpose of this chapter I would like to focus on one particular definition of leadership as formulated by Erhard *et al.*, who describe leadership as:

> an exercise in language that results in the realization of a future that wasn't going to happen anyway, which future fulfils (or contributes to fulfilling) the concerns of the relevant parties, including critically those who granted the leadership (those who lead you, and those you lead)[7]

In terms of the earlier description of the dynamics in multidisciplinary teams: the non-medical team members elect 'to grant leadership' to the team doctor – even if this is not formalized as such (another example of often held hidden assumptions). The expectation is that the doctor's expertise, based on a multifarious education and training on the one hand, and underpinned by comparatively intense legal and professional scrutiny and a detailed regulatory framework on the other, will provide clarity of thought and will facilitate a rational and balanced convergence upon a decision or action that minimizes uncertainty and risk and maximizes the well-being of patients on the one hand and of team members on the other.

Erhard *et al.* explain further:

> This definition ensures that leadership is talking about the future and includes the fundamental concerns of the relevant parties. This differs from relating to the relevant parties as "followers" and calling up an image of a single leader with others following. Rather, a future that fulfils on the fundamental concerns of the relevant parties indicates the future that wasn't going to happen is not the "idea of the leader", but rather is what emerges from digging deep to find the underlying concerns of those who are impacted by the leadership.[7]

One might equate such leadership with some sort of 'archaeological' activity (see comment below on Foucault). It places a particular burden and in a sense a privilege on the team doctor: it is simply not sufficient to provide 'medical advice' or a 'medical opinion' during team discussions. Rather, it is expected that the most senior team members (which seniority is often located in the doctor, given the assumed broad range of expertise and formalized regulatory frameworks, as described above) 'dig deep' to find what worries and concerns possibly lie beneath the surface. This interpretation of leadership resonates clearly with the perfectly reasonable need in multidisciplinary psychiatric teams to create a productive and collaborative atmosphere that secures the professional safety of its members: the team becomes a 'home' in an unpredictable world. In fact, the assumption of medical clinical leadership is recognized by modern appraisal systems, which usually invite colleagues to comment (anonymously) on various areas of professional practice, a number of which directly pertain to leadership categories, such as 'providing accessible support to team members', the 'ability to solve complex problems', the doctor's 'professional attitudes', and so on.

We have now taken the medical role from its erstwhile, somewhat caricatured, isolation of a one-man retail outlet, steeped in scientific reductionism, to the setting of a professional team, which deploys a wide variety of concepts and approaches. Along that journey the concept of clinical medical leadership arises: in the one-to-one therapeutic relationship with a patient, 'leadership' is a rather meaningless concept. Within a team it is essential. At this point the argumentation is still quite introvert, as it centres on the dynamics and the functioning of the team. However, a team operates in a wider world, and its success, efficiency and efficacy are very much influenced by that broad context. Given the previous characterization of the doctor as the practitioner who is most likely to have traversed a variety of clinical settings, teams and services, as well as being versed in a number of clinically relevant theories, practices and approaches, is it then not inevitable that such a professional ought to play a major role when services are needing to be amended, developed and configured? It is this meta-level aspect of 'being a doctor' that will now receive attention.

Clinical leadership and service development

When contacts between clinicians and patients have undergone some form of higher-level systematization, we speak of 'healthcare systems', and this clearly takes the issue of clinical leadership a level further: from the one-to-one patient-doctor relationship to the level of how healthcare is delivered in more general terms. To put it differently, we move from the above mentioned 'one-man retail outlet', via a convenience store (the multidisciplinary team) to the world of the wholesaler. The following is largely based on the author's experience of working in the British National Health Service, which is of course notable in the world as a comprehensive healthcare system, largely free at the point of delivery. However, it is hoped that the following can be applied as easily to alternative systems elsewhere in the world.

When one analyses any such healthcare system, it becomes clear that often there is much in it that is not systematic at all. Rather, over time, a complex, organically grown and interactive infrastructure develops, often reacting to a multitude of external factors (appearance of new treatments and technologies, wider political, cultural and/or economic drivers, etc.) or responding to a host of internal factors (e.g. workforce-related matters, financial pressures in a particular organization, managerial initiatives and so on) and on top of all that sometimes sprouting unexpected features and characteristics, which are often traceable to idiosyncratic, if mostly perfectly reasonable, decisions by individuals or groups. Such constellations are now recognized as 'complex adaptive systems',[8] which have the following characteristics (and I quote from Holland's paper):[8]

- The number of elements is sufficiently large that conventional descriptions cease to assist in understanding the system.
- The elements have to interact and the interaction must be dynamic; interactions often involve the exchange of information.
- Such interactions are rich, i.e. any element in the system is affected by and affects several other systems.
- The interactions are non-linear, which means that small causes can have large results.
- Interactions are primarily but not exclusively with immediate neighbours and the nature of the influence is modulated.
- Any interaction can feed back onto itself directly or after a number of intervening stages; such feedback can vary in quality; this is known as recurrency.
- They are open and it may be difficult or impossible to define system boundaries.
- Complex systems operate under far from equilibrium conditions: there has to be a constant flow of energy to maintain the organization of the system.
- All complex systems have a history: they evolve and their past is co-responsible for their present behaviour.

The result is a system that shows continuous adaptation to external and internal drivers, building upon what is already there and amending and adapting when needed. The result is often something that deviates markedly from what a service or healthcare system would have looked like had it been designed from scratch. There is one caveat: in such a 'rich' system (see Holland's use of the term), there is also a continuous threat that adaptations and amendments are not made when needed: whilst never quite in equilibrium, various components have undergone a degree of fine tuning and there will be in-built resistance to change. Because of the complexity such lagging components may not be detected for some considerable time and may only become obvious when their rigidity has led to detectable dysfunction. So what emerges is a constantly changing structure, comparable to the outward appearance and inner structure and design of Pippi Longstocking's house;[a] it is at first sight obvious that no rational architect can have designed it; yet it is much loved, serves its purpose, is flexible (if it needs to house a horse, it will) and the user/inhabitant is likely to put up with all sorts of shortcomings. One important meaning that users will attach to the structure is its historical relevance. It will to all intents and purposes resemble the complexity of an archaeological site.[b]

---

[a] A series of children's' books by Astrid Lindgren: obligatory reading material for all self-respecting adults.

[b] A seminal work by Foucault is entitled *The Archaeology of Knowledge*. Using the philosophical equivalent of archaeology allowed him to suggest the contingency of a given way of thinking by showing that previous ages had thought very differently (and, apparently, with as much effectiveness).[9] However, he critiqued himself that this method only shows the layers: it does not explain the transitions between them. He later introduced genealogical approaches to address this issue.

Accepting that the evolution of healthcare systems is to a considerable extent characterized by unplanned but rational (or planned but irrational, as the case may be) interactions, rather than cohesive and structured planning and design, we need to think through the actors who are producing this interplay and who are most likely to be behind the many decisions that are constantly taken.

In traditional models of healthcare (and in the United Kingdom this was true until only a few decades ago) the main 'operational' decisions in a particular clinical setting are likely to be taken by a few senior medical and nursing staff. In systems that are organizationally somewhat immature, most decisions will be operational: this results in the system being quite simple. Its simplicity, however, also means it is not very robust and resilient: any change, be it external or internal, is potentially able to disrupt the functioning to the point where it is defunct.

If it does survive, it will over time evolve into a more complex, more sophisticated system as described above: it gains complexity by surviving successfully, which also means it must have some degree of in-built adaptive responsiveness, much as Pippi's domicile. At some point the system (i.e. those who work in it) will recognize the need for strategic direction: it is the natural consequence of a cumulative historical experience (which actually means it has a kind of memory[c]) and the dawning realization that strategic planning will enhance the system's efficiency and ability to respond to any changes, whether expected or not. One could think of this as the system's equivalent of ourselves when we have occasion to think: 'I am not going to be taken by surprise again' or 'I could do this far better in a different way'.

At the same time that this desire for strategic steer arises, the system is likely to have gained in complexity, so that by now a far larger number of participants and/or actors are playing their part. Some of these will have specific responsibilities in making decisions or setting agendas, others may be further away from the decision-making stratum.

Particularly in a system that consists of various groups and other organizational entities (such as will be found in a mature healthcare system) it will become increasingly unclear who can provide the necessary oversight, who has the power to formulate particular strategies and make decisions, how lines of accountability are constructed, and which sources of expertise should be involved in the decision-making processes. More often than not there is an element of serendipity and randomness in the system's choice of particular staff carrying out particular tasks: whilst some level of expertise is of course usually involved, it often also depends on who is willing 'to step up to the plate', rather than people taking on responsibilities as the result of a more autocratic handing out of tasks, as is more likely in commercial environments. In other words: in a public sector organization there is some reliance on people volunteering.

When decision-making roles on strategic and operational issues are separated from clinical activity we have all too often seen that particularly doctors disengage from the process: 'I am a doctor, I treat patients and I was not trained in medical school for this'. Although particularly postgraduate specialist medical training is paying more and more

---

[c]Wegner analysed the functioning of groups, coining the term 'transactive memory systems', and showed how group members' interactions over time construct a 'knowledge-base', which includes understanding of its functional processes.[10]

attention to this issue, it is obvious that non-medical healthcare professionals generally appear less hesitant to assume the role of manager or strategic planner, and it is a recognized feature of the UK's NHS that senior managerial roles are far more often carried out by senior nursing staff, among others, than by doctors. Without casting aspersions on those who do assume those roles, it could be argued therefore that a potential rich source of expertise remains largely untapped.

Whatever the reasons underlying this phenomenon, it does lead to a particular problem. Whilst doctors arguably have received the widest and deepest training in healthcare, are often held ultimately responsible for care provided (largely as a result of legal regulatory frameworks) and – as argued above – are the likely recipient of co-workers' requests for leadership and guidance, their resulting expertise is not often put to constructive use in managing, designing and developing healthcare services. It is argued here that that may lead to design faults that could otherwise be prevented. Case Studies 6.1 and 6.2 describe these matters in a bit more detail: the first shows how clinical leadership was essential to ensure a newly funded service was targeted appropriately, and the second discusses new commissioning structures in the UK NHS (politically advertised as a way to counter the phenomenon of clinical disengagement) and debates the chance of success with regard to commissioning of psychiatric services.

Case Study 6.1 A new service configuration may be 'set up to fail' as a result of ill-thought-through service demands

A healthcare commissioning body in an area in the United Kingdom identified a sum of money to be deployed to enhance dementia services, largely in response to a newly adopted 'National Dementia Strategy'. A number of options were tabled. One of these entailed initiating a so-called 'primary care dementia service': staffed by qualified nurses who have a background in dementia care, the service was meant to achieve a number of aims, in the following order of importance:

1   increased detection rates of people with early stage dementia;
2   increased capacity in assessing eligibility for anti-dementia medication;
3   increased support for GPs in matters related to dementia.

One continuous debate, leading to identification of the first aim, was the matter of undetected and undiagnosed people with early stage dementia: estimates of prevalence in the total population indicated large numbers of undiagnosed people when compared with the number of known cases. Although recognized as valid in principle, the extent of the shortfall seemed unlikely, given that the area had had a fully staffed psychogeriatric service for more than two decades. The number of identified cases was based on a specific diagnostic coding system used by GPs. However, the commissioners were not aware (and therefore needed to be informed) that usage of the system was extremely patchy and this likely led to underestimating the actual numbers of people who had received a diagnosis. Nevertheless, there was broad agreement on the first aim being the most important one. In drafting the relevant contracts clear 'Key Performance Indicators' (KPI) were inserted, allowing monitoring of the new service's impact and ensuring that the first aim was firmly in focus.

During further discussions a number of operational questions and concerns were identified and largely addressed, but at that point the commissioners threw in a new requirement: the service should stabilize patients with known or suspected dementia with marked physical comorbidities, as these patients were most likely to be admitted frequently and repeatedly to the general hospital. Again, a perfectly laudable initiative.

However, the identified funds only provided for a limited number of staff. It had to be pointed out by the senior clinician that detection of early stage dementia and the latter requirement were not seamlessly compatible, as clinically they represented distinct patient populations. The point was made that the new requirement, however clinically relevant, could set the new service up to fail on its previously stipulated KPI. Without medical input the (non-clinical) commissioners would likely have failed to identify this and the contract would have demanded something that would never be deliverable.

One interesting issue: the whole exercise started with a pot of money: deciding what to do with it came next. That might not persuade as the most rational sequence in planning history.

Case Study 6.2 Clinical commissioning groups in the UK's NHS

In the United Kingdom a strong political agenda regarding the organization of the NHS has been enforced over the past year or so and the main components of this new structure are being put into operation, against much opposition. The politicians defend their policy by stating they want the NHS to be run by clinicians (i.e. GPs), instead of administrators, bureaucrats or, indeed, politicians, of course at the same time claiming this will decrease costs.

The thinking is that GPs will know best what their patients or patient populations need: they are now configuring 'Clinical Commissioning Groups', which will be collaborations between a number of GP surgeries and which will have wider representation from, for example, patient organizations, the voluntary sector, etc.

There are a few interesting observations to make:

1   The government claimed to consult widely, including the GPs. Most clinical leaders raised objection after objection, but they were largely ignored: although amendments were inserted, the main body of the legislation was pushed through. Apparently there is no contradiction in saying on the one hand that doctors should be 'in charge', whilst on the other hand not heeding their advice when it is not conducive to achieve the political agenda.
2   GPs have now started to form the required bodies. Obviously not all GPs will be involved: a small number will have to represent the views of their colleagues and others, and in itself that creates an organizational structure likely to resemble Pippi's outhouse. In short, the new system is likely to develop into another Byzantine structure, similar if perhaps at a smaller scale, than the one it is supposed to replace.

GPs are not specialists, yet they are tasked with commissioning specialist medical services. They will need all sorts of supporting services: contract specialists, data capturing systems, performance monitoring, epidemiological information, financial and legal experts, and so on. There are some 28 different medical specialities, so it will be impossible to have all of them represented on the new Clinical Commissioning Groups. Psychiatric services are in themselves rather Byzantine in structure: the challenge will be how specialists can empower and enable generalists to take far-reaching decisions, involving large sums of money, without making major errors. The spectre of thus far undetected hidden assumptions looms large.

At the same time it also offers a major opportunity for clinicians to become involved in service design at a far more intense level than before. Without such 'buy-in' the new system will quickly descend into chaos, given the close scrutiny of detail which will be necessary, if the example in the first case study is anything to go by.

Conclusions

A clinical leader has the opportunity to contribute to areas within healthcare that easily get 'snowed under' by the pressures of daily service delivery. In this chapter a number of areas were focused upon, each of which is likely to suffer if clinical leadership is absent or incompetent:

1 providing clarity of thought when complexity threatens to overwhelm practitioners;
2 provide a locus of professional expertise, in order to buffer against clinical uncertainty;
3 bring in knowledge about other components of a complex system;
4 foster adaptive mechanisms within the system and avoid rigidity;
5 optimal interpretation of guidelines and advice on best practice;
6 ensure non-clinical colleagues have direct access to clinical expertise;
7 ensure those who commission services and monitor service delivery have access to the relevant specialist expertise.

The list can be extended further, but the point has been made: particularly psychiatric services are often complex and Byzantine in their construction and configuration. This appears unavoidable, reflecting the complexity of our patients and their lives on the one hand, and on the other the complexity of the organ that may, in a reductionist fashion, be thought to be the seat of the disorders we deal with. We work in complex systems and it takes clinical leaders to understand that complexity, whilst at the same time understanding how to manage ambiguity, clinical uncertainty, unpredictability and variable risks.

Finally, in a constantly changing environment clinical leaders can steer the adaptive mechanisms the system deploys to remain responsive and relevant. It is precisely that role that makes our profession enthralling, no matter how many years one spends in it. Involvement as a clinical leader in that sense falls within the realm of preventative psychiatry: it decreases the risk of clinician burnout.

References

1 Laing RD. *The Divided Self. An Existential Study in Sanity and Madness*, Harmondsworth: Penguin, 1960.
2 Foucault M. *La naissance de la clinique: une archéologie du regard médical*. Paris: Presses Universitaires de France, 1963.
3 Badrakalimuthu RV, van Diest R, Bak M, de Waal HE. Problem based learning and psychiatric education. In: Gask L, Coskun B, Baron D (eds), *Teaching in Psychiatry: Putting Theory into Practice*. Oxford: Wiley-Blackwell, 2010; pp. 61–77.
4 Cook DA, Beckman TJ, Thomas KG, Thompson WG. Introducing resident doctors to complexity in ambulatory medicine. *Med Educ* 2008; **42**:838–48.
5 Somers C. Michael Jackson case points to complexity of doctor-patient relations. The Guardian 30 Sept 2011. Available at: http://www.guardian.co.uk/commentisfree/2011/sep/30/michael-jackson-doctor-patient-relationships [accessed 2 April 2013].
6 de Waal HE, Malik A, Bhugra D. The psychiatric profession: an expertise under siege? *Int J Soc Psychiatry* 2010; **56**: 647–56.

7   Erhard W, Jensen MC, Granger KL. Creating leaders: an ontological/phenomenological model. In: Snook S, Nohria N, Khurana R (eds), *The Handbook for Teaching Leadership*. Sage Publications, 2011; chapter 16.

8   Holland JH. Studying complex adaptive systems. *J Syst Sci Complex* 2006; **19**:1–8.

9   Foucault M. *The Archaeology of Knowledge* (trans. AM Sheridan Smith). London and New York: Routledge, 2002.

10   Wegner DM. Transactive memory: a contemporary analysis of the group mind. In: Mullen B, Goethals GR (eds), *Theories of Group Behavior*. New York: Springer-Verlag, 1986; pp. 185–205.

Part B
Skills Required for Leadership

Chapter 7

Communication

Levent Küey

Introduction

Among the various fundamental assets of good leadership, the quality of communication seems to be the most emphasized. Thus, effective communication could be considered as a primary attribute for good leadership; conversely, the quality of leadership depends on the quality of communication.

This chapter will mainly focus on the communication skills of a psychiatrist in the contexts of his/her work roles and environment and leadership skills.

What is communication?

Communication is defined as 'a process by which information is exchanged between individuals through a common system of symbols, signs, or behaviour'.[1] So, it is an exchange and sharing of a common system or set of symbols (e.g. language) or behaviour aiming to construct meaning. Communication is the process of interchanging such symbols between the sender(s) and receiver(s) by a wide range of means and modes in a milieu; thus the information-loaded messages are shared by the parties involved. In fact, the Latin origin of the word (*communis*) meaning 'to share', implies that the communication is completed only when the messages are perceived by the receiver. A social setting provides the context or the milieu for this social interaction, namely communication, for which at least two interacting agents are needed.

A complete communication cycle embraces, at least, the sender, the message and the receiver. Furthermore, any communication also holds certain basic elements, namely:

1 who – the person conveying the message;
2 what – the message itself;
3 to whom – the person(s) receiving the message;
4 how – the medium and the means by which the message is conveyed;
5 when – the timing of the message;
6 why – the aims of the message;
7 outcome – the effects of the message.

Leadership in Psychiatry, First Edition. Edited by Dinesh Bhugra, Pedro Ruiz and Susham Gupta.
© 2013 John Wiley & Sons, Ltd. Published 2013 by John Wiley & Sons, Ltd.

Communication as a scientific discipline

Communication as a scientific discipline and communication studies as an academic field are institutionalized across the world in many universities. The field covers a range of topics also reflecting the taxonomy of communication. Various types of communication can be classified from different standpoints, including:

- verbal and non-verbal communication;
- interpersonal, intrapersonal or organizational communication;
- intercultural and international communication;
- written, mass- or computer-mediated communication;
- face-to-face or long-distance communication.

The interpretations of communication in its context of political, cultural, economic, semiotic, hermeneutic and social dimensions are also the focus of many researches in this field. Different scientific disciplines prefer to use different classifications according to their aims and scopes.

The importance of communication for a psychiatrist

A psychiatrist can attain different professional roles for which communication skills are profoundly important to fulfil his or her aims. Working as a clinician, as a group leader of the mental health team or an interdisciplinary health team, as a researcher, as an educator, as a mentor, or as a leader in departments and organizations – all these different roles and service settings require successful communication. Yet, very few studies have been published specifically on the leadership roles of psychiatrists and the role of communication in improving their professional leadership qualities.[2]

In the field of mental health and psychiatry, verbal and non-verbal communication in an interpersonal face-to-face context becomes a priority. However, different modes of communication are used in modern psychiatric practice, besides face to face, including telephone, hands-free telephone, videoconferencing, and internet-based or tele-psychiatry.[3, 4]

In clinical settings, the main mode of communication is an interpersonal, face-to-face type involving the exchange of verbal and non-verbal messages, and influenced by various confounding factors. Hence, discussion of the features of communication taking place in the clinical setting will be presented under the following subheadings: interpersonal communication in the clinical setting; verbal and non-verbal communication in the clinical setting; and communication turning into therapeutic alliance in the clinical setting; in the last section, the communication skills for effective leadership of a psychiatrist will be deliberated.

Interpersonal communication in the clinical setting

The relation between the psychiatrist and the patient is a human interpersonal interaction set by the demands of the patient for a specific reason, namely to diminish the suffering of the patient. This aim shapes the rules and the forms of communication between the two paties. It is mainly a verbal and non-verbal communication relying on the impact of exchange of words and signs or behaviour. Some of the basic characteristics of psychiatrist-patient communication in the clinical setting can be discussed as below, also taking into consideration the general rules of basic interpersonal communication.

Psychiatrist-patient communication in the clinical setting has a clear predetermined aim, namely a therapeutic outcome for the benefit of the patient. Hence, communication turns into a therapeutic alliance in the clinical setting. Further, communication between psychiatrist and patient in this setting is inevitable. Once the interview or the clinical encounter between the psychiatrist and the patient starts both parties send and receive verbal and non-verbal messages and interpret what they have been exchanging.

The communication is an interactional joint process. Although the basic principles and framework of this communication are determined by the theoretical orientations and practice of psychiatry, it is constructed and reconstructed by both sides in the interchanging roles of sender and receiver.

Communication in this setting is also a continuous and irreversible process. The exchange of messages is a continuous flow of profoundly mingled verbal and non-verbal symbols and signs. The psychiatrist and the patient constantly express messages, and once expressed, no words or behavioural signs can be reversed. Every expression by the *sender* in this communication creates an impression on the *receiver* in a dialectical manner. None of these expressions or impressions can be deleted afterwards.

Communication in this context is a multifaceted process. The psychiatrist and the patient, although interacting as two real persons, are also both acting and reacting to each other via the imagined and internalized other. On both sides, there is a *self,* as well as a *perceived self* and an *expressed self.* In this sense, the interview room is quite crowded.

Psychiatrist-patient communication in a clinical setting is open to misunderstandings. Each verbal or non-verbal symbol used in communication is loaded with different meaning by either party. Interpretation and reinterpretation of the messages exchanged are inevitable components of communication in clinical settings, and it is the responsibility of the clinician to decode and clarify the conveyed meanings as much as possible.

The characteristics of the clinical setting provide the context of the interpersonal communication between the patient and the psychiatrist. The physical design of the interview room, and the psychological and cultural milieu provide the foundations of the communication, to be built on accordingly. The placement of chairs and the distance between them; the attitude of the clinician – whether authoritarian or liberal – or his/her cultural sensitivity and compatibility will lead to different styles of communication. Patient and psychiatrist sitting knee-to-knee in a small room, or the psychiatrist sitting in an armchair behind a walnut antique table and the patient sitting on a plain chair in front, would each create different interactional dynamics and communication styles.

The therapeutic outcome of the clinical encounter depends on the clarity of the communication, which is primarily the duty of the clinician. At times, this clarity can be hard to establish due to the psychopathology of the patient, besides the factors related to the communication skills and competency of the clinician.

Verbal and non-verbal communication in the clinical setting

The clinical setting is full of verbal and non-verbal messages, just as the sky is full of sparrows in a clear Mediterranean summer daybreak. Words and behaviours as the main means of exchanging messages between patient and clinician fill up the clinical milieu. The clinician's task is to distinguish and guide these little birds. For early career professionals this might seem like an impossible task. The clinician facing this challenge tries to identify, interpret and redirect these flying messages. The words, the conceptual constructs, loaded with overt and implied meanings, and the expressed behaviours on both sides need to be perceived and utilized for therapeutic purposes.

In a real-life situation the verbal and non-verbal communications are not two separate and independent processes; this division is made for the sake of analysis and improving our understanding from a methodological perspective. They are in fact contradictory and complementary means of message exchange. In a clinical setting, it is vital for the clinician to understand and explain the interaction of the verbal and non-verbal messages conveyed by the patient. Harmony or disharmony among the verbal and non-verbal messages can provide valuable clues. It is an important element of the psychiatric examination in assessing the mood and affective responses of the patient, which are mostly reflected by the non-verbal expressions.

On the other hand, verbal messages or the speech of the patient express the flow and content of thoughts. Here, it is not our aim to further discuss the steps and rules of psychiatric assessment, but it should be noted that a thorough understanding of the verbal and non-verbal messages expressed by the patient is crucial for a complete assessment of the mental status and emotional life of the patient. Furthermore, when it comes to the task of improving the efficiency of therapeutic interventions, the quality of the communication and the evaluation of the verbal and non-verbal messages of both sides should be followed and managed very closely by the clinician. Psychotherapy is a process of working through the meanings of communicated and even non-communicated messages. It is widely accepted that in a clinical encounter in psychiatry, considerable emphasis is placed not only on the content of the patient's verbal messages but also on observing the patient's interactions with the environment and the psychiatrist.[5] On the other hand, clinicians themselves must also be aware of their own non-verbal communications, since these can either enhance or harm the therapeutic quality of the relation.

Verbal communication

Verbal communication uses language, as an ever-evolving human-made tool, that is learned, accepted and shared by a specific group of people. It is a system of vocal and written symbols and the primary vehicle for the conveyance of meaning. Humans are not born with knowledge of a language but with the mental capacity to learn a language, by which we are socialized in a specific cultural context.

Language not only reflects what is in our minds but also reconstructs our way of mental being. As Souba says:

> This idea that reality is constituted in language is core to an ontological approach to leadership. Language reframes our observing, sense making, and feelings so we can be a different kind of leader. When we change our thinking and speaking, a different reality becomes available to us. Shifts in our mental maps generate new possibilities for desired actions and outcomes not previously accessible. The distinctions that we share with one another, with the intent of achieving mutual understanding, are those that occur in language. This common sense making is the foundation for connectivity, collaboration, and alignment, essential activities in any organization.[6]

Spoken verbal communication while conveying an informational content also conveys an emotional content; this is especially expressed in verbal tonality and in the accompanying non-verbal messages, or body language.

Since words and concepts of a given language, as a set of symbols shared in that specific society, are a priori assumed to be loaded with the same meanings, they are utilized as the essential means of interpersonal communication. When two people are talking to each other in an interpersonal communication, as occurs in the clinical setting, they both need to understand and be understood. In the clinical setting, though, these shared words and concepts of the given language not only produce the therapeutic effect but also are the source of many misunderstandings.

Misunderstandings are inevitable in interpersonal verbal communication due to the simple fact that there is no single absolute correct way of using language. Language itself is a living and evolving medium and contains diverse cultural and psychological authenticities of its users. Besides, in a given society in which the same common language is shared and considered to be the joint tool of verbal communication, there are always subgroups of people with varying jargons. In clinical settings, it is the clinician's task to overcome any potential difficulties originating from the use of jargon. The psychiatrist should minimize the use of professional and academic jargon, unless it is needed to explain and reach a common understanding of some terminology (e.g. in explaining diagnostic terms or the effects of medication).

Another challenge in verbal communication in the clinical setting is missing the meaning. Psychiatric theory is full of explanations that prove the fact that what is said does not always match what is meant. The clinician's task here is not only to hear and understand what is obviously said but also to decode the spoken words to reach their covert meaning.

Non-verbal communication

A significant means of communication, especially in face-to-face interpersonal communication as in the clinical setting, is the exchange of non-verbal messages, or the practice of so-called body language. Whether accompanying verbal messages or used separately, non-verbal behavioural expressions can convey very strong meanings.

Non-verbal communication includes facial expressions, eye movements and eye contact, gestures, and body movements and posture. Tone of voice is also considered a non-verbal cue and is known as paralanguage. Besides intonation, the volume, rate, rhythm and pitch of voice can be listed as elements of paralanguage. The same content with a lower or higher voice, with hesitation or determination, or with a slower or faster delivery, all can demonstrate different intentions and attitudes and convey different meanings.

Many researchers suggest that the majority of human communication is via non-verbal behavioural cues, with facial expressions, eye movements and eye contact constituting the primary group of these signs. Moreover, body movements and gestures are continuously sending signals to others, transferring meaning mainly about the emotions and attitude of the person.

Some pioneering research in the late 1960s suggested that the perception of the feelings of the message sender was based mainly on facial expression (55%) and vocal intonation (38%) whereas the words used had little impact (7%).[7,8] But many subsequent studies and reviews stated that these figures were misinterpreted because they were derived from research focusing only on the feelings (likes and dislikes) of the sender and not on the whole communication. This was confirmed by the original researchers that the above ratios are not applicable unless a communicator is talking about his or her feelings.[9,10]

The relative importance of verbal and non-verbal communication was further revealed by later research and reviews.[11] It seems that the quality of the human relationship may affect decoding of the non-verbal messages by the receiver. Some research focused on the relation between the relationship's well-being (e.g. in marital relationships) to the receiver's decoding skills, where, as an example, it was found that non-verbal decoding accuracy was significantly related to relationship well-being.[12]

Non-verbal messages can be under voluntary control, but mostly they are produced involuntarily or unconsciously. As with verbal communication, non-verbal communication is a continuous and irreversible process: what is expressed creates an impression on the other party and cannot be reversed.

Cross-cultural differences in non-verbal communication have attracted a lot of scientific interest; but there are also many common non-verbal cues that all cultures share and decode with the same meaning. For example, the eyebrow raise or eyebrow flash indicating a greeting when someone meets another is a common non-verbal cue across all cultures.[13]

In the clinical setting, meaning is derived by both the psychiatrist and the patient from an aggregate of verbal and non-verbal signals. It is again mainly the task of the clinician not only to correctly decode the meanings conveyed by the patient but also to grasp how the patient decodes the clinician's messages. Like in every human interaction and communication the psychiatrist-patient interaction has effects on both sides, whether these are the desired ones or not. In an effective communication the outcome reflects the effect intended by the sender of message; so in the clinical setting a well-maintained feedback loop is needed to reach this outcome.

The psychiatrist should keep in mind that non-verbal communication can, at times, replace verbal communication, or contradict the verbal message or amplify its content. The vulnerability of the patient to certain specific verbal content and non-verbal cues should be carefully identified and monitored by the clinician. Non-verbal messages are also prone to misunderstandings. Many cross-cultural and personal differences can make it difficult for the psychiatrist to obtain clear meanings.

Types of non-verbal communications

There are various classifications of non-verbal communications. Categorical classifications of non-verbal cues are mainly based on types of senses or bodily parts. A dimensional approach is also described, wherein dimensions of positiveness, potency or status, and responsiveness help to identify, describe and analyse the similarities and differences in non-verbal communication.[14]

Among the many and various types of non-verbal communication described,[13] the ones considered to be more important for psychiatrists are reviewed as follows.

Facial expressions are considered to be the primary means of conveying non-verbal communication. It is generally agreed that thousands of possible facial expressions are produced by nearly 50 facial muscles. Although non-verbal behavioural clues show great cross-cultural variation, facial expressions of sadness, anger, fear and happiness are considered to be very similar across different cultural groups.

Gestures are mainly voluntarily controlled body movements, usually of the hands, arms and head, to convey a meaning non-verbally. Pointing to someone or an object or a direction, waving, demonstrating a feeling or behaviour with hands (e.g. thumbs up or down) and nodding the head are some examples. Gestures can show variations across cultures.

Eye movements, studied under the discipline of oculesics, are powerful means of conveying many human non-verbal messages. Looking, blinking alone or with pupil dilatation, keeping or avoiding the eye contact, or staring are loaded with emotional messages, meaning interest, attraction, confidence or honesty.

Body posture and language have also been a widely researched area of non-verbal communication. Although, today they are not considered to be very definitive, some body postures, such as arm-crossing, bending forwards, the direction of the legs while sitting, can convey emotions, attitude and meaning to the receiver.

Physical touch, the importance of which has been studied widely in developmental psychology (i.e. the experiences in early childhood and infancy), conveys strong emotions, such as interest, sympathy and love, non-verbally. The form and timing of touch can convey substantial messages, especially in healthcare and psychiatric praxis. It can be therapeutic but also counter-therapeutic when used inappropriately.

Personal space (proxemics) is another effective way of expressing feelings in interpersonal relations. People usually keep a space around them and only allow certain other people to get closer, which can mean emotional closeness. Likes and dislikes can clearly be expressed in terms of personal space. How far or how close people place themselves in relation to others is the outcome of many variables including situational, personality, social and cultural factors.

Appearance, reflecting choices of clothing and hairstyles, colours, make-up and personal belongings, can demonstrate different emotional messages, beliefs, social and occupational roles, and interests. These preferences while reflecting the mood of the person simultaneously affect the interpretations and responses of receivers/observers.

Developing a thorough understanding of these and similar non-verbal forms of communicating are important for a psychiatrist both in his/her clinical practice and also for the improvement of leadership skills.

Communication turning into therapeutic alliance in the clinical setting

In the context of the clinical setting, the psychiatrist as a clinician provides mental health service. Describing, understanding, explaining and treating the patient require more than being a mere biomedical technician. The psychiatrist-patient relationship is a human relationship focused on helping the patient to resolve his or her mental difficulties or disorders. Whatever the theoretical orientation of the clinician, whether it is biological, psychoanalytical, cognitive-behavioural, socio-cultural or integrative, this specific relationship is a joint ongoing process between the two. This relationship is constructed and reconstructed to a large extent according to the verbal and non-verbal communications between the two parties.

The context and framework of the communication in the clinical setting are determined by various factors controlled by the patient and the clinician. This milieu is the setting for the communication and affects the quality of the communication. In turn, the quality of the communication determines the quality of the therapeutic effect and outcome. Thus the therapeutic quality of this communication is shaped by three factors: the clinician, the patient and the milieu.

The patient expresses his or her experience of suffering in verbal and non-verbal messages; the clinician is impressed by these messages and responds to them likewise in verbal and non-verbal forms. This process continues in cycles in a setting that should be designed specifically to benefit the psychic or mental health of the patient. As it is in general human interaction and communication, expressions and impressions do not fully overlap. But it is the task of the psychiatrist to decode the meaning of the messages in the clinical setting.

Since effective communication in the field of mental health and psychiatry aims to reach a joint understanding of what has been sent and received, expressed and impressed, and interpreted, a professional task of the psychiatrist should be to improve his or her communication skills. Such skills as non-judgemental listening, decoding and encoding, speaking, reframing and questioning, formulating, guiding and explaining are essential in building up a solid clinical alliance and therapeutic rapport. In addition, such skills are also needed for good leadership of a mental health team, or a department or a professional organization. Disappointingly many undergraduate medical and psychiatry programmes across the world lack such training; the medical students and psychiatry residents mostly try to develop their communication skills by modelling.

Communication skills for effective leadership by a psychiatrist

The communication competence of a psychiatrist, whether as a group leader of a mental health service or research team, as an educator or as a mentor, has great impact on his or her professional performance. Good leadership is in fact a matter of excellent communication competence. The qualities of good leadership are widely elaborated and discussed, mainly in the business and corporate community, where the clear conclusion is that communication competence is a prerequisite for effective leadership.[15] Different leadership dimensions have been found to be highly correlated with competent communication by leaders.

Although the importance of leadership in psychiatry is increasingly becoming a focus of scientific interest, its profile is still too low. Even in training programmes that are reportedly of high quality, two areas that residents felt least prepared for were administration and leadership skills.[16] Among the suggestions for improvement included more 'real-world' administration and leadership exposure. An enhanced training curriculum in leadership and administrative skills and medical economics was recommended. Moreover, a study of the deans of medical schools found that of the major leadership challenges, open communication was considered to be the most effective means of addressing the most complex problems.[17]

Psychiatrists frequently work as the leaders of mental health teams or interdisciplinary health teams. This type of interdisciplinary teamwork demands fine-tuned and sound leadership skills, besides effective team management, clinical supervision and explicit mechanisms for resolving role conflicts and ensuring safe practices.[18]

Another setting that could challenge the psychiatrist's leadership skills is being the director or head of a department or a professional organization. A proper question here is to ask whether psychiatrists are 'natural born' leaders or not.[19] Such a broader role as an institutional/academic leader is more complex and challenging, and the skills, competencies and training opportunities for such roles are not well defined.

A related area of concern is the discussion of who is ready or suitable for leadership in psychiatry. In deciding whether to accept or continue in a leadership position, could a useful set of guidelines for potential leaders be provided?[20] It is stated that the issues that are fundamental in deciding whether to accept or maintain a leadership position include personal appreciation of leadership style, and a leadership vision in line with the institutional vision. Putting the issues at hand into their context to make them meaningful is among the necessary skills of good leadership. Besides being able, available, and affable the leader needs to be accountable for his or her actions at the same time. The absence of accountability would make it very difficult, if not impossible, for leaders and their organizations to meet expectations. Another important asset for a leader would be the ability to develop a consistent vision including a realistic analysis of the situation and his/her skills, and the opportunities of creating the desired changes for improvement. Such a sense of vision should also embrace the realities of the network that the organization is placed in.

A visionary aspect of leadership was formulated and recommended in advice for implementing more leadership and less management.[21] This advice includes strategies for setting up the leadership team, delegating authority to these individuals, and then letting them do their work.

Conclusion

Good clinical practice and good leadership share a common feature. A competent psychiatrist in clinical practice aims to empower his or her patients and help them improve their self-resilience, but not directly to monitor or manage them. Similarly, a competent leader does not pull or push the people who are led but creates the proper structure and opportunities and a guiding milieu in which people are empowered and motivated to become future leaders themselves.

References

1   Merriam-Webster Dictionary. Available at: http://www.merriam-webster.com/dictionary/communication [accessed 3April 2013].
2   Beezhold J, Manley K, Brandon E, Buwalda V, Kastrup M. Leadership, management and administrative issues for early career psychiatrists. In: Fiorillo A, Calliess I, Sass H (eds), *How to Succeed in Psychiatry: A Guide to Training and Practice*. Chichester: John Wiley & Sons, Ltd, 2012; pp. 296–310.
3   Ball CJ, McLaren PM, Summerfield AB, Lipsedge MS, Watson JP. A comparison of communication modes in adult psychiatry. *J Telemed Telecare* 1995; **1**:22–6.
4   Ball CJ, Scott N, McLaren PM, Watson JP. Preliminary evaluation of a Low-Cost Video Conferencing (LCVC) system for remote cognitive testing of adult psychiatric patients. *Brit J Clin Psychol* 1993; **32**:303–7.
5   Foley GN, Gentile JP. Nonverbal communication in psychotherapy. *Psychiatry (Edgmont)* 2010; **7**: 38–44.
6   Souba WW. The Being of leadership. *Philos Ethics Humanit Med* 2011; **6**:5
7   Mehrabian A, Wiener M. Decoding of inconsistent communications. *J Pers Soc Psychol* 1967; **6**: 109–14.
8   Mehrabian A, Ferris SR. Inference of attitudes from nonverbal communication in two channels. *J Consult Psychol* 1967; **31**:248–52.
9   Mehrabian A. "Silent Messages" – A Wealth of Information about Nonverbal Communication (Body Language). Available at: http://www.kaaj.com/psych/smorder.html [accessed 3 April 2013].
10   Mehrabian A. *Silent Messages: Implicit Communication of Emotions and Attitudes*. Belmont, CA: Wadsworth, 1981.
11   Noller P. *Nonverbal Communication and Marital Interaction*. New York: Pergamon, 1985.
12   Carton JS, Kessler EA, Pape CL. Nonverbal decoding skills and relationship well-being in adults. *J Nonverbal Behav* 1999; **23**:91–100.
13   Knapp ML, Hall JA. *Nonverbal Communication in Human Interaction*, 7th edn. Boston: Wadsworth Publishing, 2009.
14   Mehrabian A. *Nonverbal Communication*. Aldine Transaction, 2007.
15   Flauto FJ. Walking the talk: the relationship between leadership and communication competence. *J Leadership Organiz Stud* 1999; **6**: 86–97.
16   Stubbe DE. Preparation for practice: child and adolescent psychiatry graduates' assessment of training experiences.*J Am Acad Child Adolesc Psychiatry* 2002; **41**:131–9.
17   Souba WW, Day DV. Leadership values in academic medicine. *Acad Med* 2006; **81**:20–6.
18   Rosen A, Callaly T. Interdisciplinary teamwork and leadership: issues for psychiatrists. *Australas Psychiatry* 2005; **13**:234–40.
19   Buckley PF. Reflections on leadership as chair of a department of psychiatry. The psychiatrist as a "natural born" leader. *Acad Psychiatry* 2006; **30**:309–14.
20   Greiner CB. Leadership for psychiatrists. *Acad Psychiatry* 2006; **30**:283–8.
21   Winstead DK. Advice for chairs of academic departments of psychiatry: the "Ten Commandments". *Acad Psychiatry* 2006; **30**:298–300.

Chapter 8

Leadership and Decision-Making

Dinesh Bhugra, Alex Till and Pedro Ruiz

Introduction

Leaders, whether in clinical or political settings, must make decisions that will affect the course of the organization or the country. Furthermore, these decisions may have a major impact on those who may have to carry out the orders. Decisions need to be conveyed to those within the organizations and guided to achieve the goals. Not everyone down the decision tree may agree with these, yet a leader will have to take decisions (some of which may well be unpopular) and act accordingly.

Decision-making, both in clinical and non-clinical settings, carries with it responsibilities, which include communication with patients, their carers, team workers and subordinates. In clinical decision-making, psychiatrists and other mental health professionals use a biopsychosocial model to understand aetiology and use this model to make decisions regarding clinical management. In addition, they routinely create and test hypotheses that lead to diagnosis of disorders and subsequent management. As mentioned in Chapter 1, there is a difference between decision-making and problem-solving. Problem-solving will focus on addressing problems and reaching decisions.

In this chapter we propose to address the role of the leader in making decisions, reaching out to followers and communicating these decisions effectively. We also aim to describe briefly the psychology of decision-making and differentiate it further from problem-solving. A disciplined approach is required to make clinical decisions.

Decision-making versus problem-solving

Problem-solving can be situational or have an ongoing basis. A problem brings with it a gap between what currently exists and what should be.[1] This may mean that the leader needs to be aware of the current status of the situation, the gap and the potential for reducing this gap. In theory all change offers an opportunity and problems themselves can offer an opportunity to move the organization forwards. Problem-solving and decision-making need to be seen as separate processes.[2] Barr and Dowding[2] explain that problem-solving

Leadership in Psychiatry, First Edition. Edited by Dinesh Bhugra, Pedro Ruiz and Susham Gupta.
© 2013 John Wiley & Sons, Ltd. Published 2013 by John Wiley & Sons, Ltd.

involves a fuller analysis of the circumstances related to problems. Getting to the root of the problem and finding solutions may therefore be seen as a more time-consuming process. On the other hand, the decision-making process may not take the same amount of time and energy.[3] However, in clinical decision-making, hypotheses may be generated and a diagnosis reached using collateral information and investigations, which in itself may be quite time consuming.

Barr and Dowding[2] suggest that problem management may use four approaches:

- classical management – related to optimum productivity in an organization where problem management influences the goals;
- human relations approach – impact and implications of work-based problems on people and values;
- systems approach – impact and influence on interdependence of human beings;
- contingency – combination of all these ideas.

Ultimately, the nature of the problem and what approach is used will determine success in problem management.[1]

Problem-solving can be achieved successfully if the organization or its leaders recognize the nature of the problem, assess the intelligence and impact of the problem, identify outcome criteria and generate solutions accordingly and communicate these to all concerned.[2] There is no doubt that both problem management and decision-making will be influenced by the level of previous experience and expertise. These are important factors that need to be taken into account while reaching a decision or solving a problem.

Traditionally, both processes – problem-solving and decision-making – have depended upon whether a rational or emotional approach is used. For both problem-solving or management and decision-making, the type of problem will dictate the process and the outcome. Problems can be simple or complex and may be entirely separate or embedded in each other. The solutions therefore will be effective once the type of problem is clear and the potential outcomes clearly identified. Problems can vary in their levels of complexities and intricacies, which will determine whether the decision-making is straightforward or not. Stott[4] proposes that a staged process within which problems can be solved include steps that identify, isolate, involve (others), investigate, implement and inquire (about effectiveness of the intervention). Identifying the problem and generating ideas and intervention are crucial steps in solving problems, thereby decision-making becomes a part of this process.

Psychology of decision-making

Decisions are often made in a particular context based on specific information available at that particular time when a decision is being made. Furthermore, whether a decision is ultimately good or bad can be influenced by the level of urgency and importance, as well as the process itself and the various other factors involved. A decision is a commitment to a course of action that is intended to yield results that are satisfying for specified individuals.[5] Yates *et al.*[5] asked a sample of undergraduates to describe two good and two bad decisions that they had made during the previous year. The participants were asked to rate decisions on the basis of quality (whether they saw the decision as good or bad) and on the basis of importance. Good decisions were rated at a higher dimension of quality and bad decisions were also seen as less important. The authors indicate that this may reflect cognitive dissonance. However, it is also possible that the retrospective recognition may have used misrepresentation or there may have been a selective bias. In addition, it is likely that good decisions are seen as important, whereas the reverse may not be entirely true. This 'rose-tinted' interpretation may also mean that the bad decisions are recalled more quickly.[5, 6] The key question that also needs to be explored is how to judge the quality of a decision, given the possible complex nature of this process. The quality of any decision is related not only to the desired outcome but also to the probability of that particular outcome occurring. The outcome itself will need to be looked at as it applies to the decision-maker, the leader or to others and how it affects them.[7]

The decision-making process has to incorporate objectives for the decision – what is the point and purpose of decision-making? The decision has to be made in the context for success and the issues have to be framed properly, with alternatives generated and evaluated and the best alternatives chosen.[8] In team-based decision-making, the task for the leader has to be to get the right people to participate, particularly those who may have the resources to deliver on the decisions. Within team settings the leader has to engage with opponents or find a strategy to dilute their opposition. It is helpful to listen to the opposition and attempt to understand their position. For teams to generate creative solutions, the leader must not only understand but also explain the context within which decisions will be made, delivered and acted upon. A good and effective leader will have to declare early on how the decision will be made – whether it will be based on consensus, qualified consensus, majority or directive leadership. An effective leader will generate alternatives that should represent a range of possibilities. In some settings the use of brainstorming may be effective. Team members or those who are participating in decision-making will come up with ideas, even if some are absurd. Under these circumstances the leader should take a neutral position but be able to prove these views. Within such settings individual differences can produce a creative friction, which may lead to emergence of new ideas. Good alternatives should be broadly constructed and genuine, not merely simple variations of each other. The alternatives should also be feasible. As noted in procedures based on Bayesian theory (Bayesian inference), between three and seven alternatives should be available. Depending upon the type of decision, the alternative options should include costs, benefits, feasibility, resources, ethics, etc.

The *Harvard Business Review*[8] proposes three decision-making techniques. The first one is catchball, where an initial idea is 'tossed' to a collaborator and whoever 'catches' the idea assumes responsibility for understanding and improving it. The second is point-counterpoint, where two teams are involved. One team presents the decision to the other, whose members identify one or more alternative courses of action and present their ideas to the first team in the second meeting. In the third meeting, the two teams debate the proposals and identify a common set of assumptions. The third method is intellectual watchdog, in which teams are divided into two groups. The first group develops a written proposal with recommendations, assumptions and supporting data, and presents this to the other group, who provide a written critique and present it to the first group. The first group then revise and present their proposals and so on, until decisions are agreed. A major task for the leader is to explain the rationale for a decision, and then to pass this on to the right people. A good leader will clarify which alternatives were discussed and the decisions behind those rejected, along with recognition of participants and an implementation plan and time frame. A good and successful leader will also explore any areas of uncertainty, and identify them and their potential impact. This process is important to reduce key uncertainties. Leaders must seek help if required and encourage not only evaluation of the decision but also continuous improvement.

Judgement in making decisions relies on a number of factors. A decision is defined as a commitment to a course of action;[5] judgement, on the other hand, is defined as an assessment or belief about a given situation based on the available information. In making a judgement, multiple factors from various sources of information are utilized to reach an outcome about a situation. A decision can be made using expected utility theory, which includes subcomponents of utility functions and subjective probabilities.[9] Judgement as a process includes discovery and scanning of relevant information to sift out the significant elements, then confirming the judgement along with providing and gathering feedback on the judgement reached. Exploring multiple sources of information and deciding which variables to select and what weight to give to each of these is important.[10] Information can be acquired using a number of sources, but a leader has to decide which of them to prefer over others, or to add these sources up. Certainly feedback on the decision-making is crucial in understanding whether the decision was correct or whether subsequent modifications can be made choosing other potential sources of information. Learning from feedback is not a unitary task and a number of steps may be required. Decision- making can be naturalistic, which emphasizes features of the context in which decisions are made. A recognition primed decision-making model means sizing up a situation to take the initial decision.[11-13] The second option is when a decision is made relying on the strategy to mentally simulate events leading to the situation. This approach is applied when the situation is not entirely clear. The third option is to imagine how decisions reached will play out in a given situation, allowing the decision-maker to anticipate difficulties and amend the chosen strategy (see Newell *et al.*[6] for further discussion). The role that expertise plays in making such decisions is significant and has already been mentioned. Decision-making can be understood using behavioural theory. The behaviour of a person in an organization is constructed by the organization and the position held by the individual. Thus the organization itself can dictate where decisions are made and who makes them.[14,15] Framing and reframing the problems can allow leaders to understand the extent of the problem, its complexity and potential solutions. Experts are used to reframing, and this skill as well as the underlying knowledge, are important facets of the entire decision-making process. Beach and Connolly[16] argue that the frame is a fragile thing. Emotions too will play a major role in making decisions. The mood while making decisions, past experiences and disappointments as well as creativity can all influence decisions.[17] The setting of the decision-making, whether it is within a group selectively or made by the group as a whole, needs to be considered in the context of the functions, vision and mission of the organization. Under these circumstances individual factors may be multiplied many times and a good and successful leader will have to overcome some of the inherent tensions.

Clinical decision-making

Clinical decision-making, irrespective of the medical specialty, involves exploring various hypotheses and reaching decisions on diagnosis and subsequent management. This may not always be easy. Clinicians rely on their knowledge and skills to exercise clinical judgement. Diagnosis in psychiatry brings with it specific challenges. First, the clinician has to rely on subjective reporting by the patient and in the absence of many objective tests clinicians have to reach a diagnosis. Secondly, the models often include biological, psychological, social and anthropological or spiritual dimensions and the clinician has to decide which of these models trumps others so relevant intervention can be prescribed. Cassell[18, 19] proposes that knowledge by itself does not look after patients. It is the application of knowledge that is important. Thirdly, a systematic and disciplined approach in the context of the knowledge will lead to diagnosis and subsequent management. Practical reasoning also has ethical and moral components, which are controlled on behalf of society by regulatory bodies. Scientific reasoning can be a dynamic process. This may be prevalent during a certain period but can be superseded once new discoveries challenge and change this, thereby influencing the process of decision-making.

Any method employed in understanding the process of decision-making would require breaking the latter into its constituent parts to examine the type and magnitude of risks involved, as well as the possible fallouts. Within the context of decision-making the personality of the decision-maker and the context are both important. Emotional, cognitive and philosophical factors also form a part of the decision-making process.[20] Intuition and experience combined with personal style all influence this process. The role of critical thinking is crucial for both decision-making and problem-solving. Gambrill[21] also points out that premature closure and closed questioning in a clinical encounter may lead to inadequate exploration of problems. Thus, multiple factors can affect the process of clinical diagnosis, and formulation and awareness of these factors is important to make more effective decisions.

Using a Bayes's theorem approach in actual clinical practice, decision-makers generate hypotheses and explore each, through a series of interviews supplemented by investigations to reject some of the hypotheses whilst exploring the remaining ones. Practical knowledge is affected by research data and findings, and keeping up to date for clinicians remains a key part of continuing professional development. Uncertainties in dealing with problems may well occur as a result of factors such as lack of knowledge or experience, the nature or rarity of the problem, poor information from the patient, poor motivation in reaching a diagnosis on the one hand, and difficulties in thinking such as narrow thinking, fuzzy thinking or sprawling thinking on the other.[22] Algorithms in reaching a diagnosis may be helpful, but the variables mentioned above may still create problems.

There will inevitably be differences between novices and experts in making clinical decisions. These differences can be explained on grounds of both knowledge and experience. Reasoning in order to reach a decision allows an exploration of explanations offered by the patient.[23] The clinician then goes on to develop further hypotheses if needed. Lessons in understanding the process of decision-making also incorporate professional judgement, where experience can play a significant role.

Experts and expertise

An expert is someone with specialist skills in a chosen field and who carries some specialist knowledge and technique. Their skills then gain recognition and their advice is sought widely. Expertise is therefore the accumulation of knowledge and skills characteristic of that particular field, leading to differentiation from novices or less experienced individuals.[24] These skills have to be reproducible on different occasions and the knowledge base must be up to date. Gathering of knowledge and experience is crucial.

Expertise can be understood using a number of models, which include individual differences in mental capacities. Ericsson[24] notes that expertise can be extrapolated using everyday skills in extended experiences. He also argues that expertise is qualitatively different and may be seen as an elite achievement. An expert may not perform well in every domain. Furthermore, for various reasons, they may not carry out their tasks and skills on each occasion.

Chi[25] proposes two approaches to the study of expertise, and argues that one way is to study truly exceptional people with the goal of understanding how they perform in their field. A second approach is to study experts in comparison with novices and try to understand similarities and differences. Decision-making by experts depends upon their field of expertise and what strategies they use to explore and test hypotheses and reach conclusions.

Psychological studies of experts and their expertise indicate that cognitive aspects of decision-making by experts vary. Expertise may be limited in its scope and elite performance may not transfer across domains. Expert knowledge and content matter more in expertise.[26] Intelligence, acquired knowledge and learning, as well as retention, are important in the development of expertise and skills. Feltovich *et al.*[26] argue that expertise involves larger and more integrated cognitive units, which means that with experience experts gain a larger vocabulary, which in turn helps and enables them to retain more information and patterns. Abstract representations can then be withdrawn from these large units to explain and make appropriate decisions.

Norman *et al.*[27] observe that, in medicine, expertise requires mastery of a diversity of knowledge and skills. Cognitive, motor and interpersonal skills are all critical in acquiring the status of an expert. These authors also point out that experts in medicine may have limited skills in their field. Knowledge in medicine can be of a basic mechanistic nature or focused on a particular topic. Knowledge from more formal structures may resemble a mental decision tree or algorithm, which may lead to diagnosis. A proper theoretical basis of analytical knowledge leads to the formation of concepts that may facilitate reaching a clinical diagnosis. Acquisition of technical skills, especially for craft specialists, can be demonstrated by better patient outcomes – for example, when operations are performed by surgeons who are experienced and busy.[28] Coordination of analytical and experiential knowledge is necessary and this, combined with experience, leads to better clinical decision-making.

Yates and Tschirhart[29] point out that the fundamental aspects in decision-making are identification (of the question), explanation and development. Looking at the definition of decision-making described earlier, actions are about doing things with commitment and an intention to achieve something with results that are, if not entirely satisfying, at least acceptable. A limited number of fundamental questions arise repeatedly in clinical practice. The decision processes are the means by which such cardinal issues are addressed for the problem at hand (see Yates[30] for further detailed discussion).

Expert teams, on the other hand, are effective on a number of parameters and use individual expertise to lead to a collective decision. A good leader will harness what teams 'think, do and feel'.[31] The members of the team may differentially express cognitive skills, critical knowledge and attitudes, and a successful leader will explore and find a way of harmonizing these. Teams are not static and their dynamism may itself be very helpful in reaching decisions that are appropriate for changing times. One hallmark of expert teams is their ability to be adaptive and reach timely decisions both in high- and low-pressure situations.[32] Situational cues become even more important in conditions where decisions have to be made under pressure. In teams, decision-making will still rest with the team leader, who will be held responsible for the decision.

Conclusions

Leaders will have to make decisions with the support of their teams or by themselves. The processes of solving problems and making decisions have many similarities but decision-making is more conceptual in clinical healthcare settings. Theoretical models of decision-making offer few insights into the actual processes. Knowledge, skills and expertise all contribute to successful decision-making. Leaders have to make decisions occasionally under pressure with access to perhaps limited information. Their leadership skills will allow them to ask the right questions and then make appropriate decisions. It is inevitable that other factors will play a role in reaching decisions and these may include experience, age, expertise, knowledge and skill base. Leadership does involve some amount of risk-taking once decisions are to be made. Education and training to build up the required skills and expertise will enable leaders to make fewer mistakes.

References

1 Van Gundy. *Techniques of Structured Problem Solving*. London: Van Nostrand Reinhold, 1988.
2 Barr J, Dowding L. *Leadership in Health Care*. London: Sage, 2008.
3 Tappen R, Weiss S, Whitehead D. *Essentials of Nursing Leadership and Management*. Philadelphia: FA Davis, 2004.
4 Stott K. *Making Management Work*. London: Prentice-Hall, 1992.
5 Yates JE, Veinotee E, Patalano A. Hard decisions, bad decisions. On decision quality and decision aiding. In: Schneider SL, Shanteau J (eds), *Emerging Perspectives on Judgement and Decision Research*. New York: Cambridge University Press, 2003; pp. 13–63.
6 Newell BR, Lagnado DA, Sharke DR. *Straight Choices: The Psychology of Decision Making*. Hove: Psychology Press, 2007.
7 Hastie R, Dawes RM. *Rational Choice in an Uncertain World*. Thousand Oaks, CA: Sage, 2001.
8 Harvard Business Review. *Decision Making: Five Steps to Better Results*. Boston, MA: Harvard Business School Press, 2006.

 9 Juslin P, Montgomery H. Introduction. In: Juslin P, Montgomery H (eds), *Judgment and Decision Making*. Hillsdale: LEA, 1999; pp. 1–6.

10 Dawes RM, Corrigan B. Linear models in decision making. *Psychol Bull* 1974; **81**:95–106.

11 Klein GA. A recognition primed decision (RPD) model of rapid decision making. In: Klein GA, Orasanu J, Calderwood R, Zsambok C (eds), *Decision Making in Action. Models and Methods*. Norwood, NJ: Ablex, 1993; pp. 138–47.

12 Klein GA. *Sources of Power: How People Make Decisions*. Cambridge, MA: MIT Press, 1998.

13 Lipshitz R, Klein G, Orasanu R, Salas E. Take stock of naturalisation decision making. *J Behav Decis Making* 2001; **14**:331–52.

14 Simon HA. A behavioural model of rational choice. *Quart J Econ* 1955; **69**:99–118.

15 Simon HA. Rational choice and the structure of the environments. *Psychol Rev* 1956; **63**: 129–38.

16 Beach LR, Connolly T. *The Psychology of Decision Making*. Thousand Oaks, CA: Sage, 2005.

17 Isen AM. Positive affect and decision making. In: Lewis M, Haviland J (eds), *Handbook of Emotions*. New York: Guilford Press, 1993; pp. 261–77.

18 Cassell E. *The Nature of Suffering and Goals of Medicine*. New York: Oxford University Press, 1991.

19 Cassell E. *Doctoring: The Nature of Primary Care Medicine*. New York: Oxford University Press, 1997.

20 Burstajn H, Hanin P, Gatheil T, Brodsky A. The decision analytic approach to medical malpractice law. *Med Decis Making* 1984; **4**:401–14.

21 Gambrill E. *Clinical Thinking in Clinical Practice*. Hoboken, NJ: John Wiley & Sons, Inc., 2005.

22 Perkins O. *Outsourcing IQ*. New York: Free Press, 1995.

23 Huck SM, Sandler M. *Rival Hypotheses*. New York: Harper & Row, 1979.

24 Ericsson KA. Introduction. In: Ericsson KA, Charness N, Feltovich PJ, Hoffman RR (eds), *The Cambridge Handbook of Expertise and Expert Performance*. New York: Cambridge University Press, 2006; pp. 3–19.

25 Chi M. Two approaches to the study of experts' characteristics. In: Ericsson KA, Charness N, Feltovich PJ, Hoffman RR (eds), *The Cambridge Handbook of Expertise and Expert Performance*. New York: Cambridge University Press, 2006; pp. 21–30.

26 Feltovich P, Prietula M, Ericsson E. Studies of expertise from psychological perspectives. In: Ericsson KA, Charness N, Feltovich PJ, Hoffman RR (eds), *The Cambridge Handbook of Expertise and Expert Performance*. New York: Cambridge University Press, 2006; pp. 41–68.

27 Norman G, Eva K, Brooks L, Hamstra S. Expertise in medicine and surgery. In: Ericsson KA, Charness N, Feltovich PJ, Hoffman RR (eds), *The Cambridge Handbook of Expertise and Expert Performance*. New York: Cambridge University Press, 2006; pp. 339–54.

28 Holm E, Lee C, Chassin M. Is volume related to outcome in health care? A systematic review and methodological critique of the literature. *Ann Int Med* 2002; **137**:511–20.

29 Yates JF, Tschirhart MD. Decision making expertise. In: Ericsson KA, Charness N, Feltovich PJ, Hoffman RR (eds), *The Cambridge Handbook of Expertise and Expert Performance*. New York: Cambridge University Press, 2006; pp. 421–38.

30 Yates J. *Decision Management*. San Francisco: Jossey-Bass, 2003.

31 Salas E, Cannon-Bowers JA. The science of team training. *Annu Rev Psychol* 2001; **52**:471–99.

32 Salas E, Rosen M, Burke CS, Goodwin G, Fiore SM. The making of a dream team: when expert teams do best. In: EricssonKA, CharnessN, FeltovichPJ, HoffmanRR (eds), *The Cambridge Handbook of Expertise and Expert Performance*. New York: Cambridge University Press, 2006; pp. 439–53.

Chapter 9

Team-Building in Psychiatry

Wolfgang Gaebel, Andreas Kuchenbecker, Noemi Wulff and Jürgen Zielasek

Introduction: leaders in psychiatry – as team builders and team leaders

Psychiatrists and other mental healthcare professionals may play different roles in different mental healthcare or administrative teams. According to the context, they can be leaders, managers, medical supervisors, responsible for treatment or simply colleagues. Team-related tasks play an increasing role in mental healthcare professionals' daily work. This chapter will focus on the role of psychiatrists but the basic principles outlined are also applicable to other healthcare professions.

The changing role of the modern psychiatrist: from therapist to manager?

Psychiatrists fulfil a primary role as clinicians diagnosing and treating persons presenting with mental disorders. In this clinical role, working in teams has been an increasing demand on psychiatrists coinciding with a movement to replace the medical model with a biopsychosocial model and a range of other developments in medicine.[1] Multidisciplinary clinical teams comprising psychiatrists, psychiatric nurses, psychologists and social workers are the rule in today's clinical environments, whether inpatient or outpatient settings. Increasingly, psychiatrists – and medical doctors in general – are in demand as leaders of teams not necessarily directly involved in the diagnosis, treatment and everyday healthcare of persons with mental disorders, but also with local mental healthcare organization or administration. Here, psychiatrists are needed either as experts for mental disorders or because of their individual management skills. The latter are more or less dependent on the personal communication skills or leadership skills of individuals who – by chance – are psychiatrists. The principal topic of this chapter is, however, the multitude of cases and situations in which psychiatrists and other mental healthcare professionals become team members or team leaders. This leads to a demand for professionalism in regard to teamwork. Page[2] reviewed the role of physicians in healthcare teams and concluded that the skills required to collaborate and be a team player are a core and significant part of

Leadership in Psychiatry, First Edition. Edited by Dinesh Bhugra, Pedro Ruiz and Susham Gupta.
© 2013 John Wiley & Sons, Ltd. Published 2013 by John Wiley & Sons, Ltd.

professional roles and capabilities. This, of course, also extends to other mental healthcare professionals besides psychiatrists.

Team approach in psychiatry

With the psychiatric reform process of the late twentieth century, which may be characterized as a process of decentralization and deinstitutionalization of mental healthcare, team-working has become increasingly important for psychiatrists. Rosen states that arguably psychiatry is ahead of other medical disciplines in the recognition of the multifactorial nature of mental disorders and the required multimodal interventions necessitating the involvement of multidisciplinary teams.[3] The UK's Royal College of Psychiatrists[4] identified the following professions in community mental health teams: psychiatrists, clinical psychologists, nurses, mental health workers, vocational therapists, art therapists, psychotherapists, social workers and occupational therapists. Some professional groups represented in such multidisciplinary teams, like mental health nurses, have developed increased self-assuredness following professionalization in education and organizational changes in mental healthcare. This has led to the question of whether psychiatrists are still the natural leaders of mental healthcare teams. Brimblecombe,[5] for example, investigated the changes in the relationship between psychiatrists and mental health nurses in the United Kingdom and came to the conclusion that although psychiatrists remain highly influential, there was some degree of loss of exclusive control over the mental healthcare process. The ensuing increasing demands on psychiatrists as team members – as opposed to a role as the sole leaders of mental healthcare services – have prompted an analysis of the required qualifications and job descriptions in the United Kingdom.[6] Team participation and its requirements are particularly outlined as a future aspiration for each profession in mental healthcare (e.g. availability for consultation, maintenance of a positive culture of multidisciplinary collaboration, and others; these will be dealt with in more detail later in this chapter). Much research on the role and function of mental healthcare teams cited in this chapter comes from the United States or the United Kingdom. The community-based approach towards mental healthcare brings about increased community-based mental healthcare with smaller, more locally organized mental healthcare teams. In some countries there is a trend to establish diagnosis-based expert clinics organized within centralized outpatient units,[7] although clear figures about this trend are lacking. There are many differences in the organization of mental healthcare services in the various European countries and therefore different demands of mental healthcare teams; however, common aspects of mental healthcare team leadership seem to be operative because they are based on the nature of mental disorders, the degree of professionalization of the different mental healthcare professions, and the general principles of team-building. In our opinion, these commonalities prevail over the setting-specific variables and allow the formulation of leadership tools in team-building and process guidance irrespective of the country in which psychiatric teams are formed. However, psychiatrists need to adapt these principles to the local, regional or national traditions and cultures of mental healthcare, depending on the type of setting of the team that they are leading or of which they are members (see also Chapter 6).

Team-building and team-leading as essential skills of psychiatrists

Acknowledging the increasing articulateness, assertiveness and expertise of other professions and laypersons, and following a period of neglect of professional training in administrative and management skills for psychiatrists,[8] being a team member and leading teams are considered essential skills in psychiatry including 'managing dynamics in team settings'.[4] The Union of European Medical Specialties takes a similar stance in defining 'The Profile of a Psychiatrist' as comprising, among other features, the ability to contribute effectively to interdisciplinary team activities.[9]

Although the training of psychiatrists and their hopefully optimal understanding of communication and human behaviour may make them natural team leaders ('Management is just psychiatry by other means'[10]), these key skills need to be learned and trained. Robinowitz[11] reviewed some specific attitudes and experiences of psychiatrists, which they usually gain in their clinical training. Note, however, that there may be substantial differences in the necessary attitudes towards patients as compared to colleagues. Still, some may be helpful for the psychiatrist as a team leader in mental healthcare. We have extracted the following list from this review as a guide for psychiatrists who become involved in the management of teams:

1 Understanding of individual and group dynamics.
2 Understanding of the role and impact of power and authority.
3 Understanding of systems and their management.
4 Understanding of the role that defences and transferences play in shaping behaviour.
5 Do not take some aspects of behaviour personally.
6 Understanding of the role of cultural contexts.
7 Understanding of behaviour and how to motivate and encourage change.

However, there are also some pitfalls that are specific to psychiatrists as team leaders. First of all, requirements in management and requirements as a therapist need to be separated. Secondly, administrative or strategic teams often deal with financial issues, but financial management is not a core competency of a psychiatrist. The information in the following paragraphs may support psychiatrists in developing effective team leading skills.

Team characteristics and team dynamics

Definitions: what is a team?

One frequently used definition of a team was proposed by Katzenbach and Smith:[12] 'A team is a small number of people with complementary skills who are committed to a common purpose, performance goals, and approach for which they are mutually accountable.' This describes an ideal image of a team and describes many attributes improving a team's effectiveness. However, many teams do not fulfil all of these characteristics. Katzenbach and Smith distinguish such teams from workgroups and 'pseudo-teams'. Workgroups are groups of interacting individuals who share experiences or counsel one another without following a supraordinate goal. In 'pseudo-teams', team members also do not define common goals and interact without generating added value from the team effort, which makes them even less effective than workgroups. In other definitions, interdependency of tasks is also mentioned as a key characteristic of a team.[13] Until this stage of performance and confidence is achieved, teams and workgroups often undergo several stages of team-building or team development. While team-building rather describes the process of establishing the basis for effectiveness by 'helping teams develop trust and commitment',[14] team development has its focus on enhancing performance and on developing skills, both as a group and individually (see 'Shared leadership' below).

In this chapter the term 'team' is also used for groups not fulfilling all aspects mentioned above. Still, it is recommended to every leader to reflect on whether the group of people to be led is a working group or a team and which aspects of ideal teams are missing from the group.

Structural elements of teams

Teams in mental healthcare have a range of characteristics depending on the context (e.g. organizational, diagnosis and treatment contexts). First of all, teams dealing with mental healthcare of individual patients or groups of patients may be differentiated from those serving the strategic or administrative needs of mental healthcare organizations.

Another approach to define a team's structural elements is the type of team creation. Teams may be formed by a select group of people spontaneously due to immediate demands or because of a common group interest. The team forms in reaction to this incident to identify the reasons and possible improvements to be made to the ward operating procedures. Such teams have inherently high motivation among its individual members. Other teams are created due to external demands or because others do not want to do the job. In such cases, team membership may be mandatory for some or all team members and the intrinsic individual motivation may be low. In these cases, team-building and team motivation take centre stage if the psychiatrist is the leader of such a team.

Besides these formal aspects, which are highly relevant for mental health teams, other factors such as size or decision-making techniques may be employed to define aspects of teams.[15] These may include the different goals and tasks of teams, their membership structure, their different sizes, different responsibilities, time and work cycles, and their decision-making techniques. Team leaders may interact with their teams in more directive ways or take a withdrawn attitude, only interacting when absolutely necessary. For example, a project group in a psychiatric hospital may have a very broad membership structure. It might be led by a strong leader and the team may include medical doctors, psychologists, social workers, psychiatric nurses and members of the administrative staff if standard operation procedures are to be developed. Membership may be much more limited if a more focused task is to be addressed by a team. In a day clinic, teams may be formed in order to address issues related to the community.

Similar to the wide variety of team typologies mentioned, another dimension will be the team setting. This question is specially relevant for psychiatrists because mental healthcare occurs in a wide variety of settings, mainly differentiable into inpatient and outpatient

Table 9.1 Roles of psychiatrists in teams (modified after Rosen[17])

Role designation	Example
Medical expert	Investigates mental illness, prescribes drugs and indicates psychotherapy or other therapies; explains medical terms, diagnostic and therapeutic procedures and the nature of the mental illness in question to the patient and his/her relatives as a prerequisite for informed consent and shared decision-making
Medico-legal signatory	MD qualification as the authorization for signing legal documents
Joint assessor	Participant in the biopsychosocial assessments
Teacher	Informs team members about mental illnesses, diagnosis and treatment options
Scholar	Informs team about current developments and scientific innovations in psychiatry
Generalist	Able to know and integrate expertise from several medical specialities and non-medical disciplines

mental healthcare. Another setting effect is the country in which a team is formed – there are large differences in the organizing principles of mental healthcare between different countries and such differences may be of great importance for international teams, such as research teams or teams developing international standards of care. There are few studies dealing with setting-specific aspects of mental healthcare teams, but a comparative analysis by Slade and coworkers showed that hospital settings involved less consensual decision-making than community mental health teams, and that considerable differences existed in the type of qualifications of the members of different professions in multidisciplinary mental health teams when India and Australia were compared.[16]

As mentioned in the 'Introduction' the psychiatrist may have different role functions in different settings and different teams. There is no common description or definition of the role of the psychiatrist in different settings or different teams. Rosen[17] distinguished between essential and non-essential roles of the psychiatrist (Table 9.1).

In the clinical team dealing with individual or group mental healthcare, psychiatrists will usually take over the lead because the final responsibility for treatment decisions mostly rests with them. In such teams, the psychiatrist is required both as a medical expert and as a team leader. In those teams dealing with general issues of mental healthcare, psychiatrists may be the leaders, but not necessarily so. Frequently, business administrators may take the lead in such groups. In teams not involved in mental healthcare, psychiatrists may be the leaders, but again not necessarily so, and specialists in administration, public relations or other fields may take the leadership role. In these teams, psychiatrists are needed because of their clinical expertise. However, psychiatrists may also become leaders of such teams and in these cases it will usually be their personal qualification in team leadership or their personal position in the organization's hierarchy that may advance them to the leader position. For example, in academic medicine heads of psychiatric departments may lead interdisciplinary teams dealing with administrative issues of medical education as part of their academic commitments.

Shared leadership

Leadership can also be shared by persons of different professions. Considering international mental healthcare settings, there are huge differences in the perception of shared leadership. Shared leadership may be considered as granted or as not feasible. Aspects like qualification backgrounds, cultural aspects, organizational settings of hospitals, and legal aspects of the different professions also influence the perception and effectiveness of shared leadership.

The following criteria are important for successful shared leadership:

1   The principle of shared leadership should ideally be established at all levels of the hierarchy. The hospital board should have an interdisciplinary shared leadership, representing each hospital division and also their subordinated inpatient and outpatient units.
2   A universal principle of management by objectives instills institutionally shared responsibility for dealing with the budget and the achievements of strategic and operational objectives. The institutional arrangements may be extended by personal target agreements, which are rewarded in case of achievement.
3   A recommended practice of shared leadership needs a strong commitment to the establishment and maintenance of this leadership model. It requires an intensive dialogue between leaders to clarify positions, basic principles, task distribution and the definition of joint and separate activities. As outlined before, the objectives and the strategies to achieve them, and the evaluation methods must be agreed upon. For these agreements, meeting time is required (*jour fixe*, retreats) and eventually support through external coaching. An essential feature of effective shared leadership is the definition of the decision-making process in the case of conflict and dissent.
4   It is essential to develop a (self-) critical approach to the established job-specific 'pillars' of communication within a hospital and one's own professional identity. The management of a unit of a mental healthcare organization usually requires the duality of medical-therapeutic and nursing supervision. Within the management tasks, the profession-dominated perspective is subsidiary. Also, communication between the management levels (hospital board and divisions) should not occur along the hierarchic lines of the specific disciplines but across the disciplines. Consequently, meeting and delegating practice should be closely reviewed.

Sometimes even professional associations declare shared leadership as 'state of the art'.[18] Few studies have been conducted to analyse the effects of shared leadership. A study by Steinert and coworkers in Germany has shown that this form of leadership organization may promote the satisfaction of employees and leaders.[19]

Types of collaboration in teams: interdisciplinary and multidisciplinary

Interdisciplinary interaction between healthcare professionals in psychiatric treatment is of particular importance. The quality of diagnostic assessments, the possibilities of 'understanding the case' and the effectiveness of psychiatric interventions are directly related to the success of collaboration in teams.

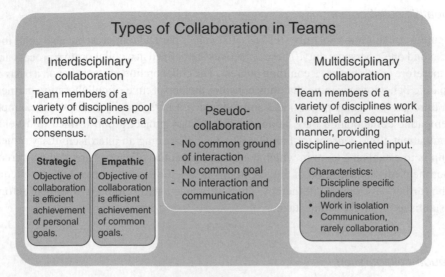

Figure 9.1   Interdisciplinary and multidisciplinary team collaboration

Many terms attempt to describe the different natures and characteristics of collaborations of professionals working in healthcare (e.g. multi-professional, inter-professional, trans-professional, multi-agency, interdisciplinary or multidisciplinary). A useful and common distinction is made between interdisciplinary and multidisciplinary teams[20] (Figure 9.1).

According to Schmitt,[20] a multidisciplinary team describes members of a team working in a parallel or sequential manner, each responsible for a different patient care need. 'Members tend to wear discipline-specific blinders and work in isolation from one another. They often communicate, but rarely collaborate'.[20] Interdisciplinary teams are also composed of a variety of disciplines and focus on outcomes, acknowledging that the participants share responsibilities. They pool information to come to a consensus (Figure 9.1). In order to reach this special quality of interdisciplinary teamwork, a mature form of collaboration is required. Spiess[21] distinguishes between strategic and empathic orientation in collaboration, while pointing out that mixed forms are possible.

Strategic collaboration

Strategic collaboration means that the involved stakeholders or employees primarily seek to achieve their own goals or partial interests, and therefore cooperate with each other. They are aware that by cooperating they are more efficient than without cooperation. For example, psychiatrists know that the compliance of the nursing service is crucial to implement their ideas of treatment. The nurses shape the daily routines of the patients and so the psychiatrist cooperates to achieve his or her own goals. On the other hand, nurses know that a certain weight and authority is given to statements made by psychiatrists and other therapists. So they introduce everyday treatment recommendations or regulations (e.g. contact with visitors) in therapeutic conversations with the psychiatrists, to get more leverage.

Empathic collaboration

Empathic collaboration not only seeks to satisfy one's particular interest but also goals that go beyond one's personal duty. These objectives are defined in a collaborative process and are therefore considered as a common interest. The collaboration partners act on a basis of empathic behaviour meaning that they consider the perspective of collaboration partners or a third party (e.g. the patient) and aim to include it in their daily actions. An example of empathic collaboration may be an interdisciplinary project group formed to develop an outpatient clinic concept for families. The goal of creating an interdisciplinary project group is to establish a team in which medical/therapeutic colleagues are also concerned about the professionalization of nursing in this new setting, while nurses have an interest in the further development of therapy. Thereby, a new interdisciplinary treatment setting is established from the initial stage.

Pseudo-collaboration

Spiess[21] describes a third style of collaboration, termed pseudo-collaboration. There is no (or no additional) common ground in the interaction between the collaboration partners. They pretend to have a common goal and a common basis for collaboration. Multidisciplinary meetings provide hardly any results. However, for the sake of giving the impression of collaboration, they are carried out. Basically, everyone is working for his or her own interests.

Team dynamics: development stages

For the purpose of this chapter team development includes team-building activities such as the initial build-up of a team. One of the basic requirements is to help teams develop trust and commitment as a basis of effectiveness.[14] Various frameworks have been developed to understand team functioning and team effectiveness. In this chapter, two frameworks will be outlined: Tuckman's stages of team development, first published in 1964, and Hale's sociometric cycle. Both first addressed group functioning and were later adapted to team performance. Tuckman's model is the most cited work to describe team development phases. It has been adapted to other leadership frameworks and suggests ideas for leadership behaviour in the different stages. Hale's sociometric cycle uses the metaphor of the four seasons to describe different stages of team development. The recommendations for leadership suggested by Hale's model deal more with adequate tools and measures than with leadership behaviour. Therefore, both models are outlined in this chapter.

According to Tuckman, a team moves through four sequential stages: forming, storming, norming and performing.[22] Sometimes also a fifth stage follows: adjourning.[23] Each of these stages has different elements of team behaviour, identity, climate and often also stage-specific tasks to fulfil. Therefore, each stage requires different leadership performance (Figure 9.2). The stages of team development may be adapted to Hersey and Blanchard's[24] model of situational leadership. This model suggests that effective leadership cannot consist of a single particular style but should be adapted to the given situation.

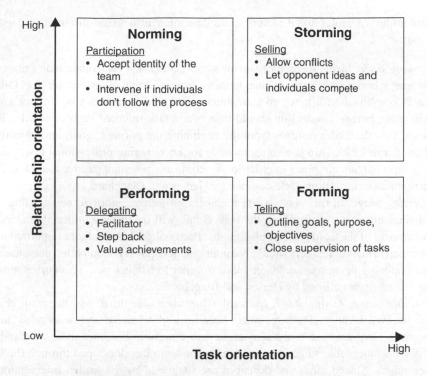

Figure 9.2 Team development stages

According to the maturity of the employee or of a group of employees, the leader emphasizes task-oriented behaviour or relationship-oriented behaviour. Hersey and Blanchard[24] describe four situational leadership styles:

- *Telling*: The leader gives an explicit task orientation by outlining goals, purpose, tasks and objectives. The work is also closely supervised. Relationships (between leaders and employees) are not in the focus of leadership performance (high task orientation/low relation orientation).
- *Selling*: Leadership emphasizes the task and the relationship. The importance of the task is explained in a supportive way. Opposing ideas and conflicts among team members have room and are dealt with (high task orientation/high relation orientation).
- *Participating*: The leader encourages shared ideas and decisions and accepts the team identity formed thereby. Relationship-oriented intervention is necessary if individuals do not follow the process of identity building (low task orientation/high relation orientation).
- *Delegating*: In this situation, the employee or the team takes responsibility for the task and the decisions made because there is sufficient ability, willingness and confidence. The leader acts as facilitator, steps back and values the team's achievement (low task orientation/low relation orientation).

This model gives recommendations for leadership behaviour towards employees in specific situations and it is also adaptable to teams (see Figure 9.2). Different degrees of team/employee professional maturity and development demand different leadership behaviour.

1   *Forming stage*: In this stage, the team members get to know each other. It describes the moment when a new unit is created within a hospital or an outpatient service. Often, this is combined with new tasks, treatments and staff members who did not know each other before. Leadership should take over a task-oriented supportive role. This means that the leader outlines from the beginning the purpose, goals and objectives of the team. Leadership is also responsible for encouraging professional discussions between the team members in order to overcome any potential passive attitudes. This correponds to the telling-style outlined by Hersey and Blanchard.

2   *Storming stage*: In this stage, team members no longer prioritize being polite and collegial but focus on fulfilling the task. Some will try to gain informal leadership and control of the team's accomplishments. Personal goals seem more important than team performance. Leaders should not intervene too quickly. Competing personalities and opposing opinions should get space in order to balance out. This correponds to the selling-style outlined by Hersey and Blanchard.

3   *Norming stage*: At this stage, team roles have been identified and the team develops its own identity. Team members become less offensive and accomplish tasks together. Decisions are more democratic and the group becomes more predictable. It is recommendable to accept the identity the team has developed through the former stages. Shared ideas and decisions are supported by the leader. Intervention is needed if individuals do not follow this process. The participating leadership style is recommended.

4   *Performing stage*: On reaching this stage the team has developed an optimum level of functioning. The awareness that the team is more effective than the sum of each member's effectiveness brings forth new ideas to accomplish the tasks. Team members cooperate, carry out their assigned roles and responsibilities, and create a relaxed climate with a high level of trust. Therefore, the team can also be a realistic role model of reciprocal understanding of the patient's social activity in the therapeutic setting.[25] Team leaders should recognize and value the achievements of the team and each individual's contribution. Leadership ideally acts as facilitator, takes a step back and shows support for the team's work. The delegating leadership style is recommended.

5   *Adjourning stage*: Tuckman subsequently described a fifth stage: adjourning. This is a stage of disclosure. New programmes or procedures demand new structures, and the team's or the unit's purpose becomes irrelevant. The climate is characterized by mixed emotions, sadness, satisfaction with the accomplished work, or lack of confidence about future tasks.

The sociometric cycle

Another very useful model is outlined by Hale[26] to assess and deal with team development stages. Hale describes a cycle of sociometric patterns, which can be used to estimate the expected changes from one to another sociometric constellation of individuals or of groups. A group of German psychodramatists centred around Lüffe-Leonard and Gabriele Birth uses these sociometric descriptions to consider organizations and derive a model of team development phases. The sociometric cycle is described metaphorically as a cycle based on the four seasons (Table 9.2).[27]

The team development stage *spring* is dominated by the spirit of change and special commitment to the team's purpose creating a strong sense of belonging (Table 9.2). In this stage, teams are often characterized by close proximity and little internal heterogeneity.

A team's *summer* is identified by rituals of consistency. The enthusiasm and turmoil of the pioneer phase gives way to solid everyday work. Working processes become systematic and better developed. It is a period of internal differentiation. Management and employees have separate functions. Roles within the team are established. Much effort is spent on describing and establishing process flows and treatment routines.

While the summer phase is fading away and the *fall* begins, the team has developed its routines and the profile of its work. This season is characterized by challenging each team member about his or her identification with the established structure and design of the team's work.

After the fall crisis, a *winter* phase of solid teamwork begins, which is peaceful and of high quality. The team winter ends with rituals of change, since it is of crucial importance that there is no conceptual and dynamic stagnation. This solid ground gives the opportunity for ideas and innovation. If these moments of development and change become evident and concrete, the team enters into a new *spring* phase and the cycle starts over again.

Methods and requirements for team leaders in team-building and team development

Here we focus on special tools to support the team development process. For more general skills, readers may find additional information in Chapter 2. While team-building relates to the initiation and inauguration phase of a team, team development deals with the subsequent stages of team activities following the inauguration of a team.

Communication skills

Performance feedback and participatory management were shown to be important pre-dictors of the development of a 'healthy' hospital organization in a prospective study in Swedish hospitals.[28] Herrman and coworkers[29] identified effective communication styles with agreements to aim for a clear and open style of communication as the key elements for effective teamwork. This includes the opportunity for all team members to con-tribute and an attitude of openness in expressing disagreement and conflict together with agreed avenues for conflict exploration and resolution. Corrigan and Garman[30] suggested that effective mental health team leaders are characterized by transactional and trans-formational leadership skills, helping their team members by goal-setting, feedback and reinforcement (transactional interaction), and by providing a view from a more elevated perspective with inspiration and intellectual stimulation (transformational interaction). The ideal would thus be a team leader motivating the team to achieve a common goal

Table 9.2   The sociometric cycle (adapted from Hale[26]) and resulting recommendations for leadership

Team stage	Possible motivational aspects	Possible discouragement
Spring	• A good pioneer stage might be the source of new strength in a phase of crises. Experiencing that working in the team can be pleasurable, inspirational and yield unconventional solutions avoids the 'daily grind' • A good social network shaped in the work environment is useful for other phases • During the pioneer stage the team learns about the value of visions. The team experiences that those who do not have the courage to dream, lack the strength to fight	• Be aware of a dynamic that leads to collective overload. The level of common standards should not be too high • The collective euphoric stage might cause blind spots • The self-regulatory function of a team is not reliable in this stage
Summer	• Make sure the tasks and roles are flexible and can undergo changes • Encourage job rotation • Use measures including team-building and team retreats (e.g. for skills analysis → who has which skills and wants to learn what . . . ?) • Closeness and distance on the job should be reviewed → use clinical supervision • Encourage objective perspective on the job • Establish employee appraisals	• Caution: inertia might be the cause of an agreeable atmosphere • After the process of internal differentiation team members might question if their resulting roles and responsibilities are sound and acceptable, whether the process was fair, and whether they are under- or over-challenged
Fall	• Use this phase as a laboratory for conflict culture → clinical supervision is a sound framework for that • Decisive leader is useful • Use conflicts as an opportunity for new positioning and decision-making → deliberate decision to stay in post	• Escalation of conflictual situations is possible • Be aware of permanent exclusion of team members • Be aware of mobbing activities
Winter	• Opportunity to tap new energy from the team • Take time for team retreat and special projects • Take time for study trips and apprenticeships in similar wards of other organizations • Job rotation • Encourage innovation workshops, new visions, the review of mission statements	• Caution that the peaceful atmosphere does not imply permanent retirement and depressive hibernation • Be aware of a tendency to individualization of employees and encourage collective reflectiveness

and guiding the team to achieve a high degree of efficiency. According to a survey of 389 staff members who provided team-based clinical or rehabilitative services, these mental health team members expected clear roles and goals, proactive and fair solutions to problems, acknowledgement of cultural diversity of the team members, efficient supervision, avoidance of autocratic leadership and avoidance of management by exception.[31]

Thus, the types of interactional necessities for team leaders are manifold and must be used flexibly depending on the actual situation. To aid teams in assessing themselves and their performance, structured video-based training programmes are available, which help not only the psychiatrist/consultant to improve his/her communicative skills but also the team to self-assess team functioning.[32] Another resource is a recent review of leadership training programmes by Beinecke[33] for the International Initiative for Mental Health Leadership.

Besides these communicative capabilities necessary for in-team communication, especially pertinent for mental healthcare teams is whether the team leadership style has a positive effect on patient outcomes. In a small study with 184 patients, Corrigan and coworkers showed that patient satisfaction with the treatment programme and patients' quality of life were inversely associated with a laissez-faire leadership type and positively associated with transformative and transactional leadership styles, explaining 40% of the total variance.[34] A larger study with 1638 seriously mentally ill persons in 44 mental healthcare team units found an association between mutual respect of team members and patient outcomes (satisfaction with housing, relations with families, social life and finances).[35]

Defining and assigning roles and responsibilities

Team role models

Besides the professional role described by the job design (see below), Belbin[36] states that team members also have specific team roles based on their behaviour rather than the job performance. He describes nine roles with different attributes resulting from studies focused on the behaviour of team members and their contribution to team effectiveness. Role diversity in a team's composition is, according to Belbin's research, contributing to a constructive and effective team.[36] The nine team roles have been modified and reduced to six roles[37] (Table 9.3).

The adaptation seems reasonable since some of Belbin's team role descriptions overlap.[37] The advantage of the reduced model is that it focuses on the description of clusters of behaviour and thereby accounts for the fact that most people have attributes of more than one role. The descriptions should therefore be used as a general framework rather than as a psychometric instrument. Role conflicts were shown to be significant factors for the development of job dissatisfaction in community mental health teams.[38] Therefore, they need to be identified and addressed appropriately by the team leader. The leader's task is to support the positive features of each role, to reduce the weaknesses and to try to have a team in which each of the described behaviour clusters are represented by team members.

Table 9.3   Summary description of team roles (modified after Gellert and Nowak[37])

Role	Characteristics	Consequences if role is not filled
Facilitator/leader	Disciplined, good overview, provides initiatives for further work, monitors agreements	No orientation, power struggles, difficult group dynamics
Coordinator/implementer	Clarifies goals, develops action plans and reasonable tasks, shows perseverance and discipline	Impractical solutions, no structure, many unfulfilled tasks
Spin doctor	Unorthodox thinking, adventurous, spontaneous and creative, tries out new solutions, confident and open-minded	New solutions never leave traditional paths, half-hearted, spiritless, mental blocks
Networking person/resource investigator	Extrovert, communicative, establishes information flows, informs on developments and tendencies, explores external support and opportunities	Redundant work, no knowledge about duties of colleagues, unknown in other departments of organization
Team worker	Integrates mavericks, perceptive and diplomatic, avoids frictions and observes team climate	Fluctuation, missing appreciation, finger pointing, repressed emotions
Specialist/completer	Polishes and perfects, concentrated until tasks are fulfilled, dedicated, highly qualified results	Mistakes, semi-finished tasks, interest lost after initial enthusiasm, reluctance to complete ideas

A useful model of effective leadership was described by Malik.[39] From his holistic and system-oriented view of leadership, he describes the basic principles of leadership and a core set of tasks and tools each leader should have a good command of, regardless of the discipline.

At this point, we will refer only to one of the tools Malik describes that is relevant to lead a team: job design and assignment control. Without defined roles and responsibilities, it is difficult to achieve objectives and goals in a team. Malik describes that not only products, but also jobs need to be designed [ref. 39, p. 298]. The objective of providing good and adequate care for the patient in itself does not say enough about the tasks and responsibilities needed to be accomplished. Therefore 'the people must organize and design the job' [ref. 39, p. 298]. The process of job design can be defined as a 'specification of the content, methods, and relationships of jobs in order to satisfy technological and organizational requirements as well as the social and personal requirements of the job holder'.[40] It is the leader's responsibility to ensure that the job of each team member is properly designed. Job designs should also be reassessed regularly because requirements may change [ref. 41, p. 262].

Special instruments/tools

Earlier in this chapter, the typical phases of team development were described and were linked to recommended methods. These methods will now be described more specifically.

Team-building workshops

Team-building workshops are recommended in the initiation phase of a new team or when a team has experienced much transition, generation change or employee turnover. Team-building workshops can be part of the project work before and during the initiation phase of a new treatment unit or during a process of reorganization. It might be helpful to use external trainers or facilitators in this process. Besides securing the outcome of such a process, a good facilitator uses tools to promote interaction, cooperation and cohesiveness. Even if external trainers are involved, it remains essential that the (future) team leader is present in this phase of conceptual clarification and team-building, as roles are established in this phase. Ideally, the presence of the leader provides clarity and certainty in this phase of fears and instability; but it surely enhances instability if the leader is not involved in this process.

Clinical supervision

Clinical supervision can and must be considered as state of the art in psychiatry. In a multicentre study conducted in Switzerland during 2002–03, Gottfried *et al.*[42] came to the conclusion that clinical supervision in psychiatry is highly valued by the staff in case- and team-based contexts. The case-based supervision takes place either in treatment settings of the team unit or across units. It is focused on a profound case understanding, the reflection of personal interests and involvement in treatment. Furthermore, it analyses team dynamics and its reflection on patients and the development and assessment of therapeutic intervention strategies. Team-based clinical supervision focuses on the dynamics of cooperation, role definitions and their clarification, and the handling of conflicts. Case-based supervision is mandatory in most mental health disciplines. In everyday clinical practice it is often decided according to the current need whether a case-based or team-based supervision or a combination of both is required. Considering Hale's team seasons, it is particularly useful to introduce team supervision in the spring phase focused on establishing, or in the constructive autumn phase with the purpose of resolving conflicts.

Team retreats

In addition to case and team supervision, days of team retreat are also very valuable. Teams get the opportunity to take a break from everyday clinical practice – often with the support of an external facilitator – in order to discuss fundamental conceptual issues. Well-established procedures can come under scrutiny, the distribution of tasks can be reviewed and treatment services can be elaborated. A team retreat experienced as constructive can be very motivating. The experience of commonly achieved successful work might in some situations be perceived as more curative (for the staff) than team-based supervision in conflict phases. Team retreat can be helpful in all the phases of team development as described by Hale. In 'team-spring' the focus of team retreats is clarification of conceptual issues and of operational and organizational structure. In 'team-summer', days of team retreat help to elaborate treatment standards, procedures, and bring treatment concepts into written forms. In the 'team-winter' phase such retreats provide space for future-oriented workshops, in which innovations and readjustments can be generated.

Employee appraisals

Standardized annual employee appraisals have value as a tool for human resource development (e.g. through a dialogue about the employee's state of mind in the workplace, requirements for training and personal career planning, etc.), but can also be used to discuss and agree upon personal goals deduced from the unit's objectives. The principle of management by objectives can be applied here. When employee appraisals are standardized, there should be clarity on the frequency (usually once a year), setting, agenda and recording of the talk. Leaders and employees should be prepared and a non-interrupted time period should be assigned.

Workplace health promotion

In particular with regards to the demographic transition in many countries (e.g. Germany, Britain, Italy), leadership will require far more awareness and instruments to adapt job assignments to elderly employees in healthcare organizations. Similar to other social working environments, not only physical exposure but also mental exposure affects the employees. In Germany, mental disorders have increased to become the main reason for occupational disabilities. A 2010 study of the Deutsche Rentenversicherung Bund (German Pension Funds) showed that mental health problems increased from 15% to 38% of all diagnoses leading to early retirement.[43] Particularly, employees working in the health and social sector are affected by absenteeism due to mental disorders, with an average of more than 1.8 days per year per employee in Germany.[44] Both organizations and leaders have to respond to this development by providing assistance and support to reduce stress in the work context. In Germany, many health insurance companies started supporting organizations through their workplace health promotion schemes (e.g. leadership training, work-balance training for employees, organizing information and awareness days in organizations, etc.).

Future perspectives

Working in teams and leading teams are key skills for all mental healthcare professionals. These skills can be learned and may be maintained by continuing education. While there is some reason to believe that psychiatrists are natural born team players, some specific aspects of the psychiatrist as a therapist may also be problematic in teams. Standard approaches to team-building and team development are available and reviewed here. The life cycles of teams can be described in terms of development stages with different leadership and communication styles. Future trends in psychiatry and mental healthcare will continue to challenge the psychiatrist as a team member or a team leader. For example, the increasing sophistication of psychiatric diagnostic and therapeutic procedures will make the psychiatrist an essential member of any mental healthcare team. In addition, the increasing need for mental healthcare will probably lead to more interest in health politics, health insurance companies and the general public in mental health issues resulting in an increasing demand for psychiatrists to join mental healthcare or general healthcare teams in clinical and non-clinical settings. Further challenges relate to the increasing numbers of different players of more professions in mental healthcare, and the question arises who is best capable of leading such teams. Acquiring management competences during medical school becomes a necessity. Conflicts between shared decision-making in multi-professional teams and final medical responsibility of the psychiatrist will inevitably arise and need to be resolved by the interdisciplinary mental healthcare teams.

References

1 Rodenhauser P. Psychiatrists as treatment team leaders: pitfalls and rewards. *Psychiatric Quart* 1996; **67**:11–31.

2 Page DW. Teams and professionalism. In: Bhugra D, Malik A (eds), *Professionalism in Mental Healthcare. Experts, Expertise and Expectations.* Cambridge University Press, Cambridge, 2011; pp. 101–11.

3 Rosen A. The community psychiatrist of the future. *Curr Opin Psychiatry* 2006; **19**:380–8.

4 Royal College of Psychiatrists. Role of the consultant psychiatrist. Leadership and excellence in mental health services. Occasional Paper OP74. London: RCP, 2010.

5 Brimblecombe NR. The changing relationship between mental health nurses and psychiatrists in the United Kingdom. *J Adv Nurs* 2005; **49**:344–53.

6 National Steering Group. (2005) Guidance on new ways of working for psychiatrists in a multidisciplinary and multiagency context. London: Royal College of Psychiatrists and National Institute of Mental Health in England. http://webarchive.nationalarchives.gov.uk/+/www. dh.gov.uk/en/Publicationsandstatistics/Publications/PublicationsPolicyAndGuidance/DH_ 4087352[accessed 10 April 2013].

7 Munk-Jorgensen P. Cider house rules. *World Psychiatry* 2008; **2**:98–9.

8 Harrison T. The role of the consultant psychiatrist in the clinical team. *Psychiatr Bull* 1989; **13**:347–50.

9 UEMS Section for Psychiatry (2005) The profile of a psychiatrist. http://www.uemspsychiatry .org/section/reports/2005Oct-PsychiatristProfile.pdf[accessed 14 May 2012].

10 Wilson DR. The seven deadly sins of academic chairs. *Acad Psychiatr* 2006; **30**:304–8.

11 Robinowitz CB. Psychiatrists as leaders in academic medicine. *Acad Med* 2006; **30**:273–8.

12 Katzenbach JR, Smith DK. *The Wisdom of Teams: Creating the High-Performance Organization.* Boston: Harvard Business School, 1993.

13 Koman ES, Wolff SB. Emotional intelligence competencies in the team and team leader. A multi-level examination of the impact of emotional intelligence on team performance. *J Manage Dev* 2007; **27**:55–75.

14   Sorrells-Jones J. Organisational dynamics. In: LancasterJ (ed.), *Nursing Issues in Leading and Managing Change*. St Louis: Mosby, 1999; pp. 125–48.

15   Team Building. World Health Organization, 2007. Available at: http://www.who.int/cancer/modules/Team%20building.pdf [accessed 4 April 2013].

16   Slade M, Rosen A, Shankar R. Multidisciplinary mental health teams. *Int J Soc Psychiatr* 1995; **3**:180–9.

17   Rosen A. New roles for old: the role of the psychiatrist in the interdisciplinary team. *Australas Psychiatry* 2001; **9**:133–7.

18   BAG Leitende Ärzte und BAG Pflegeleitungen KJP. Zielsetzungs-/ Orientierungsdaten Kinder- und Jugendpsychiatrischer Kliniken und Abteilungen in der Bundesrepublik Deutschland. 2009. Available at: http://www.bag-kjp.de/bag-zielsetzungs-und-orientierungsdaten-2009.pdf [accessed 4 April 2013].

19   Steinert T, Göbel R, Rieger W. A nurse-physician co-leadership model in psychiatric hospitals: Results of a survey among leading staff members in three sites. *Int J Ment Health Nurs* 2006; **15**:251–7.

20   Heinemann G, Zeiss A. *Team Performance in Health Care. Assessment and Development*. New York: Kluwer Academic/Plenum Publishers, 2002.

21   Spiess E. *Kooperatives Handeln in Organisationen*. München: Hampp, Mering, 1996.

22   Tuckman B. Developmental sequences in small groups. *Psychol Bull* 1965; **63**:384–99.

23   Tuckman B, Jensen M. Stages of small group development revisited. *Group Organiz Stud* 1977; **2**:419–27.

24   Hersey P, Blanchard K. *Management of Organizational Behavior – Utilizing Human Resources*. New Jersey: Prentice Hall, 1969.

25   Wulff E. Therapeutische Gemeinschaften In: Kisker KP, Freyberger H, Rose HK, Wulff E (eds), *Psychiatrie, Psychosomatik, Psychotherapie*, 4th edn. Stuttgart/New York: Thieme, 1987; pp. 411–16.

26   Hale A. Sociometric elements related to the 'Healing Circle' as presented by John Mosher. *J Group Psychother Psychodrama Sociometry* 1987; **40**:115–18.

27   Mosher J. *The Healing Circle: Myth, Ritual and Therapy*. Seattle: Blue Sky Counselor, 1990.

28   Arnetz B, Blomkvist V. Leadership, mental health, and organizational efficacy in health care organizations. Psychosocial predictors of healthy organizational development based on prospective data from four different organizations. *Psychother Psychosom* 2007; **76**:242–8.

29   Herrman H, Trauer T, Warnock J *et al*. The roles and relationships of psychiatrists and other service providers in mental health services. Royal Australian and New Zealand College of Psychiatrists. Position Statement 47b. Available at: www.ranzcp.org/Files/ranzcp-attachments/Resources/College_Statements/Position_Statements/ps47b-pdf.aspx[accessed 4 April 2013].

30   Corrigan PW, Garman AN. Transformational and transactional leadership skills for mental health teams. *Comm Mental Health J* 1999; **35**:301–12.

31   Corrigan PW, Garman AN, Lam C, Leary M. What mental health teams want in their leaders. *Adm Policy Ment Health* 1998; **26**:111–23.

32   Fichtner CG, Hardy D, Patel M *et al*. A self-assessment program for multidisciplinary mental health teams. *Psychiatr Serv* 2001; **52**:1352–7.

33   Beinecke RH. Leadership training programs and competencies for mental health, health, public administration, and business in seven countries. International Initiative for Mental Health Leadership, 2009. Available at: http://www.iimhl.com/IIMHLUpdates/20090213.pdf [accessed 4 April 2013].

34   Corrigan PW, Lickey SE, Campion JF *et al*. Mental health team leadership and consumer's satisfaction and quality of life. *Psychiatr Serv* 2000; **51**:781–5.

35   Wells R, Jinnett K, Alexander J *et al*. Team leadership and patient outcomes in US psychiatric treatment settings. *Soc Sci Med* 2006; **62**:1840–52.

36   Belbin M. *Team Roles at Work*, 2nd edn. Oxford: Butterworth Heinemann, 2010.
37   Gellert M, Nowak C. *Teamarbeit – Teamentwicklung – Teamberatung. Ein Praxisbuch für die Arbeit mit Teams*. Meezen: Limmer Verlag, 2007.
38   Carpenter J, Schneider J, Brandon T *et al.* Working in multidisciplinary community mental health teams: the impact on social workers and health professionals of integrated mental health care. *Br J Soc Work* 2003; **33**:1081–103.
39   Malik F. *Führen, Leisten, Leben – wirksames Management für eine neue Zeit*. Frankfurt: Campus Verlag, 2006.
40   Buchanan D. *The Development of Job Design Theories and Techniques*. New York: Greenwood Publishing Group Inc., 1979.
41   Sauter D. Teamarbeit: In: : Sauter D, Abderhalden C, Needham I, Wolff S (eds), *Lehrbuch Psychiatrische Pflege*. Bern: Verlag Hans Huber, 2011; pp. 254–69.
42   Gottfried K, Petitjean S, Petzold H. Supervision in der psychiatrie – eine multicenterstudie (schweiz). In: Pethold H, Schigl B, Fischer M, Höfner C (eds), *Supervision auf dem Prüfstand. Wirksamkeit, Forschung, Anwendungsfelder, Innovation*. Opladen: Leske & Budrich, 2003; pp. 299–334.
43   DRV Deutsche Rentenversicherung Bund. Rentenversicherung in Zeitreihen – Ausgabe 2010. Sonderausgabe der DRV – DRV-Schriften Band 22. Available at: http://www.deutsche-rentenversicherung.de/SharedDocs/de/Inhalt/04_Formulare_Publikationen/03_publikationen/Statistiken/Broschueren/rv_in_zeitreihen_pdf.html?nn=28150[accessed 4 April 2013].
44   BKK. Gesundheitsreport 2010. Gesundheit in einer älter werdenden Gesellschaft. Available at: http://www.bkk.de/fileadmin/user_upload/PDF/Arbeitgeber/gesundheitsreport/BKK_Gesundheitsreport_2010.pdf[accessed 4 April 3013].

Chapter 10

Coaching and Mentoring

Rebecca Viney and Denise Harris

Introduction

Coaching and mentoring have been used in the commercial sector for many years and are increasingly being used in healthcare to support and develop leaders. The development of local and national schemes to train coaches and increase coaching capacity for healthcare professionals is supported by the National Health Service Leadership Academy[1] and by initiatives such as the London Deanery Coaching and Mentoring Service.[2]

Good Medical Practice guidelines published by the General Medical Council identify that coaching and mentoring are essential to support and develop good practice:

> *You should be willing to find and take part in structured support opportunities . . . (for example, mentoring). You should do this when you join an organisation and whenever your role changes significantly throughout your career.*
>
> *You should be willing to take on a mentoring role for more junior doctors and other healthcare professionals.[3]*

In addition, the Foundation Programme Curriculum includes specific references to the importance of developing mentoring and coaching skills:

> Foundation doctors will be expected to acquire and develop the skills needed to deliver . . . mentoring effectively.
>
> Foundation doctors . . . need to understand the underlying principles of coaching and theory of feedback (e.g. Pendleton model).[4]

This chapter will examine these concepts and explore their application for leaders in psychiatry.

Definitions

It is important when defining coaching and mentoring to differentiate them from other development roles such as patronage, appraisal, educational supervision or line management. It is not teaching, telling, advising or instructing. Neither is it counselling nor therapy although the process of coaching and mentoring may identify the need for this.

Leadership in Psychiatry, First Edition. Edited by Dinesh Bhugra, Pedro Ruiz and Susham Gupta.
© 2013 John Wiley & Sons, Ltd. Published 2013 by John Wiley & Sons, Ltd.

It should be acknowledged that the precise definitions and use of the terms coaching and mentoring will vary. The activity called coaching in one organization will be called mentoring in another. Part of the reason for this is historical use of the words and their implied meaning. However, they share a common set of core skills and those offering coaching or mentoring will need to demonstrate a common set of qualities (Boxes 10.1 and 10.2).

Box 10.1   Core skills of coaches and mentors

Active listening – This is the ability to engage with and respond to what the client is saying. Attending to what is being said and managing distractions.

Observation – The client will at times display much of what they are thinking or feeling by their body language. It is essential that the coach is able to notice this and in particular when there is a mismatch between what is being said and the non-verbal cues that are being displayed.

Questioning – This is the ability to use questions to help the client to develop their thinking and to explore the issue or topic in depth.

Challenge – The mentor needs to be able to challenge the client's thinking. This may be done through questioning but also through observation and comment.

Feedback – Providing specific and constructive feedback is a necessary part of helping a client to develop.

Reflection – The coach needs to practise reflection and to foster a reflective perspective in their client.

Box 10.2   Qualities of coaches and mentors

A high level of self-awareness – It is essential that a coach is aware of his or her own reactions and weaknesses in order to manage the impact of these on the coach-client relationship. It is one of the reasons that supervision is essential.

A genuine interest in others – The focus of the discussion will be on the client's issues or goals. The mentor therefore needs to have a passion for helping other people to develop.

An open and approachable style – The client needs to feel they can trust the coach and feel safe to say what they really think. Creating that rapport is central to successful coaching.

Humility – An excellent coach will never consider that they have learnt everything. They will always be looking for new challenges for themselves. They will foster a relationship of equals with their clients.

Integrity – The client needs to feel they can believe in and trust the coach. There has to be a degree of transparency with no hidden agenda.

Confidentiality – There should be an explicit commitment to confidentiality.

Connor and Pokora[5] have offered a useful definition that emphasizes the similarities between coaching and mentoring: 'Coaching and mentoring are learning relationships which help people to take charge of their own development, to release their potential and to achieve results which they value.' The difference between coaching and mentoring usually relates to the focus and relationship between the coach/mentor and their client. The client's reason for seeking help will determine the most appropriate format.

Coaching and mentoring could therefore be seen as being part of the same continuum. The objective of both is to facilitate clients so that they are able to develop personally and professionally. For the purpose of this chapter, the terms coach(ing) and mentor(ing) will be used interchangeably. Those receiving the coaching or mentoring will be referred to as clients.

Using coaching and mentoring

All coaching relationships begin with a contract or agreement. This provides both parties with the opportunity to explore the purpose, practicalities, preferred styles and boundaries of the relationship. It helps to ensure that the relationship stays within the framework of the coaching and is a safe and effective place for the client and the coach. It is also an opportunity for both parties to decide if the arrangement will work for them or if it would be more appropriate to make alternative arrangements. Underlying all forms of coaching are certain principles, which generate its powerful impact (Box 10.3).

Box 10.3   Six principles of coaching and mentoring (Rogers, 2008[6])

1   The client is resourceful
2   The coach's role is to develop the client's resourcefulness, it is not about giving advice
3   Coaching addresses the whole person, past, present and future
4   The client sets the agenda
5   The coach and the client are equals
6   Coaching is about change

The sessions follow a format or structure so that the conversation has a focus and includes:

- a topic or goal that has prompted the request for coaching;
- exploration of that topic or goal;
- identified actions.

There are a number of models that support this structure. These will be explored in more detail later in the chapter.

In order to be effective, it is essential that the potential mentor possesses the qualities that are identified in Box 10.2. In addition, they will need to attend training that addresses the core skills in Box 10.1. It should be acknowledged that many of those qualities and skills are also essential in a clinical context for psychiatrists in order to engage with and treat their patients. However, the skills are used in a different way, the client is not 'broken' in any way and it should not be assumed that an expert clinician can automatically be a mentor.

The challenge for clinicians who become mentors is in shifting the focus of the conversation and in changing from being a problem-solver and advice-giver to a facilitator of thinking:

> A mentor does not give advice, rather helps the mentee to weigh up situations, through a process of reflection, questions, challenge and feedback allowing the mentee to come to a decision themselves. It is crucial to remember that in any mentoring relationship it is the mentee who drives the agenda, not the mentor.[7]

An important aspect of successful coaching is the ability of the coach and client to be able to develop a relationship. When it goes well this has an impact on the effectiveness of the intervention:

'I was fortunate to have met a mentor who I went along well with, and it was a right match. It has helped me significantly as mentioned above, and I'd value its contribution always in life . . . If you could find the right match, then mentoring/coaching can be life-changing.' Client

'I felt very lucky with the choice of my mentor, as I thought we were a very good fit.' Client

However, if this does not happen, the mentoring will not be successful:

'. . . I've heard negative comments from a few colleagues, which I believe were due to the fact they could not get on with their mentor, due to the personality differences.' Client

The impact of coaching and mentoring

The London Deanery recognized the potential of coaching and mentoring to support and develop doctors and dentists in order to improve the quality of patient care. The Mentoring Service (now called the Coaching and Mentoring Service) was launched in May 2008. The purpose underpinning this launch was to release the potential and enhance the careers of doctors and dentists in London in line with evidence-based best practice in coaching and mentoring.[8] The model that was used in this instance included a number of aspects essential to ensure a high quality and effective mentoring service:

- Mentors' training should be at least 3 days' duration and include observed practice and assessment of skills.
- Mentors must participate in continuing professional development and access supervision for their mentoring.
- Clients should be able to choose a mentor from any field of medicine, preferably not their own. This provides an opportunity to meet with an independent colleague who would offer an objective or alternative perspective and thus avoid the risk of collusion over the issues discussed.

The illustrations below indicate that the skills of coaching can be used in a variety of ways to support clinical leadership. The feedback is from coaches and clients who have accessed the London Deanery service.

The leader may be in receipt of coaching as a way of supporting them to manage effectively. Those who were new to consultant posts found it particularly helpful:

'I was very reassured that many people go through similar episodes of career confusion at the start of their consultant career.' Client

Alternatively, they may decide to train as a coach in order to support others or to use a coaching style to influence the culture of their team. The impact of the coaching will extend beyond that of the leader as they use the skills in other aspects of their work:

'Doing mentoring has changed the way I talk to people – patients, juniors, colleagues. Even my family has noticed!' Mentor

When asked why they had decided to train as coaches, the responses included the following:

'I decided to become a coach after I heard about coaching from a psychiatric colleague. I liked the idea of learning about a technique that is very forward focused and that attempts to change important things in someone's life.' Mentor

'I applied as a result of the failure of MTAS system, and was one of the first to be trained to help the "MTAS Victims". I thought I may become more skilled in helping Doctors in Difficulty.' Mentor

Their expectations of what the training would offer them indicated that they wanted to help others but also that they suspected it had other implications:

'I expected to find it a useful technique in my own life. It helped me make a difficult transition in my own working life.' Mentor

These examples indicate a strong interest in others and a desire to support development of their colleagues. However, the impact that it had often took them by surprise:

'I was amazed at the power of the mentoring relationship, the ability [. . .] of mentees to develop, change [. . .] as a result of reflection and facilitation.' Mentor

Those who decided to train as mentors also found that as well as being surprised by how powerful the tools were to effect change, they benefited directly from learning the new skills. It even changed their practice:

'I think this was particularly powerful for me as a psychiatrist as I stopped trying to problem solve and cure but instead was able to use the skills I learnt to help patients and mentees reflect, focus and make their own decisions. Personally at times of difficulty at work I have been able to ask myself whose responsibility this was, how much energy did I have and what was I going to do about the difficulty.' Mentor

'I now start every consultation with a question, "What would you like to get out of this meeting?" and use the appointment to come to an agreed treatment plan which I record for myself, the patient and the other concerned clinicians.' Mentor

'I felt empowered to make big changes in my working life and within my service.' Mentor

With regard to the impact for them as clinicians and leaders, they also identified a number of key factors and new insights:

'To understand that everyone has potential and the role of a leader is to allow staff to recognize and develop that potential.' Mentor

'It will make me more comfortable in mentoring juniors as it allows you to allow them to make decisions (and mistakes!). This is more in keeping with my personality, but previously I had felt it necessary to be more "intrusive" in my supervisory style. It is a relief to know that a more relaxed mode of supervision is likely to work better.' Mentor

Case Study 10.1 illustrates the personal impact that becoming a coach can have. It describes the challenge of reframing existing knowledge and expertise that one clinician experienced as she went through her training.

Potential clients may not fully understand what the process is for or how it might help them. The London Deanery Service noted that applicants mainly expected help and guidance from their mentor with a few expecting advice or practical help.[9]

'Originally I had quite different expectations as I hadn't read [the information] *properly! So, although I was up for it and aware that on some level I "needed it" I wasn't sure what I expected so went along with an open mind. I was at a crossroads really, and was thinking about the future and the next step of my career/life. I think I thought it* [the content] *would be more about work but actually it was about me.'* Client

'I did not have specific expectations, but was curious about the process. I was particularly keen on learning more about coaching/mentoring from a role model perspective.' Client

Some come knowing that they needed an external perspective to help them obtain a balanced view of their world and how they might manage the challenges they face:

'At a time of decisions and stress in work, I was looking for an independent sounding board to my concerns. My aim was to be able to distance myself from stress thus gaining perspective on my situation at the time.' Client

In particular having the opportunity to discuss things with someone who was from a different specialty and perhaps able to offer a more objective perspective was attractive:

'I was going through a difficult phase of my professional life, so my expectation was to seek an independent professional senior support and help to find my way through it. I also wanted an outside independent expert (who's not from my specialty) to have an overview of my overall performance to date, and then be able to give some guidance for my future plans.' Client

Once they have experienced mentoring, the impact on mentees can be significant particularly with regard to their self-awareness and their clinical interventions:

'It has helped me increase my reflective thinking and enhance emotional intelligence, which has and will continue to help me in working with patients as I'm more aware of myself, my strengths and my limitations. So it has given me a window through to myself. It has boosted my self-confidence in working with patients, and where it has made me realize that I'm a good doctor; it has also pointed out to me the constant need for continued professional development.' Client

'I have been feeling more positive about my work and the balance that I have in my life, which means that I can give more to patients.' Client

'I want to think I have become more reflective in my practice.' Client

It also has an impact on their work and interactions with colleagues:

'I am trying to apply some of the skills learned by role-modelling in my supervision of junior doctors. I have started to use different devices for planning and time management. I am feeling more confident about my choices of professional development.' Client

When the clients were asked what the mentor had done that helped they cited the skills that they had observed:

'He was the perfect sounding board! He facilitated the space for me to verbalize my concerns and listen to myself. This helped me validate my worries and gain perspective on them thus making them easier to live with.' Client

'[N] was neutral, unbiased and supportive, though not directive.' Client

'Listened, and reflected back what it sounded like to her – to think about what I was really saying.' Client

'She was very good at giving me feedback – I was particularly impressed by her integrating verbal and non-verbal feedback.' Client

A number of them particularly appreciated the amount of challenge they experienced or even wanted more challenge:

'It was very useful and enjoyable at the same time. I was not just blandly reassured but was challenged and made to think about myself – I did not feel criticised. I felt supported and encouraged.' Client

'The balance between being supportive and non-directive is delicate; I would like her to be even a bit more directive and critical and point out exactly where things could have been improved and what could be done in the future.' Client

---

Case Study 10.1

I first came into contact with coaching in autumn 2007 when I attended a 4-day training course provided by the London Deanery. In this my first exposure to coach training I was uncomfortably aware of the enormous challenge which it would present to my own established professional stance and identity, since I have trained and worked clinically as a psychoanalyst and psychoanalytic psychotherapist for most of my professional life. I thus approached coaching with caution and a quite conscious ambivalence, anxious about the emotional, intellectual and cognitive dissonance that involvement in this new area would generate for me personally.

I decided to respond to the challenge by immersing myself as fully as possible in every learning opportunity I could access, as a way of dealing with my own initial resistance and scepticism. In doing so, I was able to develop a range of new skills specific to coaching and add them to some of my relevant pre-existing skills, while retaining a capacity to differentiate each of these related but substantially different fields of practice.

I now feel confident in being able to practise both as a coach and coaching supervisor and am committed to continue my own development in both these areas. Regular coaching practice, close attention to feedback and my own reflective practice, in combination with my supervision have been the most formative and essential elements in the process.

Dr Nollaig Whyte

Coaching for health

There is a growing interest in the use of coaching within a clinical context and some coaches have instinctively used their coaching skills with patients as described above. Similar approaches such as Motivational Interviewing[10] and Solution-Focused Therapy[11] are already in use and there is some overlap between these and Health Coaching.

> Health coaching can be defined as helping patients gain the knowledge, skills, tools and confidence to become active participants in their care so that they can reach their self-identified health goals.[12]

These approaches are based on compelling evidence that taking a collaborative approach hugely increases the likelihood of behavioural change, whereas approaches based on telling, even where the teller is an acknowledged expert, have been shown to be largely ineffective:[7]

> Doing things to people instead of with them can be profoundly disempowering. It encourages patients to believe that professionals have all the answers and that they themselves lack relevant knowledge and skills, and hence have no legitimate role to play in decisions about their healthcare. Paternalism breeds dependency, encourages passivity and undermines people's capacity to look after themselves. It may appear benign, comfortable and reassuring, but it is a hazard to health.[13]

Case Study 10.2 illustrates how the approach works in practice and the impact it can have on patient outcomes.

Case Study 10.2

Liaison psychiatry setting – a male 20–25-year-old patient attended A&E after deliberate self-harm (OD) in a context of intermittent alcohol misuse to cope with social problems. Initially, patient thought his only way out of debt and job problems was to kill himself as perceived he had 'nothing to live for' and 'lack of control' but through coaching, with motivational interviewing style, patient decided he would address alcohol issues instead to achieve life aims of settling down with partner and earning decent income. What worked well here was my statement that we could just do a usual psych liaison risk assessment and refer him on to CMHT (thereby adding to his sense of lack of control), or we could do the consultation in a slightly different way where he might change his viewpoint. This was achieved in a 1 hour consultation in a busy A&E dept. Patient reportedly has engaged with local drug and alcohol service and not re-presented to A&E.

Diversity and equality

Another important aspect of mentoring is the opportunity it provides to address issues of diversity and equality. Professor David Clutterbuck offers the following observations about the impact of coaching on diversity:

> So much of the failure to tap into the diverse talent of employees comes down to institutionalised bias and largely unconscious barriers. Coaching and mentoring work to remove bias and reveal barriers, in several ways.

- They place people in psychologically safe situations, where they can have learning conversations with people, who they might otherwise only converse with in transactional ways.
- They help people position disadvantage.
- They help people build networks that expand the range of their career possibilities and make it possible to establish a more relevant, more visible track record.
- They help both parties in the learning relationship develop a greater appreciation of the value of diversity, both within the microcosm of their own relationship, but also within the organisation and society.
- The process of reflection gives people greater self-awareness and hence a greater appreciation of the great diversity that lies within themselves.

Professor David Clutterbuck (used with permission)

Models for coaching

There are a number of models that can be used to structure a coaching session. Coach training courses will incorporate one or more of these and the trainee coaches will be introduced to the framework whilst practising the skills they need to coach effectively. This section will outline three of the models that are currently taught.

The TGROW model

This is one of the best-known models for coaching. It is described in a number of publications and provides a simple structure for identifying and achieving goals as well as problem-solving. The acronym stands for a series of 'mini' conversations that are designed to help the client focus on achievable actions. Different writers have contributed to this model and there are several versions available.[14, 15] This version offers some alternative meanings for the letters (Box 10.4).

Box 10.4   The TGROW model

T – Theme or Topic: This stage is an exploration of what the client wants to focus on, how important and significant it is to them.

G – Goal: It is important to identify an outcome or what it is that would help the client to move forwards.

R – Reality: Identifying the limitations and restrictions the client is experiencing helps to clarify what it is that they need to address.

Options: This is the ideas stage. Ideas can be as imaginative and radical as the client wants.

W – Way Forward or Will: The Options then need to be converted into action steps that will take the client to their goal. The client also needs to identify their level of commitment to carrying out the actions.

Egan – the 'Skilled Helper' model

This model[16] has been developed over the past 30 years. The model and associated skills can be applied to coaching and mentoring and also in professional managerial and leadership roles. There are three stages in the model, each with associated tasks. The stages and tasks are designed to facilitate and enable change that the client values. Connor and Pokora[5] note that 'Egan has often stated that the model is for the client, not the client for the model' and they emphasize the importance of using it flexibly within a helping relationship characterized by respect, empathy and genuineness.

Stage one: The first stage helps the client to tell their story, to uncover any new perspectives and to focus on what will make a difference.

Stage two: The second stage helps the client to identify what they want and need in relation to the chosen aspect, and then to formulate a goal to which they can commit.

Stage three: The third stage helps the client to discover how to achieve their goal by developing and then choosing strategies for action and a realistic plan.

The CLEAR model

Peter Hawkins developed this model in the early 1980s to train coaches and coach supervisors.[17] The structure can be used in a variety of coaching contexts and works well both with individuals and when coaching teams. It is similar to GROW in that it provides a structure for coaching; however, it includes an overview of the session and incorporates the whole coaching process (Box 10.5).

Box 10.5   The CLEAR model (Hawkins and Smith, 2013[17])

Contract – Establishing expectations, boundaries, ground rules and roles

Listen – Using Active Listening skills, mirroring, reframing and making new connections to let the client know the coach has 'got their reality'

Explore – Through questioning and reflection generating new insights and options for action for the client

Action – The client chooses a way forward and agrees the first steps. This is then rehearsed live in the room

Review – This includes when the actions will be reviewed as well as an opportunity for feedback to the coach on what the client found difficult and what they would like to be different in future sessions

---

'The time for mentoring is now'

Those who deliver healthcare in the twenty-first century do so against a backdrop of constant challenge and change.[18] Working as a clinical leader in this environment requires significant levels of resilience, innovation and adaptability. This means that identifying and accessing support is more important than at any other time: 'The time for mentoring in medicine is now'.[19] The potential impact of coaching and mentoring for both clinicians and their patients can be seen from the examples above. They are powerful and useful tools for leaders that can positively impact on personal effectiveness and interactions with colleagues as well as patients.

References

1   NHS Leadership Academy. Supporting local capability. Available at: http://www. leadershipacademy.nhs.uk/areas-of-work/supporting-local-capability [accessed 4 April 2013].

2   Viney R, Harris D. Mentoring supervision for doctors and dentists in a National Health Service (NHS) Deanery. In: Bachkirova T, Jackson P, Clutterbuck D (eds), *Coaching and Mentoring Supervision Theory and Practice*. Maidenhead: Open University Press, 2011; pp. 251–7.

3   General Medical Council. *Good Medical Practice*. Manchester: General Medical Council, 2013.

4   Academy of Medical Royal Colleges. *Foundation Programme Curriculum*. London: Academy of Royal Medical Colleges, 2012.

5   Connor M, Pokora J. *Coaching and Mentoring at Work. Developing Effective Practice*, 2nd edn. Maidenhead: Open University Press, 2012.

6   Rogers J. *Coaching Skills – A Handbook*, 2nd edn. Maidenhead: Open University Press, 2008.

7   London Deanery Coaching and Mentoring. Website: http://mentoring.londondeanery.ac. uk/our-scheme/mentees/introduction-to-mentoring.

8   Viney R, Paice E. *The First Five Hundred: A Report on London Deanery's Coaching and Mentoring Service 2008–2010*. London: London Deanery, 2010.

9   Viney R, Paice E. *Reaching Out: A Report on London Deanery's Coaching and Mentoring Service 2010–2012*. London: London Deanery, 2012.

10   Miller WR, Rollnick S. *Motivational Interviewing: Preparing People for Change*. New York: Guilford Press, 2002.

11   Macdonald A. *Solution-Focused Therapy Theory, Research and Practice*. London: Sage Publications, 2007.

12   Bennett HD, Coleman EA, Parry C, Bodenheimer T, Chen EH. Health Coaching for Patients. *Family Practice Management*. American Academy of Family Physicians, 2010. Available at: http://www.aafp.org/fpm/20100900/.

13   Coulter A. *Engaging Patients in Healthcare*. Maidenhead: Open University Press, 2011.

14   Whitmore J. *Coaching for Performance – The New Edition of the Practical Guide*. London: Nicholas Brealey, 1996.

15   Downey M. *Effective Coaching: Lessons from the Coach's Couch*. New York: Texere/Thomson, 2003.

16   Egan G. *The Skilled Helper*, 9th edn. Belmont, CA: Brooks/Cole, 2010.

17   Hawkins P, Smith N. *Coaching, Mentoring and Organizational Consultancy*, 2nd edn. Maidenhead: McGraw-Hill/Open University Press, 2013.

18   Steven A, Oxley J, Fleming WG. Mentoring for NHS doctors: perceived benefits across the personal-professional interface. *J Roy Soc Med* 2008; **101**:552–7.

19   Abbasi K. Mentoring and the meaning of soul. *J Roy Soc Med* 2008; **101**:523.

Chapter 11

Leadership and Factions

Zoë K. Reed

Imagine you are in the position of your fellow consultant described in Case Study 11.1 – how would you cope? What leadership skills and competencies would you need to exercise once the situation had arisen – and what might you have exercised to prevent it arising in the first place?

Case Study 11.1

A consultant psychiatrist successfully secured a clinical director post following a restructure to bring clinical, academic and managerial leadership into a shared leadership model at the top of the service. The newly appointed top leadership team had the task of bringing together a number of specialisms from across the Trust, to enable the development of standardized clinical pathways of evidence-based interventions operating consistently across the Trust. The work involved the redesign/realignment of existing teams and services. This was a difficult task and it had to be completed in a context where a lot of money had also to be removed from the system because of the annual hospital-initiated Cost Improvement Programme (CIP) and commissioner-initiated Quality, Innovation, Productivity and Prevention (QIPP) programme requirements.

The Trust had staff and service user engagement processes and these were used to develop the revised service model. The next stage was to issue a formal staff consultation paper for those staff affected by the proposals. However, by this point, time was pressing because expenditure needed to be reduced to match the reduced Trust budget allocation. Unfortunately the negotiations with the commissioners were not finally concluded and the figures on the amount of QIPP reduction required had not been agreed. The decision was therefore taken to proceed with staff consultation but to frame the formal consultation paper on the basis of the financially worst-case scenario.

The staff response to the formal restructure proposal was to utilize some personal connections and involve the local overview and scrutiny committee as well as their professional bodies. The scrutiny committee chair called in the proposal and scrutinized the process of engagement and decision-making by the Trust in generating the proposal. He was clear from the outset that it was not the role of the scrutiny committee to determine what structures or resourcing were appropriate for a particular service. It was, however, their role to ensure that all necessary engagement and analytical processes had been carried out in coming to the decision that the proposed service redesign was the correct one. The overarching aim of the scrutiny process was to ensure that there would be no detriment to the access or quality of service available to their local citizens.

During the ensuing formal and informal meetings and committees, fault was found with every step of the Trust's processes! The NHS policy requirement to consult and involve

---

Leadership in Psychiatry, First Edition. Edited by Dinesh Bhugra, Pedro Ruiz and Susham Gupta.
© 2013 John Wiley & Sons, Ltd. Published 2013 by John Wiley & Sons, Ltd.

patients/service users was defined by the committee as those currently receiving service (as opposed to representatives/former users that the Trust had involved). The scrutiny committee was not convinced that the requirement to analyse the potential impact on people with any of the nine protected characteristics under the Equalities Act had been fully evaluated prior to decision-making. Because the service changes would affect Trust services in three London boroughs – three lots of scrutiny processes were invoked!

Within the Trust this external battering was causing concern. The Trust's reputation was being damaged by its inability to convince the scrutiny committees that it was implementing processes correctly. This was being played out publicly and was picked up in the local press. The Trust's reputation was also being damaged as a management system that could not engage with and 'control' its senior medics who chose to air their disagreement with Trust's and Commissioners' redesign plans in public. A great deal of senior time was involved in further discussions and consultations with staff, service users and voluntary organizations as a way of responding to the scrutiny committees concerns. The delay in implementing the service change in question was also leading to under-achievement of the planned expenditure reduction. This impacted the Board's confidence in the ability of Trust management to deliver the challenging scale of service reductions required to hit the budgets set in the Annual Plan. This had been submitted to the Foundation Trust regulator, Monitor, and was subject to quarterly reporting on progress.

One lesson was that in undertaking their planning the Team had not considered the power that an alliance between some staff, professional bodies, local politicians and service users could have. Another was about tone of communication – some councillors felt there was a dismissive approach in their early meetings. They felt that there was a tokenistic response to the public sector duties to effectively consult. Finally they were of the opinion that the Trust was not implementing the equalities legislation fully and were in their view (not shared by the Trust!) outwith the law in a number of technical areas. This had the effect of strengthening the resolve of the councillors to continue to use their scrutiny powers to challenge 'the NHS'.

Another aspect that had not been factored into the planning was that the councillors used this opportunity to demonstrate political differences. The committee was, as with all local authorities, politically balanced and comprised members drawn from both governing and opposition parties. The majority parties on the councils in the Trust's catchment area were made up from those in opposition. This case provided an opportunity to demonstrate fault with central government policies. The NHS was a particular bugbear for the councillors because although there were technically no reductions in expenditure in the NHS, the impact of, for example, inflation and rising cost of technology meant that there was a reduction in available funds. The councillors wanted to encourage local services to break ranks and 'admit' to cuts! The local authorities had had to implement massive cuts in their services and, because the local government leadership was from the opposition party, not the party of central government, they were free to criticize the government when carrying out their service cuts. In contrast, the Trust's commissioners insisted that the collective (commissioner and provider) stance had to be that services were simply being redesigned to improve Quality, Innovation, Productivity and Prevention (QIPP).

Being constantly under attack from multiple different interest groups proved extremely taxing for the consultant concerned! Nevertheless, he and the top leadership team were able to negotiate a way forward with the commissioners and the three London boroughs' scrutiny committees – who themselves did not agree on every point – and demonstrate that the Trust was willing to learn and revise its ideas in the light of ongoing engagement with widening groups of people.

The Team rapidly learned to adapt their style to the circumstances. They applied a number of the essential skills when leading strategic change to get things back on track. The impact of the faction fighting was that implementation of the service redesign was put back by nearly 6 months. However, the Trust learned a number of important lessons, which influenced their forward planning approaches significantly for the future.

This chapter is about how consultant psychiatrists have a crucial role to play in dealing with faction fights – such as those described in Case Study 11.1. The voice of the senior clinician is a powerful one across both the internal and external systems, and used judiciously can ensure successful navigation of such complex and multifaceted terrains. If faction fights are to be minimized, and mitigated when they do occur, then the consultant psychiatrist needs to develop and maintain a culture of openness, trust and partnership working; and this is in a context where sometimes others do not seem to be operating from those same essential principles!

So what might the skills be that will help consultants navigate the faction fighting and turn it to best advantage for their service and patients? What skills might they employ to prevent or minimize the faction fighting in the first place? The rest of this chapter will discuss a number of core skills that are essential when leading strategic change – which can often lead to faction fights of all kinds and at every level! The core skills we will examine are those that will enable you as a consultant psychiatrist to:

- See the benefit of using planned political interventions.
- Lead your service from the understanding that it is within a system.
- Make best use of time and relationships.
- Develop the most effective personal communication style.

The benefit of using planned political interventions

At the risk of stating the obvious, we have *faction fights,* the subject of this chapter, because people have different and competing interests and organizations and care systems/pathways are *not* places of unity! David Butcher contends that many managers and leaders struggle unnecessarily because they take a *rational mindset* worldview that denies the reality of *organizational politics*. Effective leaders need to keep both perspectives fully in mind and use both to guide their plans and actions. Political interventions include harnessing the power of alternative views and competing interests and to do that in a way that enables people to feel they have been part of co-creating the final solution.

The problem with this approach is that whilst it is pretty obviously the right way to go about things, it is often considered in traditional management terms to be unnecessary. The traditional rational mindset assumes that there is one right way, usually defined by those at the top of the hierarchy, and that provided it is clearly explained everyone will agree with the proposal and implement it! Organizations frequently work hard to embed the idea of a sense of unity and hierarchical control. This then means that plurality of interests and self-interest in particular is viewed as illegitimate, and those who think differently, particularly if it obviously contains components of self-interest, are considered 'off message' and obstructive.

This author argues that it is possible to see and use politics constructively and draws on David Butcher's work to explain what is meant by this approach. Despite the conventional view that 'politics is a dirty word', political processes are in fact concerned with *respecting* differences and reconciling between them to generate the best options. Butcher uses four core ideas as the basis for his book and argues that they are an essential way of thinking for effective managers, and I would contend that he offers a helpful perspective for consultants as leaders too. In drawing out points from his work, therefore, I have sometimes taken the liberty of substituting the word *leadership* for *management* where I think the points will be helpful for consultant leaders in thinking about how to tackle faction fights! Where it doesn't make sense I have left the word management in the text and invite consultant psychiatrists still to see the point as relevant to their learning.

The four core ideas about using politics that will help consultants frame their approach to the leadership task in tackling faction fights are:

- The centrality of politics to organizations and leading.
- The principled use of power.
- Balancing individual and organizational motives.
- The redefinition of leadership work.

The centrality of politics to organizations and leading

Butcher contends that organizations should more realistically be perceived of as collections of competing and mutual interest groups. And that because politics is the process through which differing perspectives are reconciled – then the use of politics when seeking to achieve change and formulate strategy is clearly *the* way of going about things. The rational mindset is sometimes insufficient to secure the outcomes wanted. In these circumstances, lobbying, positioning and behind-the-scenes alliance building are the key political activities that will need to be part of your repertoire as a successful leader. Leaders who take a political perspective will recognize that it is a good idea to foster a culture where different perspectives are welcomed. Provided the different perspectives are well intentioned, and articulated clearly, then encouraging active debate around them should result in the creation of the best solution to the change proposed. And, crucially, the creation of that solution will be seen as a joint activity.

This more political approach to leading change builds on the common sense fact that people are much more likely to be motivated to make things happen if they can see a personal relevance for doing so. In the rational model of top-down change it is unlikely that such elements would be factored into the selection of options. Quite the reverse – the need for change would usually be attributed to altruism. For example, a service change will be described as being purely in the interests of patients when in reality it serves other organizational interests (e.g. saving money), and it might be better to find a way in which it also serves the interests of the staff required to make the change (e.g. offers of more flexible ways of working or greater opportunity for academic pursuits), so that the personal relevance is evident for the implementers of the change too.

The principled use of power

Butcher argues that there have always been those who pursue power through political means – but the problem is that it is seen as being in pursuit of personal interests and conducted in a way that is seen as an abuse of power. The issue here is that within organizations, political work is not seen as legitimate and mainstream and therefore those who see the need to operate in this way do not get their voice heard when *designing* organizational change processes. Crucially, consultant leaders need to ensure that they are exercising *constructive* politics and are sure that they demonstrate in themselves and can see in others a fair balance between individual and organizational motives. Provided that is the case then political perspectives can be considered a legitimate part of the leadership strategy.

Balancing individual and organizational motives

Who defines what is in the best interests of the organization and how the process is conducted to reach that decision are the crucial factors here. Consultant leaders need to recognize that self-interest is inevitable but to ensure that it is balanced with organizational interests. Provided there is that self-conscious balance and a responsible use of power then operating politically becomes feasible.

As Butcher says, *constructive politicians* need to be able to create a meaningful justification for their agendas. He commends that the justification must be built on a clear understanding of the key business issues to be tackled and how *progress on these will be enabled through influential relationships.* I have emphasized the latter part of his advice because I would add that in the complexity of our healthcare system we need to much more explicitly think through how our plans (a) might impact and (b) might be perceived by other key players in our system – and we need to do this at the planning stage before we take the first move!

The redefinition of leadership work

Being very clear exactly what the task is that is required of leaders will be crucial in helping them decide, for example, on the relative balance of the use of their time. Some think that the currency of leadership is attention so it is vital that consultant leaders focus their time judiciously.

Butcher argues that a *constructive political* mindset redefines the basics of day-to-day managerial activity because it focuses attention on the way that the rules, roles, procedures and accountabilities are held in place. For example, in the rational model, decision-making is largely a function of hierarchy – that is, managers are given different levels of authority for decision-making. Within healthcare the current example of this is to put clinicians in charge of clinical decision-making; hence the introduction of Clinical Commissioning Groups, where groups of GPs will make the commissioning decisions, and of Service Line Management, where clinicians will be in charge of making decisions within service provision.

In Butcher's view, politically capable managers are much more critical of rational processes of corporate decision-making. In my experience, by this definition, all consultant psychiatrists operate from a political mindset! They are usually well aware that power is not always congruent with formal authority (see also Chapter 3) and will seize the opportunity to make their preferred initiatives happen regardless of accepted ways of working. However, in the main, political approaches are not accepted as a legitimate way of behaving within healthcare. Therefore it can sometimes seem to others that the psychiatrist is operating from a self-interested perspective rather than in the best interests of patients, the organization *and* self.

Butcher describes a number of activities and approaches that leaders will use when they operate from a *constructive political* mindset. Operating in the way described protects the leader from accusations of operating from self-interest. These include prioritizing working with personal agendas and building relationships and networking at all levels within the organization. This is in contrast to those who focus their time and energy on the top of the hierarchy. The *constructive political* leader will encourage debate and challenge at all levels, take an inclusive approach and involve as many people as possible. They will provide others with space and autonomy to experiment. In this way leaders will be stimulating bottom-up change and demonstrating an even-handed way of operating that will make all staff feel like they have a contribution to make to the organization.

These ideas are helpful in dispelling a number of myths about what constructive 'political' behaviours entail. In fact they are quite the reverse from the myth and are about democratizing organizations and increasing the involvement of many people in decision-making from all levels of the organization. The introduction of a constructive political approach within healthcare settings recognizes the limits of the rational, hierarchical mindset. It introduces more open and involving approaches – and argues that it is more likely that successful implementation of changes will be achieved precisely because a more political approach has been taken.

Lead your service from the understanding that it is within a system

In the business world there is an acceptance of the interdependence of organizations – both suppliers and competitors – and this has led to an increasing recognition that external stakeholders influence decision-making. Co-evolution between interdependent organizations is recognized as an acceptable development trajectory, and canny organizations are therefore constantly looking outward for both opportunities and threats. Public sector healthcare organizations are gradually becoming aware that they are not islands. However, both the size of the NHS and the commissioner/provider and primary/secondary/tertiary splits within the NHS has led many staff within it to think that the interdependence opportunities and threats are *between* organizations within the NHS. Organizations with this view can miss both opportunities and threats coming from beyond the NHS.

However, psychiatry is better placed than many other parts of healthcare to look beyond the NHS. This is because the delivery of effective healthcare for people requiring its intervention necessarily requires operating in a multi-agency context. Because it is necessary clinically for psychiatrists to be skilled in leading their service in the context that it is not an island – it is to be hoped that they can apply this approach and understanding to the process of change. Understanding that their service is connected through its people to any number of other systems that can influence positively or otherwise the chances of successful outcomes should help them in attuning their political skills and applying them to the design of service change processes.

It is possible, however, that a consultant's personal experience of being viewed as extremely powerful within the psychiatric healthcare system blinds them to recognizing that there are more powerful alliances at work that can jeopardize their plans. There is a danger that they do not apply knowledge that should be obvious to all community-based consultants, and instead assume that their hierarchical power clinically is sufficient to secure effective change, organizationally.

Because we provide services from within a connected system it is important to understand the players within the system and what their interests and agendas are. It is much easier to build relationships first based on a genuine interest in the other's issues and agendas and then return to that relationship for help to prevent faction fighting. The Chinese approach to doing business is to build the relationship first – and then see if there is some business that can be transacted. Taking this approach with our colleagues across the complex system within which we operate might stand us all in good stead.

Make best use of time and relationships

The *constructive political leadership* behaviours described above invite the consultant to think carefully about the best use of time and the most important relationships to be maintained. Constructive political behaviours become the new work of the healthcare leader – including the crucial activity of building connections and relationships outside formal arenas. All this takes time, of course, and that is time away from the clinical task. However, I would contend that the consultant is uniquely placed to build those crucial relationships and the trick therefore is to get the balance of time right.

Building and maintaining the right relationships can be most helpful in enabling the psychiatrist to move forwards on their plans without falling foul of faction fights. For example, consultants who informally briefed politicians outside public meetings, including inviting them in to view the services, experienced a much easier ride when they presented their proposals in formal settings such as council scrutiny committees. Similarly consultants who actively engage in the commissioning and contracting process are more likely to influence and shape the development of more realistic and implementable QIPP plans than those who don't.

This thinking also needs to be applied to internal stakeholders, namely staff and service users. Charles Handy, business and management commentator and author, invites us to think about staff as 'members of voluntary clubs' – a helpful metaphor for framing how to relate to them. If you want people to remain in your club and positively contribute then it is likely that you will prioritize time with them – whereas if you think about staff as 'human resources' without free will or choice you might make a different decision on balance of time. As with all initiatives involving staff, change programmes need to involve them as people and in an authentic way. So, for example, if you don't intend to change your mind then be honest and inform staff of the plan – don't ask their opinion! There are many sound business reasons for securing greater levels of employee commitment. This requires careful thinking through so that it is carried out in a *constructively political* way. The approach needs to support the self-determination within organizational limits of all staff and to pay particular attention to those with hierarchical responsibilities as well as those on the front line.

Develop the most effective personal communication style

Earlier chapters in this book have outlined why *communicating* (talking and listening; see Chapters 2 and 3) is a crucial skill required for leadership. This chapter emphasizes its relevance particularly in the leadership task of preventing faction fights and mitigating their impact when they occur. It asks you to think about your communication style particularly in the context of how people in the many different factions with a stake in mental healthcare will view you. A thought to consider is that a communication style that gives confidence in the clinical setting may not be appropriate with, for example, councillors on the local council scrutiny committees.

The case study illustrates the need for consultant leaders to consider very carefully how others view them and the impact they are having in the context of the *stereotype of their profession*. Thinking very carefully about style, tone and approach is really important for any leader. For doctors, however, there is a need to overcome the stereotype prejudice that alleges that *all* doctors are arrogant! Whilst the stereotype is largely unfounded, an astute doctor will be aware that it is always possible that what they are saying is open to misinterpretation. It will not be possible to form effective relationships with those who can impact your plans if from their first encounter with you they think you are arrogant. This stereotype is compounded since some people view the NHS as a whole and Trusts in particular as monolithic and not prepared to listen or change. Again this will colour how the consultant psychiatrist is received.

Communication is a two-way process of course and it is equally likely to damage the chances of building effective relationships if we retain stereotype views about the person we are trying to connect with. Seeing people as unique individuals, all of whom could hinder or help your plans, is crucial. Dismissing groups of people as irrelevant is also a dangerous strategy – everyone is connected to everyone else by a few short steps!

Designing for successful implementation of change

This chapter is about 'faction fights' and how to deal with them when they occur. The more strategic approach, which is recommended here, is that consultants recognize that different viewpoints and personal self-interests are endemic in every organization and system including healthcare. They are asked to remember what they know from their clinical work – that healthcare organizations exist within a much wider system. Then armed with the knowledge of the contribution that a *constructive political* mindset could bring to increasing the chances of success, consultants are asked to design and plan change programmes so they are more smoothly implemented than the one described in the case study.

The first thing to apply is the simple understanding that the right to self-organize is something most people would prefer. For example, there is much talk of 'social enterprises' as being more successful in implementing change and delivering more effective and efficient healthcare – and these are characterized as (a) smaller and (b) run on a more democratic basis than most large NHS Foundation Trusts.

At the operational level, the establishment of service line management is often promoted. This is in recognition that the best, most cost-effective decisions will only be made if clinicians and managers who make the decisions are also responsible for implementing them. The devolution of power and responsibility is also recognized as valuable at the directorate or grouping level. In successful organizations, these then seek to operate together more like a holding company or federation rather than a uniform entity.

This thinking runs counter to the prevailing way of implementing change programmes where commissioners in conjunction with provider senior managers/clinicians decide what needs to be done and then tell those affected to implement it. Worse than that even, the process of consultation about the proposal being recommended is widely perceived as a sham because the experience is that very few changes are made to such proposals despite the meetings, events, emails and discussions that ensue.

With this in mind the democratization of organizational life is something that healthcare organizations should not only aspire to – but also put demonstrably into practice! The consultant who understands the importance of taking a *constructive politics* approach needs to engage in designing processes and systems that enable more people to feel psychological ownership of the organization and its activities and plans. Developing persuasive presentational skills will be crucial so that the leader is able to achieve collaborative outcomes through personal enthusiasm, informal suggestion, logical connections and legitimizing people disclosing their motives. Working in this way will enable the consultant psychiatrist to minimize the occurrence of faction fights and mitigate their impact when they do occur.

Acknowledgement

I attended the 2010/11 Business Leaders Programme at Cranfield Management School, Cranfield University, UK. This was an impressive programme aimed at CEOs from the commercial sector, which included input from David Butcher. I am grateful for his contribution to my learning and in this chapter have drawn heavily on his teaching and the accompanying book referenced below.

Box 11.1   Some tips for successfully avoiding destructive faction fights

- Identify from the outset all the factions that could impact your plans – remember everyone is only a few steps away from someone who could hinder your plans!
- Work out how to connect with and build effective relationships – and do it before you launch your plans. Remember the Chinese approach to business – build the relationships first.
- Be comfortable with using formal and informal methods to engage and influence – be authentic; be genuinely interested.
- If you want to secure a change – very early on in your timetable, run open processes based on democratic principles and invite all the factions to participate; don't dream up ideas in private and then 'consult' with no intention of changing them.

- Be sure in your heart that you do believe that everyone you are involving does have a real contribution to make and can help you with your plans.
- As you use informal political approaches look carefully at your motives and be sure you are behaving with integrity and are carefully balancing self-interest and organizational interests.
- Be very self-aware of how others might perceive you and any stereotypes they might have of your profession or organization – and counter it through your communication style.

Recognize that faction fighting is a fact of life – that it is healthy to have opposing views but there needs to be a clear process to reconcile them – and build the time needed into your project plan.

Further reading

Butcher D, Clarke M. *Smart Management – Using Politics in Organisations*. Basingstoke: Palgrave, 2001.

Chapter 12

Leadership Outside the Clinical Team

*Juan J. López-Ibor, María Inés López-Ibor and
Blanca Reneses*

Shared leadership

Sometimes and due to a variety of reasons it may be difficult for a single leader to be effective and versatile in all situations.[1] In shared leadership more than one person provides guidance to the group as a whole, which is why it is also known as group or distributed leadership. Shared leadership is a kind of situational style as opposed to formal leadership. Even highly hierarchical organizations sometimes need to be smart and clever enough to share out the leadership role (see Chapter 2). Besides, this kind of style brings a high degree of empowerment, which is why it is highly motivating for everybody,[2,3] especially in periods of change, as nowadays.

These shared leadership teams have specific characteristics such as awareness of unity on the part of all members, the ability to act together towards a common goal and the opportunity for everybody to contribute, and learn from and work with others. However, shared leadership has the drawback that it may encourage people to abrogate their responsibility to think and act themselves, safe in the knowledge that others will act for them.[3,4]

Extended teams in healthcare settings

Shared leadership is essential in the health sector where inter-professional collaboration, a variety of resources and settings, and services provided 24 hours a day all year round are the norm. Individual leadership is typically understood as a necessary skill to be exerted within a group – in our case, within an established and well-defined clinical team, with a leader and followers performing their particular functions. But inter-professional collaboration requires that 'extended teams' are put into action. An extended team would include other clinical services (i.e. geriatrics, pain clinics), relatives of patients (e.g. participating in group sessions), educators (e.g. sharing goals in the comprehensive growth process of children) and social services staff (in rehabilitation and reintegration of patients into society).

Leadership in Psychiatry, First Edition. Edited by Dinesh Bhugra, Pedro Ruiz and Susham Gupta.
© 2013 John Wiley & Sons, Ltd. Published 2013 by John Wiley & Sons, Ltd.

Psychiatric problems are extremely common among patients seen by other medical doctors due to many reasons: comorbidity, the consequences of the stress and suffering associated with becoming ill, misdiagnosis (i.e. masked pathology), etc. This aspect of clinical practice is more often than not overlooked or not catered for. Therefore it is extremely important to be aware of the presence of psychiatric problems and engage in the promotion of mental health and psychiatric prevention as part of the consultation-liaison activities, taking into consideration the many professionals involved in these situations (medical colleagues, nurses, psychologists, occupational therapists, patient and family organizations, community services, etc.).

Clinical process management

Our experience has made us advocates of clinical process management, as distinct from the current case management. A case manager is a coordinator of resources with the principal task of detecting missing appointments and causes for non-compliance. Process management considers a disorder or a set of disorders in a comprehensive, transversal, situation-adapted and ground-breaking way. It is comprehensive because it includes every aspect of the disorder involved in the vulnerability and triggering of the process and in the strategy to recover fully or as much as possible. It is transversal because it includes the participation of several kinds of professional, each from a different perspective. It is situation-adapted because clinical process management cannot be just 'imported' and implemented; it has to be developed and continually adapted to the local situation through intensive group discussions. It is ground-breaking because it calls for leaving behind the standpoints and values of the traditional hierarchy of professions and services.

The establishment of management of a clinical process requires a team, which can take up to one year to set up. The team consists of people representing different professions and settings, and its role is to define pathways, interventions and outcomes. By the way, this group activity is, in our experience, a great opportunity for the emergence of new leaders.

The process management model integrates the clinical acumen, personal involvement, and environmental interventions needed to address the overall maintenance of the patient's physical and social mileu. Clinical case management involves several distinct activities, including: engagement of the patient, assessment, planning, linkage with resources, consultation with families, collaboration with psychiatrists, patient psychoeducation and crisis intervention.[5]

At the Instituto de Psiquiatría y Salud Mental, Hospital Clínico San Carlos we have set up two such processes, one for anxiety and depression with the cooperation of primary healthcare resources, and another for psychosis with the collaboration of social services of the Department of Family and Social Affairs.

Consultation-liaison psychiatry

Liaison services and activities have been expanding for the last 80 or so years. They have played a mediating role between psychiatry and the rest of medicine. The liaison psychiatrist is one of the few health professionals with a broad enough perspective to achieve a measure of integration of diverse data relevant to comprehensive evaluation and management of patients. Liaison activities also include teaching and research. Liaison psychiatry is an essential component in paving the way for more comprehensive views of the discipline and a tool to confront the stigma of mental diseases within the medical field.[6,7]

Comorbidity and networking

Comorbidity is so prevalent in medical care that the traditional model of teaching, research and care, the 'organic' medicine rooted in Giovanni Battista Morgagni's book *De sedibus et causis Morborum per anatomen indagatio* (1767), already over two centuries old, is being challenged. The model states that the sites and the causes of disease are the organs and they should be investigated with anatomical methods. Since then we talk about heart, or kidney, or gastrointestinal or brain disease. The model has progressively expanded to include the cellular, subcellular, molecular and genetic levels and even the mental activities. For instance, Freud regarded consciousness as a sensory organ to perceive psychic qualities;[8] furthermore, *Seele* ('soul'), the lay word generally used by Freud, is translated in French as *appareil psychique*. This 'organic' model is the origin of medical specialities, including cardiology, nephrology, gastroenterology and even psychiatry. Medical teaching is also organized along the same lines.

Nowadays the demands of care, research and even teaching, cut across disciplines, and new specialities have been created (e.g. geriatrics). Networking is the emerging trend that 'shakes' medicine as a science and as practice. An article in the *New England Journal of Medicine*[9] clearly states that: 'Thus, the network concept reveals a number of surprising connections between diseases, forcing us to rethink the way in which we classify and separate them. In the long run, networks may affect all aspects of medical research and practice.'[10] The notion is that most human diseases are not independent of each other; rather, they are associated with the breakdown of functional modules that are best described as sub-networks of a complex of genetic, regulatory, metabolic and protein–protein interactions in a cellular network that lies at the core of the pathophysiology of human diseases. On top of this are two more layers. The middle one is a disease network in which two diseases are connected if they have a common genetic or functional origin. Functional should be interpreted as relevant for adaptive purposes. Barabási quotes as an example that the genes involved in obesity are connected to at least seven other diseases (including diabetes, asthma and insulin resistance). The third level is the social network, which encompasses all human-to-human interactions (e.g. familial, friendship, sexual, and proximity-based contacts) that play a role in the spread of pathogens.

Mental disorders interact with other health conditions, and possible mechanisms have been described to explain these interactions. First is that mental disorders share certain predisposing factors with other diseases; for example, they are associated with risk factors for chronic disease such as smoking, reduced activity, poor diet, obesity and hypertension; they may have common genetic or environmental risk factors. Second is that some health conditions increase the risk of mental disorders, for example by directly disturbing the brain (through infection, inflammation, cerebrovascular disease, diabetes, etc.), or by burdening the person with the consequences of illness (trauma, difficulties of living with illness, pain, stigma, loss of social or interpersonal support) or the effects of treatment and outcome (compliance with treatment, delay in help-seeking, and reducing the likelihood of early detection and diagnosis, or both).[11]

Leadership in training and research

The burden of mental disorders has been underestimated due to an inadequate appreciation of the association between mental illness and other illnesses. For instance, depression predicts the onset and progression of both physical and social disability; conversely, many health conditions increase the risk for mental disorder, and comorbidity complicates help-seeking, diagnosis and treatment, and influences prognosis.

During the past decade many studies have been published documenting that mental disorders are more frequent and contribute to a greater burden of disease than previously thought. The three most important contributors to the burden of disease are depression (7.2% of the overall burden of disease in Europe), Alzheimer's disease/dementia (3.7%) and alcohol use disorders (3.4%). It is estimated that each year 38.2% of the European population suffers from a mental disorder (164.8 million people affected); the most frequent mental disorders are anxiety disorders (69.1 million), unipolar depression (30.3 million) and somatoform disorders excluding headache (204 million). In the World Health Organization's 2005 report the prevalence of mental disorder was 27.4% (due to 14 new disorders and inclusion of the child, adolescent and elderly populations). Besides, mental disorders are linked to many other health conditions and are among the most costly medical disorders to treat.[12] Summing up, about 14% of the global burden of disease is attributable to mental disorders.[11]

This high burden is not proportional to the resources invested in research. According to European data, neuroscience research is considerably less well supported than other comparable diseases such as cancer, with a budget of 465 million euros out of 60 650 million euros.[13]

A recent study has shown that France spends 2% of its health research budget on mental disorders, the United Kingdom 7%, and the United States 16%. Non-governmental funding ranged from 1% of total funding for mental health research in France and the United States to 14% in the United Kingdom.[14]

The Global Forum for Health Research has long highlighted the major imbalance between the magnitude of mental health problems (especially in low- and middle-income countries) and the resources devoted to addressing them. This is the so-called '10/90 gap' – that is, only 10% of global spending on health research is directed towards the problems that primarily affect the poorest 90% of the world's population.[15] The impact of the gap is particularly evident in the field of mental health.[16, 17] Therefore psychiatrists should be embarked on the fight to increase funds for research.

The Sorbonne Declaration (1998)[18] and the Bologna Declaration (1999)[19] initiated the processes of implementing a common model of university studies that had to become reality in all members of the European Community by 2010. This new model is based on a continuous learning process, whereby students are evaluated on a daily basis throughout their graduate studies and clinical practice is given greater prominence.

Another consequence of the great tide of reform now occurring worldwide in medical education is that particular attention is being paid to the so-called 'New Medicine'; curricula should focus on prevention of illness and promotion of health; this implies a high level of collaboration between future doctors and other members of the clinical teams. Psychiatry has become more important in the medical curriculum, as is stated in the Core Curriculum in Psychiatry for Medical Students of the World Psychiatric Association (WPA; 1996)[20] and the International Federation for Medical Students (1996).[21] There are three reasons for this. The first is that the general approach of psychiatry, which stresses the unity of body and mind, is important for the whole of medical practice. The second is that skills learned in psychiatry are important for all doctors (e.g. the ability to assess mental state, to communicate bad news, or to establish a good doctor-patient relationship). And the third aspect is that psychiatric problems are common among patients seen by doctors working in other fields: therefore all doctors must be able to recognize psychiatric problems not only because they are common but also because their management involves much medical time and resources. At the end of their medical training students must accept that the profession of medicine requires lifelong learning and the ability to work constructively with other health professionals, to respect patients and families, to accept the necessity of a good doctor-patient relationship, and accept the value of psychiatry as a medical discipline, by integrating humanistic, scientific and technological aspects of psychiatry.

Students should be engaged in self-directed independent learning that is problem-based (case studies, role-playing, and work in groups).

Nowadays, teaching methodology is recognized as an important activity within medical schools, and university departments and faculties should give priority to teacher training; educational development programmes are necessary in order to understand the teaching-learning process and update regularly.

Leadership and values

Value-based practice has introduced to the psychiatric and medical arena a new perspective beyond traditional bioethics. Not only ethical values, but also values of many other kinds – preferences, needs, hope, expectations, and so forth – are included in it.[22]

Patients come to a clinical encounter with unique preferences, concerns and expectations, which must be integrated into clinical decisions if the clinician is to serve those patients.[23] Furthermore, the reason why patients and patient groups, groups of relatives, ethicists and lay people may be involved in committees (e.g. research), the development of guidelines or advisory boards is to bring not only an ethical perspective but also the values of society and those that are part of their own culture and idiosyncrasy.

Value-based medicine is to values what evidence-based medicine is to facts. Both are needed for functioning more effectively with the complex and conflicting values and evidence in medicine. The need arises because decisions in medicine are increasingly made against a background of complex and often conflicting values such as clinical management, audit, quality assurance, concerns about cost-effectiveness, and the use of quality-of-life and other similar measures in preventive and public health medicine. But there are other reasons: some are to do with changes in society as a whole, the increasingly multicultural nature of society, which brings ever more diverse cultural and social values. Other more directly medical reasons have to do with changes in professional practice – the extension of multidisciplinary team-working, for example, with different clinical disciplines bringing, often, very different sets of professional values to the clinical encounter.

The most important reason, however, for the increasing importance of values in medicine has to do with the emergence of a model of patient-centred practice in which the values of individual patients are central to evidence-based clinical decision-making.

But, and this is a big but, the values of those who work in a healthcare system have to be considered. A study[24] has shown that although different members of multidisciplinary teams (psychiatrists, social workers, nurses, etc.) thought that they all had the same shared values, in practice they were often driven by very different ones.[25] Doctors were more concerned about medication, and social workers were more concerned about risk. There are also intraprofessional clashes of values (Box 12.1). So long as values do not collide with each other we are not aware of them; these differences in values were a source of failures of communication and of difficulties in teamwork and shared decision-making. Once team members were aware of these differences, they became the basis for a person-centred approach to each patient or client, in which different aspects of their individual situation could be balanced appropriately. So the hidden values, once made explicit, were changed from being a problem to an asset![25]

Box 12.1

One the meetings about development of the clinical management process of psychosis produced a very tense situation between the leaders of the group, a psychiatrist much devoted to research and an economist serving as Assistant Manager of the Institute of Psychiatry and Mental Health. Both sought the help and guidance of the Director. A conflict had arisen between two participants in the team, not between two from different professions. One was a nurse with a long career and experience in an acute ward, the other was experienced too but in a community care centre where she had been working for years. The conflict was on how to proceed with excited psychotic patient. The ward nurse pleaded passionately for contention with drugs or even physical restraint, close supervision of behaviour and compliance. The second begged for an approach that would not damage the positive relationship between patients and staff. During the next few minutes the conflicting values of the two nurses emerged – safety vs autonomy – values that were also those of their respective settings (i.e. ward vs community centre), and these had engaged the other members of the group in the discussion.

Communication skills are central to effective decision-making in value-based practice and, in particular, for bringing evidence and values together in individual cases.[26]

Leadership in society at large

Advocacy and lobbying

Psychiatry and mental health cannot be separated from each other. Although very often these two terms are used in an ambiguous way, implying that 'psychiatry' is stigmatizing (and replaced by 'mental health' or even 'psychology' in healthcare settings), we consider here another fact. Psychiatrists are not mere clinicians taking care of diseases, nor even professionals looking out for the needs of people suffering from mental disorders, be it with the collaboration of a clinical team or an extended one. A psychiatrist has to carry out other tasks in society at large as part of his or her professional responsibilities. In this context, the code of ethics of the World Psychiatric Association, the Madrid Declaration, is crystal clear: 'As members of society, psychiatrists must advocate for fair and equal treatment of the mentally ill, for social justice and equity for all'.[27] This is in agreement with the UN Resolution 46/119 of the Principles for the Protection of Persons with Mental Illness:[28] psychiatrists should oppose discriminatory practices that limit patients' benefits and entitlements, deny them parity, curb the scope of treatment, or limit their access to proper medications.

Leadership in third-party situations

Leadership in third-party situations involves, for example, psychiatrists in court procedures or in managed care decisions. There is a still ongoing discussion of the function and ethical points of reference of psychiatrists acting as expert witnesses in court procedures.[29,30] The problem is that the role and values of the clinician and the role and values of the expert witness may often collide, and that collision can harm medical ethics. This troublesome and interesting discussion turns around the acceptance of exceptional situations that a forensic psychiatrist might face. The ultimate scenario might concern the participation of a psychiatrist in the evaluation of competence of someone who is to be executed. If a psychiatrist certifies that the culprit is not insane or not insane anymore, the execution can proceed.

On one side, leaders in the field such as Appelbaum, claim that 'the forensic psychiatrist in truth does not act as a physician', he or she acts as a forensic expert, based on a non-medical ethics of 'truth' and on 'the legitimate needs of the justice system'.

On the other side, there are those who believe, based on the principles of the Madrid Declaration of the WPA and other documents, that a psychiatrist can never leave behind his or her role nor the values of the profession.

With the passage of time, several authors (including one of the authors of the present chapter) have slowly changed their position to one of accepting this exceptionalist position for forensic psychiatrists. The rationale for this is the separation between the role of a clinician taking care of a patient and the role of an expert, something that has to be clearly explained to the patient. Furthermore, the switching of roles should be strictly avoided: an expert witness deposition forbids the clinician from further treating the person concerned, and vice versa.

The obligations of organizations toward their shareholders or of the administrator regarding maximization of profits and minimization of costs can conflict with the principles of good practice. Psychiatrists working in such potentially conflicting environments should uphold the rights of the patients to receive the best treatment possible.

Third-party payers include the administration and healthcare personnel in government, social security systems or managed care companies. In this case the same principles apply to third-party payers as in the case of the judicial system.

The leader's role in the fight against the stigma of mental illness

Fighting the stigma of mental illness is a part of the mission of a psychiatry service; consequently its leader should be actively involved in this task. A stigma is a mark or sign of disgrace that usually causes negative attitudes towards those who bear it. At a conceptual level, the term can include global difficulties associated with knowledge (ignorance or lack of information), attitudes (prejudice: i.e. affective distance), and behaviour (e.g. discrimination, exclusion of regular forms of participation).[31]

A stigma can have a very negative effect on the person bearing it and also on their relatives. The idea that people with mental disorders hide their diagnosis due to shame or fear of discrimination is common. This attitude may lead them to seek less help from health services, besides other consequences.

The stigma is manifested in discriminatory behaviour, which sometimes derives from the health services themselves, in terms of a worse quality of care. Discriminatory attitudes can occur among doctors and nurses, within the family, at work or within the social environment of patients. Some studies have shown that very frequently there is a negative discriminatory attitude in health services towards patients with schizophrenia.[32–36] Data also show that mental health staff can stigmatize their patients.[34,37]

Stereotyped attitudes and prejudice from healthcare staff towards patients with schizophrenia may contribute to increased self-stigmatization, having at the same time a negative impact on the patients' help-seeking behaviour.[38] In this context, the leaders of psychiatric services can play a major role both in the field of health services and in the social environment of their patients.

In general hospitals and in primary care, interventions can be made at the following levels:

1 Favouring the integration of psychiatric care in specialized care in those countries where there is still negative discrimination.
2 Establishing processes and shared clinical protocols with other services, including primary care.
3 Leading research and innovation projects aimed at reducing the stigma of mental illness.
4 Contributing to the dissemination of good practice guidelines for health professionals and health managers.

Listed below are some examples of intervention within the social environment of patients and relatives:

1 Establishing systems of participation of patients with mental illness in health policies at high and middle levels of decision-making.

2   Favouring patients' empowerment to enable their participation in society and other fields (work, family, leisure, etc.).
3   Promoting initiatives to fight stigma by patients themselves, i.e. from the bottom up.
4   Contributing to better information about mental health stigma, and its negative consequences, for administrators and health policy-makers at national and regional levels.

In general, psychiatric services have interdisciplinary clinical teams that support these tasks. Combating the stigma of mental illness is not the domain solely of the medical profession or any other, instead it is an overarching objective affecting all professions and should permeate routine care. The role of leaders is therefore twofold. On the one hand the fight against stigma must be embedded in the everyday, meaning routine practice. On the other hand, the leader can promote specific actions to fight it according to the context in which he or she works. These specific actions include several areas: clinical practice, rehabilitation and social reintegration, research, innovation and teaching.

The international projects INDIGO[39] and ASPEN,[40] led by G. Thornicroft and other researchers in recent years, are examples of initiatives to fight stigma. These projects, especially ASPEN, include not only rigorous research on various phenomena associated with stigma but also a series of recommendations and guidelines of good practice to address stigma within the general public and health administrations.

Leadership and mass media

Society is engrained with prejudice toward mental illness, and sufferers are often widely perceived to be dangerous or unpredictable. Reinforcement of these popular myths through the media perpetuates the stigma surrounding mental illness, precipitating shame, self-blame and secrecy, all of which discourage affected individuals from seeking treatment. The involvement of the media is essential for success in any campaign to combat stigma, but, in order for the media to be used effectively, their motivations and limitations must first be recognized and understood. We refer here to three paradigmatic examples.

Too many psychiatries, too many opinions

Psychiatry is perceived to be a babelic profession, full of 'psychiatries' opposed to each other, fighting among themselves for leadership of conflicting models and roles. We have a wide spectrum of choices, including biological psychiatry, psychoanalysis, psychodynamic psychiatry, social psychiatry, community psychiatry, family psychiatry, forensic psychiatry, military psychiatry, child and geriatric psychiatry, and recently women's mental health and men's mental health too. Psychological disciplines can be added in order to create an indecipherable uproar. The consequence is that lay people perceive the lack of consensus among psychiatrists,[41] and they are not alone (Box 12.2). The mass media are full of more or less pungent descriptions and explanations, such as 'some [psychiatrists] embraced the new biological model, some still clung to the Freudian model, and a few saw mental illness as an essentially sane response to an insane world'.[42, 43]

Box 12.2

Shortly after the appointment of Gro Harlem Brundtland as WHO Director General one of the authors of the present chapter (J.J.L-I.) visited him in the author's capacity as President of the WPA in order to enhance the links of the Association with the WHO and to find avenues for collaboration in fighting the stigma of mental disorders. While preparing for the encounter, I went through Mrs Brundtland's impressive record of past achievements. She was a Norwegian Social Democratic politician, a diplomat, trained as a paediatrician, an international leader in public health and had been Minister of Health and Social Affairs and Prime Minister of Norway. The deepest worry before the visit was about the ex-premier's attitude towards psychiatry as it was public knowledge that her son Jørgen Brundtland, who had been undergoing psychiatric treatment for alcoholism, committed suicide in 1992, during her second term as Prime Minister.

And indeed the conversation started with a comment on how each individual psychiatrist conveys a very different message and that this was unacceptable for patients, families, governments and society at large. Then we went on to consider the problems of drug dependence and finally to stigma.

The WPA had launched in 1996 the 'Psychiatry Open the Doors' programme to fight the stigma of schizophrenia in spite of the prevailing pessimism surrounding this topic. The authors are inclined to think that this was part of a larger more proactive attitude as the World Health Assembly in 2011 was exclusively dedicated to mental health, considering stigma to be a major cause of discrimination and exclusion. The motto of the WHO undertaking was 'Stop exclusion, dare to care', and the logo was of a man going out through a door, leaving his shadow behind.

Fancy placebos: the antidepressant case[44]

Irwin Kirsch's book *The Emperor's New Drugs: Exploding the Antidepressant Myth*[45] has highlighted the issue of the usefulness of antidepressant medication in clinical settings, making a strong impact both among scientists and the mass media. The message is that antidepressants fall well below the criteria for clinical relevance, efficacy reaches clinical relevance only in trials involving the most severely depressed patients,[46] and that the US Food and Drug Administration (FDA) has taken an explicit decision to keep this information from the public and from prescribing physicians.

The mass media are essential to convey scientific information, but especially in the case of mental disorders, the message can be distorted due to an anti-psychiatric stigmatizing attitude on the part of the informant, the journalist or other people involved in the process. The fact is that even with information based on meta-analytical studies,[47-52] an emotion-free interpretation is not guaranteed.

Below we outline ways whereby psychiatrists can confront such biases and regain a leadership role, which really they should never lose if wanting to benefit their patients. The key elements are:

1   The design and carrying out of clinical trials does not provide enough scientific data to allow extrapolation of observations in relatively small and highly selected sample sizes to actual patients in everyday clinical practice. In reality this is not the goal of clinical trials, which are intended *just* to provide information on changes in selected rating scale items predicting an antidepressant effect. Taking information obtained

from the laboratory and using it in real life is never an easy task and short cuts have to be accepted.

2 Clinical trials samples in psychiatry are highly biased due to the need for homogenization and the limitations of the design. Studies typically do not involve large random samples, such as those carried out for metabolic or cardiovascular diseases. Studies of depression are carried out in patient samples that exclude very severely ill patients, to minimize risks (e.g. of suicide), and mild cases, to exclude possible placebo effects and also to have baseline scores in clinical cases that will enable detection of significant differences. A 50% reduction in the Hamilton Rating Scale for Depression (HRSD), a common criterion for response, is easier to demonstrate if the baseline score is 24 rather than 17.

3 We have to assume that concept, definitions, diagnostic criteria and evaluations of depressive disorders are extremely poor. The prevalence rates of unipolar depressive disorders vary markedly among sexes and regions of the world. In a WHO study, the prevalence of current major depression varied 15-fold across centres. When centres were divided into three groups according to prevalence rates, the symptom pattern or latent structure of depressive illness was generally similar at low-, medium- and high-prevalence centres. In a study depression was universally associated with disability, but this association varied significantly across centres.[53] In primary healthcare the differences are still larger. The separation of depressive illness from 'normal' depression is still an open debate. The large proportion of patients with major depressive episodes who do not receive treatment in spite of half a century of antidepressant pharmacotherapy[54] is probably a sign of the lack of clarification of these issues in the minds of patients and doctors.

4 Alternatives to conventional medicine for treatment of depression, low mood and negative feelings attract the public's attention in spite of a lack of scientific data to support their real therapeutic effects. The interest in complementary and alternative medicines grows constantly as an increasing number of people, including healthcare professionals, look at ways to improve their own lives and those of others by using a variety of such medicines.[55] The World Health Organization reports an increase in the use of non-conventional medicine, meaning traditional, complementary and alternative medicine (CAM), in countries all over the world.[56]

Complementary and alternative cures may include such things as food supplements (vitamins, other organic and inorganic substances, such as omega-3 fatty acids) and individual therapies (acupuncture, aromatherapy, herbal therapy, homeopathy, iridology, naturopathy and reflexology). In the United States, complementary and alternative therapies are used more than conventional therapies by people with anxiety and severe depression, reaching up to 53.4% of those who responded to a survey.[57] In the United Kingdom, estimates of the proportion of the general population using CAM range from 14% to 30%.[57]

Such messages are harmful for individual patients, healthcare administration, teaching and research in psychiatry, and the attractiveness of psychiatry for medical graduates. The pretext that complementary medicine has no risks and hence that alternative therapy may be a better treatment choice for depression has to be openly addressed.[46]

The challenge for the clinician is to deliver a meaningful message to his or her patients and their relatives, and occasionally to the media. In this context there is a need for further studies focusing not only on the putative drug effect but also its behaviour at large, in everyday practice, and also on alternative ways to analyse data. For instance:

1   Recent meta-analyses have shown that the more effective antidepressants were those with a side-effect profile similar to placebo.[58]
2   The 'efficacy' of non-antidepressant agents is a well-known artefact because of the problematic properties of the psychometric scales used, which include not only core symptoms of depression but also non-specific ones and even side effects,[59] besides other methodological problems.

The media and the stigma of schizophrenia

Rigorous and objective media coverage is one of the best tools to combat the stigma of schizophrenia since for most of society the media are the main source of information about health issues. Improving knowledge of schizophrenia, its symptoms and available treatments reduces that stigma. Furthermore, this type of information greatly contributes to early diagnosis of the disease, since those who are worried about experiencing the first symptoms, either in themselves or in someone close to them, will know through the media that there are treatments and that mental health professionals can help.

However, the media can also perpetuate the stigma of schizophrenia. Just as it is possible to combat stereotypes, so it is possible to strengthen them through the misuse of language or transmission of misconceptions.

There are mistakes that should and could be corrected:

1   *To describe an individual with schizophrenia as 'crazy' or define schizophrenia as 'madness'.* On the contrary, writing about 'mental illness' and the 'mentally ill' helps the understanding that there are treatments for schizophrenia and dispels the myth that schizophrenia sufferers are mentally handicapped.
2   *The use of terms such as 'a schizophrenic'.* People with schizophrenia are simply people with schizophrenia. Their illness should not be the only qualifier used to describe them.
3   *Associate schizophrenia with violent behaviour.* The vast majority of persons with mental illness never commit violent acts and, in general, are not dangerous to healthy individuals of the same population. Actually, they are more likely to be victims than perpetrators of abuse or violence, as many people still believe.
4   *Identifying people with schizophrenia as mentally handicapped.* Schizophrenia is very different to intellectual disability, which is identified usually at the beginning of childhood. Schizophrenia, however, begins in adolescence or early adulthood.
5   *Using the word 'schizophrenic' to describe things or situations.* Expressions such as 'this year's budgets are schizophrenic' trivializes the disease and gives pejorative connotations.

Migrating leaderships

The WPA Open the Doors programme in Spain in the 2000s took two major initial decisions that ultimately proved to be very fruitful. First, the headquarters of the programme was sited the leading communication consultancy in Spain and Latin America (Llorente y Cuenca). This strategy allowed more fluent communication with the mass media (e.g. organizing press conferences, interviews with experts, etc.), preparing materials (e.g. press reports) and monitoring and evaluating the outcomes of the programme. Several courses for mental health professionals and journalists were organized in certain Spanish universities.

The consultancy took care to ensure homogeneity and consistency of the message in training seminars for psychiatrists, by selecting for interviews each time different people to avoid a stereotyped image of the programme and by providing material for professionals. For instance, when the film *A Beautiful Mind* was released in Spain a dossier was distributed with information about John Nash, his illness, his Nobel Prize and all the vicissitudes concerning creativity and delusional thinking.[60] This piece of information was welcomed by psychiatrists because it provided them with interesting material and helped them when being interviewed by journalists.

The second decision was to consider the programme as limited in time. Actually the core WPA programme was also limited in time, from 1997 to 2005. In Spain the López-Ibor Foundation took care of transferring the anti-stigma activities to the Confederación Española de Agrupaciones de Familiares y Enfermos Mentales (FEAFES), which integrates most of the users' associations in Spain.

Psychiatrists as leaders in the field of health services may have the responsibility and the opportunity to contribute not only to the knowledge of their discipline but also to improve the mental health of society as a whole. To perform this task successfully they need to broaden their perspective to encompass other stakeholders and components of society, namely the mass media, lawyers, health administrators, policy-makers, other medical specialists and users' associations.

References

1   Pearce CI, Conger JA. *Shared Leadership: Reframing the Hows and Whys of Leadership.* Thousand Oaks: Sage, 2003.
2   Bens I. *Facilitating to Lead.* San Francisco: Jossey-Bass, 2006.
3   Chomsky N, McChesney RW. *Consent Without Consent. Profit Over People. Neoliberalism and Global Order.* New York: Seven Stories Press, 1999.
4   Dannhauser Z. The Relationship between Servant Leadership, Follower Trust, Team Commitment and Unit Effectiveness. Doctoral dissertation, Stellenbosch University, 2007.
5   Kanter J. Clinical case management: definition, principles, components. *Hosp Community Psychiatry* 1989; **40**:361–8.
6   Lipowski Z. Consultation-liaison psychiatry. *Psychother Psychosom* 1991; **55**:62–8.
7   López-Ibor JJ. Evaluation in consultation-liaison psychiatry. *Eur J Psychiatry* 1989; **3**:178–85.
8   Freud S. *The Interpretation of Dreams. The Standard Edition of the Complete Psychological Works of Sigmund Freud*, Vol. V (1900–1901). London: The Hogarth Press and the Institute of Psychoanalysis, 1957.

9   Barabási A. Network medicine – from obesity to the "diseasome". *N Engl J Med* 2007; **357**:404–7.

10 Loscalzo J, Barabási A. Human diseases classification in the postgenomic era: a complex systems approach to human pathobiology. *Mol Syst Biol* 2007; **3**:124.

11 Prince M, Patel V, Saxena S *et al.* No health without mental health. *Lancet* 2007; **370**:859–77.

12 Patel V, Araya R, Chatterjee S *et al.* Treatment and prevention of mental disorders in low-income and middle-income countries. *Lancet* 2007; **370**:991–1005.

13 Wittchen HU, Jacobi F, Rehm J *et al.* The size and burden of mental disorders and other disorders of the brain in Europe 2010. *Eur Neuropsychopharmacol* 2011; **21**:655–79.

14 Chevreul K, McDaid D, Farmer CM *et al.* Public and nonprofit funding for research on mental disorders in France, the United Kingdom, and the United States. *J Clin Psychiatry* 2012; **73**:e906–e912.

15 Saxena S, Paraje G, Sharan P, Karam G, Sadana R. The 10/90 divide in mental health research: trends over a 10-year period. *Br J Psychiatry* 2006; **188**:81–2.

16 McCulloch A. More investment needs to be made into mental health research. *Ment Health Today* 2009 Dec/2010 Jan: 9.

17 Tomlinson M, Rudan I, Saxena S, Swartz L, Tsai AC, Patel V. Setting priorities for global mental health research. *Bull WHO* 2009; **87**:438–46.

18 Sorbonne Joint Declaration. Joint declaration on harmonisation of the architecture of the European higher education system. Available at: http://www.bologna_berlin2003.de/pdf/Sorbonne_declaration.pdf[accessed 5 April 2013].

19 The Bologna Declaration on the European space for higher education. Available at: http://ec.europa.eu/education/policies/educ/bologna/bologna.pdf [accessed 5 April 2013].

20 World Psychiatric Association. WPA Core Curriculum in Psychiatry for Medical Students. Available at: http://www.wpanet.org/detail.php?section_id=8&content_id=111[accessed 5 April 2013].

21 International Federation of Medical Students' Associations. Standing Committee on Medical Education (SCOME). URL: http://www.ifmsa.org/Activities/Core-activities/Medical-Education [accessed 5 April 2013].

22 Fulford KW, Thornton T, Graham G. *The Oxford Textbook of Philosophy and Psychiatry.* Oxford: Oxford University Press, 2006.

23 Sackett DL, Straus SE, Scott Richardson W, Rosenberg W, Haynes RB. *Evidence-Based Medicine: How to Practice and Teach EBM*, 2nd edn. Edinburgh and London: Churchill Livingstone, 2000.

24 Colombo A, Bendelow G, Fulford B, Williams S. Evaluating the influence of implicit models of mental disorder on processes of shared decision making within community-based multi-disciplinary teams. *Soc Sci Med* 2003; **56**:1557–70.

25 Fulford KW. Values-based practice: a new partner to evidence-based practice and a first for psychiatry? *Mens Sana Monogr* 2008; **6**:10–21.

26 Hope T, Fulford KW, Yates A. *The Oxford Practice Skills Course: Ethics, Law and Communication Skills in Health Care Education.* Oxford: Oxford University Press, 1996.

27 World Psychiatric Association. Madrid Declaration on Ethical Standards for Psychiatric Practice. Available at: http://wpanet.org/detail.php?section_id=5&content_id=48. http://wpanet.org/detail.php?section_id=5&content_id=48. [accessed 5 April 2013].

28 UN General Assembly. The protection of persons with mental illness and the improvement of mental health care. United Nations, 1991. Available at: http://www.un.org/documents/ga/res/46/a46r119.htm.

29 Freedman AF, Halpern AL. Psychiatrists and the death penalty: some ethical dilemmas – a crisis in the ethical and moral behavior of psychiatrists. *Curr Opin Psychiatr* 1998; **11**:1–2.

30 Gunn J, Pellegrino E, Bonnie R *et al.* Forum – psychiatrists and the death penalty: some ethical dilemmas. *Comments. Curr Opin Psychiatr* 1998; **11**:3–11.

31 Thornicroft G, Rose D, Kassam A. Discrimination in health care against people with mental illness. *Int Rev Psychiatry* 2007; **19**:113–22.

32 Thornicroft G, Rose D, Kassam A. Discrimination in health care against people with mental illness. *Int Rev Psychiatry* 2007; **19**:113–22.

33 Fleischhacker WW, Cetkovich-Bakmas M, De Hert M *et al.* Comorbid somatic illnesses in patients with severe mental disorders: clinical, policy, and research challenges. *J Clin Psychiatry* 2008; **69**:514–19.

34 Wahl O. Mental health consumer's experience of stigma. *Schizophr Res* 1999; **25**:467–78.

35 Lawrie S, Martin K, McNeil G. General practitioners' attitudes to psychiatric and medical illness. *Psychol Med* 1998; **28**:1463–7.

36 Liggins J, Hatcher S. Stigma toward the mentally ill in the general hospital: a qualitative study. *Gen Hosp Psychiatry* 2005; **27**:359–64.

37 Ucok A, Polat A, Sartorius N, Erkoc S, Atakli C. Attitudes of psychiatrists toward patients with schizophrenia. *Psychiatry Clin Neurosci* 2004; **58**:89–91.

38 Bjorkman T, Angelman T, Jonsson M. Attitudes towards people with mental illness: a cross-sectional study among nursing staff in psychiatric and somatic care. *Scand J Caring Sci* 2008; **22**:170–7.

39 Thornicroft G, Brohan E, Rose D, Sartorius N, Leese M. Global pattern of experienced and anticipated discrimination against people with schizophrenia: a cross-sectional survey. *Lancet* 2009; **373**:408–15.

40 Lasalvia A, Zoppei S, Van Bortel T *et al.* Global pattern of experienced and anticipated discrimination reported by people with major depressive disorder: a cross sectional survey. *Lancet* 2013; **381**:55–62.

41 Menand L. Can psychiatry be a science? *The New Yorker* March 1, 2010. Available at: http://www.newyorker.com/arts/critics/atlarge/2010/03/01/100301crat_atlarge_menand#ixzz2Eo RqS1bE[accessed 5 April 2013].

42 Angell M. The epidemic of mental illness: Why? *New York Review of Books* June 23, 2011. Available at: http://www.nybooks.com/articles/archives/2011/jun/23/epidemic-mental-illness-why/?pagination=false [accessed 5 April 2013].

43 Angell M. The illusions of psychiatry. *The New York Review of Books* July 14, 2011. Available at: http://www.nybooks.com/articles/archives/2011/jul/14/illusions-of-psychiatry [accessed 5 April 2013].

44 Fountoulakis KN, Höschl C, Kasper S, López-Ibor JJ, Moeller H-J. The media and intellectuals' response to medical publications: the antidepressants case. *Ann Gen Psychiatry* 2013; **12**:11.

45 Kirsch I. *The Emperor's New Drugs: Exploding the Antidepressant Myth.* London: The Bodley Head, 2009.

46 Kirsch I. Antidepressants and the placebo response. *Epidemiol Psychiatr Soc* 2009; **18**: 318–22.

47 Barbui C, Furukawa TA, Cipriani A. Effectiveness of paroxetine in the treatment of acute major depression in adults: a systematic re-examination of published and unpublished data from randomized trials. *Can Med Assoc J* 2008; **178**:296–305.

48 Bech P, Cialdella P, Haugh MC *et al.* Meta-analysis of randomised controlled trials of fluoxetine v. placebo and tricyclic antidepressants in the short-term treatment of major depression. *Br J Psychiatry* 2000; **176**:421–8.

49 Fournier JC, DeRubeis RJ, Hollon SD *et al.* Antidepressant drug effects and depression severity: a patient-level meta-analysis. *JAMA* 2010; **303**:47–53.

50 Ghaemi SN. Why antidepressants are not antidepressants: STEP-BD, STAR∗D, and the return of neurotic depression. *Bipolar Disord* 2008; **10**:957–68.

51 Kirsch I, Deacon BJ, Huedo-Medina TB, Scoboria A, Moore TJ, Johnson BT. Initial severity and antidepressant benefits: a meta-analysis of data submitted to the Food and Drug Administration. *PLoS Med* 2008; **5**:e45.

52   Moncrieff J, Wessely S, Hardy R. Active placebos versus antidepressants for depression. *Cochrane Database Syst Rev* 2004 (1): CD003012.
53   Simon GE, Goldberg DP, von Korff M, Üstün TB. Understanding cross-national differences in depression prevalence. *Psychol Med* 2002: **32**:585–94.
54   Üstün TB, Ayuso-Mateos JL, Chatterji S, Mathers C, Murray CJL. Global burden of depressive disorders in the year 2000. *Brit J Psychiatry* 2004; **184**:386–92.
55   Van der Watt G, Laugharne J, Janca A. Complementary and alternative medicine in the treatment of anxiety and depression. *Curr Opin Psychiatry* 2008; **21**:37–42
56   World Health Organization. *WHO Traditional Medicines Strategy 2002–2005*. Geneva: World Health Organization; 2002.
57   Sharma U. *Complementary Medicine Today: Practitioners and Patients*. London: Routledge, 1992.
58   Cipriani A, Furukawa TA, Salanti G *et al*. Comparative efficacy and acceptability of 12 new-generation antidepressants: a multiple-treatments meta-analysis. *Lancet* 2009; **373**: 746–58.
59   Bech P. Rating scales in depression: limitations and pitfalls. *Dialogues Clin Neurosci* 2006; **8**:207–15.
60   La Esquizofrenia Abre las Puertas. "Una mente maravillosa" ("A Beautiful Mind"). Dossier informativo para los psiquiatras coordinadores del Programa. Available at: http://www.cat-barcelona.com/pdf/biblioteca/esquizofrenia/020214_abm_dossier_psiq.pdf [accessed 5 April 2013].

Chapter 13

Leadership in Academic Psychiatry

Dilip V. Jeste and Maja Gawronska

Leadership begins when you believe you can make a difference.

Kouzes and Posner[1]

Introduction

For academic departments of psychiatry these are both exciting and challenging times. Among the many challenges academic psychiatrists must confront are limited funding, growing competition and aging faculty, as well as keeping pace with rapid technological and scientific advances. These circumstances hold both risks and possibilities. In order to succeed and transform challenges into opportunities, academic psychiatry needs skilled leadership. While many of the same challenges are shared by leaders in other fields, the unique environment of academic psychiatry calls for a tailored approach.

The complex, multifaceted nature of academic medicine departments requires that leaders possess field-specific expertise as well as organizational and leadership knowledge.[2] In day-to-day operations, department chairs, deans, division chiefs and programme directors wear different hats on different occasions and must wear them well. They bridge students, faculty and administrators, oversee research and ensure quality of education, and communicate up and down the administrative ladder, as well as across different departments and organizations. They act as fund raisers, spokespersons and human resources managers. Some refer to their profession as 'beggar, psychologist, mediator, and maid, all in one',[3] or 'part field general, part mediator, part visionary, and part circus barker'.[4]

The plethora of skills necessary to succeed in academic leadership may seem overwhelming, particularly for physician-scientists who are promoted to leadership positions because of their demonstrated excellence in research and scholarship, but who rarely have had the opportunity to formally receive training in management and leadership skills.[5] Although some scientists may feel that such training is unnecessary as it emphasizes skills that some consider 'too soft' for those engaged in medical or basic science research,[6] lack of these skills can significantly lower the probability of achieving success in the managerial roles.

Leadership in Psychiatry, First Edition. Edited by Dinesh Bhugra, Pedro Ruiz and Susham Gupta.
© 2013 John Wiley & Sons, Ltd. Published 2013 by John Wiley & Sons, Ltd.

In fact, the Association of American Medical Colleges (AAMC) has recently highlighted concern that the average term in office for medical school deans is under 4 years.[3] A study of turnover rates for first-time chairs in academic departments of psychiatry in the United States showed that 68% of first-time chairs still remain in their position after 5 years, but only 39% are in this position at the 10-year mark.[7] Psychiatry falls between other specialities in this respect. The lowest retention rates are observed in obstetrics and gynaecology (55% at 5 years and 21% at 10 years), and the greatest managerial stability is found in neurology (69% at 5 years and 41% at 10 years) and family medicine (70% at 5 years and 38% at 10 years).[7]

Why did leaders choose to leave their position? Although explanations may vary from case to case, many chairs reported they were unable to succeed because of too many barriers, getting burned out, and being overloaded by the complexity of their tasks.[8]

Academic psychiatrists may need to learn a set of leadership skills to successfully move on to a much broader role in a challenging academic environment. In this chapter, we begin by providing a brief description of the mission of academic medicine. We then briefly describe the transition from a physician scientist to a leader. Next, we analyse the main domains of leadership in academic psychiatry: research, clinical care and teaching (including medical education, mentoring and public outreach) as well as administration and management. We then discuss strategies to promote diversity in top-level positions in academic psychiatry. Finally, we summarize the most important skills needed to succeed as a leader in academic psychiatry.

Mission of academic medicine

Medical departments and teaching hospitals come in different shapes and sizes. Yet, the commonality of their goals makes them similar across borders, cultures and specialities. Their mission encompasses several key aspects: teaching students and training clinicians, advancing scientific knowledge, and developing novel therapeutic approaches and providing excellent care for patients in need.[9, 10] In addition to training, research and patient care, physician scientists are responsible for working with communities to improve their health outcomes, and ensuring ethical expression of their profession in everyday life[11, 12] (Figure 13.1).

From physician-researcher to leader

Many physician-scientists deal with elements of these missions on a daily basis, writing scientific papers, teaching students and managing clinical trials (see also Chapter 12). However, with the transition to a big-picture leadership position, the scope and complexity of responsibilities expand markedly. Academic leaders look beyond their own research projects, department or organization. Their goal is not only to manage an effective team within their institution, but also to contribute to the overall well-being of patients, disseminate knowledge, and develop a future generation of leaders who will vigorously serve the field.

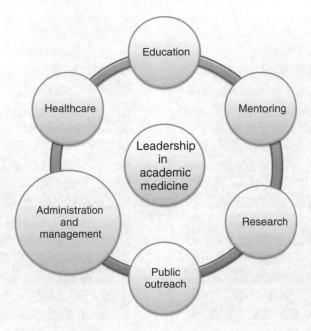

Figure 13.1 Domains of leadership in academic psychiatry

This more general role entails a whole new way of thinking. A framework adopted from Watkins aims to enumerate the changes that new leaders face.[13] In their past role, physician scientists were typically highly specialized problem-solvers, analysts working on their individual research projects or executing specific parts of larger studies. In their field of study they were most often highly competitive solo virtuosos. In order to successfully transition to their new roles as leaders in academic psychiatry, they need to orient themselves as architects, generalists and strategists who set an agenda and communicate a clear vision. They need to be more socially oriented, more interactive and prepared to work on more complex problems. In order to succeed they often need to look beyond fierce competition, and act as diplomats both within and outside their institutions. Internally, their role is more that of an orchestra conductor, who ensures not only that each individual performer excels in his or her part, but also that the parts fit together smoothly as a whole (Figure 13.2).

The British National Health Service (NHS) has developed a Leadership Qualities Framework that is specific to healthcare systems. It defines key personal, social and cognitive qualities of leaders, organized across three broad clusters: personal qualities, setting direction and delivering service:

- Personal qualities include self-belief, self-awareness, self-management, drive for improvement and personal integrity.
- Setting direction comprises sizing the future, intellectual flexibility, broad scanning, political astuteness and drive for results.
- Delivering service means leading change through people, holding to account, empowering and influencing others effectively, and working collaboratively.[14]

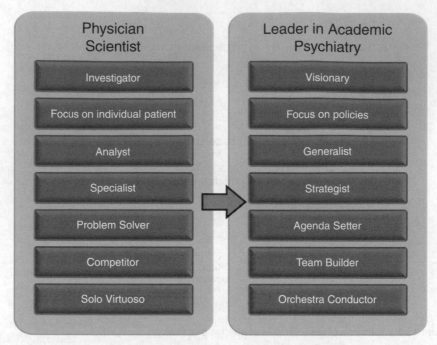

Figure 13.2 From physician-scientist to leader in academic psychiatry. Partially based on Watkins (2011)[13]

Successful leaders in academic psychiatry tend to foster these qualities while balancing the main areas of academic endeavour: research, healthcare, knowledge dissemination and administration. We will discuss each of these domains separately, although in the day-to-day work of an academic leader they are closely interconnected and interdependent worlds, and it is up to the leader to prioritize among them. We will briefly describe the main challenges associated with these domains, and discuss strategies for handling them more effectively.

Research

Great leadership starts with vision. In academic psychiatry, the vision usually revolves around advancing scientific knowledge of mental illnesses and translating the findings into better treatments that enhance patients' recovery and well-being. For example, Philippe Pinel, a French physician described as 'the father of modern, humane psychiatry', dreamed of finding medical means to alleviate the suffering of thousands of mentally ill people in the late seventeenth century. Sigmund Freud, the father of psychoanalysis, dreamed of deciphering the secrets of the human mind. Adolf Meyer, a Swiss psychiatrist who served as president of the American Psychiatric Association, was an influential advocate of the empirical approach to psychiatry during the first half of the twentieth century, envisioning a world where understanding and treatment of mental illness are based on scientific findings.[15]

> All leaders have the capacity to create a compelling vision, one that takes people to a new place, and the ability to translate that vision into reality.[16]

Leaders in academic psychiatry, who often excel in research themselves, also focus on strengthening this domain throughout their departments. This involves, but is not limited to, motivating students and faculty, ensuring adequate funding, mentoring, and overseeing the organization of studies and clinical trials. Institutional leaders are tasked with enhancing the research portfolio of multiple departments and fostering interdepartmental collaborations across the entire institution. Authors of the 'Pearls for Leaders in Academic Medicine' offer interesting strategies that leaders might use to boost the scientific output of their organization:

- Find a niche (or competitive advantage).
- Foster existing research strengths of the institution.
- Hire a renowned researcher (or a few renowned researchers), who can attract others to their department.
- Foster collaboration with researchers from different departments and institutions.
- Develop a research programme for young investigators.
- Offer attractive incentives for the most productive researchers.[3]

While individual scientists might choose research topics based on individual interests and passions, successful academic leaders tend to consider more pragmatic issues, evaluating the quality of research in their departments, the purpose and high-level goals of the research, and funding potential.

Scientific focus is critical to an institution's identity and often leads to its reputation, whether it is a university or a teaching hospital. High-quality, cutting-edge research attracts a talent pool of the best trainees, scientists and clinicians. Excelling in research opens access to funding – both government grants and money from private foundations; individual donors and industry. In fact, the most successful departments of academic psychiatry make significant financial contributions to the overall research programmes of their medical schools. Data from the US National Institutes of Health (NIH) for 2007 and 2008 showed that the top 10 academic departments of psychiatry brought in 7% to 21% of funding to the medical school. For instance, in 2009, the Department of Psychiatry at the University of California, San Diego School of Medicine, brought in more than 15% of the total NIH funding for the school.[17]

In economically challenging times, leaders of academic departments of medicine are under tremendous pressure to generate sufficient revenue to support their department missions. The competition among research institutions is fierce. Not only do they need to be faster, more effective, and more creative than their colleagues elsewhere, but also they have to keep pace with revolutionary changes in the field.

What are the attributes needed to thrive in this challenging research environment? Broad knowledge of their field, persistence and a long-term approach are crucial.[3] Research is not finished overnight. Studies or clinical trials often take years to complete. It takes many months or years of research and several revisions before a scientific paper is accepted for publication. In drug development it can take a decade or more to bring a molecule from bench to bedside.

To build a fruitful scientific career, a scientist should learn the skills that go beyond the lab bench. Particularly at the later stages of an academic career, research is rarely a solo venture. Analysis of many important research programmes shows the decisive role of human interactions and dynamics in determining the project outcomes.[18] Interpersonal skills, excellent communication talents, and the ability to collaborate with other researchers are instrumental in executing a research programme, getting peer support for the grant application, and finding new colleagues to carry out the work. In addition, researchers need the ability to publicize their work both among peers and the lay audience. Visibility in conferences, prominence in societies, and media appearances can greatly contribute to a leader's success.[19]

Knowledge dissemination

'The subject of whole-time clinical teachers [. . .] is one of great importance, not only to Universities, but to the profession and to the public at large,' wrote Sir William Osler, founder of the first residency training programme in the United States, in a letter to the President of the Johns Hopkins University in 1912. This devoted teacher also described his habit: 'After showing the treasures of my library, it is my custom to take an intelligent bibliophile to a shelf on which stand twelve handsomely bound quarto volumes, and say: "But this is my chief treasure – the 500 contributions to the scientific medicine from the graduates of the first eight years of our medical school."'[20]

Much has changed in clinical education since the early twentieth century. However, its main missions remain the same. Academic leaders are in charge of transmitting values, standards, and practices of research and healthcare from one generation of physicians to the next. Lately, teaching has become a major and growing challenge. Demand for psychiatrists is climbing worldwide. According to the World Health Organization (WHO), low-income countries have 0.05 psychiatrists per 100 000 people – a rate that is 170 times less than in high-income countries.[21] In the United States there is an estimated shortage of nearly 45 000 psychiatrists.[22] In order to meet patients' needs and enable the field to thrive in the future, present leaders must be prepared to encourage new doctors to choose a career in psychiatry. Good teaching practices are crucial in achieving this goal. Studies have shown that positive early rotation experiences and taking psychiatry electives during medical school training can positively impact the decision to enter the field of mental health.[23] Thus, carefully designed teaching programmes that provide sufficient experience and background can be critical in persuading medical students to choose less popular but much-needed specialities such as psychiatry.

To put forward a compelling vision and assemble an effective teaching programme, leaders in academic psychiatry need to think of different levels and methods of disseminating knowledge: medical education, mentoring, and public outreach.

Medical education

Medical education has witnessed several major changes over the past decade. There is an increasing focus on problem-based learning, application of new technologies, and the need for students to take more responsibility for their own education.[24] Many studies emphasize the growing bench–bedside gap, and the need to prepare doctors-to-be to deal with constantly changing medical technologies, therapies, patient demographics and prevalent diseases.[25] At the same time, in many institutions there is a greater emphasis on research over teaching. Due to financial concerns, some faculty members also feel the pressure to engage more in clinical tasks. Leaders in academic psychiatry need to overcome these shortcomings and create mechanisms to ensure that students and residents gather adequate knowledge and successfully transition to independent careers.[26]

In addition to transmitting and evaluating the required medical knowledge, the best teachers help students grow in understanding, self-awareness, moral development and the ability to relate to others. Rewarding best teachers and providing incentives to faculty for excellent teaching methods and outcomes might be essential in promoting excellence in teaching and building the department's reputation for excellence in education. Benefits of highly rated educational programmes are evident – they help attract the brightest students to such institutions.[3]

In addition to acting as teachers, academic leaders are often responsible for developing an innovative curriculum, overseeing compliance with accreditation standards, and promoting active learning using innovative methods. These leaders act as managers of learning, curriculum designers, facilitators, counsellors and evaluators, changing roles according to individual and group needs.[27]

Mentoring

Mentorship is another critical element of a teaching portfolio that must be developed by leaders in academic medicine. The word *mentor* has its origins in Homer's *Odyssey*, in which the character Mentor was described as a 'wise and trusted counsellor'.[28] A mentor in a research setting plays a variety of roles – from caring parent to friend, from counsellor to consultant, among others. Mentors provide inspiration, broaden perspective, give constructive feedback, and commit to the development of junior faculty. Good mentors tend to possess a high dose of maturity and self-confidence. The measures of a mentor's effectiveness may include the careers of his or her protégés, some of whom will hopefully outgrow their mentor and advance to higher positions in the field.[29]

Receiving adequate mentoring is of critical importance for younger faculty and students, often determining their ability to succeed in academia, as well as in clinical medicine (see also Chapter 10). Mentoring is also highly beneficial for mentors, even the busiest ones. Among the rewards successful mentors often list are fulfillment at witnessing the protégé's progress, the invaluable help provided by the protégé in staying competitive in their area of research, and satisfactory relationships that often turn into life-long friendships.[30]

Successful leaders of medical schools and graduate programmes not only catalyse the development of trainees and younger colleagues through mentoring, but also promote quality mentorship programmes in their institutions.[29] Mentoring skills can and should be evaluated and enhanced.[30]

How can leaders in academic psychiatry further foster the culture of effective mentorship in their departments? A recent study introduced a 'Conceptual Framework of Advancing Institutional Efforts to Support Research Mentorship', a tool that might be useful for institutional and/or department leaders in strengthening mentoring efforts.[31] The proposed model focuses on five key aspects associated with mentoring in research:

- *Criteria for selecting mentors:* Mentor's proficiency and interest in the protégé's area of research; experience with the institution or programme to help protégé navigate through its culture and procedures; and mentor's personal qualities, such as flexibility, patience, support and ability to communicate.
- *Incentives for motivating faculty to serve effectively as mentors:* Awards, financial incentives, and assurance that mentoring is an important part of the departmental culture.
- *Factors that facilitate the mentor-mentee relationship:* Assigning mentors, or self-identification of mentors by mentees; development of written plans that specify goals to be achieved; and policies to ensure that mentees are not exploited due to the imbalance of power between mentors and mentees.
- *Factors that strengthen a mentee's ability to conduct research responsibly:* Ways of ensuring the integrity of mentees and their adherence to stipulated rules, policies and standards of research.
- *Factors that contribute to the professional development of both mentees and mentors:* Helping mentees in networking, publishing, grant writing, developing management skills and understanding their career options.

Leaders in academic psychiatry might find it useful to apply a similar framework to facilitate and evaluate mentorship efforts. Building on this information, leaders can track, evaluate and craft plans to strengthen mentorship efforts.

Public outreach

Disseminating knowledge is not limited to medical students, fellows and colleagues. Top leaders in academic psychiatry also ensure better understanding of mental health by other medical professionals as well as the general public.

Although societal and professional attitudes toward mental health have improved considerably in recent decades, misconceptions are still prevalent in many areas. A cursory look at some statistics might be eye-opening. For instance, even though as many as one-third of the population will suffer from psychological problems at some point in their lives, only one in five will seek treatment.[32] The link between psychological well-being and general health outcomes, life satisfaction and productivity is very often overlooked. Even other physicians can forget that psychiatric problems may underlie other serious health conditions and have a large impact on morbidity and mortality. Therefore, the need for enhancing mental health literacy is evident.[33] Increasing knowledge about diagnosis, management and prevention of psychiatric disorders is an important responsibility of academic leaders.

Leaders in academic medicine should also keep in mind that good relationships with the community are beneficial in a number of ways and help promote the institution's work, trigger individual donations, and encourage the best researchers and graduate students to join the institution. In addition, public funding agencies are often interested in the broader impact of the institution's grant proposals.

In day-to-day operations public outreach requires a blend of activities, including public speaking engagements, development of public programmes for the department, interaction with media, commitment to advocacy roles, partnerships with community organizations and consultation on public policy. Outreach activities can often be coupled with fostering junior researchers' teaching and communication skills.

An outreach element that new leaders often find daunting is interacting with the media (see also Chapter 12), even though it provides opportunities to promote departments and institutions as well as one's own work. When in doubt whether to spend time on interviews, it is good to remember that reporters will tell the story with or without you. Taking the opportunity to showcase the institution's research in a local or national outlet may be highly beneficial to future interest in the institution and funding. Most academic institutions have a public relations office that will manage contacts with journalists and can even provide media training for those who do not feel comfortable in front of the camera.[3]

Healthcare

Clinical medicine is usually a major part of professional activities of physician scientists. Leaders in academic psychiatry, in addition to nurturing their research and educational enterprises, may be responsible for overseeing patient care, building well-organized teams of mental health professionals, setting goals for these teams, and training their members. Leaders who bridge research and clinical practice are in a unique position to translate findings into treatments as well as seeking novel remedies for serious problems observed in patients. Although both research and practice are focused on patient recovery, each of them is driven by unique considerations. Healthcare professionals are trained to obey rules and policies, follow the diagnostic criteria, act fast to save lives, avoid errors, and apply only those novel research findings that pass the meticulous process of clinical trials. Scientists tend to question the status quo, look for new solutions to problems, and invent therapies that might not be used in clinical care for many years.[34] Understanding and blending these approaches fuels successful academic departments of medicine.

Management and administration

It is said that leaders lead by a vision, whereas managers manage different lines of an enterprise to accomplish the vision. It is also stated that leading is like poetry, while managing uses prose.[35] In academic medicine, leaders have to blend poetry and prose at the same time. Their position usually entails a myriad of administration and management tasks. The most common ones include fundraising and budgeting, team-building, hiring and terminating, manoeuvring internal politics, and creating a strategic plan for the department/institution.[36]

Ensuring the financial stability of an academic department of psychiatry is one of the most important responsibilities of a leader, who should not only constantly monitor the available budget, but also know where and how to get additional funding. From keeping up with government grant programmes to developing relationships with the community and securing private endowments, academic leaders often play the role of fundraisers. It is worth keeping in mind that financial difficulties or challenges can bring new opportunities. Times of budget reductions, however painful, are good occasions to review what one is doing and if there is anything that should be improved.[37]

While leaders might think that they are able to do it all, the better ones choose to delegate. This is usually possible because good leaders surround themselves with good colleagues and build excellent teams to effectively fulfil their vision and the mission.[38] However, team-building in academic settings might be challenging, as faculty members often tend to think of themselves as independent contractors, and the freedom to pursue individual interests is one of their top priorities. That is why many leaders in academia refer to their job as 'herding cats'.[39] A 'cultivate and coordinate' rather than 'command and control' model of leadership might make for the most emotionally and intellectually rewarding relationship between leaders and their team members.[9,40]

Strong administration and management skills might also be invaluable while developing strategic plans for departments, programmes and institutions. Such plans detail the leader's vision for their institution and match up the vision with specific goals and resources (staff, finance, space, etc.) needed to achieve these goals. Often they also describe responsibilities of the leader and institution.[41]

Increasing diversity in academic medicine

'A blank wall of social and professional antagonism faces the woman physician that forms a situation of singular and painful loneliness, leaving her without support, respect or professional counsel', said Elizabeth Blackwell, the first woman to receive a medical degree in the United States.[42] Although a lot has changed, more than a century later scientific institutions, teaching hospitals, and universities are still not free from stereotypes, biases and sometimes discrimination. Diversity in academic psychiatry is limited, especially in leadership positions. According to different surveys, women and underrepresented minorities are not advancing through academic ranks or entering leadership positions in academic medicine at the rate of their counterparts.[43] Those who are promoted to higher positions tend to be promoted less rapidly, or quickly hit the glass ceiling. For instance, women psychiatrists account for one-third of the faculty, but only 15% of full professors.[44,45]

Increasing the diversity of leadership in terms of culture, gender, race and ethnicity has been identified as one of the goals of many prestigious professional organizations.[43] It is not just a matter of morality, social fairness or humanity; practical benefits of diverse leadership are numerous. Leaders of different backgrounds and with unique approaches can greatly enrich an organization. Different perspectives promote learning and broaden scientific inquiry. In addition, a significant proportion of researchers coming from under-represented minority groups tend to focus on minority health problems, and may possess better access to subjects or patients coming from such groups.[43,46] Other positive outcomes of diverse leadership include possibilities to improve the organization's image, obtain additional grants and attract a more diverse student, faculty and staff pool. Many studies conducted in the business environment have indicated that organizations with diverse leaderships outperform those that are more homogeneous, in areas such as productivity, effectiveness and overall job satisfaction of employees.[47]

However, students from ethnic minority backgrounds are sometimes discouraged from pursuing a career in mental health research. The reasons for low retention and recruitment rates for minority physician-scientists include a lack of exposure to appropriate role models, mentors and culture of academic medicine; a dearth of suitable mentors; and a paucity of funding required for lengthy training – a barrier to choosing an academic medicine career path, especially for those coming from lower socioeconomic backgrounds.[30] Under-represented minority members who decide to pursue this difficult career path deal with insurmountable obstacles on their way to a leadership position.

Research in the field of business and administration has suggested key strategies for attracting and retaining leaders of both genders and different racial or ethnic backgrounds at every career stage. The most successful strategies include early identification of promising minority candidates and women; removing the barriers to professional advancement for minorities, such as paucity of funds or lack of training; implementing leadership training programmes; providing young, high-potential researchers with minor administrative and managerial opportunities to hone their leadership skills; and developing mentoring programmes for minority faculty.[30]

The Four Capabilities Leadership Framework

How can leaders in academic medicine better understand their own values and skills and develop leadership capacity in an organization? The Four Capabilities Leadership Framework, a tool developed by Ancona *et al.*[48] to help understand and integrate the four critical components of leadership in a business setting, might be adopted in the area of academic medicine. It is applicable mainly to organizational cultures characterized by a motivational approach to people (coordinating rather than commanding) and environments in transition. This tool seeks to help leaders define the main components of their leadership enterprise and discover unique ways of creating change.

Leadership, as presented in the model, consists of four activities:

- *Sense making* – understanding the environment, context and external forces in which a leader is operating.
- *Relating* – building internal and external relationships.
- *Visioning* – developing a vision.
- *Inventing* – creating ways of working to complete the vision.

Leaders should draw on their unique values, skills, experiences, tactics and personality characteristics to carry out these activities and build trust, respect and authenticity in the organization.[48,49]

Attributes important for success

In a study by Keith and Buckley, US and Canadian chairs of psychiatry were asked about attributes needed for them to succeed in their roles. Forty-seven percent of respondents listed interpersonal communication; 45% strategic attributes; 36% integrity and honesty; 36% altruism, tolerance and perseverance (tolerance to blame, patience, tenacity); 22% experience and core skills; and 17% motivational attributes (ability to inspire).[50] Below we provide an extended summary of core attributes that leaders in academic psychiatry may possess and cultivate.

Visionary attitude

While all leaders communicate a shared vision,[51] academic leaders need especially deep-seated passions that are magnetic enough to motivate colleagues, junior faculty and trainees, as well as other stakeholders such as grant institutions and philanthropists.[52] A compelling vision inspires employees, and brings hope to patients. Good leaders couple their vision with a crafted strategic plan that pushes the department or institution toward realizing the vision one step at a time. In today's rapidly shifting healthcare system, academic leaders in psychiatry will need to anticipate likely changes in mental health service delivery and prepare accordingly. One expected and ongoing change is the greying of the population, especially that of mentally ill older adults.[53]

Perseverance, resilience and ability to withstand failure

A study found that 40–50% of the articles published in the top 10 psychiatry journals, ranked by impact factor, gather 30 to 50 citations within 10–15 years.[54] However, the average citation per paper in academic medicine is 0.55.[55] Academic reality is not always filled with prominent conferences, breakthrough research and international awards. Grants are rejected, hypotheses are not confirmed, studies turned down by high-quality journals of first choice, and many studies fail. Without perseverance, resilience, optimistic outlook and the ability to cope with failure, one cannot succeed in a competitive scientific milieu.[56]

Intrinsic motivation and passion for mental health

Advancing science is a calling, not a money-making proposition. Intrinsic motivation is far more important than extrinsic ones. Faculty salaries generally tend to be less lucrative than those of physicians running prosperous private practices. This is true both for those in lower academic ranks and leaders. True belief in the importance of advancing medicine is crucial not only for individual success and work satisfaction, but also for leading, motivating and engaging others in what we do.[57] Yet, success in research can be highly rewarding, especially when it leads to improving the quality of life of our patients.

Cross-cultural communication skills

The world of academia is a global village. As departments of academic psychiatry become more ethnically and culturally diverse, leaders' ability to code-switch between cultures will become critical. While leaders might share the same language, goals and vision with their subordinates or colleagues from different institutions, in order to communicate effectively they should enhance their 'cultural intelligence'. People from different backgrounds might be accustomed to different styles of leadership or work relations. Understanding these nuances will help in motivating employees and preventing misunderstandings, and allow departments of academic psychiatry to work more smoothly.[58]

Wisdom

Personal wisdom includes the traits of rational decision-making; emotional regulation; insight; prosocial behaviours such as compassion, empathy and altruism; decisiveness in the face of uncertainty; and tolerance of divergent value systems.[59,60] One may argue that these traits are essential to succeed as an academic leader too. One difference is that a good leader not only represents her/himself but also the department or institution. In other words, the leader's goal would be not only to exhibit personal wisdom but also to seek to ensure that the top echelons of the department or institution demonstrate wisdom in their behaviour, the hoped-for result being an impeccably high reputation for the organization.

Conclusions

In a dynamic and highly competitive environment, successful leaders in academic psychiatry combine the skills of good physicians, scientists, educators, mentors and managers. Physician-scientists rarely receive formal training geared towards preparing them for leadership positions. In addition to excelling in abilities required for clinicians, leaders in academic psychiatry need to exhibit a blend of management and leadership skills. These skills should be cultivated and enhanced. Successful leadership in academic psychiatry can lead to a better future, not only for a single research team, department, or medical school, but also for its students, patients, communities and, eventually, the society at large.

References

1 Kouzes JM, Posner BZ. *The Truth About Leadership: The No-Fads, Heart-of-the-Matter Facts You Need To Know*. San Francisco, CA: Jossey-Bass, 2010.
2 Bogdewic SP, Baxley EG, Jamison PK. Leadership and organizational skills in academic medicine. *Fam Med* 1997; **29**:262–5.
3 Wilson EA. *Pearls for Leaders in Academic Medicine*. New York: Springer, 2008.
4 Kelly R. *Academic Leadership Qualities for Meeting Today's Higher Education Challenges*. Madison, WI: Magna Publications, 2010.
5 Duda RB. Physician and scientist leadership in academic medicine: strategic planning for a successful academic leadership career. *Curr Surg* 2004; **61**:175–7.

6   Sapienza AM. *Managing Scientists: Leadership Strategies in Scientific Research*, 2nd edn. Hoboken, NJ: John Wiley & Sons, Inc., 2004.

7   Buckley PF, Rayburn WF. Turnover of first-time Chairs in departments of psychiatry. *Acad Psychiatry* 2011; **35**:126–8.

8   Nettleman M, Schuster BL. Internal medicine department chairs: where they come from, why they leave, where they go. *Am J Med* 2007; **120**:186–90.

9   Lee TT, Summergrad P. Leading academic departments of psychiatry. *Acad Psychiatry* 2011; **35**:71–2.

10 Meyer RE. The tripartite mission of an academic psychiatry department and the roles of the chair. *Acad Psychiatry* 2006; **30**:292–7.

11 Roberts LW, Coverdale J, Louie AK. Philanthropy, ethics, and leadership in academic psychiatry. *Acad Psychiatry* 2006; **30**:269–72.

12 Robinowitz CB. Psychiatrists as leaders in academic medicine. *Acad Psychiatry* 2006; **30**: 273–8.

13 Watkins MD. How managers become leaders. *Harvard Bus Rev* June, 2012.

14 NHS Leadership Academy. *Leadership Framework*. Coventry: NHS Institute for Innovation and Improvement, 2011.

15 Shorter EA. *History of Psychiatry: From the Era of the Asylum to the Age of Prozac*. New York: John Wiley & Sons, Inc., 1998.

16 Bennis W. Managing the dream: Leadership in the 21st century. *Training: The Magazine of Human Resource Development* 1990; **27**:44–6.

17 Pato C, Abulseoud O, Pato M. The role of research in academic psychiatric departments: a case study. *Acad Psychiatry* 2011; **35**:139–42.

18 Vaughan D. *The Challenger Launch Decision: Risky Technology, Culture, and Deviance at NASA*. Chicago, IL: University of Chicago Press, 1996.

19 Cohen CM, Cohen SL. *Management Skills for Scientists*. Woodbury, NY: Cold Spring Harbor Laboratory Press, 2005.

20 Olser W. Sir William Osler: On full-time clinical teaching in medical schools. *Can Med Assoc J* 1962; **87**:762–5.

21 Bruckner TA, Scheffler RM, Shen G *et al.* The mental health workforce gap in low- and middle-income countries: a needs-based approach. *Bull World Health Organ* 2011; **89**:184–94.

22 Faulkner LR, Juul D, Andrade NN, *et al.* Recent trends in American board of psychiatry and neurology psychiatric subspecialties. *Acad Psychiatry* 2011; **35**:35–9.

23 Silberman EK, Belitsky R, Bernstein CA *et al.* Recruiting researchers in psychiatry: the influence of residency vs. early motivation. *Acad Psychiatry* 2012; **36**:85–90.

24 Fincher RM, Simpson DE, Mennin SP *et al.* Scholarship in teaching: an imperative for the 21st century. *Acad Med* 2000; **75**:887–94.

25 Ludmerer KM, Johns MM. Reforming graduate medical education. *JAMA* 2005; **294**:1083–7.

26 Association of American Medical Colleges. *Educating Doctors to Provide High Quality Medical Care: A Vision for Medical Education in the United States*. AAMC, 2004.

27 Joyce B, Calhoun E, Hopkins D. *Models of Learning – Tools for Teaching*. Buckingham: Open University Press, 1997.

28 Homer. *The Odyssey* [trans. Armitage S]. London: Faber & Faber, 2006.

29 Sambunjak D, Straus SE, Marusic A. Mentoring in academic medicine: a systematic review. *JAMA* 2006; **296**:1103–15.

30 Jeste DV, Twamley EW, Cardenas V, Lebowitz B, Reynolds CF. A call for training the trainers: focus on mentoring to enhance diversity in mental health research. *Am J Public Health* 2009; **99**:S31–S37.

31 Keyser DJ, Lakoski JM, Lara-Cinisomo S *et al.* Advancing institutional efforts to support research mentorship: a conceptual framework and self-assessment tool. *Acad Med* 2008; **83**:217–25.

32 *Mental Health. A Report of the Surgeon General*. Rockville, MD: US Department of Health and Human Services, Substance Abuse and Mental Health Services Administration, Center for Mental Health Services, National Institutes of Health, National Institute of Mental Health, 1999.

33 Jorm AF, Korten AE, Jacomb PA *et al.* "Mental health literacy": a survey of the public's ability to recognise mental disorders and their beliefs about the effectiveness of treatment. *Med J Aust* 1997; **166**:182–6.

34 Coller BS. Translational research and the physician-scientist. In: Schafer AI (ed.), *The Vanishing Physician-Scientist*. Ithaca and London: ILR Press; 2009, pp. 67–83.

35 Bennis W. *On Becoming A Leader*. Cambridge, MA: Perseus Books, 1995.

36 Broquet KE. Leadership: from a psychiatric to an institutional perspective. *Acad Psychiatry* 2006; **30**: 289–91.

37 Liptzin B, Meyer RE. Financing academic departments of psychiatry. *Acad Psychiatry* 2011; **35**:96–100.

38 Naylor CD. Leadership in academic medicine: reflections from administrative exile. *Clin Med* 2006; **6**:488–92.

39 Scott G, Coates H, Anderson M. (2008) Learning leaders in times of change: academic leadership capabilities for Australian higher education. University of Western Sydney and Australian Council for Educational Rsearch, 2008. Available at: http://works.bepress.com/hamish_coates/3.

40 Hilosky A, Watwood B. Transformational leadership in a changing world: A survival guide for new chairs and deans. Paper presented at the Sixth Annual International Conference of the Chair Academy, Reno, NV, 12–15 Feb, 1997.

41 Munro S. A tool kit for new chairs. *Acad Psychiatry* 2006; **30**:301–3.

42 Blackwell E. *Pioneer Work in Opening the Medical Profession to Women*. London and New York: Longmans, Green and Co., 1895.

43 Institute of Medicine. *In the Nation's Compelling Interest: Ensuring Diversity in the Health Care Workforce*. Washington, DC: National Academies Press, 2004.

44 Association of American Medical Colleges. *Directory of American Medical Education*. AAMC, 2011.

45 Bickel J, Wara D, Atkinson BF *et al.* Increasing women's leadership in academic medicine: report of the AAMC Project Implementation Committee. *Acad Med* 2002; **77**: 1043–61.

46 Nivet MA. Minorities in academic medicine: review of the literature. *J Vasc Surg* 2010; **51**:53S–58S.

47 McCuiston VE, Wooldridge BR, Pierce CK. Leading the diverse workforce: Profit, prospects and progress. *Leadership Organiz Dev J* 2004; **25**:73–92.

48 Ancona D, Kochan T, Scully M, Van Maanen J, Westney E. *Leadership in an Age of Uncertainty. Managing for the Future: Organizational Behavior and Processes*. South-Western College Publishing, 2005.

49 Ancona D, Malone TW, Orlikowski WJ, Senge PM. In praise of the incomplete leader. *Harvard Bus Rev* 2007; **85**:92–100.

50 Keith SJ, Buckley PF. Leadership experiences and characteristics of chairs of academic departments of psychiatry. *Acad Psychiatry* 2011; **35**:118–21.

51 Anthony WA, Huckshorn KA. *Principled Leadership in Mental Health Systems and Programs*. Boston: Boston University Center for Psychiatric Rehabilitation, 2008.

52 Munro S. Balance, safety, and passion: three principles for academic leaders. *Acad Psychiatry* 2011; **35**:134–5.

53 Jeste DV, Alexopoulos GS, Bartels SJ *et al.* Consensus statement on the upcoming crisis in geriatric mental health: Research agenda for the next two decades. *Arch Gen Psychiatry* 1999; **56**:848–53.

54 Hunt GE, Cleary M, Walter G. Psychiatry and the Hirsch h-index: The relationship between journal impact factors and accrued citations. *Harv Rev Psychiatry* 2010; **18**:207–19.
55 Thomson Reuters. Essential Science Indicators Database. Available at: http://thomsonreuters.com/products_services/science/science_products/scientific_research/research_evaluation_tools/essential_science_indicators/[accessed 15 April 2013].
56 Tasman A. Reminiscences and reflections on leadership. *Acad Psychiatry* 2011; **35**:129–33.
57 Weiss RL. Leadership in academic psychiatry: the vision, the 'givens,' and the nature of leaders. *Acad Psychiatry* 2009; **33**:85–8.
58 Molinsky AL, Davenport TH, Iyer B, Davidson C. Three skills every 21st-century manager needs. *Harvard Bus Rev* 2012; **90**:139–43.
59 Meeks TW, Jeste DV. Neurobiology of wisdom: A literature overview. *Arch Gen Psychiatry* 2009; **66**:355–65.
60 Jeste DV, Harris JC. Wisdom – a neuroscience perspective. *JAMA* 2010; **304**:1602–3.

Chapter 14

Taking People With You

David M. Ndetei and Patrick Gatonga

Introduction

As has been reiterated in previous chapters of this book, the field of mental health presents some of the most challenging leadership encounters. These challenges range from the management of patients whom many societies regard as outcasts, an enormous workload on mental health professionals, the stigma that straddles all stakeholders and population groups, to the scarcity of every resource required to address the growing burden of disease. While all these challenges present unique opportunities, the human resource challenge is regarded as the most important.[1,2] Thus, to the mental health professional, knowing how to provide effective leadership requires an appreciation of the value of people. One has to recognize the value not only of one's own colleagues but also of people at all levels of the mental healthcare system. This means regarding the patient, family, community, other healthcare workers, government and all other stakeholders as part of a large treatment model. Exploitation of the opportunities that exist within this model can be a very fruitful venture.

Which people?

The importance of the role people play is not unique to the mental health profession. It applies to all areas and sectors.[3] Take, for example, the ordinary day of an employee in the bakery who has to report to work by 8.00 am every weekday. Assume she is married and the mother of two children. Thus she has to run two institutions, family and work. In the family she has to learn how to develop a home environment in which everyone is happy. Note that her system of work is not just the internal environment at the bakery, but also the external environment that includes her family. Whenever she leaves home happy, knowing that she has left behind a happy, contented family, she is bound to have a more productive day at work. If she heads her department at work, she is more likely to be more effective in her work and interact amiably with her team. This team then becomes motivated and is happy to have a leader who is approachable, friendly and happy. She is able to facilitate a calm working environment. Notice that the success of her department

Leadership in Psychiatry, First Edition. Edited by Dinesh Bhugra, Pedro Ruiz and Susham Gupta.
© 2013 John Wiley & Sons, Ltd. Published 2013 by John Wiley & Sons, Ltd.

at the bakery depends on how she is able to effectively value the people in her family and at work, taking them along with her so that they can be part of her success. In other words, one must look at every system both internally and externally. The people in both environments are key to the success of the system. Similarly, in the mental healthcare system, a great leader must recognize the influence of various people who may be direct or indirect stakeholders in the system.

Of course there are elements that vary from profession to profession and industry to industry. For example, the dynamics of a singer's professional system must be different from that of a psychiatrist who has to attend to patients who are mentally ill and are facing the even bigger challenge of societal neglect. Nevertheless, people are still the most important resource in any system, and knowing how to take people with you then becomes an essential skill that must be possessed by any leader, particularly in mental health.

Let us now consider a typical example of a mental health scenario that is common in many countries. You are the chief psychiatrist at a large city hospital in Kerala state in India. The ward round for your department has just begun. The history is nothing new to you; you have come across many of its kind. A family brings a patient to the hospital complaining that the patient is talking a lot and making too much noise. They also complain that the patient is very dirty and has not taken a shower for several weeks (you actually had suspected this upon meeting the patient!). They then tell you that the patient does not listen to anyone. On the night before his admission the patient appeared very reserved and was found in his bedroom about to commit suicide by hanging himself. The relatives have since abandoned the patient hoping that the hospital would take care of the patient. Actually, your staff are complaining that there are far too many abandoned patients, and there are not enough staff to take care of them. The psychiatric ward has four nurses, two clinical psychologists and you – the only psychiatrist. The ward has 52 patients but a capacity of only 26 beds. More than half of the admitted patients have been abandoned by relatives. You recall that you sit on the hospital management board in the capacity of a head of department. The challenges facing your department have been overwhelming. Yet, you understand that the hospital statistics show a much greater burden of acute illnesses such as diarrhoeal diseases and HIV/AIDs. Over the last decade or so, most financial and other resources have been channelled towards the more visibly debilitating diseases. You have attempted to secure some resources for your department but all your efforts have come to naught. As you continue with the ward round, you look around and all you see is four members of your staff looking at you hopefully to guide on management decisions for every patient whose psychiatric history is read out. You notice that while making choices on the best drugs to administer, you are stuck with just a few options. The hospital has only managed to secure a few first-generation generic drugs. As you raise your head to respond to one of your clinical officers' questions, you almost feel helpless once you notice that you are like five small boats sailing in troubled waters. There are patients walking around you in all directions. Some are shouting; others are naked; others are showing side effects from out-of-date first-generation drugs. Their relatives have been overdosing them with drugs with the presumption that they will get better so long as they are on drugs. You almost feel like your career is worthless. What do you do? Where do you begin?

Valuing your team

Case Study 14.1

A well-known mental health centre run by a large hospital in New York has grown tremendously. After the retirement of its administrative leader, the human resources department hired a new administrator to head the centre, a well-known psychiatrist called Dr Cameron. He has been hired on a part-time basis due to other professional commitments at the university and in his private practice.

The centre's popularity has been growing over time. Many local citizens and foreigners have sought psychological treatment at the centre. In order to manage the increased patient load, Dr Cameron increases the number of staff psychologists from four to eight. He adds another five intern psychologists in order to boost the centre's capacity.

Due to his commitments, Dr Cameron reschedules supervision meetings with the psychologists to evenings, once every 2 weeks. However, the atmosphere at the meetings now becomes very tense. Many of the psychologists try to discuss their patients, but the time scheduled for these meetings is insufficient to accommodate all 13 psychologists. Additionally, the psychologists have different professional philosophies about treatment plans. Some favour a psychoanalytic approach while others are for a cognitive approach.

Some young practitioners are voicing complaints that the supervision meetings are useless because Dr Cameron has no time to help them with the most challenging patient dilemmas. Consequently, only four psychologists attend the supervision sessions.

Recently, the general manager of the hospital has held two meetings with all Mental Health Center staff including Dr Cameron and the psychologists. The discussion is centred on the drastic drop in the number of patients applying for treatment at the centre.

Case Study 14.1 illustrates how good teamwork guided by a visionary leader can lead to successful mental health intervention strategies. It also illustrates how the converse can be disastrous. The point to take home is that teams present an opportunity for leaders. A good leader recognizes that the team he/she leads is a valuable asset. This team should function as a unit. A good team's unity is easily evidenced as work performance is streamlined with no redundancies between or among members. Team members also form coherent bonds, with every member clearly recognizing their function in the team. Importantly, members fully understand the overall goal of the team and are inspired to go beyond achieving that goal (see also Chapter 9). To achieve this, leaders and potential leaders in mental health should develop the tactics discussed below.

Empowering the team

Empowerment is one of the greatest drivers of performance for any team member.[4] Once team members are empowered, they are motivated to perform and deliver beyond expectation. Mental health professionals can be empowered by making them realize their abilities and talents. This is done through constant appraisal and emphasis on their positive aspects. For instance, the team leader in a mental health team could recognize the counselling abilities of a team member, or the talent for treatment insight in another. Yet another team player could be good at communicating with patients, and so on. Given the constant challenges of mental health professionals in dealing with disturbed patients, anxious families and stigmatized illnesses, empowerment of mental healthcare professionals becomes an important motivator in the profession.

Good leaders also recognize their team members' best lines of growth. This requires keeping them in close contact and adopting an open-door policy to enable team members to open up. However, a delicate balance should be struck so as not to imply any sense of micromanagement. Such a perception could lead to negative opinions and provoke adverse reactions from team members.

Some of the signs that a team is empowered include autonomy of work, initiative and innovation. Empowered team members are able to work independently without supervision. If left to themselves, they ensure that the work runs smoothly and efficiently. They feel free to innovate and come up with new ideas. For instance, a good team may come up with innovative ways of providing psychosocial support to patients and families so as to treat the family as a whole. They may also develop creative ways of tackling psychosocial problems that occur commonly among the mentally ill patients in their unit.

Developing relationships

Team management and leadership are the most critical ingredients of a successful mental health system.[5] This partly involves developing good relationships with the team. The fact that mental health professionals are scarce makes them not only marketable professionals but also often indispensable. One of the shortcomings of this reality is that these professionals could easily develop eccentric approaches to their work, and care little about the good of the team. In some countries, these team members also run their own private practices into which they are bound to invest more time and concentration. As such, team leaders should aim to build good relationships so that team members care about the good of the team as a whole. This applies to players at all levels and in all sectors, both public and private (see Chapter 9).

Perhaps the great question running through one's mind is how to build such relationships. Many studies have shown that good teamwork is enhanced by team-building activities. These activities need not be task-based outdoor activities; they can also include such activities as continuous medical education on current issues in mental health. Other forums for career development and breakfast meetings are additional ways to create cohesive bonds among team members and thus strengthen relationships among them.

Effective communication

Every book on leadership has 'communication' as part of its content.[6] Therefore in this case the topic may sound like a cliché. However, the peculiarities of the broader medical profession and mental health in particular make this an important point to note. Most leaders in healthcare, especially mental health, attain their status by virtue of their more superior training. The medical culture also has an additional characteristic of possessing a strict hierarchical culture. For instance, the head of the team may be appointed on the basis of being the longest serving psychiatrist or the psychiatrist with the highest academic achievement. Though this tendency for managerial appointments is being questioned in terms of its effectiveness, it is still prevalent in almost all countries, and is so engrained in many countries that it is the norm rather than the exception. One of the shortcomings of this strategy is that persons appointed in this manner have an inherent tendency to be arrogant and disregarding of their juniors' feelings and opinions.

Mental health leaders need to communicate effectively with their team members in order to win their support and cooperation. While support may be granted to the leader out of fear on the part of the juniors, the vision of a mental health team cannot be realized without effective communication between the leader and the rest of the team. Thus leaders need to allow members to speak their minds freely. Leaders, for their part, should provide a confident, clear, accurate, honest and forthright response.

Willingness to serve team members

Mental health team leaders are often called upon in crises. These crises range from hospital emergencies to disasters. For instance, one may be called to attend to a violent patient or to provide support in the case of a tragic natural disaster. While some may be crises that require the intervention of a leader, others may be crises that other team members can handle. Again, drawing from the rigidity of the medical professional hierarchy, a leader may be naturally inclined to feel like a subordinate when asked to attend to some duties that others could attend to. However, leaders should place themselves in such a position that they can serve others not only when called upon, but also when they sense the need. This not only provides the team members with reassurance but also encourages them to develop themselves further, grow in the profession and serve in the team.

Taking the mentally ill patient with you

The individual patient

What do you do if somebody has no insight of their mental illness? What do you do if a patient's anxiety disorder is affecting their lives? What do you do if a patient's involvement in a tragedy causes a persistent post-traumatic disorder?

Many a time, solutions to these problems lie within the patient. Being a leader in mental health does not mean that your leadership is just confined to leading fellow professionals or colleagues. It also means leading the patient into finding a lasting solution. It means knowing that the patient should be part of the treatment programme, not a mere recipient.

Mental health problems require a tremendous amount of patient involvement. They also involve helping the patient to learn how to cope with daily challenges as well as how to develop sustainable strategies for themselves. Sometimes we fail in achieving the results we want simply because we forget that the patient is a client. Like any successful business operator will tell you, putting the client first is key to success. It is best to tailor services to clients' needs, allowing them to communicate their perceived needs. It is only through engaging them in this manner that we can get to know whether or not we meet their expectations.

Mentally ill patients need to be involved in their own treatment. Although there may be exceptions where this is not entirely possible, many mentally ill patients are capable of being involved in their own treatment. It is important that mental health leaders develop programmes to promote patient education as well as self-help programmes for patients with mental illness.

The synergy of support groups

Leaders can also explore the opportunities to enroll patients into support groups. Support groups for mental health provide mutual support and peer support.[7] Mutual support is a process by which people voluntarily come together to help each other address common problems. The members could be sharing the same type of problem or not. Peer support is social, emotional and instrumental support that is mutually offered or provided by persons with similar mental health conditions where there is some mutual agreement on what is helpful.

Examples of existing groups are Emotions Anonymous, the Depression and Bipolar Support Alliance (DBSA), GROW, and Recovery International. Mental Health America (MHA) and the National Alliance on Mental Illness (NAMI) are large organizations based in the United States, and other local organizations exist in different countries and regions. The role of the leader is to provide a link between patients at the health facility or community and these support groups.

Building partnerships with families and the community

The burden of mental illness is enormous and growing. Furthermore, some mental illnesses that are prevalent in an area reflect the nature of the external environment in which the patient lives. This environment could be the cause of maladaptive behaviour evident in the patient. The environment consists of families and the community – the people with whom the patient is in day-to-day contact. For instance, in a community where consumption of drugs such as alcohol is highly prevalent, then members of the community are likely to present with drug- and substance use-related mental disorders. In a community where poverty is rife, then there are likely to be disorders like depression and schizophrenia triggered by these environmental constraints. Indeed, a good mental health leader recognizes that the dynamics of mental illness are broad and varied.

As such, good leadership entails involvement of the family and the community. The healthcare facility should not be an island or institution where mentally ill people are dumped with the hope of recovery after some time. The community should be educated to realize that mental illness is an illness not only for the patient but also for the community.

Ways of building partnerships with families and the community are many. For instance, for illnesses that do not require hospitalization, families can be encouraged to provide support to the patient while he or she is still at home. They are guided on how to do this. It is then up to the leader of the mental health team to facilitate ways in which families are educated about mental illnesses once they bring a patient to the hospital. While doing so, good leaders also ensure that a rapport is struck between the patient and mental health professionals so as to establish mutual trust and partnership. This can be done through encouraging other professionals in the team to do so and by serving as an example oneself. One must also have sound judgement on which families qualify for being allowed to take care of the patient at home. Some families, given this opportunity, may actually aggravate an existing situation.

The community at large is also an important component of mental illness management. As patients attend the hospital for various illnesses, mental health professionals should provide integrated services for screening mental illnesses especially where it is suspected that there may be existing risk factors. This, however, cannot take place without a good leader backed by an empowered mental health team. Several opportunities exist to provide these kinds of services. Importantly, screening does not require a trained mental health professional. It can be done by general health workers who are taught how to use various screening tools for common mental health disorders. Many mental health leaders such as heads of departments have the privilege of sitting on such forums as hospital committees. They therefore have the opportunity to propose the implementation of integrated mental health services that address the specific needs of a community.

There are examples of successful community involvement in mental healthcare. The World Health Organization (WHO) task-shifting model has been adopted in several developing countries including Brazil, Kenya, Nigeria and India. This has served to improve the availability of human resources to address the growing mental health burden. The model has proved to be effective particularly where visionary mental health leaders provide appropriate leadership to ensure successful and sustainable implementation of this model.

Building partnerships with NGOs

Mental health leaders recognize that team effort, family and community participation are crucial for a successful mental healthcare system. Additionally, they recognize that the system requires more support from other stakeholders particularly in terms of resources to aid in implementation of effective programmes.

Many non-governmental organizations (NGOs) created to improve mental health mobilize resources from different parts of the world in order fulfil their objectives. These NGOs seek the collaboration of reputable institutions that provide mental healthcare. Good leaders in such institutions therefore would take advantage of these existing opportunities. It is through such collaborations that major programmes can be designed and implemented. The organizations come with a wealth of human, financial and other resources that provide the necessary expertise and experience to boost mental healthcare in hospitals and communities. Such organizations include Global Mental Health in the United Kingdom and Africa Mental Health Foundation in Africa. Opportunities of this nature also provide avenues for career development and broadening experience for team members at local health facilities. It is therefore prudent that a leader of a mental healthcare provision team recognizes such opportunities and utilizes them.

In the United Kingdom, for example, mental health services are undergoing change with the creation of more foundation trusts. This change has additionally brought a need for business intelligence so that information is available on care delivered, the outcomes and the financial costs. This gives clinicians a more comprehensive understanding of the care delivered, empowering them to make more meaningful decisions, and to work more closely with commissioners to shape future healthcare delivery.

Building partnerships with the local administration and government

Here we must emphasize again that mental health issues are very broad, straddling a variety of sectors. Patients with mental illnesses may not just require treatment at a health facility for them to get well. Often they require social support. A wise leader takes cognizance of this fact. The leader should understand that in order to achieve a permanent solution to a patient's problem, various elements in the patient's life have to be addressed. Failure to realize this results in patients presenting to health facilities many times over. This happens because their risk factors are not fully addressed. Consider Case Study 14.2.

Case Study 14.2

Michael Smith lost his parents through a tragic accident in London when he was 9 years old. He was the only child. He was then taken in by an uncle's family. Michael's new 'parents' divorced 3 years after he started living with them. He then chose to live with the uncle. His uncle, distressed by the divorce suit, took to drinking and stopped taking care of Michael, who was attending middle school at the time. Michael soon began taking alcohol himself. After completing high school, Michael worked at a local supermarket. He spent most of his money on alcohol. He landed in trouble regularly at work due to his drink problem. After a short while he was fired. He got other jobs, but his drink problem would soon see him kicked out. Eventually, he was jobless and addicted to alcohol.

One day, on his way to his house, he collapsed on a pavement near a park. Passers-by called an ambulance, which took him to hospital. After receiving emergency treatment he was stabilized and admitted to the general ward. Later, after a full medical history was obtained from him, he was transferred to the psychiatric unit where he was scheduledto receive treatment for alcohol dependence. He was, however, jobless and had little hope for success in life despite continued assurance that he could overcome the problem.

As a leader of the psychiatric unit in Case Study 14.2, what would you do to solve Michael's problem? Remember that if Michael is offered treatment for his alcohol dependence problem, he will recover but will likely return to his alcohol consumption habits. Again, remember that your unit will have many other patients with similar problems as well as others with different problems that require your attention.

As a leader, you cannot do everything alone. You need to take people with you! With a good mental health team at the local hospital, the team can take care of the acute needs as well as the rehabilitation needs at the hospital. Keep in mind that you need to support the team so that the patient does not return to hospital time and again because of the same problem. This is where other stakeholders come in. As a leader, you need to create partnerships with local authorities and government to provide social support to needy patients. For instance, the government could provide jobs and schooling opportunities for patients in order to fully address their needs and risk factors. Through the local authorities, follow-up is also easier since these authorities usually have good grass roots knowledge of community members.

The desirable outcome for the individual in Case Study 14.2 is that the patient's alcohol dependence problem is fully treated. At the same time, it is desirable that the patient's social problems are treated, including getting a job. Of course there is no drug that can treat his job problem! This is where leadership plays a critical role in building partnerships with job providers. It is not just jobs that patients need. It could be education through special schools, particularly for children and disabled persons.

Looking beyond borders

With globalization, geographical boundaries have been breached or supplanted by modern technology and cultural mingling throughout the world. Many industries now operate globally, and mental health needs to borrow from them. Several opportunities exist for leaders to explore, and there are many willing partners in global mental healthcare. They come from different countries, some of which have experience with developing and implementing successful intervention strategies for mental health. These open doors for continual learning by mental health teams in various parts of the world. For instance, there are opportunities to learn about innovative research models and programmes that can aid in reducing the mental health treatment gap as well as boosting human capacity to address the mental health burden. Spotting such opportunities and exploring them is in the province of a mental health leader. Indeed, that is where the future lies; taking people with you, beginning with the patient next to you and going beyond borders to overseas colleagues and partners.

References

1 Saxena S, Thornicroft G, Knapp M, Whiteford H. Resources for mental health: scarcity, inequity, and inefficiency. *Lancet* 2007; **370**:878–89.
2 Bartlett CA, Ghoshal S. Building competitive advantage through people. *MIT Sloan Management Review* 2002; Winter. Available at: http://iic.wiki.fgv.br/file/view/Bartlett+%26+Ghosal+2002.pdf [accessed 15 April 2013].
3 Drake RE, Goldman HH, Leff HS *et al*. Implementing evidence-based practices in routine mental health service settings. *Psychiatric Serv* 2001; **52**:179–82.
4 Levi D, Slem C. Team work in research and development organizations: the characteristics of successful teams. *Int J Ind Ergonom* 1995; **16**:29–42.

5 Feldman F, Khademian A. Inclusive management: building relationships with the public. UC Irvine: Center for the Study of Democracy, 2002. Available at: http://escholarship.org/uc/item/7rp1985z [accessed 15 April 2013].
6 Fletcher M. The effects of internal communication, leadership and team performance on successful service quality implementation: a South African perspective. *Team Performance Management* 1999; **5**:150–63.
7 Broadhead WE, Kaplan BH, James SA *et al.* The epidemiologic evidence for a relationship between social support and health. *Am J Epidemiol* 1983; **117**:521–37.

Chapter 15

Leaders and Managers: A Case Study in Organizational Transformation – the Sheppard Pratt Experience, 1990–2011

Robert Roca and Steven S. Sharfstein

Introduction

The psychiatric hospital in the twenty-first century is a complex and ever-changing organization. The organizational dynamics expressed by the relationship among leaders, managers and healthcare workers are a special challenge during this era of major reform. When there is a paradigm shift in the economics of care and market survival strategies, the leader of the organization (such as the psychiatric hospital) takes on a Darwinian perspective as he/she witnesses the demise of sister institutions in the face of such challenges. But, the changes and challenges are not only in the realm of economics. In hospital psychiatry, there are many complexities, including the use of medications that stabilize severe symptoms and enable rapid discharge but have significant side effects; legal and regulatory issues relating to the rights of patients that make it difficult to treat very ill individuals who refuse care; and new ideas contained within the community mental health ideologies, such as the concept of 'recovery'.

This chapter will look at the various roles of leaders and managers in the context of a case study of one psychiatric hospital in the United States with a 120-year history of patient care. The first part will review the role of the psychiatric hospital in the United States as the provider of long-term, institutional care for the first 100 years of its existence, and the new roles for the psychiatric hospital that emerged following deinstitutionalization (which began 50 years ago). We will then embark on a case study of Sheppard Pratt, a private, not-for-profit hospital located in Baltimore, Maryland, that moved away from long-stay inpatient care and underwent a major reinvention in the context of changes that began in 1990 as the result of managed care. The case study will highlight the various roles of leaders and managers in this transformation; the skills of the physician leaders in the organization, including the CEO and medical director (who are both physicians), in implementing these changes; and the ongoing tensions moving forwards into the twenty-first century.

Leadership in Psychiatry, First Edition. Edited by Dinesh Bhugra, Pedro Ruiz and Susham Gupta.
© 2013 John Wiley & Sons, Ltd. Published 2013 by John Wiley & Sons, Ltd.

The evolution of the psychiatric hospital in the United States

There are two distinct subtexts in the story of hospital psychiatry in the United States. Beginning in the late eighteenth and early nineteenth centuries, public institutions, funded primarily by the states and counties, were established to provide care to a diverse population of patients with behavioural disorders sufficiently severe to preclude residence in the community. Many of these patients had schizophrenia and other conditions for which there was no effective specific treatment, and many patients remained hospitalized indefinitely. By 1955, the peak of 'asylum' psychiatry in the United States, more than half a million individuals resided in state and county mental hospitals.

Over the same period of time, private psychiatric hospitals came on the scene for the treatment of patients with less severe conditions and with the financial resources to pay for care. Many of these were founded by philanthropists who were moved by the plight of the mentally ill and drawn to establish institutions grounded in the humane principles of 'moral treatment'. As psychoanalytic theory became the dominant force in US psychiatry in the early part of the twentieth century, many of these private hospitals became bastions of long-term psychoanalytically informed inpatient care. Length of stay was measured in months or years. With the inception of private health insurance, these facilities became accessible to persons who were not wealthy. By the 1970s and 1980s, inpatient psychiatric care was in demand, and the private hospitals flourished.[1]

The landscape began to change for the public hospitals in the 1950s. With the advent of antipsychotic medication, psychiatrists were able to offer treatment that ameliorated delusions and hallucinations, and it became possible to consider discharging patients for whom custodial inpatient care had previously been a life sentence. Over the next few years, there were legal challenges to long-term inpatient confinement. In addition, there was an ideological shift in favour of community-based care emphasizing strengths rather than impairment and focusing on helping 'consumers' attain achievable life goals rather than settling for patienthood as their principal identity. As a result of all these factors, there were only 60 000 patients in public hospitals by 2010.[2]

The landscape changed radically for private psychiatric hospitals in the late 1980s. Payers and employers grew impatient with paying for long-term hospital care and began to apply the methods of 'managed care' to reduce their costs. Case managers working for the payers reviewed cases concurrently and challenged the 'medical necessity' of hospitalization at the time of admission and throughout the stay. Hospitals were not reimbursed for care that did not meet stringent medical necessity criteria, requiring strong evidence that outpatient treatment was not a safe alternative. Over the course of only a few years, hospitals experienced markedly diminished lengths of stay; psychiatric beds lay empty, and hospital revenues plunged. Facilities began to close, and it became clear to hospital leaders that survival would require a radical change in course.[1]

Sheppard Pratt in 1990

In the 1850s, a successful Quaker businessman named Moses Sheppard met Dorothea Dix, a passionate advocate for the humane treatment of persons with mental illness. As a result of this experience, he decided to establish the Sheppard Asylum in Baltimore as a centre for the compassionate treatment of the mentally ill. By the time its doors opened in 1891, the Asylum had been renamed the Sheppard and Enoch Pratt Hospital in recognition of a substantial gift from Enoch Pratt, another Quaker philanthropist from Baltimore.[3]

Like most similar institutions, Sheppard Pratt was profoundly affected by the psycho-analytic movement in the early part of the twentieth century and became a centre for long-term, psychoanalytically oriented hospital care. For decades, 322 beds remained filled with patients who stayed for months and left when they were well or when their funding ran out, whichever came first. The principal tasks of the CEO were keeping the beds filled with paying patients and keeping expenses under control. There was little need for entrepreneurial creativity. The most notable initiative in these years was Sheppard Pratt's collaboration in the 1970s with the local public mental health authority to co-sponsor a community mental health centre as a public-private partnership, the only such arrangement in the nation.

In the late 1980s, Sheppard Pratt, like all similar institutions, began to feel the seismic impact of the managed care revolution. By the early 1990s, the waiting list had gone away and beds lay unoccupied. Threatened by shrinking revenue and burdened by high fixed costs, Sheppard Pratt experienced increasing and unsustainable financial losses, and the need for change became urgently apparent.

This new environment made new demands on leaders. No longer was it sufficient to understand how to deliver long-term inpatient care to a reliable stream of paying clients. Leaders now needed to be knowledgeable about other care delivery models, to understand finance and marketing, to be adept at helping staff make the transition to the new realities, and to recognize and release staff members who were unable or unwilling to make the transition. They also needed to be prepared to be vigilant and flexible so that they could make further course adjustments as circumstances continued to change.

Sheppard Pratt's transformational response to this crisis began in 1992 when the Board of Trustees named Steven S. Sharfstein, MD, as the fifth director in the 100-year history of the institution. In the 6 months prior to accepting this challenge, the new CEO was sent to the Harvard Business School for the Advanced Management Program to provide him with the substrate of skills needed for the kind of changes anticipated. This programme offered a basis for understanding the management challenges and financial issues in an environment of convulsive change and also encouraged a spirit of entrepreneurial creativity and courage. Dr Sharfstein's background as a community psychiatrist, public health administrator and researcher on the economics of psychiatric care gave him a unique perspective on the changes that needed to happen.

Changing vision and strategy

It was clear that the new circumstances called for a fundamental re-examination of the vision and strategy of a century-old institution. The challenge was to identify financially viable solutions that were consistent with a mission inspired by nineteenth century Quaker ideals. This meant developing mission-consistent programmes that would provide revenue streams adequate to cover their own direct costs as well as corporate overheads, and operating them in a manner that did not compromise safety and effectiveness.

What emerged was a vision of a 'hospital without walls', a community mental health *system* focused on providing comprehensive services to a geographically dispersed community of need. This was not a surprising vision in light of the fact that the new CEO was a psychiatrist who was trained in community psychiatry and was confident that excellent care could be provided in a continuum of care in which the hospital was used primarily for short-term containment and crisis stabilization and the remainder of the treatment was provided in less restrictive (and less expensive) environments, such as day treatment and intensive outpatient settings.

The strategy supporting this vision included reorienting most inpatient units to crisis stabilization rather than long-term care, creating day hospital and intensive outpatient programmes throughout the region, and identifying new mission-consistent activities that would diversify sources of revenue.

Some of these strategies were successful. Residential and educational programmes were developed for youths whose psychiatric symptoms rendered them unsafe in the community. Day school programmes were created for children who were able to live in the community but had developmental problems and/or psychiatric symptoms that made them inappropriate for mainstream schools. These programmes met Sheppard Pratt founder's imperative 'to meet a need that would not otherwise be met' while providing funding from a new revenue source (i.e. the school system).

Encouraged by the success of the community mental health partnership experiment with the local public mental health authority, Sheppard Pratt acquired several smaller, economically challenged non-profit organizations that offered psychiatric rehabilitation, supervised housing and outpatient services to persons with serious and persistent mental illness. These arrangements allowed the smaller 'affiliate' organizations to remain true to their mission, made them profitable by enabling them to reduce overhead expenses, and provided Sheppard Pratt with yet another revenue stream.

Even as general inpatient units emptied in response to the pressures of managed care, demand for inpatient care remained strong in certain niches. There was a persistent need for inpatient services for patients who could not be treated safely in the community and who were not appropriate for general inpatient psychiatric units. These included children, the very elderly, aggressive psychotic patients, persons with comorbid developmental disability, and persons with complex post-traumatic syndromes. Units serving many of these populations had already been established at Sheppard Pratt, and some had regional and even national referral bases. Other special groups of patients remained unserved, and during this time, units were developed to accommodate some of them (e.g. adolescents with developmental disabilities complicated by severe behavioural problems). In the course of making such adjustments to the market, Sheppard Pratt moved incrementally down a strategic road that sought to identify and distinguish the inpatient hospital as a place where clinicians and payers could refer their most difficult cases. Many of these patients had Medicare, which was, for the most part, not managed. Others had commercial coverage from companies desperate to find a source of definitive care for patients with special needs who had repeatedly failed short-term inpatient treatment efforts in other facilities. The result was a large cohort of challenging patients who required longer lengths of stay, thereby helping maintain the inpatient census (and associated revenues), and whose positive outcomes earned Sheppard Pratt a reputation as a high-quality institution capable of treating patients who had fared poorly elsewhere.

During this period we also discovered that general hospitals with psychiatric units often found it difficult to recruit psychiatrists and otherwise manage their behavioural health programme. A number of those hospitals approached Sheppard Pratt to take on physician recruitment and the management of part or all of the service. The contracts generally involved physician recruitment and were structured to cover their direct costs as well as a portion of corporate overhead expense. But beyond this, the contracts differed significantly because the wishes of each host hospital were unique. To grow this line of business, leaders needed to build the contract to the particular specifications of the customer. This strategy succeeded in securing several such contracts in the region and resulted in new revenues as well as heightened visibility in the community and the emergence of a network of care, with the most difficult cases being referred from the general hospitals to the specialty hospital for tertiary care.

Not every strategy was successful. Early in the managed care revolution, it was expected that fee-for-service payment would rapidly give way to capitation arrangements that would fund the creation of outpatient networks capable of managing psychiatric conditions in the community while greatly reducing the need for hospitalization. In anticipation of this development, the Sheppard Pratt Health Plan was created as a means of obtaining and managing capitation contracts. The thought was that vertical integration would provide clinical, financial and competitive advantages, and day hospital and outpatient services were expanded throughout the region. But, it turned out that Sheppard Pratt was not competitive with large insurance companies for these capitation contracts. When Sheppard Pratt Health Plan did secure contracts, the capitation rates were so low that they did not cover the costs of care, in part because of adverse selection (i.e. the patients with psychiatric illness preferentially selected the company with which we contracted precisely because they knew they needed to use the psychiatric benefit) and, in part, because Sheppard Pratt, with its reputation on the line, was not very good at denying care. Most of the remaining outpatient work was reimbursed at discounted fee-for-service rates that did not cover the costs of the outpatient network. After several years of losses, it became clear that the Health Plan was a failed experiment. It was sold, and the majority of outpatient centres were closed and their patients were transferred to the clinics operated by Sheppard Pratt's community affiliates.

As these events unfolded, it became clear that inpatient care was not going away. This was partly a result of the fact that the new economics of mental healthcare did not fund outpatient care sufficiently to make it viable. So, outpatient services closed and patients in crisis had nowhere to go except emergency rooms, where they waited for many hours – and sometimes for days – until an inpatient bed was found. Accordingly, the demand for inpatient care began to increase in the early 2000s, and so did the need for crisis services by which patients could get access to these inpatient resources. In this setting, it made sense to restore bed capacity, and this was undertaken. It also seemed strategic to improve access to inpatient care by creating an in-house crisis assessment programme that would allow patients who were judged (or judged themselves) in need of hospital care to come directly to the hospital for evaluation rather than go to an emergency room. Over the years, Sheppard Pratt developed increasingly accessible and patient-friendly crisis evaluation services and discovered that the majority of these patients qualified for treatment on the inpatient or day hospital services. As of this writing, the hospital service is busier than it has been in years and functions as the economic engine of the health system. At the same time, the schools, residential programmes, general hospital contracts and affiliate programmes are pulling their own weight and helping cover corporate overheads. Sheppard Pratt today is the leading behavioural healthcare organization in the state, treating more than 50 000 individuals annually in many locations. It operates two specialty psychiatric hospitals, 12 schools and two residential treatment centres for adolescents; it has contracts with six general hospitals; it employs nearly 3000 personnel, including 92 psychiatrists; and has an annual operating budget of $270 million per year.

Lessons in leadership over the past 20 years – a personal reflection

The last 20 years taught us at least three important lessons about leadership. First, it clearly was important to have a vision and to devise strategies supportive of that vision. But it was even more important to maintain a high level of vigilance and recognize when a strategy was not working so that prudent, mission-consistent adjustments could be made. This was the single most important task of leadership.

Second, it was critical to find ways of managing fixed costs in an environment of fluctuating volumes of service and revenues. Since salaries were the single greatest source of expense, it was essential to keep salary costs as low as possible consistent with maintaining service capacity and quality. The latter – maintaining service quality – was important not only because of our moral and professional obligation to do so, but also because our reputation for high quality was a source of competitive advantage and thus vital for business success. One implication of this was that staffing costs could not be reduced in a manner that compromised clinical outcomes or detracted from the experience of patients, referrers and payers. This moved us to look for opportunities to reduce fixed staffing costs, mainly in administrative areas responsible for functions that could be redistributed to other departments. The result was the elimination of several costly administrative positions and their support staff, usually on the occasion of a retirement.

This approach proved to be a source of significant fixed-cost savings but made it vital to find effective ways to reassign the responsibilities of the administrative staff and departments that were eliminated. This was accomplished in two ways. First, the oversight responsibility for these functions was shifted to other high-level executives, who now had larger portfolios and more direct reports. Second, and more important, since high-level executives now had much more to look after, it was essential to give their mid-level managers more responsibility and authority in their areas of control. For this to be successful, mid-level managers needed more, and more timely, high-level information, assistance and support from leadership, and a sense of personal accountability for the performance of their department.

The redistribution of the duties of the Chief Administrative Officer (CAO) of the hospital provides an illustration of how this worked. During her tenure, the hospital CAO served as the point of contact between the leaders of the health system and the managers of the hospital programmes. She met regularly with unit managers to review their financial statements, to solve operational problems, and to convey messages from other top leaders.

When she retired, and when it was determined that the CAO position would not be filled, it was essential to find a new, time-effective means of linking unit management and top leadership. The oversight responsibility for the hospital programmes was shifted to the medical director and the chief nursing officer, both of whom already had many other duties. They both believed that the functioning of the units and the communication between top leadership and unit management would be greatly enhanced by bringing these groups together on a regular basis. At their suggestion, we established the practice of half-hour bimonthly meetings of top leaders, including the CEO and Chief Financial Officer (CFO), with the managers of each clinical programme for the purpose of familiarizing leaders with the priorities and needs of the unit management and familiarizing the unit managers with the perspectives of the health system leadership. Each meeting began with an opportunity for the unit managers to talk about their unit and make known their outstanding needs, particularly those calling for intervention by health system leaders (e.g. physical plant repairs that had been requested but not yet completed). This proved popular and highly effective. The other central element of each meeting was a detailed review of the most recent financial statements. Initially, this was led by the CFO; however, this responsibility eventually shifted to the unit managers. The result of this shift was an unprecedented level of understanding of the financial statements on the part of the unit managers and a new sense of personal responsibility and accountability for the financial performance of the unit. With this shift, the role of the top leadership became one of providing information and support to the unit managers in their efforts to run their units effectively and efficiently. As of this writing, this redistribution of duties – a flattening of the management structure – has worked well in both operational and financial terms.

The third important lesson was that the boundary between leaders and managers must be permeable. That's not to say that leadership and management aren't different concepts and activities. Leadership is being exhibited when good ideas are expressed in a way that provides direction to others and motivates them to engage in effective action on behalf of those ideas. Management involves controlling operations in the service of executing a plan. Concisely, leadership provides guidance and management oversees implementation. Leadership is usually the responsibility of top executives, particularly the CEO, and management is usually the job of the directors of the various operational departments and divisions. But, surviving in this tumultuous period has called upon managers and leaders to move deftly between roles in response to shifting internal and external realities. We found that we needed managers who were able to think independently and lead their people – and sometimes the entire organization – in new directions. And, we have needed leaders who were willing to roll up their sleeves, master the details, and understand their business sufficiently well to manage operations.

Lean times ahead

The next 20 years are likely to be as dynamic as the last, driven by the urgent need to rein in costs while improving quality and value. In the United States, healthcare consumes nearly 17% of gross domestic product (GDP), and the per capita expenditures on healthcare greatly exceed those in any other nation. Despite this, health outcomes in the United States are not the best in the world by any objective measure.[4] While there is disagreement about how best to go about reforming healthcare, all parties agree that we must contain the costs of healthcare while improving outcomes. This means that leaders and managers will need to find ways of doing a better job with fewer resources in an environment where the processes and products of healthcare are likely to be more closely scrutinized and perhaps regulated than ever before.

As always, it's not clear what is actually going to happen. One possible scenario is suggested by the recently implemented Patient Protection and Affordable Care Act (signed by President Obama in 2010). The Act proposes a number of innovations in the organization and funding of healthcare, including so-called Accountable Care Organizations (ACO), which would bring providers together to increase the integration of services and hopefully both improve outcomes and reduce wasteful spending. Some leaders have started to take their organizations aggressively down this road and are starting to form ACOs. Others recall the early days of the managed care revolution and are reluctant to make large investments in one particular vision of the future, particularly in view of political forces pushing to block the implementation of the new law.

What are other potential scenarios? Independent of the Act, a lively debate on reform includes discussions of bundling payments for hospitals and doctors, tying reimbursement to measures of quality, creating incentives for the adoption of electronic health records, and many more ideas, including adopting a single-payer reimbursement system. What are leaders to do in such an unsettled and dynamic landscape? It is going to remain critical for leaders to keep a close eye on the match between their organization and demands of the external environment so that thoughtful and timely strategic realignments and adjustments can be made. And, in the lean times to come, it will be critical for leaders to get everyone in the organization focused on improving value. This means that everyone will need to know where the organization is trying to go (vision), how it is trying to get there (strategy) and their role in that strategy. And while each role will be unique in many respects, everyone's role will include identifying problems in quality (including waste) in their area of responsibility and taking the initiative to solve those problems. This will require that leaders effectively communicate the vision and strategy of the organization and ensure that staff have training in systematic and proven methods of recognizing and solving problems.

We started down this road in 2006. The Medical Director (Robert Roca), who was at the time completing an MBA, recruited a business school instructor to conduct a practicum on rapid-cycle performance improvement methods for health system leaders and managers. This experience spawned an interest in adapting Toyota Production System ('Lean') methods to our environment and led to the decision to train staff at every level in this use of Lean tools. We engaged a consultant to help us get fully underway. In the first year, we saw encouraging results of this effort in terms of staff engagement and morale at every level; willingness to initiate and take responsibility for problem-solving; success in problem-solving; and appreciation of the power and effectiveness of diverse (e.g. doctors, vice-presidents, housekeepers), egalitarian, multidisciplinary teams guided by a systematic methodology.

Key initial projects included improving communication with referring psychiatrists at the time of hospital discharge and ensuring that patients did not receive foods to which they were allergic. Subsequently, we focused on reducing the loss of patients' belongings, improving the process of employee orientation, and streamlining and error-proofing clinical workflows related to involuntary hospitalization and treatment planning. We are continuing to monitor the outcomes of these and other early projects. But perhaps the most important goal of all has been to create a culture committed to continuous improvement using Lean methods. This means ensuring that everyone believes that it is the job of every employee to identify and take advantage of opportunities for improvement. It also means making a special commitment to staff training and to developing a cadre of experts to train staff and lead projects. As of this writing, four staff members have become certified instructors and trained over 200 staff members from every corner of the health system. The result of this effort is a growing workforce of quality improvement enthusiasts who are ready and willing to participate in improvement projects and, over time, may themselves be capable of *leading* such efforts in their areas of responsibility.

Conclusion

In the past 20 years, psychiatric hospitals have witnessed a tsunami of change, and the future promises to be just as dynamic. Surviving will require vigilant, flexible leadership and management committed to unceasing efforts to improve effectiveness and efficiency. As we have learned, there are distinctions between leaders and managers, and physician executives need to understand the differences – as well as the circumstances under which the boundaries become blurred. The primary role of leaders is to establish a vision and set a strategy for achieving success, but leaders must be mindful of management issues. The main role of managers is to implement the strategies that have been selected to realize the vision and to make it happen according to a plan established and modified over time by key groups within the organization as the environment changes. But, of course, accomplishing this involves a measure of leadership. Our example of the Sheppard Pratt Hospital transforming itself into the Sheppard Pratt Health System as the world of reimbursement changed radically in the 1990s illuminates these processes at work.

The experience taught us that our work as psychiatrist administrators required the vocabulary, perspectives and skills that are at the heart of a business education. It is no accident that the two authors of this chapter have had business school experience; Robert Roca received an MBA at Johns Hopkins, and Steven Sharfstein received training at Harvard's Advanced Management Program. We not only learned about the distinction between leadership and management but also evolved and developed specific technical skills, such as financial management, which are essential in the process of evolving the vision and a strategy for achieving that vision. Specific clinical skills, such as those learned in group processes, are also useful here as the operation of a complex organization consists of ever-evolving groups of clinicians and administrators who need to solve problems, develop effective change strategies, and identify and meet the needs of our primary 'customers' (i.e. patients and their families) as well as the needs of personnel and staff.

The final lesson was that, with preparation, vigilance, flexibility, hard work and a little luck, it is possible to survive even a tsunami of change.

References

1 Geller J. History of hospital psychiatry and lessons learned. In: Sharfstein SS, Dickerson FB, Oldham JM (eds), *Textbook of Hospital Psychiatry*. American Psychiatric Publishing, Inc., 2009; pp. 1–20.
2 Foley DJ, Manderscheid RW, Atay JE *et al.* Highlights of organized mental health services in 2002 and major national and state trends. In: Manderscheid RW, Berry JT (eds), *Mental Health, United States, 2004*. Rockville, MD: U.S. Department of Health and Human Services, 2002; pp. 200–36.
3 Forbush B. *Moses Sheppard: Quaker Philanthropist of Baltimore*. J.B. Lippincott Co., 1968.
4 Davis K, Schoen C, Stremikis K. Mirror, Mirror on the Wall: How the performance of the U.S. health care system compares internationally, 2010 update. The Commonwealth Fund, 2010. Available at: http://www.commonwealthfund.org/~/media/Files/Publications/Fund%20Report/2010/Jun/1400_Davis_Mirror_Mirror_on_the_wall_2010.pdf[accessed 1 May 2013].

Chapter 16

Burnout and Disillusionment

Wulf Rössler

Introduction

Mental health issues, particularly those in the workplace, have recently received considerable attention from the general public due to the industrial world's transformation to a service-based economy. There has been a movement toward integrating well-established concepts of occupational psychology with the current concepts of mental disorders, for example the association between job strain and depression.[1] Workers in high-strain jobs report more stress and job dissatisfaction, which, in turn, is associated with higher levels of perceived stress, a poorer perception of one's mental health, and more claims for disability days.[2] Thus, measuring job dissatisfaction in the workplace can be a useful tool for detecting depression.

Within the occupational context, burnout, as a syndrome of emotional exhaustion, has become a favoured concept. In a Finnish study, it was significantly associated with job strain and was believed to be an intermediary between stress and depression.[3] Subsequently, depression is now considered a risk factor for job loss and unemployment. Depression results in increased turnover rate and lower pay, possibly because of the employee's poor performance and discrimination due to the stigma of depression.[4] The risk for burnout is significantly higher in certain occupations, notably among healthcare workers.[5]

The concept of burnout

The term was introduced in a 1960 novel by Graham Greene – *A Burnt-Out Case* – in which a disillusioned architect leaves his job and moves to a leper colony in Africa in an attempt to overcome burnout. Freudenberger,[6] a US psychiatrist, was one of the first scientifically to describe job burnout as a psychological syndrome in response to chronic interpersonal stressors in the workplace. Pines *et al.*[7] defined burnout as a state of physical, emotional and mental exhaustion, while Maslach and Jackson[8] characterized it in three key dimensions: overwhelming exhaustion from chronic interpersonal stress; feelings of

Leadership in Psychiatry, First Edition. Edited by Dinesh Bhugra, Pedro Ruiz and Susham Gupta.
© 2013 John Wiley & Sons, Ltd. Published 2013 by John Wiley & Sons, Ltd.

cynicism and detachment from the job; and a sense of ineffectiveness and lack of personal accomplishments at work (Box 16.1).

Box 16.1   Items from the Maslach Burnout Inventory

Emotional exhaustion

I feel emotionally drained from my work.
I feel used up at the end of the workday.
I feel fatigued when I get up in the morning and have to face another day on the job.
Working with people all day is really a strain for me.
I feel burned out from my work.
I feel frustrated by my job.
I feel I'm working too hard on my job.
Working with people directly puts too much stress on me.
I feel like I'm at the end of my rope.

Depersonalization

I feel I treat some recipients as if they were impersonal objects.
I've become more callous toward people since I took this job.
I worry that this job is hardening me emotionally.
I don't really care what happens to some recipients.
I feel recipients blame me for some of their problems.

Personal accomplishment

I can easily understand how my recipients feel about things.
I deal very effectively with the problems of my recipients.
I feel I'm positively influencing other people's lives through my work.
I feel very energetic.
I can easily create a relaxed atmosphere with my recipients.
I feel exhilarated after working closely with my recipients.
I have accomplished many worthwhile things in this job.
In my work, I deal with emotional problems very calmly.

According to Maslach *et al.*,[9] exhaustion represents the individual-stress dimension, that is, an inability to cope with work problems that subsequently consumes one's emotional and physical resources. Cynicism embodies the interpersonal context, corresponding to a negative response to various aspects of the job. The sense of reduced efficacy or accomplishment applies to the self-evaluation dimension, relating to feelings of incompetence and a lack of achievement and productivity.

The first phase of burnout research in the 1970s was mostly exploratory, intending to describe this phenomenon. Preliminary investigations were rooted in the care-giving professions and human services, emphasizing the relationship between provider and client. Such research originated from a bottom-up approach derived from people's workplace experiences. This is one reason why the concept of burnout remains so popular in the general population. In the 1980s, the focus shifted to more empirical research that involved questionnaires and surveys within larger populations. The scale still most widely used is the Maslach Burnout Inventory (MBI).[8] In the 1990s, the concept was extended to professions beyond the human services.[9]

Although this research has been greatly expanded during the last few decades, several issues are still debated:[9]

- Is the burnout phenomenon distinctly different from other constructs such as depression, chronic fatigue or neurasthenia?
- How is burnout related to individual factors, demographic characteristics (age and gender), personality traits (e.g. hardiness, self-esteem, coping style, locus of control) and attitudes toward one's job?
- Are the three dimensions of burnout independent, or do they tend to develop over time and follow a particular order?
- Which job characteristics predestine one for burnout (e.g. workload; time pressures; absence of social support, especially from superiors; a lack of adequate information; conflicting or ambiguous roles; no responsibility in decision-making; or a lack of autonomy)?
- Which occupational characteristics are associated with burnout – emotional challenges, frequency of contact with people, or severity of problems?
- How is burnout related to job performance (i.e. presenteeism, absenteeism, intention to leave one's job as well as dissatisfaction and reduced commitment to that job or organization)?
- Which organizational characteristics are associated with burnout (hierarchy, rules of communication, fairness, values, career opportunities or job security)?

Extensive evidence already supports most of these issues but cannot be discussed within the limits of this review. However, the majority of these topics also apply to burnout in physicians in general and mental health workers in particular.

Doctors in distress

In an editorial for *The Lancet* in 2011, Devi[10] stated that, 'physicians have worryingly high rates of suicide and depression when compared with the general population. . . . The problem seems to start at medical school but exact causes are still unknown. At medical school, competitiveness, the quest for perfection, too much autonomy coupled with responsibility, and the fear of showing vulnerability, have all been cited as triggers for mental ill health. . . . It seems that students remain scared of stigmatisation and adverse effects on their careers if they seek help for any mental health issues.'

A physician's ill health is not only a personal problem but also might affect the general quality of healthcare provided to one's patients. Wallace and colleagues[11] have reviewed evidence for the impact of workload, stress and related topics on physicians' health, such as fatigue, burnout, depression or substance use. The most relevant factors are shown in Box 16.2.

Box 16.2   Workplace stressors, contextual factors, and the impact of physicians' individual factors on personal health and quality of care (adapted from Wang[25])

Workplace stressors

- Workload
- Work hours
- Long shifts
- Fatigue
- Emotionally stressful interactions
- Cognitive demands/need for quick processing
- Increased patient-care demands
- Information overload
- Restricted autonomy
- Structural and organizational changes

Contextual factors

- Confidentiality issues
- Culture of medicine supporting self-neglect
- Remuneration issues
- Growing bureaucracy
- Increased accountability
- Cost control
- Conflict between patients' and organization's needs

Physicians' characteristics

- Indifference to personal needs
- Neglect of self-care
- Conspiracy of silence
- Predisposing personality traits

Outcomes

- Job dissatisfaction
- Substance use
- Relationship troubles
- Depression
- Burnout
- Risk of suicide
- Reduced productivity
- Reduced quality of patient care
- Increased risk of medical errors

In a Canadian study, 64% of physicians indicated that their workload was too heavy; 48% reported that this burden had increased within the past year.[12] Aside from the influence of an extensive workload, many working hours, or long night shifts, specific stressors are associated with the medical field. Physicians work in emotionally demanding environments with patients, families or other medical staff. They must make quick decisions while faced with a frequent overload of information that can have a decisive impact on the lives of their patients. All of these stressors must be weighed against a rapidly changing organizational context in medicine. Today, economic objectives have taken priority over medical values. This perspective conflicts with almost all values of importance that are instilled during a physician's training. These factors contribute to a cycle of stress and reduced quality of care. In fact, disillusioned physicians are quite likely to change their discipline or leave the medical field entirely. In a Canadian survey, 50% of physicians each week considered leaving academic medicine, while 30% thought about abandoning medicine altogether.[12]

Stress and burnout in mental health workers

In principle, mental health workers experience similar work stressors and have the same contextual factors as professionals from other medical disciplines. However, stressors specific to the psychiatric profession have also been identified.[13] These stem from the stigmas often attached to this profession, especially because of demanding relationships with patients, challenging interactions with other mental health professionals in multidisciplinary teams, personal threats from violent patients, and legalistic frameworks. Professionals who are part of community teams experience heightened levels of stress and burnout as a result of greater workloads, increasing administrative requirements and fewer resources. Other specific stressors include struggles with time management, inappropriate referrals, safety issues, role conflict and ambiguity, a lack of supervision, and generally poor working conditions.[14]

These sources of stress and their outcomes, particularly in the psychiatric field, have been systematically reviewed by Fothergill *et al.*[15] Other frequent and continuing complaints among mental health workers have been the negative characteristics of patients and their relatives,[16] a lack of positive feedback, low pay and a poor work environment.[17] Patient suicide is another major stressor, with the majority of mental health workers reporting post-traumatic stress symptoms after a patient suicide.[18] These work-related stresses and symptoms of burnout are common among younger psychiatrists.[19]

Social support from one's own family members or colleagues is critical to the capacity for dealing with work-related problems, especially in the case of a patient suicide.[17] Nevertheless, psychiatrists tend to keep such problems to themselves, a strategy quite common throughout the medical field. Positive predictors for coping are good self-esteem, a manageable workload, productive attitudes toward superiors, and active involvement within the organization.[20] However, approximately 25% of all psychiatrists in the United Kingdom have scored above the threshold for vulnerability to psychiatric morbidity.[19] In a German survey among psychiatrists, 44.6% indicated they had already suffered from a depressive episode.[21]

Factors that contribute to job satisfaction include having a variety of tasks, being valued by and receiving support from others, and being informed about the entire organization.[22]

How to deal with burnout?

Most burnout interventions focus on the individual and appropriate coping strategies. The primary goal is to enable an individual to handle the challenges of the job. However, there is room for improvement. Most of these interventions, for example better time management or training in interpersonal and social skills, are not specifically tailored for (mental) health workers even though they might also suit their employment needs. Instead, they focus on reducing the number of hours worked, and achieving better management of the workload and related time pressures. The intention is to learn to concentrate on the essentials of the profession, set priorities and complete tasks.

Most of these interventions must be evaluated within the context of predisposing personality traits. For example, it is well known that neuroticism is significantly associated with a tendency toward burnout. Such approaches are meant to improve work behaviour but not to change one's personality. These interventions also must fit within the background of different work-related attitudes, such as having unrealistic expectations toward the job.

Young doctors[23] are especially vulnerable to these unrealistic expectations. Skovolt[23] has described in detail the various steps followed from job entry to becoming an autonomous, self-responsible professional. Ultimately, the goal is to develop confidence in one's ability to conduct one's own work and to have control over the results. Although a professional should be authentic and follows his or her own work style, in reality, young doctors are confronted with many unexpected challenges. This is particularly true in psychiatry, where they often must deal with chronic, treatment-resistant patients who do not really appreciate the psychiatric help offered. Often, that treatment is applied involuntarily, adding another stressor to the patient-doctor relationship. Thus, the first year(s) after entering a job are often characterized by disillusionment. The model of an imbalance between effort and reward postulates that, when great efforts are expended but low rewards received, this is likely to provoke negative emotions and sustained stress responses. Conversely, positive emotions evoked by appropriate social rewards will promote well-being and good health. Such rewards are exemplified by salary, esteem and career opportunities (including job security), with each component having an influence on the quality of one's health.[24]

This effort–reward model must also be tested within the organizational context, where the potential value for interventions can be remarkable but is generally difficult to realize. Most organizations are quite reluctant to make changes. However, as it becomes more difficult to recruit young doctors (in particular in psychiatry), those organizations must create a more attractive work environment. In this respect, much has been accomplished in central Europe, where salaries have been increased, working hours limited, and the length of night shifts reduced in many psychiatric hospitals. These young doctors also must have superiors who care for them, provide good supervision, and support them when they deal with difficult situations. If these goals are achieved, the new professionals have a better chance of surmounting their inevitable work problems and accessing the fascinating world of psychiatry fearlessly and with curiosity.

References

1   Sanne B, Mykletun A, Dahl A, Moen B, Tell G. Testing the Job Demand-Control-Support model with anxiety and depression as outcomes: the Hordaland Health Study. *Occup Med (Lond)* 2005; **55**:463–73.

2   Shields M. Stress and depression in the employed population and unhappy on the job. *Health Rep* 2006; **17**:11–38.

3 Ahola K, Honkonen T, Kivimäki M *et al.* Contribution of burnout to the association between job strain and depression: the health 2000 study. *J Occup Environ Med* 2009; **48**:1023–30

4 Lerner D, Adler DA, Chang H *et al.* Unemployment, job retention, and productivity loss among employees with depression. *Psychiatr Serv* 2004; **55**:1371–8.

5 Bender A, Farvolden P. Depression and the workplace: a progress report. *Curr Psychiatry Rep* 2008; **10**:73–9.

6 Freudenberger H. The staff burnout syndrome in alternative institutions. *Psychother Theory Res Pract* 1975; **12**:72–83.

7 Pines A, Aronson E, Kafry D. *Burnout. From Tedium to Personal Growth.* New York: Free Press, 1981.

8 Maslach C, Jackson S. *Manual Maslach Burnout Inventory.* Palo Alto: Consulting Psychologists Press, 1986.

9 Maslach C, Schaufeli WB, Leiter MP. Job burnout. *Annu Rev Psychol* 2001; **52**:397–422.

10 Devi S. Doctors in distress. *Lancet* 2011; **377**:454–5.

11 Wallace JE, Lemaire JB, Ghali WA. Physician wellness: a missing quality indicator. *Lancet* 2009; **374**:1714–21.

12 Canadian Medical Association. *Guide to Physician Health and Well Being: Facts, Advice, and Resources for Canadian Doctors.* Ottawa, ON: Canadian Medical Association, 2003.

13 Margison F. Stress in psychiatrists. In: Firth-Cozens RPJ (ed.), *Stress in Health Professionals.* Chichester: John Wiley & Sons, Ltd, 1987.

14 Edwards D, Burnard P, Coyle D, Fothergill A, Hannigan B. Stress and burnout in community mental health nursing: a review of the literature. *J Psychiatr Ment Health Nurs* 2000; **7**:7–14.

15 Fothergill A, Edwards D, Burnard P. Stress, burnout, coping and stress management in psychiatrists: findings from a systematic review. *Int J Soc Psychiatry* 2004; **50**:54–65.

16 Dawkins J, Depp FC, Selzer N. Occupational stress in a public mental hospital: the psychiatrist's view. *Hosp Community Psychiatry* 1984; **35**:56–60.

17 Dallender J, Nolan P, Soares J, Thomsen S, Arnetz B. A comparative study of the perceptions of British mental health nurses and psychiatrists of their work environment. *J Adv Nurs* 1999; **29**:36–43.

18 Chemtob C, Hamada R, Bauer G, Kinney B. Patients' suicides: frequency and impact on psychiatrists. *Am J Psychiatry* 1998; **145**:224–8.

19 Guthrie E, Tattan T, Williams E, Black D, Bacliotti H. Sources of stress, psychological distress and burnout in psychiatrists. *Psychiatric Bull* 1999; **23**:207–12.

20 Thomsen S, Dallender J, Soares J, Nolan P, Arnetz B. Predictors of a healthy workplace for Swedish and English psychiatrists. *Br J Psychiatry* 1998; **173**:80–4.

21 Braun M, Schonfeldt-Lecuona C, Freudenmann RW *et al.* Depression, burnout and effort-reward imbalance among psychiatrists. *Psychother Psychosom* 2010; **79**:326–7.

22 Clark G, Vaccaro J. Burnout among CMHC psychiatrists and the struggle to survive. *Hosp Community Psychiatry* 1987; **38**:843–7.

23 Skovolt T. *The Resilient Practitioner: Burnout Prevention and Self-Care Strategies for Counselors, Therapists, Teachers, and Health Professionals.* Boston: Allyn & Bacon, 2001.

24 Siegrist J, Starke D, Chandola T *et al.* The measurement of effort-reward imbalance at work: European comparisons. *Soc Sci Med* 2004; **58**:1483–99.

25 Wang J. Work stress as a risk factor for major depressive episode(s). *Psychol Med* 2005; **35**:865–71.

Chapter 17

Gender Issues Related to Medical Leadership with Particular Reference to Psychiatry

Marianne Kastrup and Klement Dymi

Introduction – historical background

Women have in all times had leadership positions, but according to the website Worldwide Guide to Women in Leadership,[1] it was around the time of World War I that we first saw the emergence of females in government. In 1924, a Danish woman became the first democratically elected female minister. However, it took until 1960 before a woman was elected as prime minister – in Sri Lanka – and in 1974 the role of national president was filled by a woman for the first time – in Argentina. In 1999, Sweden became the first country to have more women than men as ministers in government. And in August 2011 there were globally a total of 12 women as national presidents and a further 12 women as prime ministers.

Similar developments have been observed in all areas of society and in most parts of the world, including in medicine. Women have been part of the healing profession since early civilizations. When the first universities were created in the eleventh century women were not generally allowed to enter – with few exceptions, such as the University of Bologna in Italy. However, in the Islamic empires during the same period women were often treating other women with the acceptance of society.[2]

Historically, there has been a conflict within the medical discipline between the more traditional – folkloristic – approach to treatment carried out to a large extent by women, and the more professional, academic approach and expertise undertaken by men.[3] This conflict in Europe between the lay women healers and the male medical profession was, among other things, an aspect of the witch hunt that ravaged Europe between the late fifteenth and the early eighteenth centuries. The witches had often extensive knowledge of herbs, whereas many male professionals derived their knowledge from astrology. One consequence of the witch hunt was that the male physicians gained superiority in status and power over the female healers – a position that remained for centuries and to a large extent exists to the present day.

Leadership in Psychiatry, First Edition. Edited by Dinesh Bhugra, Pedro Ruiz and Susham Gupta.
© 2013 John Wiley & Sons, Ltd. Published 2013 by John Wiley & Sons, Ltd.

Nowadays, it is still apparent that female doctors do not have positions that are equal to those of their male colleagues in most parts of the world, and that the preponderance of males increases the higher the position in the medical and academic hierarchy.

The present chapter will provide an overview of the current status of women in the medical hierarchy, and discuss possible barriers – structural and personal – hindering women from reaching leadership positions, as well as strategies to reach a more equitable position of the two sexes. The chapter also reflects personal experiences (M.K.) within the field.

Present status

Today in most Western countries we see that women comprise more than half of the students in medical faculties as well as among medical graduates.

Medical students

Medical students – whether male or female – enter medical schools with similar intelligence capacities but women are more likely to leave medical schools for 'non-academic' reasons than men.[4] As a typical example, in Denmark during the twentieth century there was a steady increase in the proportion of women entering medical school, reaching a level of about 65% by the 1980s.

One reason for the increasing proportion of female students may be that the restricted admission criteria to medical schools tend to favour young women graduating from high school with higher marks than men. With this increasing proportion one could anticipate that it is only a matter of time before women and men will occupy similar proportions of leadership positions.

Medical graduates

Looking at a World Health Organization (WHO) overview of the gender ratio of physicians we see a preponderance of female doctors primarily in the former Communist countries of Eastern Europe, and a male:female ratio ranging from 1.4:1 in Western countries to 2.6:1 in the United States and 5.4:1 in Japan.[5]

Once graduated, female graduates are more likely to experience unemployment or part-time employment than male graduates,[6] a finding also reported among US medical graduates.

A questionnaire sent in 2001 to 707 male and 707 female Danish physicians showed that female physicians experienced relatively more stressors in relation to their daily life and health while their male colleagues primarily experienced stressors in relation to their working life. Further, female physicians had more than twice the risk of being daily stressed compared to male physicians, even when controlled for a number of possible indicators in relation to daily life, working conditions and health.[7] Such results could indicate that female doctors are relatively more sensitive toward domestic stress factors and react more to domestic/familial responsibilities, but further research is needed regarding possible biological explanations too.

Leadership

In a survey of all Norwegian doctors, male doctors were more likely to have leadership positions (14%) compared to women (5%), the highest percentage being in academic positions.[8] A possible period effect – that it is easier to reach leadership positions today compared to 10 years previously – was tested but did not change the estimated probabilities.

Distributing the proportion of female leaders according to how large the percentage of women was in the specialty showed a slight, but not significant increase in probability of leadership with increased proportion of women in the specialty. Such findings indicate that it is not easier per se to attain leadership positions in female-dominated specialties, as one might expect.

In psychiatry, which is one of the specialties with a consistently high proportion of women, a US survey among academic positions demonstrated that women comprised 10% of the psychiatric faculty, but only 3% of full professors.[9]

In a survey among members of the Danish Psychiatric Association, male psychiatrists overall were reported to be involved in more research activities, and had more international publications than their female colleagues.[10] And yet there seems to have been relatively little effort to engage women in scientific authorship.[11] On the contrary, data suggest that women are largely excluded from decision-making in medical research.[8] Furthermore, female psychiatrists are less likely to teach in medical schools and less likely to engage in various extracurricular activities, such as emergency work or alcohol clinics.[12]

In the workplace we also see that male psychiatrists experience more support than their female colleagues and report greater job satisfaction, indicating that women may have to fight more for their successes.

Many of the findings above are not recent, and it may be questioned whether they still are valid. Yet, despite the advancement of women in medicine in most areas of the world their advancement in leadership positions has not followed at the same speed.[13]

Psychiatric leadership

However, when focusing on psychiatrists in leadership positions it has been shown that female psychiatrists who reached leadership positions were more active with respect to, for example, research or educational activities than their male counterparts, indicating that it takes relatively more for women to reach a leadership position.[10] Similar findings have also been reported regarding female CEOs from Canada.[14]

Traditionally, three reasons are typically advanced to explain the lack of female leaders: (i) women have not been in the medical field sufficiently long to reach such positions; (ii) they do not compete for family reasons; and (iii) they lack the required leadership skills.[13] In their overview, Carnes and co-workers[13] argue against these presumptions, concluding that data suggest that the failure of women to advance is largely due to the systematic disadvantages women face daily when carrying out their work, rather than the above reasons.

In the American Management Association, on the other hand, it has been reported that women in leadership positions are more likely to give up a home function for an important work function and more likely to state that they get most of their life satisfaction from their jobs, compared to their male colleagues.[15] This could be taken as a yet another indication that women who have managed to climb in the hierarchy are willing to (or need to) sacrifice more regarding their private life but also that this dedication to their professional career may add to their quality of life. These findings could be interpreted in line with the findings of Kastrup and Petersson.[10]

Surveys

In order to get an overview of the status regarding current female leadership two approaches were used. One was to undertake a search for published research carried out in the field of female medical leadership as well as reviews covering the area (September 2011). The second was to circulate to a number of psychiatric associations a brief questionnaire about statistics regarding female positions in psychiatry (Summer 2012).

The literature search gave few hits, particularly of a very recent origin. One may wonder what this indicates. Is this a reflection that the topic is no longer considered of particular relevance because with an increasing proportion of female doctors the proportion of female leaders will inevitably increase and result in an equitable representation of women among leaders? Is this an issue no longer giving rise to any concern? Furthermore, is it not an issue of sufficient interest to be the subject of research and published in medical journals? If this is the case we may have to look elsewhere if we want to get current views of the field.

An interesting finding is that there were several publications on the above-mentioned topics in the 1980s, and to some extent in the 1990s, when in many Western countries we saw an increasing trend of female doctors climbing the hierarchical ladder. This was related to the Women's Lib movement, with a focus on gender-related health topics. We saw at that time an emergence of equal opportunity committees as well as committees on women's health. As a co-founder of some of these I (M.K.) still recall the very sparse number of male colleagues who felt inclined to participate in or support this development. On the contrary, such initiatives were very often met with certain ridicule, which might have prevented some from joining. On an anecdotal level, the 100-year anniversary of the first Danish female graduating as a physician took place in 1985, and was celebrated with an all-female issue of the journal of the Danish Medical Association. But there was deep concern from the male editors, who feared for the publication's scientific quality having women solely responsible for the issue.

Today one may hypothesize that the mainly male editors of medical journals do not think that the issue of female physicians is worth including in their journals because what indeed is the problem? According to a vast majority of the medical establishment it is an indisputable fact that qualified leaders will reach the top, irrespective of gender. It is only a matter of time until we see a larger proportion of women at the top of the medical hierarchy – and if not it is because women are unwilling to reach for the top – a point of view that frequently is not, based upon an extrapolation of the trend seen hitherto.

Data on how female psychiatrists stand in relation to leadership are lacking. We attempted to get an overview by a brief e-mail questionnaire sent to a selected list of high-level (mainly) female professionals in positions of leadership in psychiatry-related organizations, but the response was limited.

Those leaders that answered did not have specific data on the matter and could give only approximate figures. About 30–60% of the registered members in the responding leaders' organizations were females, and most leadership positions within their own organizations were held by women, but they did not provide any data on how many, or what percentage, of the members (formally trained psychiatrists) that actually have positions of leadership in their work/professional activities (academic or executive) were women. The respondents had, however, a positive view about the possibilities for women psychiatrists to rise to leadership positions. The low response rate may be interpreted in many ways, but it may show also a lack of interest in this issue, or reluctance among female leaders to discuss leadership.

Among the comments received it was mentioned that many women enter psychiatry due to the less and more easily controlled hours of work, and many are not interested in contributing the extra amount of work needed to move into higher levels of administration. It was also noted that in some countries males had to serve in the armed forces, which could be time consuming and a hindrance for male advancement compared to some of the responsibilities women are faced with.

Barriers

A main question is whether women today – despite their increasing presence and role/visibility in the medical world – do in fact have the same opportunities as their male colleagues or whether the barriers they are exposed to prevent them from realizing their potentials.[8] No one denies that women and men face different kinds of obstacles on their way to the top. But women encounter particular barriers. Some barriers are related to structural matters, others to organizational factors and others to personal factors.

Structural barriers

The relative paucity of female medical professionals reaching leadership positions could be the result of structural constraints. The impediments may not be very visible or obvious, but rather may be an integral part of the medical hierarchical system; obstacles that impede women's careers more than men's are both intrinsic and extrinsic.[16] They may be related to the often subtle ways used in the selection process when someone is recommended for promotion or participation in research projects, when the 'system' tends to favour individuals who in their mentality/attitudes resemble those already in power, reflecting a reluctance of those in power to accept new approaches or points of view. This implies among other things that men are given an opportunity to progress and succeed whereas women hit the 'glass ceiling' and progress no further.

One should be aware that being part of a minority population leads to increased focus and attention being paid to that population, and that this may inhibit successful integration in the majority culture. In the competitive academic world where research productivity is a prerequisite for top positions, women often perform tasks that may be referred to as 'institutional housekeeping'.[17]

Interestingly, the above scenario contrasts with statements such as: women have particular negotiating skills; they are better at solving conflicts in daily working situations; they are more likely to exhibit flexibility when seeking a compromise; and they may be more adept at consensus seeking – all traits that in modern leadership are highly valued as alternatives to previous patriarchal leadership models.

In overcoming the structural hurdles that impede the professional progress of women towards leadership positions, many myths will have to be slain.[18] Statements like 'women are more emotional', 'women are less secure of themselves', 'women are their own worst enemies', 'women are not as effective as men' or 'women are dedicated to service' are still trotted out, and women are frequently subjected to double standards such as 'damned if you do, damned if you don't'.

It has also been demonstrated that a so-called negative stereotyping threat exists – whereby groups who are characterized by negative stereotypes perform below their ability in that domain – and this may be an important factor in explaining the under-representation of women in leadership positions.[19]

Concern is also expressed that with the increasing proportion of women in medicine the profession may end up as undervalued and under-respected, in line with other professions dominated by women.[20]

Organizational

In a survey among CEOs in US hospitals women comprised 26% of the leaders. They reported gender-specific obstacles and emphasized that women received 19% less in salary compared to male colleagues,[21] a fact that is frequently reported and explained on the basis that males seem better in negotiating special rewards for particular services thus ending up with a total salary exceeding that of their female counterparts. Medical organizations are not sufficiently aware of such gender-specific problems, which were emphasized by, among others, the Commission of Graduate Medical Education in 1995 when asking for gender pay equity.[22] This finding is also seen among female faculty members, who are consistently paid less than men.

A further organizational barrier relates to maternity leave politics. Extended maternity leave on the one hand facilitates women's job opportunities but may also be a disadvantage if it is used to push women aside. The same goes for part-time employment options, which may hamper women's careers as women traditionally are more likely to take such opportunities. One may, however, argue that from a career point of view women are late bloomers who, once their familial duties are reduced, can develop hitherto unfulfilled potentials and overtake their male colleagues.

Familial/individual/personal barriers

Should we acknowledge that there are inborn gender differences that are likely to continue and that the preponderance of males in almost all leadership positions is a reflection thereof? The two sexes may have differences in personality traits that account for differences in achievement. Women are often said to be more inclined toward person-centred areas while men are more task- and result-oriented and focus on hard-core academic success. And are women as ambitious when it comes to taking on leadership responsibilities?

These and similar questions have repeatedly been asked in a justification of how things are. Again and again it is emphasized that female physicians more than male physicians are caught in the complex web of family commitments, emotional caretaking and stress factors, but also a wish for influence and academic achievement. Even in relationships where both partners have similar education and able to strive for the same positions, women are more likely, even today, to prioritize greater family commitment.

Data on how subordinates view male versus female leaders are diverse – some find that gender makes no difference in leadership ability; other reports indicate that female subordinates perceive leaders as less effective if they exhibit 'feminine' traits; and yet others suggest that female leaders showing 'masculine' traits, though seen as more effective, are not perceived as having any greater leadership ability. On the other hand, men are shown as effective irrespective of whether they show 'masculine' or 'feminine' characteristics, but women are effective, only seen as effective if they show 'masculine' traits.[23]

Strategies to move forwards

Many initiatives have been undertaken to overcome the skewed sex ratio in medical leadership. Some of these initiatives have been directed to society at large and are typically of a structural nature; others have been directed towards the individual woman improving the possibility and opportunities for her to climb the hierarchical ladder.

According to the EU commissioner for legal matters, Viviane Reding,[24] there are four structural reasons why and how we should break the glass ceiling for female leadership. First of all there is a clear economic reason: if more women join the workforce more persons are part of the labour market. Secondly, it has been shown that increasing female leadership positions in fact increases the economic capacity of the organization. Thirdly, female quotas have been introduced in some countries to be used as a possible – albeit debatable – means to get more women in leadership positions including on boards. And finally, the population in Europe is overall in favour of gender equality and there is a prevailing belief that women possess the same competencies as men with respect to leadership abilities.

In their overview, Carnes and co-workers[13] list a series of recommendations to move ahead and emphasize the need to recognize the impact of socialized gender differences and prioritize a professional and personal work/life balance together with a systemic change for the advancement of medical women.

In the Chief Medical Officer's Annual Report,[25] it was recommended that in order to increase female leadership one should improve access to mentoring and encourage women into leadership, but also encourage part-time working and refresher training and more practical arrangements to ease daily stress – such as access to child care.

Structural

Structural efforts may include changes in legislation that facilitate women's career fulfilment and work in various ways. Among them are legislative initiatives that have an impact on women's opportunities to combine career and family life. We have in a number of countries seen improvements in maternity leave – both with respect to length of the leave and to the social benefits available. Other innovative approaches include the introduction of mandatory paternity leave, and improved access to kindergartens or other day-care institutions. Further we also see a growing acceptance of part-time career patterns, thereby providing more women with opportunities to fulfil their career ambitions at a more flexible pace.

Efforts have been made in some countries to adjust the labour market to the influx of qualified women by, for example, introducing an equal opportunities policy with a positive gender discrimination favouring women.[8] A possible solution to increase the hiring of female faculty members would be to establish workshops focusing on this prior to recruitment. This has been the case at the University of Wisconsin-Madison, resulting in increased gender diversity.[26]

Organizational

The establishment of mentorship is a way forward; this involves a relationship between a senior and a junior person with the aim to provide advice and emotional support and give honest feedback.[23] Having a mentor has always been a useful way to progress one's career. Traditionally it may have been informal and not called a mentorship, but increasingly formal mentoring programmes have developed in academic or clinical settings for particular groups/populations or as a general offer.[23] This development recognizes that having a mentor – typically a respected senior colleague who has achieved what you aspire to – with whom you may share your plans and a set common goal is a very fruitful step forward. Successful mentoring requires that the mentor and mentee agree on the goals as well as on the more practical aspects, and that the mentor takes on the responsibility to keep the mentee on track. Mentoring of young male doctors can help them to understand the advantages in working for a more equal distribution of domestic responsibilities, which may result in better opportunities for their female partners.

From an organizational point of view, modern management promotes leadership characterized by acting as a role model, by creating an atmosphere of trust and respect, and having the ability to communicate values and goals – all areas in which women are strong and which should be more prominent.

Individual

The question is, what does it take to be a successful female leader? North[27] has provided a list of character traits as well as advice to the individual woman on how to climb the medical hierarchical ladder. Among the advice given is that women should from the very start, make up their mind about how much and what are they willing to sacrifice, because without sacrifices she (or he for that matter) will not succeed. It is a myth to think that the winner can take it all.

It has also been found that women and men differ in their ability to delegate. Women may tend to stay involved and, unlike men, find it difficult to accept that delegation results in independence.[23]

Women should also learn to be more willing to take risks and develop an ability to feel comfortable outside the safety zone if they feel they are on the right track, and reduce their consensus-seeking behaviour. Having said that, women should not bend and make compromises that go against their principles, but keep their integrity whatever it costs. Women should use to their advantage their better emotional and communication skills, which should make them better equipped to negotiate, to solve conflicts, and to play an ambassadorial role in the community, etc.[27]

A successful personal strategy is also to be careful in which battles you pick.[27] Many women tend to direct their focus on details, which may be a disadvantage in managing large organizations where it can be necessary to view the overall picture and not get absorbed in details.

Thus, the potential female leader will not only keep her eye on the overall picture, but also exhibit a genuine enthusiasm and belief that the organization will succeed thereby inspiring others in her organization and creating an atmosphere of commitment. Finally, the advice is to maintain good humour – it is critical not to take things too personally, but look on the 'bright side of life'.

Where do we go from here?

The question remains why are there so few women leaders even in countries where gender equality is at its greatest? Should we be satisfied with the present situation? Or should we create institutional environments that are able to use the talents of both men and women, and a healthcare system that is responsive to the needs of both sexes.[13]

If women are to crash through the glass ceiling, organizations have to provide better opportunities for mentoring and networking combined with flexibility in work structures.[16] As professional psychiatrists we should acknowledge that effective leadership could with profit include both 'masculine' and 'feminine' qualities.[23]

What to do if you wish to assume higher professional and social responsibility and develop in that direction? Here are a few clues to ponder:

• Find a mentor whom you trust and who is willing to spend some time with you.
• Become part of a team in an area that has your interest, but do not be too choosy – you will find that almost any topic grows in interest.

- Find a support group of other female colleagues.
- Do not take things too personally but face challenges with good humour and choose your fights carefully, as there may be many.

References

1 Worldwide Guide to Women in Leadership. Website: http://www.guide2womenleaders.com/ [accessed 17 April 2013].
2 Wikipedia. Women in medicine. Available at: http://en.wikipedia.org/wiki/Women_in_medicine [accessed 17 April 2013].
3 Ehrenreich B, English D. *For Her Own Good. 150 Years of the Experts' Advice to Women.* London: Pluto Press, 1979.
4 Leason J, Gray J. *Women and Medicine.* London: Tavistock Publications, 1978.
5 World Health Organization. Gender distribution by occupation. Available at: http://apps.who.int/globalatlas/docs/HRH/HTML/Sex_occ.htm [accessed 17 April 2013].
6 DADL. *Meritering og videreuddannelse* [Merit and postgraduate education]. Report of the Danish Medical Association Committee of Equal Rights. Copenhagen: Danish Medical Association, 1986.
7 Hargreaves M, Petersson B, Kastrup M. Kønsforskclle i stress blandt læger [Gender differences in stress among doctors]. *Ugeskr Læg* 2007: **169**:2418–22.
8 Kværner K, Aasland O, Botten GS. Female medical leadership: Cross sectional study. *Brit Med J* 1999; **318**:91–4.
9 Robinowitz CH, Nadelson C, Notman M. Women psychiatrists in the US. *Am J Psychiatr* 1981; **138**:1357–61.
10 Kastrup M, Petersson B. Working conditions of male and female psychiatrists. *Acta Psychiatr Scand* 1986; **74**:84–90.
11 Benedek EP. Editorial practices of psychiatric and related journals: Implications for women. *Am J Psychiatr* 1976; **133**:89–92.
12 Petersson B, Kastrup M. Mandlige og kvindelige psykiatere [Male and female psychiatrists]. *Ugeskr Læg* 1986; **148**:1710–14.
13 Carnes M, Morrissey C, Geller SE. Women's health and women's leadership in academic medicine: Hitting the same glass ceiling? *J Women Hlth* 2008; **17**:1453–62.
14 Storch J. Women executives in Canadian hospitals. *Healthcare Management Forum* 1989; **3**:22–5.
15 Powell GN, Posner B, Schmidt WH. Women: the more committed managers? *Manag Rev* 1985; **74**:43–5.
16 Madsen MK, Blide LA. Professional advancement of women in health care management: a conceptual model. *Top Hlth Inf Manag* 1992; **13**:45–55.
17 Bird SLJ, Wang Y. Creating status of women reports: Institutional housekeeping as women's work. *NSWA J* 2004; **16**:194–200.
18 Wiggins C. Female healthcare managers and the glass ceiling. *Hospital Topics* 1991; **69**: 8–15.
19 Burgess DJ, Josseph A, van Ryn M, Carnes M. Does stereotype threat affect women in academic medicine? *Acad Med* 2012; **87**:506–12.
20 Lyon DS. Where have all the young men gone? Keeping men in obstetrics and gynecology. *Obstet Gynecol* 1997; **90**:634–6.
21 Collins S, Matthews E, McKinnies R, Collins K, Jensen S. Chief executive officers in US hospitals. *Health Care Manag (Frederick)* 2009; **28**:134–41.

22   Council on Graduate Medical Education. *COGME Fifth Report: Women and Medicine*. US Department of Health and Human Services, Public Health Service Health Resources and Services Administration, 1995.

23   Rubens AJ, Malperin MA. Mentoring in healthcare organizations. Implications for female healthcare managers. *Hospital Topics* 1996; **74**:23–8.

24   Reding V. The glass ceiling for women in boards should be broken now [glasloftet for kvinder i bestyrelser skal brydes nu]. *Politiken* 2012; **14** July: pp. 3–4.

25   Broad M. Breaking down the barriers to female medical leadership. Hospital Dr, 2009. Available at: http://www.hospitaldr.co.uk/features/breaking-down-the-barriers-to-female-medical-leadership [accessed 17 April 2013].

26   Sheridan JT, Fine E, Pribbenow CM, Handelsman J, Carnes M. Searching for excellence and diversity: Increasing hiring of women faculty at one medical center. *Acad Med* 2012; **85**:999–1007.

27   North MA. A formula for success for women (and men) in leadership. *Healthcare Financial Management* 2006; October: pp. 118–20.

Chapter 18

Leadership for Good versus Good Leadership in Mental Health

Sidney H. Weissman and Kenneth G. Busch

Introduction

In this chapter we will address what is meant by leadership for 'good' versus what is 'good leadership' in mental health. Prior to our discussion of these concepts we must first define what we mean by the terms 'good' and 'right'. After addressing the complexities of defining 'good' and 'right' or 'rights' we will examine how these terms apply in our complex and varied societies. With this background we will then examine the construct 'leadership'. We will conclude by addressing 'good leadership' in mental health versus leadership for 'good' in mental health.

Issues in defining a 'good' and a 'right'

We will begin by offering a preliminary definition of what is meant by a 'good'. This is a question which has daunted philosophers for centuries. We will start with Aristotle, who said that happiness is the 'good'.[1] In today's language we would interpret the concept of happiness as referring to well-being and that it occurs as the consequence of activity that uses one's talents on behalf of a favoured or beneficial end.

John Stuart Mill distinguished the means required to generate three different pleasures ('goods'): the moral, intellectual and anima.[2] Mill additionally addressed both the 'good' and the means to attain it through 'good leadership'. The principal source for the concept of the 'social good' is Plato's Republic.[3] The 'social good' is best understood as an interlacing of the elements of a society and the functions of the community in such ways that the well-being of each is conditional on the well-being of all.

Now we will move from addressing the construct of the 'good' to addressing a related construct, the idea of a 'right'. In the Western world the definitions of 'rights' have two principal sources. First is the Old Testament, which contains precepts as laid down in the Ten Commandments, as promulgated by Moses. Second is the work of Immanuel Kant and his construct the 'categorical imperative'.[4] This is the rule that no one can do anything

Leadership in Psychiatry, First Edition. Edited by Dinesh Bhugra, Pedro Ruiz and Susham Gupta.

if everyone could not do it without harm to others. Elements of these philosophers' views of 'good' and 'right' punctuate our contemporary views of the 'good'.

Contemporary issues in defining the 'right' or 'rights' of individuals

As we examine varied definitions of 'right' or 'rights' we will observe that many factors impact on both definitions and how a society implements them. Further, the definitions of 'rights' or a 'right' in a society may change over time. Whereas today in the United States women can vote, they did not have this 'right' 100 years ago. This was once an accepted view of the 'rights' of women, which seems far removed from the United States today. Slavery, the extreme denial of human 'rights', still exists in parts of the world. In some countries immigrant workers are not afforded the 'rights' of citizens. 'Guest' workers are frequently imported to a country to accomplish tasks that a country's citizens are not interested in performing. Although frequently brought into a country as contract employees, which implies that they have 'rights', these workers are often treated in many ways as slaves with limited or no 'rights'. These absences of what some would consider basic human 'rights' are frequently either obscured or denied in some societies, or accepted as a reasonable way to treat those who differ from the most powerful elements of the society. In this context 'rights' translates as a protection for all citizens or residents of a country from potential abuse and exploitation.

'Rights' also represent a society's legal standards. The ability to file a suit alleging that one has been harmed is a 'right'. Differing societies will define what actions by others against oneself can lead to litigation or indeed criminal action. Protection against intrusion by a society's government in personal or political activity is also a 'right' not necessarily enjoyed by all citizens in all countries.

In the United States some states have passed laws that enable an individual to carry a concealed firearm, which they can use to defend themselves if they feel they are being attacked. Some see this as a 'right' of individuals to defend themselves if or when attacked. Others see it as abusing the rights of the unarmed citizen. In situations of conflict between an individual with a concealed weapon and an unarmed citizen, where the weapon is used to inflict a mortal wound, only the armed individual can present their view of what occurred. Some see the law as giving legal authority or 'rights' to the individual with a weapon to act without restraint and remove from the unarmed the 'right' to live in safety.

As we examine issues in healthcare from the perspective of the 'good' and the 'right' and what constitutes 'good leadership' we need to keep in mind the difficult issues involved in assessing and determining what is 'good' and 'right'.

'Rights' in healthcare

In healthcare the struggle to define 'rights' is complicated by there being a number of differing views. Further, the various 'rights' at times compete with one another for a society's resources to ensure their viability. Additionally, not everyone agrees on what is their society's core view of 'rights' in healthcare. In large pluralistic societies, people frequently disagree on what are individuals' healthcare 'rights'; For example, in the United States although the United States Supreme Court ruled that the right to abortion is a legal right of every US woman, a minority of the population vigorously and at times violently disagrees. They feel that the ultimate healthcare 'right' which exists for every member of a society is the protection and preservation of each human life. They see the human foetus at any stage of development as a person who has 'rights' that must be protected by society. They have coined the term 'pro-life' to make their point.

In contrast individuals who favour a woman's 'right' to have an abortion see a quite different ultimate 'right'. For these individuals the ultimate healthcare 'right' is for every citizen to be able to make their own decisions regarding their individual healthcare. This 'right' gives every woman in all situations the responsibility to direct her healthcare. Pregnancy is one element of a woman's healthcare. Every woman can then determine how she wishes to deal with a pregnancy. They would agree with 'pro-life' advocates of a societal role to protect life. They would not, as 'pro-life' advocates do, define the foetus at conception as a human life. Further they would see an ultimate 'good' in women's healthcare as the protection of the 'right' of every woman to make decisions to control all medical aspects of her life without government or societal interference. They have coined the term 'pro-choice' to highlight their view of the 'right'.

The 'right' to healthcare

Since everyone will at some time in their lifetime need healthcare one might ask if it is an individual's 'right' to receive competent healthcare at a level that their society can afford. In some countries healthcare is provided to all citizens through varied schemes. In these countries it is seen as a 'right' of every citizen to obtain competent healthcare. Further it is held that minimal differences in quality should exist between the healthcare available to wealthy or poor citizens of the country. In other countries, either because of poverty or limited resources, quality healthcare is only available to a small segment of the population. In still others healthcare is not considered a 'right' of each citizen. Unique economic and societal imperatives in every country will determine how and where citizens access healthcare.

Parallel 'goods' in healthcare

In healthcare we not only confront disagreements about how to judge and make critical decisions regarding what is 'right' – as we observed in discussing abortion above – but we also observe the existence of a number of what we will call parallel 'goods'. For example, are a society's healthcare needs best met by focusing resources on clinical care, the education of healthcare professionals or research? Various society members or health-care leaders may argue for the focus to be on one of these to a greater or lesser extent than the others. In each of these respective areas there may be further disputes as to what is the 'good'. In addressing clinical care should funds be used to focus on general healthcare needs for the many or the special healthcare needs of the few, or should funds be divided equitably between them? For example, should we develop programmes for organ or tissue transplantation that aid a few, or – if resources are limited – use these funds to enhance the care of individuals with chronic diseases such as diabetes?

In the area of medical education we see similar conflicts. Are a society's needs best met by focusing resources on educating doctors to be specialists or on training doctors in primary care? Even if it is agreed that a society needs more primary care practitioners to meet its healthcare needs, some would argue that the additional practitioners should be either advanced nurse practitioners or physician assistants, not only medical doctors.

When we address how we should fund research the same question arises of what is the pre-eminent 'good'. Should we allocate resources equally to all areas of research or focus primarily on basic research, or translational research or clinical research? In allocating limited resources, each point of view has its advocates. We do not intend to answer these questions here but to show that when we talk of obtaining the 'good' this construct has many different meanings and supporters. Every society must develop mechanisms to examine all of the 'goods' that impact on healthcare for its citizens. Then it must implement procedures to select how to use resources to meet the society's own unique goals or 'goods'.

Historically societies have tended not to give equal emphasis to all healthcare issues. Mental healthcare, because of the stigma that is frequently attached to mental illness, is often seen by many as not being a societal or healthcare 'good' that needs significant resources. In Britain the slogan 'No Health Without Mental Health' is an attempt to position mental healthcare as a 'good' to be valued and mandated by society. By doing this mental health supporters hope to increase the resources that are committed to mental healthcare.

Even within the mental health fields there is disagreement as to how resources should be utilized. Some argue that the major portion of resources devoted to mental disorders should be focused on individuals with serious mental illness. Specifically we should focus clinical and research resources on individuals with schizophrenia or other seriously disabling mental disorders. Others argue that resources should be shared equally to treat individuals with mental disorders. Clearly again each society must decide on its unique priorities in addressing its multiple healthcare needs.

Even when a healthcare 'good' for a society is essentially agreed the implementation of policies and actions to attain it is not easily accomplished. Many of the decisions as to how to use a society's limited resources or which 'good' to address are made by doctors, hospital administrators or local health authorities in isolation without direct or clear societal input. Each of these agents may be able to commit significant societal healthcare resources without any outside review. When a physician makes decisions alone with their patient, the outcome may commit significant societal resources without any societal input or knowledge. This decision is by definition undemocratic from the perspective of other members of the society. On the other hand if society develops models of how resources are to be used in treating differing illnesses the individual has limited power in determining their healthcare. This may also be seen as undemocratic. In some societies mechanisms exist to address the potential conflict between the 'good' for the individual to obtain the best medical care and the 'good' for society to monitor and control the use of resources. In a representative democracy, elected representatives are charged with developing policies to resolve the conflict between these two 'goods' in healthcare. Frequently the resolution focuses only on how to utilize limited resources.

In some circumstances when processes are seemingly in place to best implement a society held 'good' the actual implementation of these policies does not always work as planned. Again using the United States as an example, the salaries of doctors working in hospitals as residents (house officers) are paid for by the US federal government using funds from a federal programme. This programme is designed to ensure an adequate number of well-trained physicians in the United States. While the federal government pays the salary of each resident the hospital determines how to apportion the residents between various medical specialties. Public health officials may feel that in the region surrounding the hospital a shortage of primary care doctors exists. They will argue that the hospital should increase the number of resident positions in primary care. The residents from this hospital when they graduate will likely practise in the region of the hospital, reducing the primary care physician shortage and thereby enhancing patient care.

The hospital may argue that training resident doctors in certain specialties will increase the hospital's capacity to treat specific well-paying groups of patients. This added hospital revenue will allow the hospital to treat needy individuals who otherwise could not afford to obtain medical care. Failure to categorically define how federal funds are to be used allows this argument to arise between competing 'goods'. In the United States today each hospital accepting federal funds is free to make its own determination of what is 'good' without societal input.

Leadership

As we address leadership we must assert that 'good leadership' may not be leadership for the 'good'. World history is populated with individuals who in their country were perceived by its citizens at the time as effective or 'good' leaders but in fact led their countries into ruin. Some national leaders in addition to causing the ruin of their own countries provoked wars that led to the destruction of other countries resulting in enormous loss of life.

Before continuing we must address what we mean by leadership, although other definitions have been described elsewhere in this volume. A leader is someone who can present an opinion of how to understand and act on an issue or problem in such a way that others will carry out the actions that they propose or support. In any country or organization knowledgeable and capable leaders are vital. Leaders must be able to prioritize the resources that are available to them in sustaining their organization and then be capable of proposing and implementing policies. 'Good' leaders must have the ability to make critical decisions and accept responsibility for their actions in a complex and changing world. The capacity to be a 'good' leader does not mean that one is leading for the 'good'.

To accomplish these tasks leaders must be able to connect to those whom they lead. Followers of a leader may develop powerful feelings regarding their leader. Psychoanalysts[5] using psychoanalytic terms describe the psychological relationship that may develop between 'leader' and 'follower' from the perspective of the follower as an idealizing transference. This transference creates a special view of the leader in the eyes of the follower. In some situations the follower will carry out the leader's proposed actions without considering their ramifications.

In situations where the 'followers' respond because of their 'feelings' toward the leader the leader must interact with the 'followers' in a manner that sustains their view and addresses their psychological needs and stated desires. In these situations leaders actively encourage their followers' idealizations. This ensures that in complex situations the 'followers' will support the leader's actions without question. If the leader both appears to correctly respond to situations and concurrently engages followers' idealizations, the leader will maintain his or her authority. The relationship between leader and follower may be maintained even in situations where the outcomes of decisions made by the leader are disastrous if the 'idealization' of the leader remains intact.[6]

An example of this can be seen near the end of World War II in Europe. In 1944 it was clear that Germany would be defeated and Berlin would be occupied by Soviet troops. With defeat inevitable, Hitler gave orders to destroy the infrastructure of Berlin as Soviet troops advanced, and with the outcome clear German soldiers followed his orders. Just as Hitler ordered, they destroyed much of the city to slow the Soviets' inevitable advance.

As powerful as the idealizing transference is, it should be noted that its presence does not ensure that a leader will retain power and authority indefinitely even when their policies and actions have been correct. In a democracy the idealizing transference that has empowered the leader in the eyes of voters in one situation may not necessarily transfer to another. The unique demands of a new situation may cause followers (voters) to feel that the attributes of the leader do not fit the needs of leadership in the new situation. The events in post-World War II Britain are an example. Winston Churchill by all accounts served as an extraordinary prime minister during World War II. After the war he was immediately voted out of office when the British electorate felt he could not effectively address the problems of post-war Britain. Churchill's election defeat was perceived as startling by the rest of the world; citizens elsewhere maintained their idealization of Churchill.

Leaders need special abilities to accomplish the tasks of leadership. A leader must be able to project a sense of competence that they have the ability to solve problems. We frequently refer to this as charisma. A leader needs to understand what elements of a problem they do not understand. If a leader feels their authority is threatened in their attempts to understand a problem the leader may seek counsel from someone who will agree with whatever the leader proposes. Advice so obtained may not help solve a problem but will ensure the high standing of the adviser with the leader. However, leaders with a sense of confidence and actual respect for others will find the most competent and knowledgeable individuals to assist in their responses to critical issues. The questions for 'followers' when their 'leader' is dealing with a complex problem is to appreciate how the leader goes about obtaining counsel to address a problem and then how the leader in fact resolves the problem. 'Followers' must appreciate that the solution to a problem should remain their leader's chief agenda item, not maintaining their 'idealization'.

'Good' leaders in medicine

In medicine 'good leadership' involves, besides all the other requirements of leadership, two variables. First is the competency of the leader with respect to their skills and knowledge of medicine, and second is their ability to engage others in broader problem-solving activities. An example of the distinction between these two skills can be observed in military hospitals near the front line in a war. Here the triage physician is responsible for assessing every casualty brought to the military hospital. This physician assesses the patient's treatment needs in terms of urgency and their likelihood of surviving an operation. The treatment decisions are based on the soldier's injury and the available clinical resources. The triage physician must not only be able to effectively evaluate each soldier's needs but also must be able to effectively communicate his or her treatment recommendations to the medical staff. Resources in these situations are frequently limited and not all soldiers are always treated. Some are sent for treatment while others are left to die. Statistics on patient survival allow triage physicians to be graded on the effectiveness of their decision-making capacity. For these physicians explicit data exist to evaluate them as practitioners and as clinical leaders.

The administrative functions of running and managing a front-line military hospital are not performed by the triage physician but by others. Differing parameters of effectiveness are used to assess the hospital commander's effectiveness and leadership skills. In the military hospital the effectiveness of each physician in critical leadership roles can be assessed by data.

In many medical situations, both clinical and administrative, we do not have access to data which allow us to assess the competence of our leaders. At times an immediate action is needed and complex explanations are not possible. In these situations followers' responses are either based on prior knowledge of the leader's competence in similar situations or on positive or negative 'feelings' (transferences) about the leader. In these latter situations some 'followers' will rely on their positive feeling 'idealization' to support the leader. Others will not.

'Good' leaders in mental health

In a field as broad as mental health we need a number of 'good leaders' with varied skills. Different leaders will address specific issues, goals or 'goods'. The first goal a 'good' leader must address, as noted above, is making mental healthcare in all of its aspects a critical concern of society. This is an overarching goal in addressing mental healthcare that must be met before other mental health goals can be accomplished. Our leader or leaders will need to find ways to translate mental health issues into terms understandable by all elements of society. These leaders will need to use a vast array of techniques to engage society in valuing mental healthcare. One element of this leadership will be to engage the government in identifying adequate resources for mental healthcare. Another element of good mental health leadership is to create situations where mental health practitioners attain a voice in the political system where they can advocate for the 'good'.

To accomplish this leaders and practitioners must be able to effectively work with media, allies, stakeholders, elected officials and government agencies. They must specifically develop relationships with varied policy-makers so that they can aid in the development of mental health policy. The leaders who can accomplish this will use either their own appeal to the public or the resources of professional associations in their country to advocate for these priorities.

The next goal of a good mental health leader will be to address the tensions inside the mental health community. Here the leader will need to work to create an environment where all of the sciences that inform us of the potential causes of mental disorder are addressed. A leader or leaders will need to ensure that varied treatment modalities used in mental health are all valued. Talking therapies and the use of medication must all be considered psychotherapies since each affect the psychological functioning of an individual. Addressing each of these concerns may be most difficult for members of the psychiatric community.

In academic settings leaders must work to ensure that all medical students and health science students receive adequate basic training in psychiatry. They will also need to ensure that psychiatric residency training is broad based and inclusive of the varied disciplines that inform us regarding mental health (see also Chapter 13).

There is not one set of characteristics to identify these varied leaders. No specific algorithm will determine who can rise to the challenge of becoming an effective leader. Just as it is difficult if not impossible to predict who will be a 'good' leader it is equally difficult to determine what is 'good' and 'right' in the many and varied cultures and environments in which we live. The limited resources in mental healthcare underline how understanding what is 'good' and 'right' poses a critical challenge to each of us and to our leaders as we care for our patients.

Leadership for the 'good' in mental health

We have now discussed the difficulties that are involved in determining the 'good', the 'right' and being able to lead. We will now address these issues explicitly for mental health. First we must acknowledge that although our general principles will be the same in all countries their implementation may vary from country to country and even for districts or institutions within a country. Our first goal is to ensure that the mental health needs of a country's citizens are a healthcare priority. Once mental healthcare is established as a healthcare priority, that is as an essential 'good', then resources have to be made available to ensure that adequate clinical services are available for all citizens on an equal basis. In addition to providing basic mental health services some countries will be able to fund research into mental health issues. For wealthy countries research may include basic neuroscience or genomics. Other countries with limited resources may only be able to address clinical research. All countries will need to assess the epidemiology of mental disorders within their borders. This knowledge is critical if essential mental healthcare is to be provided to their citizens.

To accomplish this greater awareness of the importance of investment in mental health-care, leadership can be provided by various members of every society. It is likely that mental health workers will have a key role in pressing for the implementation of this 'good'. But many others will need to be involved. In developing leadership at a societal level it may be useful to enlist as leaders visible and important members of the society whose family members or themselves have experienced a mental illness. They more than any other group may be able to address the need for mental healthcare and by example reduce the stigma associated with mental illness.

In focusing their society on the importance of addressing mental illness, mental health workers will need to address all avenues that deal with mental disorders. These include hospitals where patients are treated, medical schools where curricular issues are discussed, and most critically the elected or appointed officials of the country's government.

We have not addressed issues of preventive care. Clearly this is a 'good'. But it is difficult to address preventive care in a society with extremely limited resources. We do not need any studies to know the harmful effects on a child's growth and development if the child is homeless, hungry or unable to attend a school because there is none.

Conclusion

Just as it is difficult to determine the 'good' and the 'right' in the many circumstances in which we address mental health it is equally difficult to predict who will be a 'good' leader. Because of limited resources in mental healthcare an understanding of these difficulties in determining the 'good' and the' right' and who will be 'good leaders' poses a critical challenge to each of us as we care for our patients.

References

1   Aristotle. *Ethics, Basic Works of Aristotle* (ed. R. McKeon). New York: Random House, 1941; pp. 937–8.
2   Mill JS. *Utilitarianism*. Indianapolis, IN: Hackett, 2001; p. 8.
3   Plato. *Republic* (trans. F. Cornford). Oxford: Oxford University Press, 1941; pp. 53–275.
4   Kant I. *Critique of Practical Reason* (trans. L.W. Beck). New York: Macmillan, 1985; p. 19.
5   Basch MF. A comparison of Freud and Kohut, apostasy or synergy? In: Detrick DW, Detrick SP (eds), *Self Psychology Comparison and Contrasts*. Hillsdale, NJ: The Analytic Press, 1989; p. 15.
6   Han H, Andrews KT, Ganz M, Baggetta M, Lim C. The relationship of leadership quality to the political presence of civic organizations. *Perspectives on Politics* 2011; **9**:45–59.

Chapter 19

Acquiring Leadership Skills: Description of an International Programme for Early Career Psychiatrists

Norman Sartorius

Introduction

Leaders are people who are characterized by features that make it probable that others will follow them almost regardless of the direction that they propose to take. Among the features likely to characterize most leaders are self-confidence (i.e. behaviour that gives the impression that the leader knows where to go and how best to get there), determination in the pursuance of goals, willingness to make personal sacrifices in order to make progress, and endurance and energy that are superior to those of the other members of the group. Not all these traits are present in all leaders – indeed, sometimes only one is sufficient.

In addition to leadership skills that can be acquired there are other characteristics of leaders that are important but usually cannot be gained through training. These include behaviour shaped in early childhood, personal experience, physical and mental stamina, cognitive capacity and the ability to handle competing demands at the same time.

Developing leadership is of particular importance in the field of mental health. Mental disorders are a problem of major public health importance. They are highly prevalent and can have severe consequences. They cause a great deal of suffering for those who are ill and for those who care for them. Their prevalence is likely to increase in the years to come. Their treatment is possible and the results of treatment in terms of a significant reduction of symptoms and the prevention of impairment are better than those obtained by the treatment of other serious non-communicable diseases. Yet, despite the importance of such disorders and the availability of the means to deal with them, most people with severe mental disorders do not receive treatment. The main reason for this is the stigma attached to mental illness – a stigma that indicates that the mentally ill are incurable, often dangerous and in general unlikely to be ever again useful to society.

Yet despite the severe obstacles that stigmatization places before anyone intending to develop a mental health programme, there are examples of successes even in countries in which the resources that can be used for mental health programme development are severely restricted. Some of the numerous examples include: the introduction of mental

Leadership in Psychiatry, First Edition. Edited by Dinesh Bhugra, Pedro Ruiz and Susham Gupta.
© 2013 John Wiley & Sons, Ltd. Published 2013 by John Wiley & Sons, Ltd.

health elements into the primary healthcare system in Iran; the extension of mental health services into rural areas in Ethiopia relying on a small but dedicated group of nurses trained in mental health; the remarkable work done by mental health assistants in Zambia; the village care system in Nigeria;[1] the programme of extension of mental healthcare in Senegal, the Philippines, Colombia and India;[2] the programmes of promotion of mental health in the north of Pakistan; and the programmes in Colombia,[3] Bolivia and other countries in Latin America[4] and in other countries.[5] Although different in style most of these successes have been linked to charismatic leaders rather than to structural and enduring changes of the health system. Also, most of these highly encouraging programmes have been limited to an area in the country or to a particular mode of service provision, for example, the involvement of nurse practitioners in mental healthcare. The 'export' of strategies and techniques developed for use in one setting to the totality of a country or to a region is often difficult and when successful, often of short duration. The pioneering efforts of leaders who managed to make a difference rarely find an echo and acceptance in areas in which there are no leaders who could learn from achievements of others and develop them further and wider.

The recognition of the fact that leaders make the difference and are necessary for progress led to a variety of efforts to create leaders, usually without much success. There is a huge literature on leadership qualities and many highly commercialized agencies provide training that –they promise – will make the participants become leaders.

While it is probably unrealistic to expect that leaders can be created, it is certainly true that those who have leadership potential can be equipped with skills that will make them more effective once they take a leadership position. Most of these skills will also be useful for those who are not leaders, nor want to become one.

A first group of skills that can make leadership more effective and easier are communication skills. These include the skill of listening to others and understanding what they are saying or want to say; the skill of presenting one's plans or goals in a way that will make others want to participate in them or share them; and the skill of limiting the amount of information being offered to others to digestible quantities. Some people seem to have been born good communicators; the majority, however, have to be taught communication skills. This can be done and usually takes a relatively short time.

The second group of skills concerns the discovery of those who are likely to share the vision and to participate in the venture that the leader wishes to undertake. It is rarely possible and usually not necessary to have all members of a group become enthusiastic about a particular goal or plan: convincing a small proportion of the group to follow the leader's ideas is usually sufficient. Penfield, a social scientist in Canada, once analysed voting behaviour and established that, in groups of people who are not committed to any particular line of action, it usually suffices to have on one's side the square root of the total number of those who need to accept a proposal. Thus, to move a group of 100 people in a particular direction, it is sufficient to have 10 who believe in the proposal made by the leader. The corollary of this rule is, of course, that the proportion of people whom a leader should convince in order to move the mass in a particular direction will diminish with the growth of the group as a whole. Thus, to convince 25 people, the leader has to convince five – or 20% – to become fervent followers; to lead one million people, the leader has to be certain of having 1000 people on side – or only 0.1% of the total. This rule explains how it is possible for leaders to get very large groups of people to accept their proposals while relying on a relatively small group of firmly committed followers.

The third group of skills concerns the timing of a leader's action. This is probably the most difficult skill to acquire because it depends on several other skills that need to be acquired– such as the ability to simultaneously assess (several) trends of behaviour in a particular group of people and to interpret these assessments in the context of the leader's plans and of the broader environment that might influence the members of the group that is to be steered in a particular direction.

These considerations led me to design an educational programme whose main objectives were to provide young psychiatrists with some of the skills that would help them in their professional development and to bring them together under conditions that would be likely to facilitate the creation of networks of young psychiatrists and the collaboration between them.[a]

The programme had two components: first, intensive interactive courses during which psychiatrists who were early in their career (ECP) acquired leadership skills; and second continuing support and mentorship when necessary and possible, following the workshops. The programme started during my presidency of the World Psychiatric Association (WPA) and for the first few years was conducted under the aegis of the WPA and in collaboration with WPA member societies. Subsequently the programme was conducted by the Association for the Improvement of Mental Health Programme (AMH), a not-for-profit non-governmental association located in Geneva. Since its beginning we organized more than 60 courses in Asia (China, India, Indonesia, Japan, Korea, Singapore), the Americas (Chile, Mexico), Europe (Belarus, Croatia, Czech Republic, France, Germany, Hungary, Latvia, Poland, Romania, Russia, Serbia, Slovakia, Turkey), Africa (Kenya, Nigeria, Ethiopia) and the Middle East (Egypt, Tunisia) involving more than a thousand young psychiatrists from some 80 countries. In some instances the courses helped in the initiation of national and international associations of young psychiatrists (e.g. in Japan and Korea) and led to collaborative studies that strengthened the networks and produced publications in international scientific journals as well as in local professional journals (e.g. see Gater et al.,[6] Jordanova et al.[7] and Hashimoto et al.[8]). Figure 19.1 shows the countries from which participants have attended the AMH Leadership course.

The faculty for the courses usually involved two internationally well-known experts[b] and two leading experts from the country in which the course was held. Over time the curriculum of the courses changed in the light of the experience and observations and suggestions made by the members of the faculty and the participants: yet, the basic structure of the courses remained the same.

[a]The programme was directed at psychiatrists early in their career although many psychiatrists at more advanced stages in their career could benefit from the courses: the problem, however, is that most often they do not believe that they need to learn any such skills at their age and position.

[b]Professors Sir David Goldberg and G. Thornicroft were the international expert members of the faculty in numerous courses, and their contributions to the programme were of particular value. Professor J.E. Cooper, D. Bhugra, E. Chiu, J. Furedi, C. Hoeschl and J. Libiger were members of the faculty for some of courses and added significantly to their success.

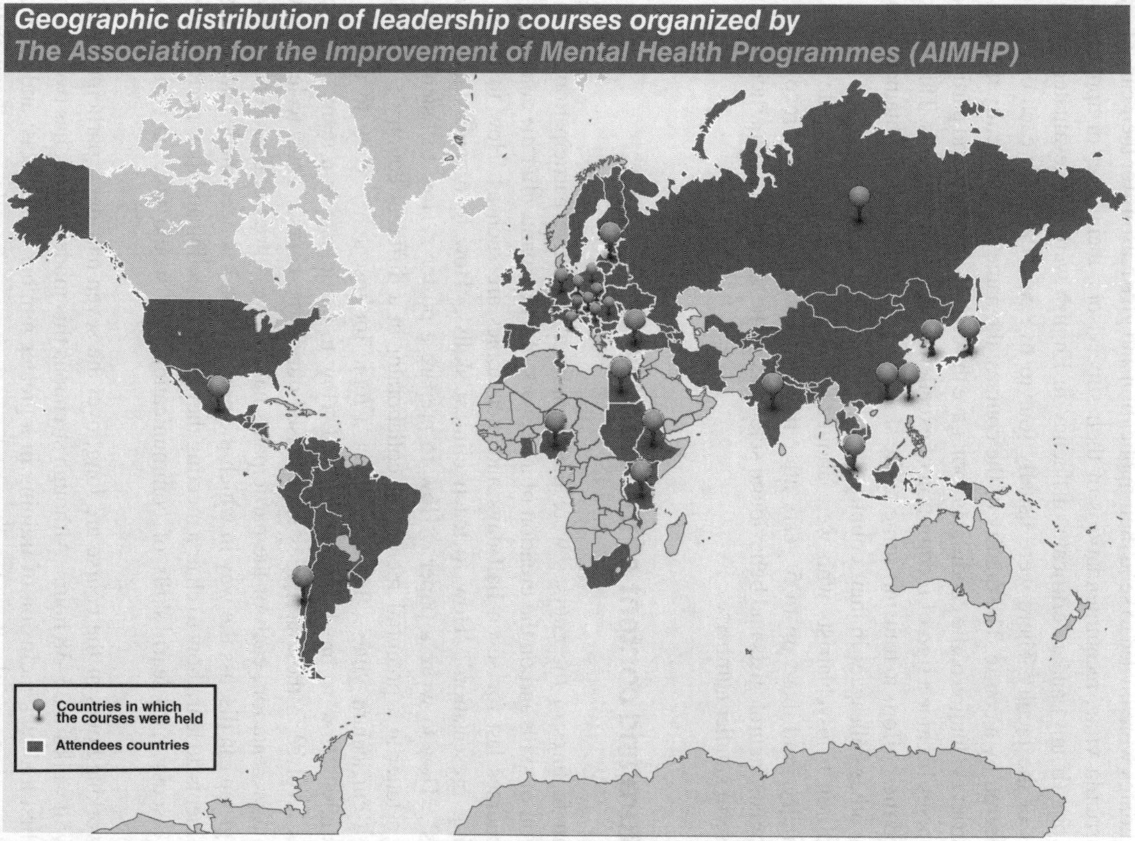
Geographic distribution of leadership courses organized by
The Association for the Improvement of Mental Health Programmes (AIMHP)
Countries in which the courses were held
Attendees countries

Figure 19.1 Countries from which participants have attended the AIM Leadership courses. Countries in bold type are those where courses have taken place. With kind permission from Alejandro Hernandez

Selection of the participants

In order to make the teaching as useful as possible the selection of the participants was given particular attention. Societies of psychiatry were invited to participate in the selection, and in the early years of the programme regularly co-sponsored the courses. The candidates were invited to send their application and give reasons for their candidacy. Their curricula vitae, recommendations of their supervisors, their letter of application, publications (if any) and a certificate of fluency in English were then evaluated by the members of the faculty. There were usually four to five candidates for each of the 16 places offered by a course. The quality of the courses, the names of the faculty members and the strict evaluation of the candidates soon gave the courses prestige, and participation in the courses became a sign of recognition of excellence for the participants. This in turn facilitated their efforts to transmit some of the skills and information they obtained in the course to other colleagues in their country.

In addition to psychiatrists who were about to complete their postgraduate training in psychiatry (and those up to 5 years after they obtained the specialty recognition), psychologists, neurologists and behavioural scientists of the same age also participated in the course in smaller numbers.

Structure and content of the courses

The main features of the courses were their emphasis on active participation, on the acquisition of skills and on the creation of a network of participants after the course.

The courses last for seven half-days and their topics are such as 'How to make a convincing presentation', 'How to teach clinical skills', 'How to organize and chair meetings', 'How to write a paper', 'How to prepare a poster', 'How to listen', 'How to write a letter to a potential mentor or collaborator in a different country', 'How to prepare a curriculum vitae', 'How to select a topic for research', 'How to design a simple study', 'How to break bad news', and 'How to participate in a team'. Each of the skills involved in these activities is exercised during the course. Thus, to learn how to make a presentation, each of the participants has to give a brief oral presentation so that the group can discuss the way in which the presentation has been made and suggest improvements; to learn how to chair a meeting they chair a meeting and their performance is then discussed; to learn skills of communication they would take part in various role plays.

The working hours of the course are long; over the seven half-days, participants and faculty will work for 35–38 hours. Although strenuous this mode of work has two advantages – first it allows inclusion of training in a greater number of subjects; and second, perhaps more importantly, the intensive common activity significantly contributes to the bonding among the participants and their readiness to remain in contact and work together after the course. The active involvement of participants in all sessions – by reducing the number of lectures to a minimum and by avoiding other forms of passive learning – made long hours of work easier to follow.

All members of the faculty were present in all sessions. All the meals were taken together and – since the courses were often held in a location that was some distance from major town attractions – the faculty was also approachable before and after the course hours. This allowed considerable one-to-one teaching and advice on specific issues of interest to the participants.

The considerable attention given to the room, seating and other arrangements for each of the courses served to teach ways in which the environment of an encounter can be made to support the conduct of the meeting and the achievement of its objectives.

Outcome and follow-up of courses

The courses have been evaluated by the participants and the ratings of the course were constantly high. The participants made comments and suggestions about the courses and these were used to streamline and improve the curricula and organization of the courses over the years. Numerous participants also wrote glowing letters after their return home, telling us that the course was very useful for them in their daily work and in developing programmes. In several instances the courses were repeated by the participants in their countries (e.g. Croatia, Indonesia, Malaysia and Serbia), and in at least two countries they have become a regular event: in Japan the Japanese Young Psychiatrist Organization (JYPO) has conducted courses every year since 2001, first mainly involving Japanese participants and more recently also participants from other countries in the Far East. In Germany the first four courses were conducted under the auspices of the Brandenburg Academy of Sciences focusing on participants from the countries in the Balkans; subsequently, and now for the 11th consecutive year, the University Department of Psychiatry at Charité conducted the course (the Berlin Summer School) involving students from many European countries.[9]

The participants in the courses also undertook joint research on topics identified during the time that they were together at the course. The studies done so far involved participants from different countries – the first such publication brought together researchers from countries that had never before published any joint paper.[7] Some of the papers resulting from the network's collaboration received international recognition – thus the work on pathways to care conducted in Croatia, Serbia, the former Yugoslav Republic of Macedonia and Romania received the Best Young Psychiatrists' Scientific Investigation Award during the World Congress of Psychiatry in 2005. In addition to studies of pathways to care carried out in the Balkan countries, studies using the same methods were done by young psychiatrists in Japan, Mongolia, Nepal,[8] China, Indonesia, Italy and other countries. Other studies focused on: patterns of prescription of treatment for severe mental illness in different countries;[7] the image that psychiatrists have in the eyes of colleagues in other disciplines; and the evaluation of psychiatric services by people who received treatment in these services.[c] In numerous instances the faculty members provided advice to the participants about studies that they have undertaken on their own.

---

[c]Papers describing the results of these studies are in preparation.

Conclusion

The courses providing professional skills, including those enhancing leadership potential, have proved to be useful to psychiatrists in different parts of the world. By now young psychiatrists from over 80 countries have participated in the courses and it is likely that many of them have transmitted what they have learned to others. This, however, is not sufficient. The acquisition of leadership and other professional skills should become a routine and obligatory part of postgraduate training in psychiatry because this may help to develop strong mental health programmes useful to the mentally ill and to the further development of psychiatry as a discipline.

References

1 Gureje D, Alem A. Mental health policy developments in Africa. *Bull WHO* 2000; **78**:475–82.
2 WHO. *Mental Health Care in Developing Countries: a Critical Appraisal of Research Findings*. Geneva: World Health Organization, 1984.
3 Climent CE, de Arango MV, Plutchick R, Leon CA. Development of an alternative, efficient, low cost mental health delivery system in Cali, Colombia, Part I: The Auxiliary Nurse. *Soc Psychiatry* 1978; **13**:29–35.
4 Alarcon RD, Agnilar Gaxiola SA. Mental health policy development in Latin America. *Bull WHO* 2000; **78**: 483–90.
5 Cohen A, Kleinman A, Saraceno, B (eds). *World Mental Health Casebook*. New York: Kluwer Academic/Plenum Publishers, 2002.
6 Gater R, Jordanova V, Maric N *et al.* Pathways to psychiatric care in Eastern Europe. *Brit J Psychiatry* 2005; **187**:248–55.
7 Jordanova V, Maric NP, Alikaj V *et al.* Prescribing practices in psychiatric hospitals in Eastern Europe. *Eur Psychiatry* 2011; **26**:414–18.
8 Hashimoto N, Fujisawa D, Giasuddin NA *et al.* Pathways to mental health care in Bangladesh, India, Japan, Mongolia and Nepal. *Asia Pac J Public Health* 2010; December 15, SAGE e-pub; doi: 10.1177/1010539510379395.
9 Mihai A, Ströhle A, Maric N, Heinz A, Helmchen H, Sartorius N. Postgraduate training for young psychiatrists – experience of the Berlin Summer School. *Eur Psychiatry* 2006; **21**:509–15.

Chapter 20

Leadership, Ethics and Managing Diversity

Julio Torales, Hugo Rodriguez and Dinesh Bhugra

Introduction

Leaders have a responsibility to lead but they also need to ensure that they have followers. Most of the time leaders lead from the front, though occasionally they have to act as shepherds and shepherd their followers from behind. They are also shepherds of values for the organization and the culture. Their passion and courage will enable them to engage their followers so that their vision can be realized and delivered. One of the most important roles the leader can perform is that of shepherd of ethics and human rights, while ensuring that their leadership style fits in with the culturally and socially acceptable ethical framework.

With the ever increasing movement of people around the globe, it is inevitable that leaders need to become aware of the cultural values and norms of the people they lead. It is possible to be aware of cultural diversity, and leaders must take this into account for purposes of engagement as well as explaining their vision. Countries have dealt with the processes of mass migration in different ways. For example, the United States follows the melting pot notion, Canada the rainbow nation, while Britain uses multiculturalism. These terms bring with them different levels of understanding and acceptance by the society into which the migrants settle, thereby emphasizing certain expectations more than others. For leaders from the new society, these values and expectations will raise specific issues.

Leadership can be seen to have at least two dimensions: technical and ethical. Often the ethical dimension is ignored or not studied to the same degree as the technical dimension. Ethical and moral domains are also important for the understanding and functioning of the leader.

All leaderships should be ethical, irrespective of the context. Integrity is the hallmark of the professional, and an ethical framework is critical in maintaining the integrity of the profession. Dealing with individuals from other cultures and societies may be problematic if the leader does not understand their cultural and social norms. Embedded within the ethical framework is the issue of basic human rights. Especially in mental health clinical practice, the leader must be aware of ethical and human rights issues.

Leadership in Psychiatry, First Edition. Edited by Dinesh Bhugra, Pedro Ruiz and Susham Gupta.
© 2013 John Wiley & Sons, Ltd. Published 2013 by John Wiley & Sons, Ltd.

With increasing globalization and movement of people across the world, it is likely that both leaders and their followers may come from different cultural backgrounds, and this may raise specific expectations and issues. Dealing with diversity can include managing varying expectations about cultural values, gender, sexual orientation, language and religion, among others. Even when the leader and the followers come from the same culture or society, there may still be regional differences related to socioeconomic status, educational status and dialects, all of which may lead to confusion, especially in communication. Furthermore, ethical dilemmas across cultures can raise specific issues, which a leader must be able to manage and deal with appropriately and sensitively. Both written and oral communications become extremely important in this context. In this chapter, we aim to highlight some of the ethical issues along with human rights and managing diversity, whether it is related to culture, religion or sexual orientation. Gender has already been discussed in this volume by Kastrup and Dymi (see Chapter 17). We propose to outline some of the basic principles in this context.

What are human rights?

Simply defined, human rights relate to basic freedoms – to ensure that human beings can speak freely, flourish in their own environment and live freely. The tension here is about the social context in which they live. Basic human rights also include encouraging and supporting individuals to achieve their full potential and be active members of the society in which they can participate fully. Being given due dignity and respect is part of basic human rights. Human rights are also about protecting humans from harm, which raises specific issues about both self-harm and harm to others (deliberate or accidental). This is at the core of clinical psychiatric practice and is also a part of the technical competence of the leader. These rights are about ensuring that individual members of society, especially those who are vulnerable, are protected from exploitation and poor treatment. Human rights date back millennia and, in spite of several attempts to ensure that these are universal, their acceptance remains extremely patchy around the globe and sometimes even in the same country in spite of legal frameworks.

Human rights and ethics are interlinked in a number of ways. Ethics dictate rules of conduct, and professional ethics are basically appropriate ways of managing professional responsibilities. Some of these issues have been dealt with in Chapter 3. An awareness of ethical issues and potential for conflict is an important aspect of any communication in clinical settings. Taking into account the patient's world view (in a similar way to that of the follower) can facilitate communication and mutual understanding. The ethical dilemmas in mental health settings are probably more demanding, even if these are not sufficiently clear at times.

Quality of leadership is bound into the moral values of the individual, of the society they come from and of their followers. Moral values of the leadership and those embedded in the culture and society also add to the moral fibre of the leader.[1]

Ethical principles consist of values that are culturally imbibed and are often a result of developmental experiences through the family, schools, peers, universities, friends, etc. These will be further strengthened by academic and social environmental influences, giving the society values that are fair, equitable and healthy.[2] For example, as will be described later in this chapter, sociocentric societies may have a more informal framework for dealing with ethical and legal matters.

Models of leadership are discussed elsewhere in this volume, but the relationship model (i.e. the relationship between leaders and their followers) is generally non-coercive, generating a true exchange of ideas and values between the two parties. However, on occasion the leader may have a larger role in influencing followers. The intrinsic motivation to lead or be led will dictate values and possibly ethical dilemmas. Leaders may share the values of their followers and through the process of leadership ensure that these values are consistent with one another.[2, 3] The simple implementation of reward and punishment is not sufficient in itself to achieve the commitment of the leaders, and other strategies may be indicated.

Dealing with diversity

Communication across cultures is strongly influenced by cultural norms and values. If the leaders and followers are from different cultural backgrounds, it is likely that miscommunication may occur.[3, 4] Taking parallels with psychotherapy across cultures, there are certain basic issues in dealing with diversity that need to be remembered (see also Chapter 7). The basic operation of communicating across cultures deals with identifying the problem and clarifying the message and then implementing the solution. Within such communication the leader-follower dyad will be important, as will the dialogue that will create maps for communication, which will provide a clear framework for communication and sharing of the vision of the leader. The task in the specific cultural context is to comprehensibly and meaningfully explain the vision and the aims. Built within such communication is the emphasis that the leader may place on the need for change as well as the degree of change required.

Cultural differences depending upon types of culture have been defined by Hofstede, who describes various dimensions of cultures that also determine the characteristics of cultures.[5] Thus cultures may be sociocentric or egocentric, masculine or feminine, uncertainty avoidant or not, among other types. These dimensions will affect both the leaders and their followers. Not all members of a sociocentric culture will be sociocentric. However, the leader must be aware of their own personal strengths and weaknesses as well as those of the cultures they come from and cultures they may be working in (if these are different), and manage these characteristics appropriately. It is possible that there may be members of the team who come from different cultures thereby creating a potential for tensions if the communication is not clear. Therefore, in team-working, concepts of the self on the part of the leader must be understood in the context of the concepts of self of the other members. Ethnic and racial identities, along with cultural identities, a grasp of language and an awareness of non-verbal communication, all become important.

To complicate matters further, the organizational culture will also play a role in ensuring that its staff are able to manage organizational cultural identities. Cultural appropriateness in managing people's expectations is vital for leaders to deliver their own vision.

Healthcare is a social process[6] and mental healthcare more so. The beliefs, expectations and personal resources of those who seek help have to be taken into account within the ethical and human rights framework of the service provider. The common task is to negotiate an understanding of the problem, making sense of the experience and moving the agenda for the organization forwards (or delivering the organization's mission) at the same time. In the way clinicians deal with patients, a common (communicating) language may or may not work but the leaders must be aware that the language they are using may not be clear to their followers, and the followers' language may be misunderstood by the leader. Negotiating across these boundaries of language and culture is an important first step in engaging the followers or the team. Role culture or team culture will bring with them their own values and expectations, as outlined by Handy.[7] In this chapter, we do not propose to highlight all the aspects of dealing with diversity but chiefly point out their importance in the role of the leader. Furthermore, the culture of the organization as well as that of the healthcare system have to be placed into context and taken into account, ensuring that leaders are well equipped to deal with them.

Role of the leader and ethics

Within the framework of ethics, several attributes of leadership have been identified.[8] These include character, courage, credibility, communication, knowledge, commitment and understanding of the groups and followers.

Character refers to the will and habits of the leader; a strong will makes it possible to traverse difficult situations so giving followers confidence in their leader. On occasion it is difficult to know what exactly character refers to. Courage allows the leader to be bold and act accordingly in achieving the objectives of the organization and the team so that followers are fully engaged in these endeavours. The leader must have credibility, which is about being acceptable to followers and vice versa. Communication of passion and vision is at the core of the leader-follower relationship, and it is imperative that leaders have the ability to communicate clearly and succinctly (also see Chapter 7). Communication also involves listening carefully to the followers as well as to other stakeholders. There is an urgent and pressing need for the leader to listen carefully and also to ensure that individuals know that their views are being heard, even if no action is taken or is possible. Knowledge or technical competence has already been discussed in earlier chapters. Leaders must also be aware of gaps in their knowledge and have the humility to seek help as and when required. The wisdom to know when they don't know something is an important part of the role of the leader. Total commitment to the organization and its aims and values makes the leader an ethical individual who does not have hidden agendas. Other stakeholders must recognize this commitment if they are to accept their leaders and follow them. A full understanding of the organization and other needs of stakeholders will stand the leader in good stead so that appropriate support and guidance are available to the followers. The leader has to be an ethical person who is fully aware of values and morals.[8]

Managing the ethical framework and diversity is a key aspect of successful leadership. The importance of the ethical framework is at the heart of professionalism, where governance and regulatory bodies may have a role to play. A successful leader can be defined as someone who manages to achieve the best from people and inspire them to deliver the aims of the team or the organization. Sometimes, in certain situations, it may not be possible to achieve these aims, but a simple containment of anxieties of the followers may well be enough. Managing cultural and sexual diversity, while putting aside one's personal values and prejudices, makes for better engagement and a better leader. Ethical principles also apply to the just distribution of finite resources in managing people and other resources.[9] Thus in professional settings the leader has both professional and personal ethics to manage and these are central.[10] The leader must manage ethical values at both personal and professional levels, though it may not always be easy to do so.

Conclusions

Leadership and professionalism, as well as the profession itself, are learnt by observing and teaching. Communication with stakeholders is a key responsibility both of the clinician and the leader. Managing diversity and an awareness of what moral values cultures may carry with them are crucial in achieving the goals set by and for the organization. In addition, the role the leader plays in developing as well as managing the ethical framework for the organization is inherent in leadership values and mores. Learning these values through one's own culture and also the culture of the organization allows the leader to be both pragmatic and sensitive in dealing with various issues, including potential conflict.

References

1 Perles GSM. Etica y liderazgo empresarial: una complementariedad necesaria. *Papeles de Etica, Economía y Dirección* 2000; **5**:1–14.
2 Prieto A, Zambrano E. Ethics and transformational leadership in teaching. *Telos* 2005; **7**:81–91.
3 Bhugra D, Bhui KS. *Cross-Cultural Psychiatry: A Practical Guide*. London: Arnold, 2001.
4 Bhugra D, Bhui KS. Psychotherapy for ethnic minorities. *Brit J Psychother* 1998; **14**:310–26.
5 Hofstede G. *Culture's Consequences*. Thousand Oaks, CA: Sage, 2001.
6 Waxler-Morrison N. Introduction. In: Waxler-Morrison N, Anderson JM, Richardson E (eds), *Cross-Cultural Caring: A Handbook for Health Professionals in Western Canada*. Vancouver: University of British Columbia Press, 1990; pp. 8–10.
7 Handy C. *Understanding Organisations*. London: Penguin, 2005.
8 Moreno CM. Claves para el liderazgo ético. *Capital Humano* 2004; **183**:84–8.
9 Armstrong D. Embodiment and ethics: constructing medicine's two bodies. *Sociol Health Ill* 2006; **28**:866–81.
10 Roberts LW, Hoop JG. *Professionalism and Ethics*. Washington, DC: American Psychiatric Publishing, Inc., 2008.

Part C
Learning Materials

Chapter 21

Assessment Tools

Cindy L. Ehresman

Assessment of leadership can encompass purposes as wide-ranging as determining who to hire and where to place the newly hired person within the organization or practice, who to promote into positions of increased responsibility, development of the members' leadership capacity, and methods for assigning and appraising individual and team performance. The leadership dimensions that are typically assessed include measures of leadership potential, leadership competencies for current and future positions, and more elusive leadership qualities and characteristics such as measures of individual character, values and ethics. These constructs may all have uses appropriate for a psychiatry practice. This wide variety of reasons for measuring leadership makes it critical to begin by determining the purpose for the assessment.

As varied as the purposes for assessing leadership, the tools used for assessment encompass an equally broad spectrum, and choosing the appropriate instrument will depend on the intended use of the results. This chapter identifies some of those tools along with a short review of the applicability of each to a practice. Additional resources are presented to help facilitate their use.

Uses of leadership assessment in a practice

Medical practices experience unique pressures and demands from serving individuals who seek them out, often for relief from illness and injury. Although centred on healing, the mental health organization comprises team members of varying abilities and leadership capacities. In recognition of the importance of maximizing the potential of each employee, assessing leadership for selection, for development and for performance evaluation are all valid. Contemporary leadership researchers often recognize the increasing importance of teamwork and collaborative work environments as we move from the old hierarchical, command-and-control style of management to the shared leadership of engaged and participative organizational members. The knowledge, skills and abilities of those designated as leaders remain important to the success of the team but current research indicates that the perspective of how leadership emerges or how group members share in the leadership

Leadership in Psychiatry, First Edition. Edited by Dinesh Bhugra, Pedro Ruiz and Susham Gupta.
© 2013 John Wiley & Sons, Ltd. Published 2013 by John Wiley & Sons, Ltd.

process in groups working together to accomplish a common goal is increasingly important.[1] This leadership potential of individuals and teams can be intentionally developed through interventions that must necessarily begin with assessment of competencies and capacity.

What to assess

Assessment of leadership capacity or potential is not based only on observed performance in a current position. Leadership is developed over time, enhanced by developmental programmes and experiences, and therefore identified competencies can be assessed early on as predictors of an individual's future performance. Dimensions associated with leadership that are commonly assessed, both for selection and for development purposes, include:

- communication skills
- motivation to lead
- drive/results orientation
- team skills
- problem-solving and innovation
- influencing others
- tolerance for stress
- integrity/ethics.

While this list of dimensions includes those most frequently assessed in leadership research, this chapter will focus primarily on those instruments more widely used for selection, development and performance appraisal.

Tools for assessing leadership: selection, development and performance

Leadership assessment tools typically serve one of three functions:

1 Assisting in the selection of leaders, either through external hiring or internal promotion.
2 Developing leadership capacity/potential.
3 Evaluating leader performance and helping with future performance improvement.

Some leadership assessment tools serve more than one of these functions.

One of the primary uses of assessment is to predict an organizational member's capacity to hold future leadership roles within the practice. Selecting the right new-hire or the best person for promotion into a leadership role requires the right tools to assess leadership capacity. Tools used primarily for selection purposes include structured interviews, various tests of potential, including tests of cognitive abilities, personality tests and situational judgment tests. Additional assessment tools are used for both selection and development. These include assessment centres and other simulation methods.

Leadership assessment tools are also used to identify strengths and weakness in leadership competencies for developmental purposes. Methods such as multisource ratings, often referred to as 360-degree feedback, and various measures of leadership style and leadership competencies are also used as developmental assessment tools. Some of the additional assessment instruments that we will discuss, such as measures that focus on key aspects of leadership – ranging from emotional intelligence to conflict management to leadership skills/competencies – can all be a part of leadership development efforts in psychiatric practices.

Finally, some of these leadership assessment tools and methods are used to evaluate leader performance. Most notable would be the multisource ratings, which were originally developed as an alternative to the traditional top-down performance evaluation for managers/leaders.

Additionally, the process of assessing particular leadership behaviours signals which of these are highly valued to the organization. As with most things, that which gets measured gets the most focus. By including particular constructs in interviews, in developmental activities and in performance evaluations, team members can construe what the practice most values. There are seemingly as many instruments and methodologies employed as there are consultants and agencies, but the most commonly used are detailed in this section.

Interviews

Perhaps the most familiar form of assessment is the interview. Face-to-face or virtual interviews can be useful for evaluating candidates' interpersonal, communication and teamwork skill level and also to determine the amount of existing job knowledge. When selecting new members of a practice or evaluating candidates for promotion within the practice, structured interviews that focus on those traits and skills related to current and potential leadership as well as the needed job competencies can lead to better selection, and eventually improve leadership performance in the practice. The use of common questions for all candidates provides higher validity and more useful information for selection.[2,3] In addition to experience-based questions, situational questions can also be used. In a situational interview, the interviewer(s) might pose the same hypothetical scenario and ask each candidate to describe how they would approach the situation. A rubric for scoring the best answers to interview questions (both situational questions and questions on leadership experience/competencies) will lead to better prediction of successful leadership.

Tests of cognitive ability

General intelligence (the ability to acquire new skills) stands as a significant predictor of success in the workplace, predicting the emergence and effectiveness of leadership, particularly with complex and intellectually challenging tasks.[2,4] Due to the potential for adverse results for minority groups, cognitive ability should be one of a suite of assessment tools and not used as a stand-alone determinant. Clinicians will likely be aware of some of the more commonly used or preferred instruments such as the Wechsler Adult Intelligence Scale (WAIS) and the Stanford–Binet Intelligence Scales, but there are cognitive ability tests that are better suited to the workplace, and these include the Wonderlic measures (see Appendix 21.1) and other instruments.

Simulations/assessment centres

Assessment of leadership competencies can be accomplished through simulations of job-related tasks such as in-basket activities, leaderless group discussions, oral and written communication exercises, and problem-solving exercises. This standardized form of behaviour measurement is usually associated with the multiple-rater format of an assessment centre. Assessment centres are used for both selection and for developmental purposes. The design of the assessment centre will necessarily be dependent on the intended use and can include interviews and psychological tests along with the simulations. Rater training is a critical component of assessment centres and ratings are often assigned through a series of consensus-building sessions among raters.

While assessment centres enjoy strong validity and are reported to do a good job of predicting future performance, particularly for those competencies assessed, they have been criticized for failing to measure complex constructs such as leadership.[5-7] They are notoriously heavy consumers of resources, both time and money, and designing and operating an assessment centre is unlikely to prove beneficial to most practices. An alternative to operating an assessment centre is to make use of the services of companies who specialize in providing these services, including computer-simulated assessment centres (see Appendix 21.1).

Situational judgement tests

Situational judgement tests (SJTs) are an additional form of simulation that presents a scenario and asks the respondent to evaluate (make a judgement about) the situation and choose his or her solution from the listed selection. In this way the applicant displays relevant knowledge, skills and abilities (KSAs) by declaring how they would behave in a particular situation. SJTs are frequently crafted in such a way that the respondent selects which of the listed answers is the most correct as opposed to choosing the answer that represents the way they would actually respond. This form of test construction is done in order to reduce faking.[8] SJTs can be paper and pencil based, computer based, or administered via an interactive video.

While SJTs are considered to have low physical fidelity (how well the simulation matches a real situation), particularly as compared to an assessment centre, they have high psychological fidelity. SJTs have been in use since the 1920s and are favoured by industrial/organizational psychologists for their ability to measure several independent constructs at the same time (such as agreeableness, conscientiousness and cognitive ability) and also because they are less likely to exhibit race and gender differences than interviews and cognitive tests.[8,9] This multidimensional form of assessment has demonstrated correlations with constructs including cognitive ability, the Big Five personality factors and job performance. The most commonly assessed constructs include agreeableness, conscientiousness, emotional stability, extroversion, job experience, openness, leadership and interpersonal skills.[8,10] SJTs are typically a low-cost (once initial development is accomplished) and effective method of assessing leadership for both selection and development purposes. Because most SJTs target specific job-related constructs, they are typically developed in-house and are proprietary. Industrial/organizational consulting psychologists and human resource management companies may provide test development tailored to the individual practice (see Appendix 21.1).

Personality tests

Companies and other types of organizations, along with numerous consulting agencies, now administer personality tests as commonly as clinicians use them to assess psychiatric patients. Personality tests, measuring psychological dispositions, attitudes and motivations, are a predictor of leadership style. Leadership style in turn predicts the attitudes of followers and the functioning of work groups. These attitudes and performance factors ultimately predict the overall performance of the organization.[11] This linkage of leader personality to organizational success makes personality testing for selection (as well as for leader development) a valuable part of the assessment toolkit. There are many choices when selecting instruments for assessing personality and a few of those designed specifically for use by businesses are identified below.

The research on the linkage of the Big Five personality traits (neuroticism, extraversion, openness, agreeableness, conscientiousness) to leadership has enjoyed a revival in recent years. Meta-analyses show that the Big Five do a good job of predicting leadership emergence and effectiveness and are linked to transformational leadership[4] (see Appendix 21.1).

Multisource ratings (360-degree feedback)

As a leadership development tool, multi-rater assessments have proliferated at an astounding rate. Also commonly called 360-degree feedback or multisource feedback (MSF), the process provides the subject with anonymous feedback from multiple sources at multiple levels. An example might be the practice manager who receives feedback from superiors, subordinates, peers and customers/clients about job-related skills and behaviours (e.g. knowledge of business, ability to communicate effectively, drive/results orientation, time management). The raters submit their completed surveys for scoring to a central location (often an outside consultant or agency). Results from the multiple levels are consolidated by a knowledgeable facilitator, who prepares a report and reviews it with the subject of the ratings. Ideally the feedback then serves as the basis of a development plan to improve effectiveness.

This process of providing formal feedback through an anonymous structure where skills and behaviours are presented in well-defined blocks gives raters more opportunity for objectivity and accuracy. This in turn makes the feedback richer and more likely to provide the input needed for a development plan.[12] Another benefit of MSF is that the items assessed provide clues for the participants about which behaviours and skills are valued by the organization and how they measure up to those standards.

Research on the effectiveness of MSF for developmental purposes concluded that moderately positive results could be expected but failed to find evidence of large-scale improvements in performance.[13] Additionally, the process is time and effort intensive and research on participants who received negative feedback revealed some long-term behavioural effects.[13] However, using a sound MSF instrument as part of an overall leader development programme offers an opportunity for formal assessment based on multiple perspectives. Best practice for implementing an effective MSF program entails an eight-step process:[12]

1 Determine the purpose for the assessment and the organizational context.
2 Determine the target population.
3 Select the MSF instrument best suited to accomplish the goals.
4 Effectively communicate to all organizational members involved.
5 Undertake appropriate data collection.
6 Provide feedback.
7 Ensure the feedback is correctly interpreted.
8 Construct a development plan based on the feedback.

The use of MSF for performance evaluation requires additional consideration. Because performance appraisals are generally associated with promotion, planning for reduction in force, and compensation, they rely heavily on supervisor input. The effectiveness of MSF relies in good part on anonymous feedback, and researchers have identified issues associated with MSF responses when the rater is aware that it will impact administrative decisions.[13] It is recommended that MSF be used primarily for developmental purposes (see Appendix 21.1).

Measures of leadership style/leadership competencies/leadership traits

Multifactor Leadership Questionnaire

Although measures of leadership style are more commonly used for leadership research, they are also useful as a means of providing feedback for developmental purposes.[2] One of the better-known and psychometrically sound instruments is the Multifactor Leadership Questionnaire (MLQ). The MLQ has been refined several times since initial development in the mid-1980s. In addition to numerous research studies and use by consultants and human resource professionals, it has also been used extensively in studies of leadership in mental health, healthcare, service and other public sector settings.[14]

The current form of the MLQ (5X) measures leadership styles ranging from passive to transformational by measuring components of behaviour. The prominent four behavioural components of transformational leadership (idealized influence, inspirational motivation, intellectual stimulation, and individualized consideration) along with two of the dimensions of transactional leadership (contingent reward and management by exception) and the behavioural aspect of no leadership (laissez-faire) comprise the self-report and rater versions of the instrument (see Appendix 21.1).

Authentic Leadership Questionnaire (ALQ)

Fuelled in part by the spate of contemporary scandals in the business, government and religious sectors, leadership researchers have begun to focus on the authenticity of leaders. With roots stemming from the research on transformational leadership, the relatively new concept – authentic leadership – is receiving considerable attention. Too new and too complex for a simple definition, authentic leadership can be summarized as a complete understanding of one's beliefs and inclinations – both the positive and the negative – and an alignment of this understanding with demonstrated behaviour.[15] Authentic leadership is the subject of research from three different viewpoints: (i) the intrapersonal perspective (leader's self-knowledge, self -regulation, and self-concept); (ii) the interpersonal perspective (relationships between leaders and followers); and (iii) the developmental perspective (leader's ethical and psychological qualities form the basis for leadership authenticity growth potential).[16]

Although researchers generally agree that context may impact the interpretation of authentic leadership, measurement of four factors may be accomplished through the Authentic Leadership Questionnaire (ALQ). The four factors addressed are:

1 *Self-awareness* – the degree to which the leader recognizes his or her own strengths and weaknesses and the impact these have on others.
2 *Relational transparency* – the degree to which the leader shares a true version of his or her self.
3 *Internalized moral perspective* – the degree to which the individual uses a self-regulatory process of using his or her own ethical and moral standards rather than being guided by circumstances.
4 *Balanced processing* – the degree to which the individual analyses and processes the opinion of others before making a decision, including those that disagree.

Both self-report (ALQ Self-Only Report) and multi-rater (ALQ 360 Multi-Rater Report) versions are available and may be useful for leadership development (see Appendix 21.1).

Perceived Leader Integrity Scale (PLIS)

The Perceived Leader Integrity Scale (PLIS) is a psychometrically sound multi-rater format (feedback from multiple levels) developed to provide feedback on a leader's perceived integrity, ethics and destructive behaviour that may be useful for leadership development purposes within a practice. There is also a shorter (eight-item) version available at no cost via the internet but the authors caution that it does not provide enough detail for developmental purposes (see Appendix 21.1).

Thomas-Kilmann Conflict Mode Instrument

The Thomas-Kilmann Conflict Mode Instrument (TKI) is based on the Blake and Mouton Managerial Grid (now termed 'Leadership Grid'), a model of five conflict-handling styles (competing, collaborating, compromising, avoiding and accommodating). This well-established assessment tool can help facilitate interpersonal and team dynamics within the practice as well as provide leadership development feedback to individuals (see Appendix 21.1).

Other popular tools

This listing of assessment tools is certainly not comprehensive. There are other widely available and popular instruments that are purported to relate to leadership but lack the validating research. Emotional intelligence is an example of this, with extensive popular press literature and a bevy of instruments that claim to measure this trait, but lacking the definitive supporting research linking it to leadership competence[4] (see Appendix 21.1).

Another popular instrument, the Myers-Briggs Type Indicator (MBTI), has produced contradictory results in research attempting to link the 16 personality types identified by the test to leadership.[4] Based on Jung typologies, the instrument consists of a series of questions with results that purport to identify worldview and decision-making qualities of the respondent (see Appendix 21.1).

The DISC® behavioural style instrument is based on the four quadrants of dominance/drive, inducement/influence, submission/steadiness and compliance/conscientiousness. The model specifies that each individual displays all four styles but in varying degrees of intensity. While DISC® is quite popular and widely available via consultants who are authorized to administer and interpret the results, there is little empirical research supporting the instrument's development.[4] However, practitioners report anecdotal success by combining DISC® (measures of behaviour) with the Workplace Motivators Report (measures of motivation) along with the Hartman Acumen Capacity Index (measures of clarity of thought). These three instruments together form the TTI TriMetrix® HD system for use in evaluating the whole person (behaviours, motivators, acumen and competencies), which is useful for job fit/hiring, coaching individuals and team development (see Appendix 21.1).

How to use leadership assessment in your practice

The dynamic nature of leadership and the complexity of the construct necessitate multiple methods of assessment rather than selection of only one – whether of those listed or one of the many others available. Table 21.1 gives a summary of the tools identified in this chapter. No single assessment tool can measure the full range of an individual's existing leadership competencies or his/her capacity for future leadership roles within the practice.

The use of leadership assessment for the purposes of hiring and promotion can be useful in building a team of members who possess those competencies and capacities valued most by the practice. The proliferation of available programmes utilizing multisource ratings (360-degree) makes this a potentially valuable assessment tool, particularly for those

Table 21.1 Selected tools and applications for leadership assessment

Tools for leadership assessment	Used for selection	Used for development	Used for performance evaluation
Interviews	X		
General intelligence test	X		
Simulations/assessment centres	X	X	
Situational judgement tests	X	X	
Personality tests	X		
Measures of leadership style/competencies/traits			
Multisource ratings (360°)		X	X
Multifactor Leadership Questionnaire		X	
Authentic Leadership Questionnaire (Self-Report)		X	
Authentic Leadership Quotient (Multi-Rater Report)		X	
Perceived Leader Integrity Scale		X	
Thomas-Kilmann Conflict Mode Instrument		X	
Measures of emotional intelligence	X	X	
Myers-Briggs Type Indicator	X	X	
DISC/TriMetrix	X	X	

members already in leadership roles, and potentially for performance evaluation as well. Assessment of leadership is most powerful when it goes beyond a decision-making tool and is combined with a leadership development plan. The snapshot provided by any assessment is just that, a moment in time, and the next step is to evaluate the results of the assessment to determine what future contributions the individual might bring to the organization.

Appendix 21.1 Sources of tools for assessing leadership

Tests of cognitive ability

Wonderlic Cognitive Ability Tests
Wonderlic Inc., 400 Lakeview Parkway, Suite 200, Vernon Hills, IL 60061, USA. (877) 605-9496. Website: http://www.wonderlic.com/

Assessment centres

DDI Assessment Center
Development Dimensions International (DDI), World Corporate Headquarters and Center for Learning & Technology, 1225 Washington Pike, Bridgeville, PA 15017-2838, USA. Tel: (800) 933-4463 or 412-257-0600. Fax: (412) 220-2942. Website: http://www .ddiworld.com/

Situational judgement tests

Loganberry Limited, 50 Broadlands Avenue, Chesham, Buckinghamshire, HP5 1AL, UK. Telephone: 07740 197680. Website: http://www.loganberrylimited.co.uk/index.html

Personality tests

Predictive Index® System
PI Worldwide, 16 Laurel Ave., Wellesley Hills, MA 02481, USA. Telephone: +1-781-235-8872. Toll-free (USA): 800-832-888PI. Website: http://www.piworldwide.com/

Hogan Personality Inventory (HPI)
Hogan Assessment Systems, 2622 E. 21st St., Tulsa, OK 741148, USA. Telephone: 800.756.0632. Website: http://www.hoganassessments.com/

Multisource rating

Benchmarks®
Center for Creative Leadership, One Leadership Place, P.O. Box 26300, Greensboro, NC 27438, USA. Telephone: 1 336 545 2810
   Center for Creative Leadership. EMEA, Rue Neerveld 101–103 Neerveldstraat, B-1200 Brussels, Belgium. Telephone: 32 (0) 2 679 09 10. Website: http://www.ccl.org/leadership/index.aspx

Measures of leadership style/leadership competencies/leadership traits

Multifactor Leadership Questionnaire (MLQ)
Mind Garden, Inc., 855 Oak Grove Ave., Suite 215, Menlo Park, CA 94025, USA.
Telephone: (650) 322-6300. Fax: (650) 322-6398. Website: http://www.mindgarden.com

Authentic Leadership Questionnaire (ALQ)
Mind Garden, Inc., 855 Oak Grove Ave., Suite 215, Menlo Park, CA 94025, USA.
Telephone: (650) 322-6300. Fax: (650) 322-6398. Website: http://www.mindgarden.com

Perceived Leader Integrity Scale (PLIS)
For more information or permission to use in your practice, contact S. Bartholomew
Craig, PhD (bart_craig@ncsu.edu). The short version is available at http://www.sbcraig.
com/plis/

Thomas-Kilmann Conflict Mode Instrument (TKI)
CPP, Inc., 1055 Joaquin Road, Ste. 200, Mountain View, CA 94043, USA. Telephone:
(650) 969-8901. Toll-free: (800) 624-1765. Fax: (650) 969-8608. Website: https://www.
cpp.com/en/tkiproducts.aspx?pc=142

Other popular instruments

*Mayer-Salovey-Caruso Emotional Intelligence Test (MSCEIT) and EQ-i 2.0 Emotional
Quotient-Inventory*
Multi-Health Systems Inc., P.O. Box 950, North Tonawanda, NY 14120-0950, USA.
Telephone: 1.800.456.3003. Website: http://ei.mhs.com/
   MHS Inc., 3770 Victoria Park Ave., Toronto, Ontario, M2H 3M6, Canada. Telephone:
1.800.268.6011.
   MHS (UK), 83 Baker Street, London, W1U 6AG. Telephone: (0)845 601 7603.

Myers-Briggs Type Indicator
MBTI® Master Practitioner Referral Network, 2815 NW 13th Street, Suite 401,
Gainesville, FL 32609-2878, USA. Telephone: 866.526.6284 (USA and Canada). Web-
site: http://www.mbtireferralnetwork.org/

DISC® and TriMetrix® HD
TTI Performance Systems, Ltd, 17785 North Pacesetter Way, Scottsdale, AZ 85255, USA.
Telephone: 1-800-869-6908. Website: http://www.ttiassessments.com/

References

1   Day D, Gronn P, Salas E. Leadership capacity in teams. *Leadership Quart* 2004; **15**:857–80.
2   London M, Smither JW, Diamante T. Best practices in leadership assessment. In: Conger J,
   Riggio R (eds), *The Practice of Leadership: Developing the Next Generation of Leaders*. San
   Francisco: Jossey-Bass, 2007; pp. 41–63.

3   Bass BM. *The Bass Handbook of Leadership: Theory, Research & Managerial Applications*, 4th edn. New York: Free Press, 2008.

4   Antonakis J. Predictors of leadership: the usual suspects and the suspect traits. In: Bryman A, Collinson D, Grint K, Jackson B, Uhl-Bien M (eds), *The Sage Handbook of Leadership*. Thousand Oaks, CA: Sage Publications, 2011; pp. 269–85.

5   Lance C. Why assessment centers do not work the way they are supposed to. *Ind Organiz Psychol* 2008; **1**:84–97.

6   Lowry P. The assessment center process: assessing leadership in the public sector. *Public Pers Manag* 1995; **24**:443–50.

7   Lowry P. The assessment center process: new directions. *J Soc Behav Pers* 1997; **12**:53–62.

8   McDaniel MA, Nguyen NT. Situational judgment tests: a review of practice and constructs assessed. *Int J Select Assess* 2001; **9**:103–13.

9   Ployhart R, MacKenzie W. Situational judgment tests: a critical review and agenda for the future. In: Zedeck S (ed.), *APA Handbook of Industrial and Organizational Psychology*, vol. 2. Washington, DC: American Psychological Association, 2011; pp. 237–52.

10 Christian M, Edwards B, Bradley J. Situational judgment tests: constructs assessed and a meta-analysis of their criterion-related validities. *Pers Psychol* 2010; **63**:83–117.

11 Hogan R, Kaiser RB. What we know about leadership. *Rev Gen Psychol* 2005; **9**:169–80.

12 Chappelow CT. 360-degree feedback. In: McCauley CD, Van Velsor E (eds), *The Center for Creative Leadership Handbook of Leadership Development*, 2nd edn. San Francisco: Jossey-Bass, 2011; pp. 58–84.

13 Atwater LE, Brett JF, Charles AC. Multisource feedback: lessons learned and implications for practice. *Hum Resour Manage* 2007; **46**:285–307.

14 Aarons G. Transformational and transactional leadership: association with attitudes toward evidence-based practice. *Psychiatr Serv* 2006; **57**:1162–9.

15 Caza A, Jackson B. Authentic leadership. In: Bryman A, Collinson D, Grint K, Jackson B, Uhl-Bien M (eds), *The Sage Handbook of Leadership*. Thousand Oaks, CA: Sage Publications, 2011; pp. 352–64.

16 Northouse PG. *Leadership Theory and Practice*, 6th edn. Thousand Oaks, CA: Sage Publications.

Chapter 22

Learning Materials

John P. Baker

Introduction

The intent of this chapter is to provide the reader with additional resources and references for further leadership development and thought regarding the various leadership aspects discussed in this text. This chapter does not duplicate the material provided by each author in their respective chapters, but attempts to enhance the reader's understanding of the material by suggesting additional references, case studies, guides, exercises and ways to apply the information discussed in each chapter. The purpose of these learning materials is to allow those interested in further development of specific subject areas additional means for increased experiential application and understanding.

Chapter 1: What is Leadership?

1 Rost (1991) provides an extensive discussion on the definition of leadership in his book, *Leadership for the Twenty-First Century* (ISBN 0-275-94610-X).
2 The following website provides an overview of leadership and classic theories: http://www.nwlink.com/~donclark/leader/leadcon.html.
3 With a mentor or in a small group, define leadership in your context. Next, define the competencies and skills a leader must have to succeed in your context.
4 Avolio (2011) provides an overview of leadership development in his book, *Full Range Leadership Development* (ISBN 978-1-4129-7475-2).

Chapter 2: What Makes a Leader? Leader Skills and Competencies

1 McGuire and Rhodes (2009) provide 'Helpful Sources of Studies on Intelligence and Brain Research' as an appendix in their book, *Transforming your Leadership Culture* (ISBN 978-0-470-25957-3).

Leadership in Psychiatry, First Edition. Edited by Dinesh Bhugra, Pedro Ruiz and Susham Gupta.
© 2013 John Wiley & Sons, Ltd. Published 2013 by John Wiley & Sons, Ltd.

2   Hughes, Ginnett and Curphy (2009) provide a list and explanation of leader skills in Part Four of their text, *Leadership Enhancing the Lessons of Experience* (6th edn; ISBN 978-0-07-340504-9).
3   Pierce and Newstrom (2008) provide 15 exercises focused on the practice of leadership in Part Two of their text, *Leaders and the Leadership Process* (5th edn; ISBN978-0-353028-4).
4   The following website provides a discussion regarding general leadership skills and competencies: http://www.shrm.org/research/articles/articles/pages/leadershipcompetencies.aspx.
5   Rath (2007) provides an online self-assessment of a person's strengths in his book, *Strengthsfinder 2.0* (ISBN 978-1-59562-015-6). This empirically based assessment was developed using Gallup Poll data and is the focal point for Rath's argument that leader development should focus on improving strengths rather than weaknesses.

Chapter 3: Medical Professionalism, Leadership and Professional Judgement

1   The following website provides insights to leadership and professionalism in the medical profession: http://www.ncbi.nlm.nih.gov/pubmed/17051276.

Chapter 4: Leadership Theories and Approaches

1   Northouse (2013) provides an excellent overview of leadership theories and approaches in his text, *Leadership Theory and Practice* (6th edn; ISBN 978-1-4522-4466-2). For each theory or approach discussed, Northouse provides several case studies and a self-assessment instrument for readers to gain insight to his/her ability in the discussed leadership theory or approach.
2   Yukl (2009) provides an excellent general text on leadership titled *Leadership in Organizations* (ISBN 978-0-1324-2431-8). The text includes various case studies and discussion questions regarding most leadership theories and approaches addressed in this publication.
3   Leader analysis exercise. Discuss the leadership of the following public figures. Discuss the traits of the leader and the leadership theory or approach that best illustrates the leadership style of the leader.
   a   George Washington
   b   Abraham Lincoln
   c   Martin Luther King
   d   Steve Jobs
   e   Warren Buffett
   Solution for Leader Analysis Exercise:
   a   George Washington: honest, patriotic, selfless, humble. He illustrated path-goal leadership as he provided the correct leader behaviours to motivate the Continental Army to achieve victory (goal) for independence.

b Abraham Lincoln: honest, visionary, humble. He illustrated transformational leadership through his leadership during the Civil War as he did not want a divided United States and knew the implications of a divided Union.

c Martin Luther King: inspirational, charismatic, visionary. Transformational leadership is easily illustrated by MLK as he created a clear, distinct vision for racial relations within the United States and inspired others to achieve that vision.

d Steve Jobs: intelligent, visionary, self-centred, driven. Steve Jobs best illustrates both transformational leadership and path-goal. Transformational leadership is illustrated in his intense desire and passion to achieve his vision and his driving people to go beyond what they thought they could invent. Path-goal is evident; a discussion on the leader behaviours illustrates the use of directive and achievement-oriented behaviors.

e Warren Buffett: intelligent, visionary, pragmatic, disciplined. Buffett illustrates Leader Member Exchange (LMX) theory as he chose companies for their strengths and had a close in-group that he depended on to run his companies. Path-goal leadership is also illustrated by Buffett.

4 Mind Garden Inc. offers various leadership assessment instruments including the Multifactor Leadership Questionnaire used to assess transformational leadership: http://www.mindgarden.com/.

5 *The Leadership Challenge* (ISBN 978-0-7879-8492-2), a *New York Times* best seller, is an empirical model of leadership developed by Kouzes and Posner based on over 25 years of research. Assessment and additional materials supporting the Leadership Challenge model are available at the following website: http://www.leadershipchallenge.com/WileyCDA/.

Chapter 5: Clinical Leadership

1 Carter, Ulrich and Goldsmith (2005) in their book, *Best Practices in Leadership Development and Organization Change* (ISBN 0-7879-7625 3), highlight the successful leadership practices and advice from successful organizations, several in the healthcare field. The authors have founded the Best Practices Institute; for more information visit www.bpinstitute.net.

2 McKinsey and Company, a for-profit organization, provide the McKinsey Quarterly, a free, electronic journal focused on the healthcare industry: http://www.mckinseyquarterly.com/When_clinicians_lead_2293.

Chapter 6: Leadership and Clinician Engagement in Service Development

1 The Department of Health and Human Services for Tasmania provided information regarding a leadership development programme based on enhancing clinical engagement: http://www.dhhs.tas.gov.au/career/home/career_development__and__

advancement/management_and_leadership_development_program/clinical_engage
ment/_nocache?SQ_DESIGN_NAME=v2.

Chapter 7: Communication

1   Hamilton (2011) provides detailed information on communication styles in her text, *Communicating for Results A Guide for Business and the Professions* (9th edn; ISBN 978-1-4390-3643-3).

2   Hackman and Johnson (2004) provide a text titled *Leadership: A Communication Perspective* (5th edn; ISBN 978-1-57766-579-3) that provides readers with a communication-focused perspective on leadership. Each chapter includes application exercises and suggested movies that further illustrate leadership communication concepts.

3   Stone, Patton and Heen (1999) provide a unique insight to communicating effectively as a leader in their book *Difficult Conversations How to Discuss What Matters Most* (ISBN 978-0-14-311844-2).

4   The following website provides an overview regarding the impact of communication on the leadership process: http://www.nwlink.com/~donclark/leader/leadcom.html.

Chapter 8: Leadership and Decision-Making

1   Denhardt, Denhardt and Aristigueta (2009) provide a text titled *Managing Human Behavior in Public and Nonprofit Organizations* (ISBN 978-1-4129-5667-3) that includes an overview chapter (Chapter 5) on decision-making applicable to most organizational settings.

2   Johnson's text, *Meeting the Ethical Challenges of Leadership Casting Light or Shadow* (ISBN 978-1-4129-8222-1), provides a chapter on various ethical perspectives that impact leadership and making decisions.

Chapter 9: Team-Building in Psychiatry

1   Acona and Bresman (2007) provide insight to developing and leading virtual teams in their book titled *X-Teams* (ISBN 978-1-59139-692-5).

2   Levi (2011), in his book titled *Group Dynamics for Teams* (ISBN 978-1-4129-7762-3), provides insight to team leadership and includes many exercise and assessment tools along with case studies. Levi also provides in an appendix a guide to student team projects.

3   LaFasto and Larson provide a team leader assessment tool titled 'The Collaborative Team Leader', in their book *When Teams Work Best* (2001; ISBN 978-0-7619-2366-4). The tool includes both a team leader self-assessment and team member assessment of the leader.

Chapter 10: Coaching and Mentoring

1   Zachary provides application guidance for mentoring in several books, including: *Creating a Mentoring Culture* (ISBN 0-7879-6401-8), *The Mentor's Guide* (ISBN 978-0-90772-6) and *The Mentee's Guide* (ISBN 978-0-470-34358-6).

2   The following website for the National Mentoring Partnership Program provides various tools and suggestions for effective mentoring: http://www.mentoring.org/. Although focused on youth mentoring, the processes and materials can generalize to other contexts and situations.

Chapter 11: Leadership and Factions

1   Stanford University discusses six common pitfalls to avoid when negotiating in a business environment: http://www.gsb.stanford.edu/news/research/hr_negotiation_strategy.shtml.

2   The Negotiation Experts provide pre-negotiating strategies and discuss other aspects of negotiating at their website: http://www.negotiations.com/articles/negotiation-strategy/.

Chapter 12

Given the broad topic of this chapter, the other leadership chapters contain information regarding effective leadership strategies when engaging leadership outside the clinical team.

Chapter 13: Leadership in Academic Psychiatry

1   The *Academic Leadership Journal in Student Research* (http://www.academicleadership.org) is an online, international, peer-reviewed, open-access journal dedicated to advancing research on academic disciplines.

Chapter 14: Taking People With You

1   Appreciative inquiry (AI) is the process of changing attitudes, practices and behaviours through appreciative conversations and relationships. Cooperrider, Whitney and Stavros (2008) provide a text titled *Appreciative Inquiry Handbook* (2nd edn; ISBN 978-1-57675-493-1) that includes a detailed discussion of AI, case studies and exercises aimed at enhancing a leader's ability to lead change with, not against, people.

Chapter 15: Leaders and Managers: A Case Study in Organizational Transformation

1   Drucker, considered by many as the father of management in Western cultures, provides insight to leadership from a management perspective in his book *Drucker on Leadership, New Lessons from the Father of Modern Management* (ISBN 978-0-470-40500-0).

Chapter 16: Burnout and Disillusionment

1   Stallard, Dewing-Hommes and Pankau (2007) provide insights and ideas to reignite passion and enthusiasm in organizations in their book, *Fired Up or Burned Out How to Reignite Your Team's Passion, Creativity, and Productivity* (ISBN 978-07852-2358-0).

Chapter 17: Gender Issues Related to Medical Leadership

1   The Pew Research Center (http://www.pewsocialtrends.org/) provides various reports on aspects of gender and leadership.
2   Zichy provides an analysis of women and leadership in her book, *Women and the Leadership Q, The Breakthrough System for Achieving Power and Influence* (ISBN 0-07-135216-3). Zichy focuses most of her discussion on analysing women leaders from various segments of society.

Chapter 18: Leadership for Good versus Good Leadership in Mental Health

1   Cuilla has written several books on ethical leadership, including: *The Ethics of Leadership* (ISBN 978-0-15-506317-4), *Ethics, the Heart of Leadership* (ISBN 0-275-98252-1) and *The Working Life, The Promise and Betrayal of Modern Work* (ISBN 0-609-80737-4). Cuilla draws from classical texts to create discussions regarding modern-day issues.
2   *Ethics for the Real World: Creating a Personal Code to Guide Decisions in Work and Life* by Howard and Korver (ISBN 978-1-4221-2106-1) guides readers through the process to develop a personal ethics code. The format of this publication allows readers to quickly understand the critical importance of developing a personal code of ethics then provides a useful format and process for developing their own code.

Chapter 20: Leadership, Ethics and Managing Diversity

1 Johnson provides a text that addresses the ethical implication of leadership. His book, *Meeting the Ethical Challenges of Leadership Casting Light or Shadow* (ISBN 978-1-4129-8222-1) discusses ethical aspects of leadership, group dynamics, organizational climate, diversity and crisis. Johnson also provides an overview of the ethical perspectives most used by leaders. The content of the book includes case studies and self-assessments for each chapter.

2 Price has written a text on ethical leadership titled *Leadership Ethics, An Introduction* (ISBN 978-0-521-69911-2). Price's text provides a greater examination of the philosophical aspects of leadership ethics rather than the practical application as in the Johnson text.

Chapter 23

Conclusions

Dinesh Bhugra, Susham Gupta and Pedro Ruiz

Leadership has personal, social and cultural aspects to it, and any successful leader will need to take these into account when discharging their role. Leadership theories offer some direction and explanation about the role of leaders. However, these theories indicate that there are indeed different ways of looking at approaches to leadership, from the trait approach – looking at how great leaders function – to the style of leadership and using skills approaches, contingency theory as outlined by Baker in this volume. These theories point out the strengths and pitfalls of certain approaches. In addition, the components of these theoretical approaches enable us to explore both in-groups and out-groups, which can strengthen or weaken the leader. An inspirational leader can motivate the people around them both emotionally and intellectually with increased influence. As Baker (see Chapter 4) highlights, charismatic leadership is strongly related to transformational leadership. Transformational leadership is about an ability to communicate a desirable vision of the future to which both leaders and their followers are committed, and to use strategic approaches to achieve those aims.

Not every clinician would wish to be a leader, and not every leader will be successful or transformational. However, it remains vital that all clinicians are aware of what leadership roles are and what responsibilities these roles carry with them. The leadership roles for clinicians can be very local, that is, within the team or within the department, or at broader levels at regional, national or international levels. Furthermore, the skills required vary, but awareness of the qualities and types of leadership enables clinicians to develop and deliver services that will be acceptable to patients and their carers.

Inherent in clinical leadership is technical competence – an awareness of the subject as well as recent advances so that stakeholders can have the confidence in the clinical leadership. The expertise required in leadership is about self-awareness and confidence in decision-making processes so that both leaders and their followers are able to sign up to this vision. Medical models of leadership have been used in a number of medical specialties – surgery and anaesthesia, to name but two. Medical professionals, by virtue of their technical competence, can manage to deal with uncertainty and ambiguity, which are a key part of psychiatric practice, and by and large psychiatrists are very good at managing that.

Leadership in Psychiatry, First Edition. Edited by Dinesh Bhugra, Pedro Ruiz and Susham Gupta.
© 2013 John Wiley & Sons, Ltd. Published 2013 by John Wiley & Sons, Ltd.

In the twenty-first century, clinical practice as well as healthcare systems are likely to change further although these changes have already started, no matter what specialty in medicine is talked about. For psychiatry, medical innovations such as pharmacogenomics and therapy without therapists (web-based therapies) will be important. This will be compounded by changing social and psychological structures. Increasing use of social media, increased globalization and urbanization are important in changing expectations of patients, the way patients perceive the medical profession, and how the latter responds. It is likely that healthcare systems will have to change, as a result of burgeoning costs and an increase in longevity, which will be accompanied by chronic and comorbid conditions. Hence clinicians must lead in developing and delivering alternative models that will be acceptable to patients and their carers on the one hand and to society as a whole on the other. A major challenge for clinical leaders is to renegotiate this social contract.

The skills and competencies required for leadership are both flexible and accessible, and some of these skills can be easily acquired. The challenge is for clinicians to be interested in the role of leader in the first place and then have easy access to training. It is in the interest of employers to ensure that such training is available at multiple levels according to need.

Leadership skills are needed outside the clinical team as well. In an era of economic downturn, it is important that clinicians work with society at large and stakeholders in particular (e.g. policy-makers) to advocate on behalf of their patients and seek fair and equal treatment, social justice and equity. The term parity of esteem has been used. Although there are clear problems with this usage, this is being accepted in a number of settings. Leadership roles in settings such as judicial systems have been covered by López-Ibor *et al.* in this volume (see Chapter 12). Dealing with prejudice, discrimination and stigma is part of the leader's role and responsibility. Understanding anti-stigma campaigns, evaluating them and making sense of the evaluation is important for the team in general and for the leader in particular. On occasion a leader will have to manage shared leadership so that the team members can move together. Academic leadership, whether in conducting research and leading research teams or taking on leadership through editorship of a journal, carries with it responsibilities of exploration and communication.

Leadership skills, whether they are purely clinical, academic or a mixture of the two, can be learned. However, a key is to engage individuals at an early stage of their career, even at the undergraduate level. It is important that potential high flyers be identified at an early stage and then coached and mentored appropriately.

Teaching of medical and clinical leadership skills can take many shapes. The underlying skills are identifiable; they can be taught at different levels and can be supplemented according to experience required. The challenges related to a clinician's role in leadership are many, but through project management, shadowing and mentoring these can be overcome. It is important that these opportunities are made available at all levels of training. Coaching, peer support, learning from colleagues and other disciplines with focused training and converting the training to experience and expertise thus can provide a linear growth in leadership skills. There will be challenges and opportunities for clinical leaders in a number of areas in the next few decades. These will include the impact of globalization and urbanization, the emergence of new technologies, making health a commodity, and competing demands for shrinking resources. These challenges can be opportunities, provided that leaders are willing to engage and lead. Using various educational and assessment tools can demonstrate the positive and negative aspects of an individual's personality, skills and competencies so that appropriate training can then be put in place.

Every clinician in psychiatry has the potential and possibility of leading their clinical team through the various challenges they will face by employing a combination of innovation, engagement and inspiration. The ultimate goal is to improve the services that will be acceptable and emotionally accessible both to patients and their carers and will be used appropriately.

Index

Leadership in Psychiatry, First Edition. Edited by Dinesh Bhugra, Pedro Ruiz and Susham Gupta.
© 2013 John Wiley & Sons, Ltd. Published 2013 by John Wiley & Sons, Ltd.